Six Days
of Awful Fighting:

Cavalry Operations
on the Road to Cold Harbor

Other work by Eric J. Wittenberg:

Five or Ten Minutes of Blind Confusion: The Battle of Aiken, South Carolina, February 11, 1865 (2018)

We Ride a Whirlwind: Sherman and Johnston at Bennett Place (2017)

Holding the Line on the River of Death: Union Mounted Forces at Chickamauga, September 18, 1863 (2018)

The Union Cavalry Comes of Age: Hartwood Church to Brandy Station, 1863 (Second ed. 2017)

Out Flew the Sabers: The Battle of Brandy Station, June 9, 1863 (with Daniel T. Davis, 2016)

The Second Battle of Winchester: The Confederate Victory that Opened the Door to Gettysburg (with Scott L. Mingus, Sr., 2016)

The Devil's to Pay: John Buford at Gettysburg. A History and Walking Tour (2014)

Protecting the Flank at Gettysburg: The Battles for Brinkerhoff's Ridge and East Cavalry Field (Second Edition, 2013)

The Battle of White Sulphur Springs; Averell Fails to Secure West Virginia (2011)

Gettysburg's Forgotten Cavalry Actions: Farnsworth's Charge, South Cavalry Field and the Battle of Fairfield (Second Edition, 2011)

The Battle of Brandy Station: North America's Largest Cavalry Battle (2010)

Like a Meteor Blazing Brightly: The Short but Controversial Life of Colonel Ulric Dahlgren (2009)

One Continuous Fight: The Retreat from Gettysburg and the Pursuit of Lee's Army of Northern Virginia, July 4-14, 1863 (with J. David Petruzzi and Michael F. Nugent, 2008)

Rush's Lancers: The Sixth Pennsylvania Cavalry in the Civil War (2007)

Plenty of Blame to Go Around: Jeb Stuart's Controversial Ride to Gettysburg (with J. David Petruzzi, 2006)

The Battle of Monroe's Crossroads and the Civil War's Final Campaign (2006)

Little Phil: A Reassessment of the Civil War Leadership of Gen. Philip H. Sheridan (2002)

With Sheridan in the Final Campaign Against Lee (2002)

Glory Enough for All: Sheridan's Second Raid and the Battle of Trevilian Station (2001)

At Custer's Side: The Civil War Writings of James Harvey Kidd (2001)

Under Custer's Command: The Civil War Journal of James Henry Avery (2000)

Six Days
of Awful Fighting:

Cavalry Operations
on the Road to Cold Harbor

Eric J. Wittenberg

FOX RUN
PUBLISHING
QUALITY PUBLISHING ONE BOOK AT A TIME

© 2020 by Eric J. Wittenberg

Publisher's Cataloging-in-Publication Data
provided by Five Rainbows Cataloging Services

Names: Wittenberg, Eric J., 1961- author. | Powell, David A., 1961- writer of foreword.
Title: Six days of awful fighting : cavalry operations on the road to Cold Harbor / Eric J. Wittenberg ; foreword by David A. Powell.
Description: Burlington, NC : Fox Run Publishing, 2020. | Includes bibliographical references and index.
Identifiers: LCCN 2020952442 (print) | ISBN 978-1-945602-16-0 (hardcover) | ISBN 978-1-945602-17-7 (paperback)
Subjects: LCSH: United States--History--Civil War, 1861-1865--Cavalry operations. | Virginia--History--Civil War, 1861-1865--Campaigns. | United States--History--Civil War, 1861-1865—Campaigns. | Sheridan, Philip Henry, 1831-1888. | Sheridan, Philip Henry, 1831-1888. | Cold Harbor, Battle of, Va., 1864. | BISAC: HISTORY / United States / Civil War Period (1850-1877) | HISTORY / United States / State & Local / South (AL, AR, FL, GA, KY, LA, MS, NC, SC, TN, VA, WV)
Classification: LCC E476.52 .W57 2020 (print) | LCC E476.52 (ebook) | DDC 973.7/37--dc23.

Cover design by Sandra Miller Linhart

Published by
Fox Run Publishing LLC
2779 South Church Street, #305
Burlington, NC 27215
http://www.foxrunpub.com/

"Hell is empty and all the devils are here!"
The Tempest, Act 1, Scene 2

For Susan, with gratitude for all that you do to make what I do possible.

Table of Contents

List of Maps

List of Images

Author's Preface

Most students of the American Civil War know about the terrible fighting that occurred at Cold Harbor in Hanover County, Virginia, from June 1–3, 1864. However, few know about the severe cavalry combat leading up to the battle of Cold Harbor. From May 27 to June 1, the Cavalry Corps of the Army of the Potomac and the Cavalry Corps of the Army of Northern Virginia slugged it out at places like Hanovertown, Haw's Shop, Matadequin Creek, Hanover Court House, Ashland, and, finally, Cold Harbor itself, setting the stage for the well-known infantry battle that broke out on the afternoon of June 1, 1864.

Edward L. Wells of the 4th South Carolina Cavalry provided the best explanation for why these cavalry battles are worthy of study. "The cavalry engagements preceding Cold Harbor were not isolated fights, but the smaller links in the chain of scientific maneuvers leading up gradually to this crowning event," he wrote years after the war. "They were minor parts of a grand and symmetrical whole."[1] Wells was absolutely correct in his analysis. One cannot truly understand how the battle of Cold Harbor played out unless one also understands how the armies got there. This book will get the armies to the battle of Cold Harbor.

This is the first monograph dedicated to telling the story of these largely overlooked cavalry battles. After introducing the competing forces of horse soldiers, and also discussing the significance of the mounted actions that occurred during the earlier phases of the Overland campaign, we will then examine each of the engagements in detail. The May 28, 1864, battle of Haw's Shop was considered the harshest cavalry battle of the war to date; however, it was quickly eclipsed two weeks later by the battle of Trevilian Station. Haw's Shop marked Maj. Gen. Wade Hampton's emergence as the new commander of the Army of Northern Virginia's Cavalry Corps in the wake of the death of the lamented cavalry chief, Maj. Gen. J. E. B. Stuart, 16 days earlier.

Familiar characters such as Philip H. Sheridan, Fitzhugh Lee, George A. Custer, and David M. Gregg play significant roles in these

---

1. Edward L. Wells, *Hampton and His Cavalry in '64* (Richmond, VA: B. F. Johnson Publishing Co., 1899), 185–186.

battles. So, too, do lesser known participants such as Brig. Gen. Matthew C. Butler and his large, inexperienced brigade of South Carolina cavalrymen, Capt. Oliver Cushman of the 1st Vermont Cavalry, Maj. John B. Millen of the 20th Georgia Battalion of Cavalry, and Lt. Col. Erastus Blakeslee of the 1st Connecticut Cavalry, the last three of whom were casualties of these engagements.

Approximately 70 photographs grace this book's pages. Twenty-five of Edward Alexander's excellent maps are included, all of which make it easier to understand the engagements. Many of my recent works have included research from walking and driving tours. I wish I could have included tours of the battlefields addressed in this book, but nearly all of the battles occurred on what is now private property. As a result, it is not possible to tour them in any detail. Only the battlefield at Cold Harbor is public property and readily accessible. Please respect the private property rights of the owners. Consequently, I regret there is no tour included in this book.

A brief note about sources is appropriate here. Robert E. L. Krick, the gifted National Park Service historian at the Richmond National Battlefield park, maintains a large collection of primary source material at the park's headquarters at Chimborazo. I drew upon the collection in writing this work, but it is important to note that the copies contained in the files at Chimborazo are often not the original sources for those materials, which can be found in other places. For ease of citation, if something came from the files at Chimborazo, it is noted as such, even though the originals may be housed elsewhere.

As with every project of this type, I am grateful to many people for their assistance. As mentioned, Edward Alexander's outstanding maps add to the narrative, and I appreciate Edward's support. David A. Powell, my friend and co-author, gave me valuable feedback on the manuscript and wrote the foreword that follows. Robert E. L. Krick took me to see battlefield sites, provided some primary sources, and carefully reviewed the manuscript for accuracy. So, too, did my friend Gordon C. Rhea, the dean of students of the Overland Campaign. Emmanuel Dabney, another National Park Service historian, obtained a number of primary source materials for me from various repositories in the Richmond area.

Professor Christopher Stowe also rounded up primary source material, as did J. Keith Jones. Tom Elmore made a special trip to Charleston, South Carolina, to obtain primary source material for this book and to provide me with items from his hometown of Columbia. Ken Lawrence, the authority on all things pertaining to the 6th Ohio Cavalry, provided a number of images and some useful primary source information, including material on the death of his ancestor, Maj.

Delos R. Northway, and I am grateful for that. Adolfo Ovies provided extremely useful food for thought about the evolution of cavalry tactics, and I am grateful for his input. Michael Block provided an image of Maj. Richard Falls of the 1st Pennsylvania Cavalry. My friend Melissa Weeks also rendered very useful editorial feedback that makes this a better read.

This is now my third book project with my friends from Fox Run Publishing. Fox Run creates a quality book and strongly supports the efforts of authors. My editor, Heather Ammel, amply proves the truth of the old cliché that a good editor can make a mediocre book good and a good book excellent. Heather makes my work better, and I appreciate that. Keith Jones did a fine job of laying out this book and readying it for publication.

And, as always, I remain grateful to my long-suffering but much-loved wife, Susan Skilken Wittenberg, without whose infinite patience for my need to tell these stories of the American Civil War, none of this would be possible.

Eric J. Wittenberg
Columbus, Ohio

Foreword

By David A. Powell

"Who ever saw a dead cavalryman?" So runs the adage, supposedly attributed to both Union General Joseph Hooker and President Abraham Lincoln, which became a common refrain among Federal infantrymen in the first half of the Civil War. The implication inherent in that phrase suggests that by the 1860, the technology of war had evolved to the point that the hard work of battle fell heavily on the infantry and the artillery, not *l'arme blanche*. Hooker is said to have used it as a taunt to inspire a greater degree of aggressiveness in his horsemen prior to the Chancellorsville campaign, almost certainly to his later regret.

But if by the beginning of the American Civil War the age of the massed heavy cavalry charge, with rank upon rank of breastplate-clad *cuirassiers* thundering down on unfortunate infantry, had passed, it is not true that cavalry itself was a thing of the past. Outside of pitched battles, much of the hard work of campaigning fell disproportionately on the mounted force, as demonstrated in the day-to-day clashes resulting from armies maneuvering for advantage. The cavalry, then, bled and died in affairs of outposts, in screening actions, and in fighting for time until the heavy legions could come up. Their fights, though smaller and less remarked-on, nevertheless proved equally bloody over the long haul.

The literature of our Civil War remains heavily focused on tactical narratives describing the big battles – and quite often, the smaller battles as well. It is a quirk of the genre that campaign narratives are much rarer. Thanks to that quirk, the cavalry's role in those operations has suffered from a degree of relative neglect, due to its unusual pride of place in conducting operational maneuver. More so, perhaps, because much of the work on cavalry that does exist has tended to focus on the flash – raids, deeds of daring, and the like.

Eric Wittenberg has bucked that historical trend, and in so doing has done much to highlight the role of cavalry throughout his extensive writing career. His work on cavalry operations in the Gettysburg Campaign, and especially his study of Union General John

Buford at that engagement, stands as a testament to both his love of the cavalry and his skill at telling the cavalry's story.

In *Six Days of Awful Fighting*, Eric has given us an excellent volume detailing another chapter in the ongoing combat between the Union cavalry of the Army of the Potomac and its opponent of long standing, the Cavalry Corps of the Confederate Army of Northern Virginia. *Six Days* explores a week's worth of engagements at the end of May 1864: engagements that led up to and culminated in the full-scale battle of Cold Harbor, June 1-3, 1864. It is a story of daily fighting, hard and heavy; which easily lays to rest the canard quoted above. Here were found plenty of dead cavalrymen on both sides.

This work also demonstrates why studying cavalry operations is so important. It opens a door into that operational narrative so important to try and understand the how and why of the large-scale maneuvering of mid-nineteenth century field armies. Each of these cavalry actions marks a move in the week-long chess game between Ulysses S. Grant, seeking to gain position or turn a flank, and Robert E. Lee, in thwarting those efforts. Time and again, cavalry leaders had to size up a fluid, ever-changing tactical situation and make the correct countermove. At the sharp end of that process, the action was furious, bitter, and bloody.

The men of the cavalry in both armies are well represented here. The Federal cavalry was on the ascendant, now usually more numerous, better mounted, and better armed then their opponents. It was not always so: in 1861 and 1862 the Union cavalry was often frittered away on lesser duties, not concentrated for use and to maximize striking power. Not until 1863 did the Union cavalry come into its own to slug it out, toe to toe, with the Rebels. By 1864, with the new seven-shot Spencer repeating carbine coming into widespread issue, the blue troopers could often deliver superior firepower on the battlefield.

But the Confederate Cavalry Corps remained a formidable opponent. Despite the shocking loss of their commander J.E.B. Stuart, mortally wounded at Yellow Tavern on May 11 and dying the next day, the Confederates persevered. South Carolinian Wade Hampton, unexpectedly thrust into Stuart's role, proved more than capable, maturing into an outstanding corps commander in his own right. Given how little time he had to adjust to his new responsibilities, his performance leading up to Cold Harbor was impressive. In the days and months to come, Hampton would further grow into the role.

Opposing Hampton was Philip Sheridan, determined to prove that the Union cavalry could be an aggressive, concentrated offensive force instead of being largely wasted on escort and screening duties. Under Sheridan, the cavalry gained confidence and often dominated the battlefield. Though Sheridan was far from the perfect cavalryman – he had very little experience with cavalry prior to the fighting described here – he and his troopers pushed the Rebel cavalry to their limits. In that sense, these six days represent a tipping-point in the balance of power between the Union and Confederate cavalry forces.

Of course, Wittenberg describes each of the actions included in considerable tactical detail as well. Those who crave the blow-by-blow and shot-by-shot narrative will find it here. By digging into a plethora of sources, both official and unofficial, Wittenberg has produced a vivid portrait of the numerous encounters encompassed over the course of this bloody week. The men on both sides were justly proud of their efforts, and their combat records, and took pains to record those deeds. By mining those accounts, Wittenberg has given us an unprecedented examination of what happened.

As I read this work, one of the things which struck me was the number of green troops involved, especially on the Southern side. While it is well established that a number of Union infantry units involved in Grant's 1864 Virginia Overland Campaign, having been drawn out of their comfortable Washington defenses for this effort, were effectively new to combat; by 1864 it is generally acknowledged that the Confederates had few new troops left to commit. In fact, many Confederate regiments were drawn from the coastal regions of the deep south, especially from South Carolina, and rushed northward to Virginia that spring to offset the large numbers of Federals swelling Grant's ranks. A considerable number of those units were either newly formed or had so far seen little action other than comfortable garrison duty. Among them were several regiments of cavalry. At least one brigade of green South Carolinians found themselves thrust immediately in the thick of the fighting described here, with mixed results.

In my own work on Chickamauga, I have come to appreciate the nuances and intricacies of following the cavalry in order to fully understand the larger operational picture, and how, quite often, that cavalry story makes for remarkably exciting reading in its own right. In the narrative that follows, Eric Wittenberg has given us another superb monograph on Civil War cavalry operations, the life of the cavalry in the field, and further insight into the operational context of one eventful week in that most costly of campaigns: 1864 in Virginia.

CHAPTER ONE

The Army of the Potomac's Cavalry Corps, May 1864

The Army of the Potomac's Cavalry Corps came of age in 1863. After enduring 18 months of the Army of Northern Virginia's cavalry riding literal rings around it, the Federal army's high command fixed the problems with its organization, and the Union horse performed admirably during 1863. In February of that year, Maj. Gen. Joseph Hooker, commanding the Army of the Potomac, for the first time massed all mounted forces assigned to the army into a single cohesive corps. Almost immediately, morale improved, and so did the performance of the blue-clad horse soldiers. On June 9, 1863, the Army of the Potomac's cavalry fought Maj. Gen. J. E. B. Stuart's vaunted Army of Northern Virginia's cavalry to a tactical draw. The 14-hour slugging match left Stuart happy to see the Federals withdraw.[1]

Twelve days later the Union cavalry scored its first battlefield victory, defeating Stuart at Upperville in the Loudoun Valley of Virginia.[2] Then, at Gettysburg on July 1, Brig. Gen. John Buford's troopers held off almost 10,000 Confederate infantry long enough for the Army of the Potomac's I Corps to arrive. A few days afterward, Stuart suffered another loss, on East Cavalry Field, to Brig. Gen. David M. Gregg's troopers. The opposing forces tangled nearly 20 times while retreating from Gettysburg, and the fighting continued for most of the fall. By the end of 1863, the Army of the Potomac's Cavalry Corps had achieved parity with its Southern counterpart.

And then disaster struck. Buford, generally considered the best Union cavalry commander, died of typhoid fever on December 16, at the age of 37. Then, in February 1864, ambitious Brig. Gen. Judson Kilpatrick, commanding the Army of the Potomac's Third Cavalry Division, received permission to lead a raid toward Richmond to free prisoners of war from Libby and Belle Isle Prisons. Kilpatrick led one

---

1. For a detailed discussion of the development of the Army of the Potomac's Cavalry Corps in1863, see Eric J. Wittenberg, *The Union Cavalry Comes of Age: Hartwood Church to Brandy Station, 1863* (2nd ed.)(Charleston, SC: The History Press, 2017).
2. For the most detailed treatment of the battle of Upperville, see Robert F. O'Neill Jr., *The Cavalry Battles of Aldie, Middleburg and Upperville: Small but Important Riots, June 10–27, 1863* (Lynchburg, VA: H. E. Howard, 1993).

Lt. Gen. Ulysses S. Grant, overall commander of the Union armies.

(Library of Congress)

of the raid's columns while 21-year-old Col. Ulric Dahlgren, a dashing one-legged soldier, led the other. The expedition not only left Dahlgren dead and shrouded in ugly controversy, but it also achieved none of its objectives and severely damaged Kilpatrick's already questionable credibility. Major General Alfred Pleasonton, commanding the Army of the Potomac's Cavalry Corps, shouldered much of the blame for the miserably unsuccessful raid, even though he had openly opposed the plan.[3]

The entire Army of the Potomac was in a state of flux that winter. Army commander Maj. Gen. George G. Meade frustrated President Abraham Lincoln, who considered Meade too cautious. When Meade went into winter camp in November 1863, after the army's victory at the Second Battle of Rappahannock Station, Lincoln's frustration boiled over. Lincoln and Secretary of War Edwin M. Stanton goaded Meade into moving against Gen. Robert E. Lee in December, but the aborted campaign, known as the battle of Mine Run, failed to drive Lee's army away. The president's irritation grew, as he realized that Northern voters had grown war-weary and expected victories. Something had to change.

Major General Ulysses S. Grant, commanding the Union armies in the Western Theater, delivered the desired change. Grant, a grim, determined warrior who had never lost a major engagement, thrashed Gen. Braxton Bragg's Army of Tennessee at Chattanooga in November 1863. Grant's political patron, Representative Elihu Washburne of Illinois, introduced legislation to revive the long-dormant rank of lieutenant general—last held by George Washington—with the intention of promoting Grant to the lofty rank. Grant would then outrank everyone, enabling him to develop and implement a strategy for winning the war.

3. For a detailed treatment of the Kilpatrick-Dahlgren raid, see Bruce M. Venter, *Kill Jeff Davis: The Union Raid on Richmond 1864* (Norman: University of Oklahoma Press, 2016).

On March 4, 1864, writing to his good friend Maj. Gen. William T. Sherman, Grant stated that "the bill reviving the grade of lieutenant general has become a law and my name has been sent to the Senate." He then received orders "to report to Washington immediately in person, which indicates either a confirmation or likelihood of confirmation."[4]

Grant was right. Throngs of civilians and politicians greeted him as the Union's savior. The Army of the Potomac's grizzled quartermaster, Brig. Gen. Rufus Ingalls, Grant's roommate at the United States Military Academy at West Point, told Meade, "Grant means business."[5] Grant's long-time friend Lt. Gen. James Longstreet, who was the Army of Northern Virginia's senior corps commander, echoed a similar sentiment. "That man will fight us every day and every hour until the end of the war," he warned.[6] Lieutenant Colonel Theodore Lyman, one of Meade's staff officers, described the grim-faced new general-in-chief eloquently: "He habitually wears an expression as if he had determined to drive his head through a brick wall, and was about to do it."[7] Grant's single-minded determination would change the face of the war in Virginia.

Congress quickly approved Grant's promotion, and the newly minted lieutenant general began crafting a strategy for the coming spring campaign season. Grant realized the only way the North could win was to wear down the South, which would require non-stop campaigning on all fronts against a Confederacy already straining its war-making capacity. Grant decided to coordinate all of the Union armies in the field to bring each of the Union's resources to bear.[8]

Grant planned a series of coordinated, simultaneous assaults on all fronts. In the West, Sherman would launch a campaign intended to capture the important logistics center of Atlanta and destroy Gen. Joseph E. Johnston's Army of Tennessee. Major General Nathaniel P. Banks would lead an expedition designed to seize the important

4. William S. McFeely, *Grant: A Biography* (New York: W. W. Norton & Co., 1982), 151.
5. Bruce Catton, *Grant Takes Command* (Boston: Little, Brown & Co., 1968), 163.
6. Horace Porter, *Campaigning with Grant* (New York: The Century Co., 1906), 47.
7. George R. Agassiz, ed., *Meade's Headquarters, 1863–1865: Letters of Col. Theodore Lyman from the Wilderness to Appomattox* (Boston: Atlantic Monthly Press, 1922), 81.
8. *The War of the Rebellion: A Compilation of the Official Records of the Union and Confederate Armies*, 128 volumes in 3 series (Washington, D.C.: United States Government Printing Office, 1889), Series 1, Vol. 36, Part 1, 12 (further references will be to the "OR." In addition, unless otherwise noted, all references will be to Series 1 of the OR).

*Maj. Gen. George G. Meade,
commander, Army of the
Potomac.*

(Library of Congress)

manufacturing town of Shreveport, Louisiana, an operation already planned and approved before Grant's promotion. Banks would then advance on the critical port city of Mobile, Alabama. Other Union forces would move on Charleston, South Carolina, pinning down the Confederate coastal garrisons.

In the East, Maj. Gen. Franz Sigel, a politically influential German immigrant, was tasked with clearing Confederates from the crucial Shenandoah Valley before advancing on Richmond from the west. Meanwhile, the Army of the James, commanded by Maj. Gen. Benjamin F. Butler, a prominent Massachusetts politician and War Democrat, would advance on Richmond from the east. Grant intended to travel with the Army of the Potomac, which would bear the brunt of the fighting in the center, with Sigel flanking the Confederates on their left and Butler to their right and rear.[9]

Meade, who nominally remained the Army of the Potomac's commander, received peremptory orders from Grant: Lee's Army of Northern Virginia would be his objective—wherever Lee went, Meade would follow.[10] Before the spring campaign began, Meade reorganized the Army of the Potomac from five infantry corps to three—the II, V, and VI.[11] He also reorganized the Cavalry Corps.

9. Ibid., 14–18.
10. Ibid., 15.
11. The I Corps, which had been battered at Gettysburg and was too small to stand as an independent corps, was reorganized into two divisions and transferred to the V Corps. Major General William H. French, an unreliable alcoholic, commanded the III Corps. French performed poorly during the Mine Run campaign, despite outranking all of the army's corps commanders. Meade finally rid himself of French by splitting up the III Corps. The First and Second Divisions were transferred to the II Corps, becoming its Third and Fourth Divisions. The Third Division was assigned to the VI Corps,

Dissatisfied with the Cavalry Corps' performance, particularly after the Kilpatrick-Dahlgren raid debacle, Meade relieved Pleasonton with the approval of Secretary of War Stanton.[12] A cavalry officer observed, "Even [Pleasonton's] success and the proofs he had given of the value of the cavalry, when properly used and led, were not sufficient to overcome the force of traditions and customs, and among higher authorities the idea still prevailed that the mounted force was secondary to, and should be used for the protection, convenience, and relief of the infantry." He concluded, "Serious differences of opinion between Generals Meade and Pleasonton had from time to time occurred, and at last had gone so far that the latter . . . could no longer retain his command."[13]

Who would replace Pleasonton? Buford was dead and Kilpatrick had been banished to the Western Theater. Gregg, commanding the Second Cavalry Division, was the senior subordinate, but he lacked an aggressive spirit even though he was competent. No other qualified candidates existed within the Army of the Potomac's Cavalry Corps.[14] In an early interview with Lincoln, Grant expressed dissatisfaction with "the little that had been accomplished by the cavalry so far in the war, and the belief that it was capable of accomplishing much more than it had done under a thorough leader. I said I wanted the very best man in the army for that command." The army's chief of staff, Maj. Gen. Henry W. Halleck, asked, "How would Sheridan do?" Grant replied, "The very man I want."[15]

becoming that corps' Third Division. Thus, the incompetent French was left without a command.

12. George Meade, ed., *The Life and Letters of George Gordon Meade*, 2 vols. (New York: Charles Scribner's Sons, 1913), 2:185. There is some dispute about precisely who was responsible for Pleasonton's relief from command.

13. Henry E. Davies, *General Sheridan* (New York: D. Appleton & Co., 1895), 92–93. Also, Pleasonton testified against Meade before the Congressional Joint Committee on the Conduct of the War in the winter of 1864. He stabbed his commander in the back by claiming Meade had intended to retreat at Gettysburg and that he had encouraged Meade to counterattack after the repulse of Pickett's Charge. This enraged Meade, whose support was the sole reason why Pleasonton still commanded the Cavalry Corps. Once Meade withdrew his support, Pleasonton had no remaining support in the army's high command. He was removed and sent to Missouri, where he spent the remaining balance of the war.

14. Gregg may have resented being passed over for corps command. When he realized Sheridan was not competent to command the Cavalry Corps, his bitterness may have boiled over. Gregg resigned his commission in the winter of 1865, just before the war's final campaign, and never fully explained his reasons, only stating he had pressing business at home. Exasperation at being passed over for corps command twice (it happened again in the fall of 1864) probably factored into the decision to resign his commission. He never served in the army again.

15. Ulysses S. Grant, *Personal Memoirs of Ulysses S. Grant*, 2 vols. (New York: Charles L. Webster & Co., 1885), 2:133.

Maj. Gen. Philip H. Sheridan, commander of the Cavalry Corps, Army of the Potomac.

(Library of Congress)

Major General Philip H. Sheridan was largely a mystery to his new command. Colonel Charles Wainwright, a pithy artillerist, reflected, "I know nothing ... of ... [Sheridan], but a change I think was needed; neither Pleasonton nor [Maj. Gen. George] Stoneman proved themselves equal to the position."[16] Brigadier General Henry E. Davies, who commanded a brigade in Gregg's Second Cavalry Division, observed only the fittest leaders in the Cavalry Corps survived, which ensured that its prior leadership came from the corps' ranks. Consequently, little was known of Sheridan's prior service in the Western Theater. Davies said, "It was not known that he had ever served with or in command of cavalry, and the prejudice ... among mounted troops against being placed under the orders of an officer whose experiences from the Army of the Potomac had previously suffered had not induced the belief that the West was the point of the compass from which the advent of wise men bringing rich gifts of victory and success was to be confidently expected."[17] Captain Charles Francis Adams of the 1st Massachusetts Cavalry, grandson and great-grandson of United States presidents, recalled that Sheridan "was essentially an Irish adventurer—a species of brilliant Charles O'Malley; with a well-developed natural aptitude for military life, he was not conspicuous for character."[18]

16. Alan Nevins, ed., *A Diary of Battle: The Personal Journals of Colonel Charles S. Wainwright, 1861–1865* (New York: Harcourt, Brace & World, 1962), 341. Major General George Stoneman was appointed the original commander of the Army of the Potomac's Cavalry Corps when Hooker ordered its formation in February 1863. Stoneman left the army to go on medical leave for treatment of a terrible case of hemorrhoids on May 15, 1863, and never returned to the Army of the Potomac. Pleasonton began as temporary commander, and then became permanent commander of the Cavalry Corps in August 1863, after the Gettysburg campaign.
17. Davies, *General Sheridan*, 93–95.
18. Charles Francis Adams, *Charles Francis Adams 1835–1915: An Autobiography* (Boston: Houghton-Mifflin, 1916), 158. Adams referred to a fictional Irish dragoon and adventurer named Charles O'Malley who

At first blush, Sheridan was an illogical candidate to command the Army of the Potomac's Cavalry Corps. Born in County Cavan, Ireland, on March 6, 1831, the diminutive Irishman graduated from West Point in 1853, ranking in the bottom third of his class. He served in the Fourth Infantry in the Pacific Northwest for most of his antebellum army career, and after service as a staff officer during the early days of the Civil War, he received a commission as colonel of the 2nd Michigan Cavalry in 1862. For 90 days he commanded a demi-brigade of two cavalry regiments. He held this command for only three months before being promoted to brigadier general of volunteers and given command of an infantry division. He performed particularly well at the 1862 battle of Stones River when his division's stand saved the Army of the Cumberland. Under Grant's watchful eye, Sheridan also led the successful assault up Missionary Ridge during the November 1863 battle of Chattanooga. Grant marked the brave and aggressive young man for advancement.[19]

Thus, when Sheridan received the appointment to command the Army of the Potomac's Cavalry Corps, he had precisely 90 days' experience commanding cavalry. Colonel Horace Porter, one of Grant's staff officers, observed that the new cavalry chief "had been worn down almost to a shadow by hard work and exposure ... he looked anything but formidable as a candidate for a cavalry leader."[20]

General Meade was not impressed. "His determination to absorb everything done is so manifest as to have attracted the attention of the entire army," he told his wife.[21] Sharing similar sentiments, Sheridan's West Point classmate Maj. Gen. David S. Stanley claimed Sheridan "was wholly unacquainted with books but was very observant and very energetic. I think his success was owing to a certain audacity and ... a perfect indifference as to how many of his men were killed if he only carried his point."[22]

Major James H. Kidd, commander of the 6th Michigan Cavalry in the spring of 1864, recorded his observations:

supposedly served in the British army during the Napoleonic Peninsular War. See Charles Lever, *Charles O'Malley: The Irish Dragoon*, 2 vols. (Dublin: William Curry, Jun & Co., 1841).

19. Roy Morris Jr., *Sheridan: The Life and Wars of General Phil Sheridan* (New York: Crown Publishers, Inc., 1992). For more on Sheridan's performance at Missionary Ridge, see Wiley Sword, *Mountains Touched with Fire* (New York: St. Martin's Press, 1995).
20. Porter, *Campaigning with Grant*, 23.
21. Meade, *Life and Letters of George Gordon Meade*, 2:271.
22. David S. Stanley, *Personal Memoirs of Major-General David S. Stanley* (Cambridge, MA: Harvard University Press, 1917), 23.

[Sheridan] was square of shoulder and there was plenty of room for the display of a major general's buttons on his broad chest. His face was strong, with a firm jaw, a keen eye, and extraordinary firmness in every lineament. In his manner there was an alertness, evinced rather in look than in movement. Nothing escaped his eye, which was brilliant and searching and at the same time emitted flashes of kindly good nature. When riding past or among his troopers, he had a way of casting quick, comprehensive glances to the right and left and in all directions. He overlooked nothing. One had a feeling that he was under close and critical observation, that Sheridan had his eye on him, was mentally taking his measure and would remember and recognize him the next time. No introduction was needed.[23]

The bandy-legged little Irishman did not make a good first impression on Lincoln, who commented that Sheridan was "a brown, chunky little chap, with a long body, short legs, not enough neck to hang him, and such long arms that if his ankles itch he can scratch them without stooping." Grant quickly retorted, "You will find him big enough for the purpose before we get through with him."[24]

The Army of the Potomac's Cavalry Corps consisted of three divisions. Two of those divisions, the Second and Third, had two brigades each, while the First Division had three. Except for the Reserve Brigade, assigned to the First Division, all of these units consisted of volunteer cavalry regiments. The Reserve Brigade consisted of three small regiments of Regular Army cavalry assigned to service with the Army of the Potomac, providing a solid, professional nucleus to the Cavalry Corps. The Northern horsemen carried pistols, sabers, and a variety of breech loading carbines, and some carried the seven-shot Spencer repeating carbine.

After the disastrous Richmond raid, Kilpatrick had been exiled to the Western Theater, serving under Sherman for the rest of the war. At Grant's insistence, Sheridan assigned brash, young Brig. Gen. James H. Wilson to command Kilpatrick's Third Cavalry Division. Wilson's assignment enraged Brig. Gen. George A. Custer, who had briefly commanded the Third Division during the summer and fall of 1863 and outranked Wilson, a man with no experience commanding troops in the field. Further, Custer and Wilson had despised each other ever

23. James H. Kidd, *Personal Recollections of a Cavalryman in Custer's Michigan Brigade* (Ionia, MI: Sentinel Printing Co., 1908), 298.
24. Morris, *Sheridan*, 1.

since their days at West Point, making for a toxic environment. Davies, the Third Division's other brigadier general, also outranked Wilson. Sheridan assigned Davies to command a Second Division brigade, replacing wounded Col. John B. McIntosh, who then assumed command of a Third Division brigade upon returning to duty. Custer's entire brigade was transferred to the First Division, and Col. George H. Chapman's brigade was transferred to the Third Division to replace Custer's brigade.

Another outsider, Brig. Gen. Alfred T. A. Torbert of Delaware, a member of the West Point class of 1855, assumed command of Buford's First Division, displacing its senior brigadier, Wesley Merritt. Torbert's "qualifica-

Brig. Gen. Alfred T. A. Torbert, commander of the 1st Division, Cavalry Corps, Army of the Potomac.

(Library of Congress)

tions as a cavalry commander were not remarkable," an officer of the 6th Michigan Cavalry noted.[25] "He was a handsome, dashing fellow, at this time, a beautiful horseman, and as brave as a lion; but his abilities were hardly equal to such large commands."[26] An officer of the VI Corps, who observed Torbert in the field many times, recalled, "General Torbert ... was a very handsome man and the best-dressed officer in the army. He had magnificent horses, a saddle which was said to have cost five hundred dollars, with accouterments to match, and whenever he passed a reviewing stand it usually caused a sensation."[27]

Earlier in the war, Torbert competently commanded New Jersey infantrymen, but he had no experience commanding cavalry. Custer, nevertheless, seemed pleased with his new commander. "Everything is

25. Kidd, *Personal Recollections*, 261.
26. E. R. Hagemann, ed., *Fighting Rebels and Redskins: Experiences in Army Life of Colonel George B. Sanford, 1861–1892* (Norman: University of Oklahoma Press, 1969), 224.
27. Thomas W. Hyde, *Following the Greek Cross, or Memories of the Sixth Army Corps* (Boston: Houghton Mifflin, 1894), 180–81.

Brig. George A. Custer, commander of the Michigan Cavalry Brigade, 1st Division, Cavalry Corps, Army of the Potomac.

(Library of Congress)

arranged satisfactorily now," he told his wife, Libbie. "I take my Brigade and join the First Division Cavalry Corps under General Torbert, an old and intimate friend of mine, and a very worthy gentleman."[28] Custer and his four fine regiments of Michigan cavalry—the 1st, 5th, 6th, and 7th—achieved great things while attached to the First Division.

Custer, at the tender age of 24, was on the way to a spectacular career. Graduating at the bottom of his West Point class in 1861, Custer's legendary good luck placed him in a coveted staff billet with the Army of the Potomac's first commander, Maj. Gen. George B. McClellan. He was then assigned to Pleasonton's staff, where his boldness and courage caught the cavalry chief's eye. Shortly after Pleasonton assumed corps command, he arranged for Custer's promotion from temporary captain to brigadier general of volunteers,

28. George A. Custer to Elizabeth Bacon Custer, April 16, 1864, in Marguerite Merrington, ed., *The Custer Story: The Life and Letters of General George A. Custer and his Wife Elizabeth* (New York: Devin-Adair Co., 1950), 89.

on June 28, 1863. Tall, brash, handsome, athletic, and a born horseman, "the Boy General with the Golden Locks," as Custer was known, had not disappointed.

"This officer was one of the funniest-looking beings you ever saw, and looks like a circus rider gone mad!" Lieutenant Colonel Lyman exclaimed. "He wears a huzzar jacket and tight trousers, of faded black velvet trimmed with tarnished gold lace. His head is decked with a little gray, felt hat; high boots and gilt spurs complete the costume, which is enhanced by the General's coiffure, consisting in short, dry flaxen ringlets! His aspect, though highly amusing, is also pleasing, as he has a very merry blue eye, and a devil-may-care style."[29]

Custer was the quintessential hussar.[30] He preferred hell-for-leather mounted charges rather than the dismounted infantry-style tactics Sheridan and Torbert favored. Evolutions in technology triggered extreme changes in cavalry tactics, and mounted combat quickly fell from favor. In some ways Custer had an antiquated approach to combat, advocating a rapidly fading style.

A trooper in the 7th Michigan adoringly described his brigadier as "the idol of his troopers and the terror of his foes."[31] Commanding one of Custer's regiments, Kidd wrote to his father in June 1864: "So brave a man I never saw and as competent as brave. Under him a man is ashamed to be cowardly. Under him our men can achieve wonders."[32] One of Sheridan's staff officers, Capt. Frederic C. Newhall, described Custer as "quick as a flash, daring and reckless almost without equal, yet showing coolness and judgment in some tight places."[33] His "Wolverines," as Custer called his Michigan men, performed

29. Agassiz, *Meade's Headquarters*, 17.
30. Hussars were European light cavalry who did the bulk of their fighting mounted. They had the reputation of being the dashing but unruly adventurers of their respective armies, known for being hard-fighting, hard-drinking, womanizing swashbucklers. According to prototypical French hussar Gen. Antoine Charles Louis de Lasalle, who died in battle at the age of 34, "Any hussar who is not dead by the age of thirty is a blackguard." They were known for their rapid charges in tight formations against enemy infantry or cavalry units. The U.S. Army never formally adopted hussar regiments, but its prewar light cavalry units often employed these tactics. Other than being a teetotaler, Custer embodied many hussar traits.
31. William F. Kenfield, "Trevilian's Station," in William O. Lee, comp., *Personal and Historical Sketches and Facial History of and by Members of the Seventh Regiment Michigan Volunteer Cavalry, 1862–1865* (Detroit: Ralston Co., 1901), 239.
32. Eric J. Wittenberg, ed., *One of Custer's Wolverines: The Civil War Letters of Brevet Brigadier General James Harvey Kidd, Sixth Michigan Cavalry* (Kent, OH: Kent State University Press, 2000), 88.
33. Frederic C. Newhall, *With General Sheridan Lee's Last Campaign* (Philadelphia: J. B. Lippincott, 1866), 228.

Col. Thomas C. Devin, commander of the 2nd Brigade, 1st Division, Cavalry Corps, Army of the Potomac.

(Library of Congress)

spectacularly at Gettysburg and in the months following. His brigade was the envy of the Army of the Potomac.[34]

The First Division also included Col. Thomas C. Devin's small veteran brigade. Known as "Buford's Hard Hitter" or "Old Warhorse," Devin was 41 years old and had no formal military training. Prior to the Civil War he painted houses in New York City and was the captain of a company of militia cavalry. "I can't teach Devin anything about cavalry," Buford once said. "He knows more than I do."[35] Another described Devin as "of the school of Polonius, a little slow sometimes in entrance to a fight, but, being in, as slow to leave a point for which the enemy is trying."[36] Devin was older than the other cavalry commanders and long overdue for promotion. Buford's death cost Devin his strongest advocate, and his lack of professional military training also hindered him.[37]

34. There are, of course, dozens of published biographies of George A. Custer. So many, in fact, that it is hard to keep them straight. For those interested in a balanced but thorough treatment of Custer's life and career, the author recommends Jeffry D. Wert, *Custer: The Controversial Life of George Armstrong Custer* (New York: Simon & Schuster, 1996). For those interested in a detailed study of Custer's exploits in the Civil War, there is no better source than Gregory J. W. Urwin, *Custer Victorious: The Civil War Battle of George Armstrong Custer* (East Brunswick, NJ: Associated University Presses, 1983).
35. Edward G. Longacre, *The Cavalry at Gettysburg: A Tactical Study of Mounted Operations during the Civil War's Pivotal Campaign, 9 June–14 July 1863* (Rutherford, NJ: Fairleigh Dickinson University Press, 1986), 51.
36. Newhall, *With General Sheridan*, 228.
37. Ezra J. Warner, *Generals in Blue: Lives of the Union Commanders* (Baton Rouge: Louisiana State University Press, 1964), 124. Devin's long-overdue promotion did not come until the winter of 1865, many months after John Buford's untimely death.

Devin's small veteran brigade consisted of his own 6th New York Cavalry, the 4th New York Cavalry, the 9th New York Cavalry, and the 17th Pennsylvania Cavalry, all veteran commands. Only the 4th New York Cavalry had a bad reputation; in the fall of 1863, Buford took away its regimental colors for failing to meet his expectations in battle.

The Third, or Reserve Brigade, consisted of the 1st, 2nd, and 5th U.S. Cavalry, the 6th Pennsylvania Cavalry, and the 19th New York Cavalry, also known as the 1st New York Dragoons. This brigade originally consisted of only Regular regiments, but the 6th Pennsylvania joined the brigade in the spring of 1863, and the 1st New York Dragoons joined that fall.

Brig. Gen. Wesley Merritt, commander of the Reserve Brigade, 1st Division, Cavalry Corps, Army of the Potomac.

(Library of Congress)

Many Regulars had accepted commissions in volunteer regiments, which drained their effective strength. The Regulars had not been used well during the early phases of the war, leaving their ranks thin. The 6th U.S. Cavalry became so depleted during the Gettysburg campaign that it ceased to be an effective fighting unit and served as Cavalry Corps headquarters' escort for the remainder of the war. When Stoneman massed the Cavalry Corps in the winter of 1863, Buford assumed command of the Reserve Brigade at his request. He reorganized and trained the Regulars, casting them in his mold—steady, competent, and reliable. One Regular described the Reserve Brigade as the Army of the Potomac's "Old Guard."[38]

Thirty-year-old Wesley Merritt commanded the Reserve Brigade. The talented, professional soldier graduated West Point in the class of

38. Theophilus F. Rodenbough, "Sheridan's Richmond Raid," in Robert U. Johnson and Clarence C. Buel, eds., *Battles and Leaders of the Civil War,* 4 vols. (New York: Century Publishing Co., 1884–1888), 4:188 (unless otherwise noted, the four-volume set of Battles and Leaders will hereinafter be referred to as "B&L").

Col. J. Irvin Gregg, commander of the 2nd Brigade, 2nd Division,
Cavalry Corps, Army of the Potomac.

(USAHEC)

1860.[39] He rose through the ranks quickly, receiving promotion to brigadier general of volunteers on June 28, 1863, along with Custer and Elon J. Farnsworth. After Buford's death, Merritt commanded the First Division until Torbert's assignment and then returned to command the Reserve Brigade. Bigger and better things awaited this fine young officer, who ended up accumulating 43 years' service in the Regular Army. After triumphantly accepting Manila's surrender during the Spanish-American War, he retired as the second-ranking officer in the army. A staff officer recorded that Merritt "had a constitution of iron, and underneath a rather passive demeanor

39. Kidd, *Personal Recollections*, 238–39. The only full-length biography of Merritt is Don Albert, *Brandy Station to Manila Bay: A Biography of General Wesley Merritt* (Austin, TX: Presidial Press, 1980).

concealed a fiery ambition. He was and is, I am glad to say, a successful and very able soldier, and well deserves the high rank he now holds in the regular army of the United States."[40]

"He has an army reputation as a cavalry officer second to none," war correspondent Charles A. Page recalled about Merritt, "and is admired by his fellow-soldiers for his gallantry under fire and for the rare good judgment shown in the splendid manner in which he handles his troops on all occasions."[41] Captain Theophilus F. Rodenbough, who succeeded Merritt in command of the 2nd U.S. Cavalry, thought Merritt was "the embodiment of force." Rodenbough considered him "one of those rare men whose faculties are sharpened and

Brig. Gen. David M. Gregg, commander of the 2nd Division, Cavalry Corps, Army of the Potomac.

(Library of Congress)

whose view is cleared on the battlefield. His decisions were delivered with the rapidity of thought and were as clear as if they had been studied for weeks. He always said that he never found that his first judgment gained by time and reflection." He continued, "In him a fiery soul was held in thrall to will. Never disturbed by doubt, or moved by fear, neither circumspect nor rash, he never missed an opportunity or made a mistake."[42] One of Custer's officers observed, "Modesty which fitted him like a garment, charming manners, the demeanor of a gentleman, cool but fearless bearing in action, were his distinguishing characteristics."[43]

Brigadier General David M. Gregg, another professional soldier, commanded the Second Cavalry Division. Gregg and Torbert were West Point classmates, and the modest Pennsylvanian was a first cousin

40. Hagemann, *Fighting Rebels and Redskins*, 225.
41. Charles A. Page, *Letters of a War Correspondent* (Boston: L. C. Page & Co., 1899), 293–4.
42. Theophilus F. Rodenbough, "Some Cavalry Leaders," in Francis Trevelyan Miller, ed., *The Photographic History of the Civil War*, 10 vols. (New York: The Review of Reviews, 1911), 4:278.
43. Kidd, *Personal Recollections*, 238–39.

of Andrew Gregg Curtin, wartime governor of the Keystone State. When war broke out, Gregg was a first lieutenant in the 1st Dragoons. He transferred to the newly formed 6th U.S. Cavalry in 1861. On January 24, 1862, he became colonel of the 8th Pennsylvania Cavalry and was then named brigadier general of volunteers on November 29, 1862. By the spring of 1864, at the age of 31, Gregg had already commanded a division for more than a year; no Union officer commanded a division of cavalry longer than Gregg. "He was the only division commander I had whose experience had been almost exclusively derived from the cavalry arm," Sheridan recalled.[44]

The men fondly remembered Gregg as "tall and spare, of notable activity, capable of the greatest exertion and exposure, gentle in manner but bold and resolute in action. Firm and just in discipline, he was a favorite of his troopers and ever held, for he deserved, their affection and entire confidence." Gregg knew the principles of war, remaining always ready and able to employ them. Endowed "with a natural genius of high order, he [was] universally hailed as the finest type of cavalry leader. A man of unimpeachable personal character, in private life affable and genial but not demonstrative, he fulfilled with modesty and honor all the duties of the citizen and head of an interesting and devoted family."[45]

Major General James H. Wilson penned, "In General David McM. Gregg . . . the cavalry had one of its best officers." Continuing, he wrote, "He had always belonged to that branch of the service, and was noted for sterling ability and great experience. Steady as a clock and as gallant as Murat, it has often been said that he was the best all-'round cavalry officer that ever commanded a division in either army."[46]

Calm, quiet, modest, and highly competent, Gregg's forethought and good execution led to a spectacular Federal victory against the vaunted Confederate cavalry at Gettysburg on July 3, 1863. A former officer later commented that Gregg's "modesty kept him from the notoriety that many gained through the newspapers; but in the army the testimony of all officers who knew him was the same. Brave, prudent, dashing when occasion required dash, and firm as a rock, he

---

44. Philip H. Sheridan, *Personal Memoirs of P. H. Sheridan*, 2 vols. (New York: Charles L. Webster & Co., 1888), 1:352.

45. "David McMurtrie Gregg," Circular No. 6, Series of 1917, Military Order of the Loyal Legion of the United States, Commandery of Pennsylvania, May 3, 1917, 2.

46. James H. Wilson, *Under the Old Flag: Recollections of Military Operations in the War for the Union, the Spanish War, the Boxer Rebellion, etc.*, 2 vols. (Westport, CT: Greenwood Press, 1912), 1:364.

was looked upon, both as a regimental commander and afterwards as Major-General, as a man in whose hands any troops were safe."[47]

Gregg's Second Division consisted of two brigades. The First Brigade, which included the 1st Massachusetts Cavalry, the 1st New Jersey Cavalry, the 6th Ohio Cavalry, and the 1st Pennsylvania Cavalry, was a veteran unit Davies commanded. A 28-year-old lawyer from New York City, Davies served with the 5th New York Infantry early in the war. He was then appointed major of the 2nd New York Cavalry, in which he served under Kilpatrick's command. Davies advanced through the ranks of lieutenant colonel and colonel, before receiving a promotion to brigadier general of volunteers in the fall of 1863. Rodenbough described Davies

Brig. Gen. Henry E. Davies, commander of the 1st Brigade, 2nd Division, Cavalry Corps, Army of the Potomac.

(Library of Congress)

as "polished, genial, and gallant."[48] Newhall remembered him as "earnest and dashing, always getting horses killed and balls through his boots; a strict disciplinarian and efficient in camp and field."[49] Davies eventually earned a promotion to major general of volunteers, rendering outstanding service in the war's closing days.

Gregg's first cousin, Col. John Irvin Gregg, commanded the Second Brigade. Unlike his cousin, the 37-year-old General Gregg was not a professional soldier by trade. When the war with Mexico broke out in 1846, J. I. Gregg enlisted in a Pennsylvania volunteer infantry regiment and quickly became an officer. After honorable service in the Mexican–American War, he returned home to Pennsylvania, where he

---

47. Samuel P. Bates, *Martial Deeds of Pennsylvania* (Philadelphia: T. H. Davis & Co., 1875), 722. There is no satisfactory full-length biography of Gregg available. The only published biography is Milton Burgess, *David Gregg: Pennsylvania Cavalryman* (privately published, 1984).
48. Rodenbough, "Sheridan's Richmond Raid," 188.
49. Newhall, *With General Sheridan*, 229.

owned and operated an iron foundry. When the Civil War began, he joined his cousin in the newly formed 3rd U.S. Cavalry, which was redesignated as the 6th U.S. Cavalry in the fall of 1861. In November 1862, Governor Curtin commissioned him colonel of the new 16th Pennsylvania Cavalry, and Gregg served with distinction. He assumed command of a brigade in his cousin's division in the spring of 1863. By the following spring he had commanded a brigade for about a year, during which time he performed well in combat, earning a reputation for being "steadfast" and "cool as a clock, looking out from under his broad slouch-hat on any phase of the battle."[50] His veteran brigade consisted of the 1st Maine Cavalry, 10th New York Cavalry, 2nd Pennsylvania Cavalry, 4th Pennsylvania Cavalry, 8th Pennsylvania Cavalry, 13th Pennsylvania Cavalry, and his own 16th Pennsylvania Cavalry.

Brigadier General James Harrison Wilson commanded the Third Division. Wilson was born on his father's farm near Shawneetown, Illinois, on September 27, 1837. He spent a year at McKendree College in St. Clair County, Illinois, before enrolling at West Point in 1855. In those years West Point was a five-year academy, which is why Wilson, who ranked sixth in his class, graduated in 1860, along with Wesley Merritt and Confederate Maj. Gen. Stephen D. Ramseur. Since he graduated at the top of his class, he was assigned to the topographical engineers, serving at Fort Vancouver in the Department of Oregon. During the winter of 1861 and 1862, he served as the chief topographical engineer of the Port Royal, South Carolina, expedition of the Department of the South. Wilson then took part in the reduction of Fort Pulaski, Georgia, at the mouth of the Savannah River. During the 1862 Maryland campaign, Wilson became an aide-de-camp to Maj. Gen. George B. McClellan and witnessed the battles of South Mountain and Antietam.

When his time with McClellan ended, he transferred to Grant's headquarters in the West and performed engineering duties as a staff lieutenant colonel. Throughout the entire Vicksburg campaign, he served as inspector general of the Army of the Tennessee. On October 30, 1863, he was promoted to brigadier general of volunteers, the only officer from Grant's staff ever promoted to troop command. Wilson remained on staff duty through the battle of Chattanooga and then served as chief engineer for Sherman's force, which was sent to relieve Knoxville. On February 17, 1864, Wilson was appointed chief of the Cavalry Bureau in Washington, D.C., where he demonstrated a superior ability for organization and administration. Finally, that spring, Grant assigned him command of the Third Cavalry Division,

50. Rodenbough, "Sheridan's Richmond Raid," 188; Newhall, *With General Sheridan*, 229.

succeeding Judson Kilpatrick and demonstrating why Wilson was often called "Grant's pet."[51]

Wilson "was a brilliant man intellectually, highly educated, and thoroughly companionable," former assistant Secretary of War Charles A. Dana remembered.[52] Major General David S. Stanley, who served with Wilson in the Western Theater from 1864 to 1865, described Wilson as "young, intelligent, and very ambitious."[53] Wilson could also be brash and abrasive, though. His biographer, Edward G. Longacre, observed that he "was often imperious and outspoken, to the extent that he fully alienated as many people as he attracted."[54] Reflecting similar sentiments, Custer and Wilson despised each other from their days at West Point, and Custer refused to serve under an officer junior

Brig. Gen. James H. Wilson, commander of the 3rd Division, Cavalry Corps, Army of the Potomac.

(Library of Congress)

to him in rank. To resolve the problem, the Michigan Cavalry Brigade was assigned to the First Division, and the First Brigade of the First Division, commanded by Col. George H. Chapman of the 3rd Indiana Cavalry, transferred to the Third Division.

George Henry Chapman was born in Holland, Massachusetts, on November 22, 1832. When he was six years old his family moved to Indiana, where his father and uncle published newspapers in Terre Haute and Indianapolis. Chapman attended the Marion County Seminary before becoming a navy midshipman in 1847. He resigned after only three years and followed his father into the newspaper

51. Warner, *Generals in Blue*, 566–68.
52. Charles A. Dana, *Recollections of the Civil War* (New York: D. Appleton, 1898), 62.
53. Stanley, *Personal Memoirs of Major General David S. Stanley*, 190.
54. Edward G. Longacre, *From Union Stars to Top Hat: A Biography of the Extraordinary General James Harrison Wilson* (Mechanicsburg, PA: Stackpole, 1972), 14.

Col. George H. Chapman, commander of the 1st Brigade, 3rd Division, Cavalry Corps, Army of the Potomac.

(NARA)

business, publishing the *Indiana Republican*, all while studying law. He was admitted to the bar in 1857, followed a few years later with an appointment to assistant clerk for the House of Representatives. By October 1861, Chapman resigned his position to accept a commission as a major in the 3rd Indiana Cavalry. Before long, he was promoted to lieutenant colonel in 1862 and to colonel in 1863, all while uniformly earning the praises of his superiors. He participated in the campaigns of Second Bull Run, Antietam, Fredericksburg, Chancellorsville, and Gettysburg. Chapman was a capable, dependable cavalry officer who led a veteran brigade consisting of the 8th New York, 3rd Indiana, 2nd Ohio, and 1st Vermont, which was one of the best volunteer cavalry regiments in the Union service.[55]

Colonel John Baillie McIntosh, at 35 years old, commanded the Second Brigade. McIntosh was the son of a Regular Army officer and served in the prewar navy. One of his brothers, Confederate Brig. Gen. James M. McIntosh, was killed in the March 1862 battle of Pea Ridge. Although not a West Pointer, McIntosh received a commission as a lieutenant in the 2nd U.S. Cavalry in 1861, and he compiled a distinguished record of service in the Civil War. He received a brevet to major for his service during the 1862 Peninsula campaign and succeeded William Woods Averell as colonel of the 3rd Pennsylvania Cavalry in November. With the formation of the Army of the Potomac's Cavalry Corps, McIntosh assumed command of Averell's 1st Brigade.[56] He was a "born fighter, a strict disciplinarian, a dashing leader, and a polished gentleman," although the men of his brigade did

55. Warner, *Generals in Blue*, 80–81. Chapman was promoted to brigadier general of volunteers on July 21, 1864.
56. Ibid., 300–301.

Col. John B. McIntosh, commander of the 2nd Brigade, 3rd Division, Cavalry Corps, Army of the Potomac.

(Library of Congress).

not particularly like him.[57] McIntosh proved himself a reliable and competent brigade commander, perhaps the finest in the Army of the Potomac. His brigade consisted of the 1st Connecticut, 2nd New York, 5th New York, and 18th Pennsylvania.

The Army of the Potomac's Cavalry Corps also included two brigades of horse artillery commanded by captains James M. Robertson and Dunbar R. Ransom. Each brigade consisted of six batteries of horse artillery.[58]

57. Mark M. Boatner III, *Civil War Dictionary* (New York: David McKay, 1959), 534.
58. Historically, two types of field artillery served with the armies: mounted artillery and horse artillery. With mounted artillery, teams of eight horses or mules drew the guns; teams of horses and mules also drew the limbers and caissons. The soldiers assigned to man the guns of mounted artillery either walked or rode on the caissons and limbers.

With horse artillery, each man assigned to the battery had his own mount, meaning that they were able to keep up with cavalry as it moved in the field. Essentially, horse artillery was a hybrid of cavalry and artillery. Dennis Hart Mahan, who taught military tactics at West Point and also translated French military manuals, defined the role of horse artillery:
The horse-artillery is held in hand for decisive moments. When launched forth, its arrival and execution should be unexpected and instantaneous. Ready to repair all disasters and partial reverses, it, at one moment, temporarily replaces a battery of foot, and at the next is on another point of the field, to force back an enemy's column. In preparing the attacks of cavalry, this arm is often indispensable and always invaluable; brought with rapidity in front of a line, or opposite to squares of infantry, within the range of canister, its well-directed fire, in a few discharges, opens a gap, or so shakes the entire mass, that the cavalier finds but a feeble obstacle, where, without this aid, he would in vain have exhausted all his powers.
Dennis Hart Mahan, *Elementary Treatise on Advance-Guard, Out-Post, and Detachment Service of Troops and the Manner of Posting and Handling Them in the Presence of the Enemy* (New York: Wiley, 1847), 47. The men were trained to move from place to place and then to quickly dismount, unlimber, and aim their guns, meaning that they could be brought to bear

Lt. Alexander C. M. Pennington, commander, Battery M, 2nd U. S. Artillery.

(Library of Congress)

The batteries comprised two sections of three-inch ordnance rifles, which were lightweight, highly accurate mobile cannons. All but one of the 12 batteries was Regular Army; only Capt. Joseph W. Martin's 6th New York Light Battery consisted of volunteers. The Regular batteries, most of which were commanded by West Point-trained career artillerists, were extremely capable. Lieutenants commanded 10 out of the 11 Regular batteries; Captain Alanson M. Randol, commander of combined Batteries H and I, 1st U.S. Artillery, was the only exception. Batteries often served with specific cavalry brigades. For example, Lt. Alexander C. M. Pennington's Battery M, 2nd U.S. Artillery, usually served with Custer's brigade.

Thus, Sheridan inherited a command that had been forged in battle and that was largely led by competent veteran officers who had proven their mettle during 1863's hard campaigns. The Army of the Potomac's Cavalry Corps had already shed the unflattering cliché, "Whoever saw a dead cavalryman?" The Yankee troopers were reasonably well mounted and superbly equipped. Custer's brigade and some other units carried seven-shot Spencer repeating carbines. One Regular gave a description of employing the Spencers: "The workmanship of the gun was indifferent, but it did, notwithstanding, excellent service and gave an immense advantage to the troops armed with it. [They] could throw in a tremendous fire when necessary, with great effect upon the enemy, who was naturally very often deceived in his estimate of the force opposed to him, judging by the unremitting incessant rattle along the

quickly and effectively in the field. Highly proficient, well-trained batteries of horse artillery could do so in about a minute.

line that he was contending with at least a division" when only a brigade faced them.[59]

Confederate trooper Edward Laight Wells, of Charleston, South Carolina, later observed that troops armed with Spencers "ought to have been equal to at least double their number carrying only muzzle-loaders."[60] Another Rebel trooper less elegantly described the Spencers: "You'uns load in the morning and fire all day."[61] Compared with the single-shot carbines most gray-clad horse soldiers carried, Yankee troopers enjoyed a significant advantage in firepower.

Unlike their Southern counterparts, the Federals also had plenty of supplies, including remounts. Excessive winter picketing, combined with the arduous Kilpatrick-Dahlgren raid, took a severe toll on the Cavalry Corps' mounts. Sheridan keenly noted the deteriorated state of the horses in the spring of 1864. Just after the conclusion of the Gettysburg campaign, the army created the Cavalry Bureau, which provided plenty of mounts for the burgeoning ranks of Union horse soldiers. While not a perfect institution by any means, the Cavalry Bureau successfully supplied ample fresh horseflesh for the Army of the Potomac's Cavalry Corps.

Once the reorganization of the Cavalry Corps was completed, Sheridan assessed the status of his new command. Appalled by the state of his corps and the wretched condition of its mounts, Sheridan faulted excessive picketing during the winter months that had inflicted a severe toll on both man and beast. Consequently, the Cavalry Corps' horses "were thin and very much worn out by excessive, and, it seemed to me, unnecessary picket duty." Sheridan continued, "However, shortly after my taking command, much of the picketing was done away with, and we had two weeks of leisure time to nurse the horses, on which so much depended."[62] As the horses rested, Sheridan developed a new approach for his troopers.

In his posthumous memoirs, Sheridan claimed he faced resistance from General Meade. The traditional role of cavalry in the Napoleonic model was scouting, screening, and reconnaissance. Fighting was secondary—the cavalry's primary role was leading the way for the infantry while preventing the prying eyes of the enemy from finding

59. Louis Henry Carpenter, "Sheridan's Expedition Around Richmond May 9–25, 1864," *Journal of the United States Cavalry Association* 1(1888), 301.
60. Edward L. Wells, *Hampton and His Cavalry in '64* (Richmond, VA: B. F. Johnson Publishing Co., 1899), 95.
61. Samuel Harris, *Personal Reminiscences of Samuel Harris* (Chicago: The Robinson Press, 1897), 31.
62. OR 36, 1:787.

the army's main body.[63] Sheridan had an entirely different and revolutionary vision for the cavalry.

According to Sheridan, he laid out his "idea as to what the cavalry should do, the main purport of which was that it ought to be concentrated to fight the enemy's cavalry. Heretofore, the commander of the Cavalry Corps had been, virtually, but an adjunct at army headquarters—a sort of chief of cavalry—and my proposition seemed to stagger General Meade not a little." Little Phil continued, "I knew that it would be difficult to overcome the recognized custom of using the cavalry for the protection of trains and the establishment of cordons around the infantry corps, and so far as subordinating its operations to the main movements of the main army that in name was it a corps at all, but I still thought it my duty to try."[64] In fact, Meade opposed Sheridan at every juncture, creating a great deal of friction and stress in their relationship.

A Regular Army officer described Sheridan's vision for the Cavalry Corps: "Sheridan insisted that his cavalry should not be

---

63. Union cavalryman Bvt. Maj. Gen. William W. Averell described the traditional role of cavalry:

> Reliable information of the enemy's position or movements, which is absolutely necessary to the commander of an army to successfully conduct a campaign, must be largely furnished by the cavalry. The duty of the cavalry when an engagement is imminent is specially imperative—to keep in touch with the enemy and observe and carefully note, with time of day or night, every slightest indication and report it promptly to the commander of the army. On the march, cavalry forms in advance, flank and rear guards and supplies escorts, couriers and guides. Cavalry should extend well away from the main body on the march like antennae to mask its movements and to discover any movement of the enemy.
>
> Cavalry should never hug the army on the march, especially in a thickly wooded country, because the horses being restricted to the roads, the slightest obstacle in advance is liable to cause a blockade against the march of infantry." Moreover, "in camp it furnishes outposts, vedettes and scouts. In battle it attacks the enemy's flanks and rear, and above all other duties in battle, it secures the fruits of victory by vigorous and unrelenting pursuit. In defeat it screens the withdrawal of the army and by its fortitude and activity baffles the enemy.

In addition to these active military duties of the cavalry, it receives flags of truce, interrogates spies, deserters and prisoners, makes and improves topographical maps, destroys and builds bridges, obstructs and opens communications, and obtains or destroys forage and supplies.

Edward K. Eckert and Nicholas J. Amato, eds., *Ten Years in the Saddle: The Memoir of William Woods Averell, 1851–1862* (San Rafael, Calif.: Presidio Press, 1978), 328–9.

64. Sheridan, *Personal Memoirs*, 1:354–55.

separated into fragments but should be concentrated 'to fight the enemy's cavalry.'" Sheridan intended the Cavalry Corps be just that—a fully integrated corps that acted independently of the main body of the army. By keeping the enemy cavalry occupied, Sheridan would not have to worry about performing the traditional roles of cavalry.[65]

When the Army of the Potomac set out for its spring campaign in the first days of May 1864, it boasted one of the largest and most powerful fighting cavalry commands the world had ever seen. With a well-equipped, well-led, and well-mounted force of more than 10,000 horsemen, Sheridan champed at the bit to try out his theory and pitch into the Confederate cavalry. He would not have to wait long to seize his opportunity.

65. Charles D. Rhodes, "Cavalry Battles and Charges," in Francis Trevelyan Miller, ed., *The Photographic History of the Civil War*, 10 vols. (New York: Review of Reviews Co., 1911), 4:240–42.

CHAPTER 2

Opening Moves: The Overland Campaign Begins

The Army of the Potomac moved out of its winter camps around Brandy Station in Culpeper County, Virginia, before midnight on May 3, 1864. The two armies clashed in the Wilderness on May 5 and 6, inflicting massive casualties on each side.[1] The Wilderness was a thick bramble of secondary forests filled with dense undergrowth. As the Federals and Confederates learned a year earlier at the battle of Chancellorsville, the Wilderness was not conducive for maneuvering or fighting. Early on the morning of May 5, Brig. Gen. James H. Wilson's Third Cavalry Division got its chance to shine when Maj. Gen. George G. Meade allowed Maj. Gen. Philip H. Sheridan to launch an offensive with his horse soldiers.

When Meade called Brig. Gen. Alfred T. A. Torbert's First Cavalry Division up to support Sheridan's proposed attack, Wilson shifted his division south of the Catharpin Road to cover the II Corps' movement. In his first action commanding troops in the field, Wilson did not do well. Engaging with Confederate Brig. Gen. Thomas L. Rosser's Virginia cavalry brigade, Wilson's troopers had a furious fight. Accurate horse artillery fire aided Rosser's Virginians in shattering Wilson's line and driving his men from the field, which prevented Wilson from warning Meade that the Army of Northern Virginia blocked his path.[2] The new division commander did not enjoy an auspicious debut. Rosser's success permitted Maj. Gen. Fitzhugh Lee to move his division of Confederate cavalry to Todd's Tavern, at the critical intersection of the Catharpin and Brock roads, where it could block the Army of the Potomac's direct route around the Army of Northern Virginia's right flank to Spotsylvania Court House. Thus, Sheridan's aggressiveness and inexperience in turn caused the equally inexperienced Wilson to suffer a serious defeat at the hands of the Southern horse soldiers. Another division of the Cavalry Corps should have performed that important role, not the inexperienced Wilson's. Brigadier General David M. Gregg's division had been nearby, and its veterans could have performed this duty easily.

---

1 Parts of the Wilderness battlefield overlapped with the 1863 Chancellorsville battlefield.

2 Gordon C. Rhea, *The Battle of the Wilderness, May 5–6, 1864* (Baton Rouge: Louisiana State University Press, 1994), 115–17.

The Wilderness' densely wooded terrain forced the horse soldiers to fight on foot, requiring Meade's battle plan to preclude a major role for cavalry. Instead, the army commander wanted Sheridan to perform conventional cavalry duty by protecting the Army of the Potomac's wagon trains. The aggressive Sheridan, chafing under the restrictions, complained, "I cannot do anything with the cavalry except to act on the defensive. Why cannot infantry be sent to guard the trains and let me take the offensive?" Meade gave Sheridan permission to detach portions of his command for secondary operations, such as severing lines of communications, but these orders did not placate his unhappy subordinate.[3] With little help from Northern cavalry, the Army of Northern Virginia defeated the Army of the Potomac in two days of brutal, close combat. Displeased with Meade's conduct of the battle, Lt. Gen. Ulysses S. Grant began directing the army's movements himself, creating an awkward command structure.

Instead of pulling back to lick his wounds like his predecessors had, Grant sidled around Lee's right flank, trying to interpose the Army of the Potomac between Lee and Richmond by occupying the critical crossroads town of Spotsylvania Court House. In the vanguard of the Northern advance, Sheridan's horsemen fought and scouted, losing crucial engagements along the Plank Road on May 5 and at Todd's Tavern on May 6 and 7.

On May 8, with Brig. Gen. Wesley Merritt in temporary command of the First Division, the Reserve Brigade led the division's advance along the Catharpin Road, with Devin's brigade following. The 6th Pennsylvania Cavalry of the Reserve Brigade led the advance westward. It was the Regulars' turn to lead the First Division into the sparring ring on the morning of May 8. "We had certainly not advanced a mile, and daylight had scarcely broken when we were again as heavily engaged as on the previous evening," Capt. George Sanford, First Division staff, wrote.[4]

Merritt reported, "On advancing the leading brigade (the Reserve) was immediately engaged, soon very heavily with the enemy's dismounted cavalry and infantry."[5] He ordered two of Col. Thomas C. Devin's regiments to support the Reserve Brigade. "Dismounting Ninth New York Cavalry and Seventeenth Pennsylvania Cavalry, sent them in on the right and left of the Reserve Brigade," Devin recalled.[6] Devin's men moved into position and attacked the Confederates. "Our

---

3 *OR* 36, 2:428, 513, and 515.
4 E. R. Hagemann, ed., *Fighting Rebels and Redskins: Experiences in Army Life of Colonel George B. Sanford, 1861–1892* (Norman: University of Oklahoma Press, 1969), 228.
5 *OR* 36, pt.1, 811–12.
6 Ibid., 834.

line was formed with [George A.] Custer's brigade of Torbert's division on the right; Colonel Gregg's brigade of General Gregg's division next; then General Merritt's brigade of the 1st Division and, on the extreme left, Davies' brigade of Gregg's division," the historian of the 6th Pennsylvania Cavalry described. "General Merritt held the right, where combat was hottest. The Reserve Brigade suffered the most, as it was most hardly pressed, and most nobly did they meet the desperate onslaught. Our cavalry were all dismounted, for the contest occurred mostly in thick woods, where horses could not be used to advantage."[7]

"For perhaps an hour or more we managed to make some slight progress, but then by the increasing weight of fire it became evident that [J. E. B.] Stuart had been re-enforced by the Confederate Infantry," Capt. George B. Sanford recalled, adding that "our advance came practically to a standstill."[8] Devin reported, "The enemy was driven back to a strong position, barricaded along his whole front, which he succeeded in holding until the cavalry was relieved by the Fifth Corps, when the brigade was ordered to retire."[9]

The narrow bridge over the Chickahominy created a bottleneck that slowed the advance of the Federal cavalry by pinching the column into a single file. Both Merritt's and Gregg's troopers waited for their opportunity to cross in fields on either side of the road. Just then, the van of Maj. Gen. Gouverneur K. Warren's V Corps appeared, which cost the Army of the Potomac any opportunity to seize Spotsylvania Court House. "Merritt's cavalry became inextricably entangled with Warren's infantry," Maj. James H. Kidd, 6th Michigan Cavalry, declared, "so that neither one reached Spotsylvania, as they were both expected to do, Gregg was neutralized."[10]

At that moment, Sheridan reined in and found Merritt in a heated argument with Warren, an engineer "who had no great love for cavalry" and who was "making complaint that the cavalry were obstructing his infantry column."[11] Warren was livid, and for "years afterwards complained bitterly of the way in which [Merritt] and Gregg delayed the march of his weightier columns," Wilson recollected. "He always contended that the cavalry should have kept together on the left flank and given the infantry clear road."

---

7 Samuel L. Gracey, *Annals of the Sixth Pennsylvania Cavalry* (Philadelphia: E. H. Butler & Co., 1868), 238–39.
8 Hagemann, *Fighting Rebels and Redskins*, 228.
9 *OR* 36, pt.1, 834.
10 Kidd, *Personal Recollections*, 285.
11 Hagemann, *Fighting Rebels and Redskins*, 229; Sheridan, *Personal Memoirs*, 1:367.

Maj. James H. Kidd, commander,
6th Michigan Cavalry.

(Bentley Library, University of Michigan)

A few minutes later Meade arrived[12] and informed Sheridan that he had changed Merritt's and Gregg's orders. He had ordered Gregg "simply to hold Corbin's bridge, and Merritt to move out in front of the infantry column marching on Spotsylvania."[13] Sheridan somehow managed to hold his notorious Irish temper. "I made some strong remonstrances against the course that had been pursued, but by then it was too late to carry out the combinations I had projected the night before," Sheridan lamented. "I drew Merritt off the road, and the leading division of the Fifth Corps pushed up to the front."[14]

The bulk of Warren's infantrymen arrived "in good style as usual" and tried to force their way through the mass of horse soldiers along the road, evidencing the rivalry between infantry and cavalry that marked the war.[15] "A little after daylight the infantry came up," Lt. Charles H. Veil of the 1st U.S. Cavalry remembered. "Brigadier General John C. Robinson's division was leading with him riding at the head . . . As he rode by where I was, I heard him say to someone, 'Oh, get your d____d cavalry out of the way. There is nothing ahead but a little cavalry. We will soon clean them out.' I thought to myself, 'Old man, you will find something more than a little cavalry on ahead.' He went on and in, but less than fifteen minutes afterward I saw them carry my General Robinson back on a stretcher with a leg shot off."[16]

This episode plainly demonstrates not only the friction between the infantry and the cavalry, but also how incessant conflict between

---

12 Wilson, *Under the Old Flag*, 1:395.
13 Sheridan, *Personal Memoirs*, 1:366.
14 Ibid.
15 Hagemann, *Fighting Rebels and Redskins*, 229.
16 Herman J. Viola, ed., *The Memoirs of Charles Henry Veil: A Soldier's Recollections of the Civil War and the Arizona Territories* (New York: Orion Books, 1993), 38.

Meade and Sheridan ultimately cost the Army of the Potomac. When Sheridan's troopers failed to clear the road from the Wilderness to Spotsylvania, that crucial thoroughfare remained in Confederate hands, permitting Fitzhugh Lee's cavalry to seize the important crossroads at Todd's Tavern before the Army of the Potomac could do so.[17] The road to Spotsylvania Court House was not cleared because Sheridan neglected to act promptly after receiving orders on May 8.[18] With Meade failing to win the race to Spotsylvania Court House, the two armies fell into a bloody and brutal stalemate, slugging it out for nearly two weeks.

The evening of May 8, annoyed by the cavalry's failure, Meade summoned Sheridan to his headquarters. Sheridan, in turn, was furious that Meade had issued direct orders to one of his subordinates outside the normal chain of command. There, "a very acrimonious dispute took place between the two generals." Meade told Sheridan, in no uncertain terms, that he was unhappy with the cavalry's performance, which sparked an extended argument.[19]

Sheridan later recounted telling Meade that he had "broken up my combinations, exposed Wilson's division, and kept Gregg unnecessarily idle, and ... such disjointed operations as he had been requiring of the cavalry . . .would render the corps inefficient and useless." According to Sheridan, the discussion took on a loud and ominous tone. " One word brought on another until, finally I told him that I could whip Stuart if he (Meade) would let me, but since he insisted on giving the cavalry directions without consulting or even notifying me, he could thenceforth command the Cavalry Corps himself—that I would not give it another order."[20] In a towering fit of pique, Sheridan stormed out of the meeting, leaving Meade sputtering with rage.

Meade, perhaps wanting to relieve the little Irishman of command for insubordination, went directly to Grant's nearby tent and recounted what had occurred to the commanding general. Grant listened silently until Meade mentioned Sheridan's desire to whip Stuart's cavalry. "Did Sheridan say that?" Grant inquired. "Well, he

17 Little has been written on the brutal fighting at and near Todd's Tavern, the substance of which strays beyond the scope of this study. For the most comprehensive work on Todd's Tavern to date, see Rhea, *The Battle of the Wilderness.*

18 Andrew A. Humphreys, *The Virginia Campaign of 1864 and 1865: The Army of the Potomac and the Army of the James,* 2 vols. (New York: Charles Scribner's Sons, 1883), 1:60–72.

19 Porter, *Campaigning with Grant,* 83–84.

20 Sheridan, *Personal Memoirs,* 1:368–69.

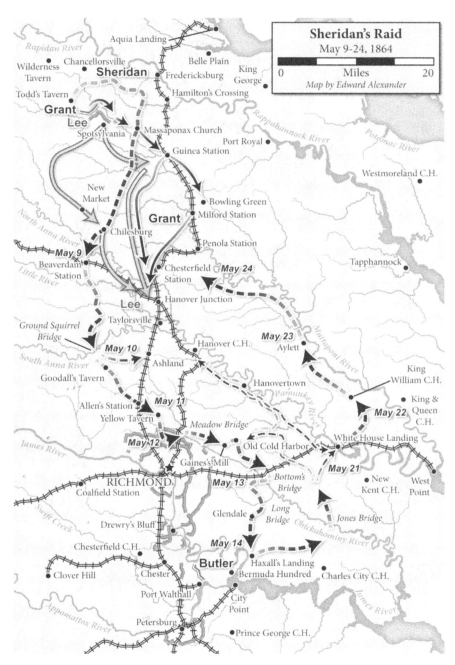

Sheridan's May Richmond Raid.

generally knows what he is talking about. Let him start right out and do it."[21]

An elated Sheridan summoned his subordinates that night. "We are going to fight Stuart's cavalry in consequence of a suggestion from me," he said. "We will give him a fair, square fight; we are strong, and I know we can beat him and in view of my recent representations to General Meade I shall expect nothing but success." The enemy cavalry would be the primary target of the expedition. "Our move," Sheridan ordered, "would be a challenge to Stuart for a cavalry duel behind Lee's lines, and in his own country."[22]

With his entire corps in tow, Sheridan set out the next day to whip Jeb Stuart and his vaunted cavalry. Encountering a small force of enemy horsemen, the Federals pushed

Maj. Gen. J.E.B. Stuart, former commander, Cavalry Corps, Army of Northern Virginia.

(Library of Congress)

---

21 Porter, *Campaigning with Grant*, 84. There is no evidence that Meade specifically intended to relieve Sheridan and replace him with Gregg, the senior division commander. This seems to have been the case. However, Sheridan was Grant's choice to command the Cavalry Corps, not Meade's. The two men had already had some friction in their relationship about Sheridan's ideas for the use of the Cavalry Corps. Meade likely saw Sheridan's actions as a direct challenge to his authority, and he acted strongly. Further, Sheridan had failed in his mission to clear the way for the infantry's advance to Spotsylvania Court House via Todd's Tavern. Obviously, Grant disagreed with the army commander's assessment, something that undoubtedly angered Meade a great deal. An early account from Bvt. Lt. Col. Carswell McClellan, a cavalry staff officer, accused Sheridan of being both a liar and insubordinate. McClellan claimed that Grant rewarded Sheridan's insubordination of refusing to obey the lawful orders of his commanding officer, Meade, by permitting Sheridan to cut loose from the army in independent command rather than punish him for insubordination. See Carswell McClellan, *Notes on the Personal Memoirs of P. H. Sheridan* (St. Paul, MN: Press of Wm. E. Banning Jr., 1889), 25.
22 Sheridan, *Personal Memoirs*, 1:370–71.

through their thin ranks. "Keep moving boys," Sheridan roared. "We're going on through. There isn't cavalry enough in the Southern Confederacy to stop us."[23]

When word of Sheridan's departure reached Stuart, he gathered part of his command for a forced march and intercepted Sheridan's line of advance at Yellow Tavern on the Telegraph Road, a few miles north of Richmond. During a day of intense fighting on May 11, Stuart suffered a mortal wound. The plumed cavalier died in Richmond the next day while the Army of Northern Virginia clashed in the Bloody Angle of the Mule Shoe salient at Spotsylvania. Sheridan's troopers swept aside the smaller Confederate force, opening the road to Richmond. The Northern troopers pushed on to the first line of defenses surrounding Richmond but were repulsed and failed to seize the Confederate capital.

Instead, Sheridan moved to link up with Maj. Gen. Benjamin F. Butler's Army of the James, which was operating on the north side of the peninsula east of Richmond. "It is possible that I might have captured the city of Richmond by an assault," Sheridan claimed in a note to Meade, "but the want of knowledge of your operations and those of General Butler, and the facility with which the enemy could throw in troops, made me abandon the attempt."[24] Given the strength of Richmond's defenses, his relatively small force of horsemen likely could not have taken the city, and even if they had captured it, they could not have held it.[25] Instead, Sheridan and his horsemen turned northeast.

Fitzhugh Lee's cavalry had laid a trap for the unsuspecting Federals at Meadow Bridges, an important crossing over the swampy Chickahominy River, just outside Richmond's defenses. By May 12, Sheridan's men were nearly out of food, forage for their horses, and ammunition, and the gray-clad horse soldiers had hemmed them in. One of Devin's New Yorkers called it "the tightest place in which the corps ever found itself," and a Maine trooper recalled it as "the most

---

23 Stephen Z. Starr, *The Union Cavalry in the Civil War*, 3 vols. (Baton Rouge: Louisiana State University Press, 1981), 2:297.

24 *OR* 36, 1:778.

25 After the failure of the Kilpatrick-Dahlgren raid, the Confederate government evacuated the prisoners of war from Richmond and sent them to prison camps throughout the Deep South, including a newly built camp at Andersonville, Georgia, so that the Union high command would not be tempted to try another raid to free the prisoners. Thus, had Sheridan forced his way into Richmond that day, he would have accomplished little other than gaining the publicity value of seizing the Confederate capital.

foreboding experience of my army life."[26] As Sheridan pushed toward Meadow Bridges, the initial Confederate line, manned largely by clerks from Richmond, shattered, but as the Federals pressed on, Confederate resistance stiffened. Elements of Brig. Gen. George A. Custer's Michigan Brigade cleared the causeway over Meadow Bridges, establishing a fragile bridgehead to safety across the Chickahominy.

Gen. Robert E. Lee, commander, Army of Northern Virginia.

(Library of Congress)

Sheridan recognized he had a tenuous position and fretted about his predicament. Fitzhugh Lee's cavalry division had joined the fray, as had more infantry from Richmond. The concentrated firepower from the Spencer carbines of Custer's Wolverines held the Confederate horsemen at bay long enough for Federal pioneers to repair the railroad span across the Chickahominy. The Northern cavalrymen then streamed across the bridge and, with the Reserve Brigade leading, launched a desperate attack, clearing the way for the Union cavalry to escape. Sheridan proudly watched his troopers file across the bridge to safety.[27]

By May 14, the Cavalry Corps had safely made its way to Butler's base at Haxall's Landing on the James River. The horsemen remained there for several days, resting and refitting. Five days later, the bulk of the brutal fighting at Spotsylvania was over, and on May 19, Grant

---

26 Alonzo V. Foster, *Reminiscences and Record of the 6th New York V. V. Cavalry* (Brooklyn, NY: privately published, 1892), 75; Edward P. Tobie, *History of the First Maine Cavalry* (Boston: Press of Emery & Hughes, 1887), 266.

27 Gordon C. Rhea, *To the North Anna River: Grant and Lee, May 13–25, 1864* (Baton Rouge: Louisiana State University Press, 2000), 46–56. Rhea's account is the only detailed tactical treatment of the important engagement at Meadow Bridges.

ordered Meade to move his entire army southeast of Spotsylvania to the North Anna River.

Four days later, the Army of the Potomac attempted to cross the North Anna, but a stout Confederate defense located on a dominating ridge overlooking Ox Ford thwarted it. The Confederates held a nearly impregnable position; however, the Federals avoided massive casualties only because Major General Warren, V Corps commander, refused to attack. Had cavalry accompanied the army at the North Anna, the Northerners might not have advanced blindly into a trap. After disengaging, Grant again sidled around Robert E. Lee's right flank and headed for Richmond, with the Army of Northern Virginia in pursuit. The Cavalry Corps did not rejoin the Army of the Potomac until May 25. "Just returned from 'Sheridan's Great Raid,'" Lt. Edward Granger, who served on Custer's staff, reported on May 25. "Don't know how long we shall stay here. Don't know anything, except that Grant is whipping Lee thoroughly."[28]

As part of his grand strategy, Grant sent Maj. Gen. Franz Sigel's army up the Shenandoah Valley, intending to deprive Lee of his primary source of supplies and provender. When a scratch-Confederate force defeated Sigel at New Market, Virginia, on May 15, Grant replaced Sigel with Maj. Gen. David "Black Dave" Hunter, a man whom Confederate cavalry Brig. Gen. John D. Imboden derisively described as "a human hyena."[29] Hunter consolidated his command and advanced toward Staunton, intending to destroy the vital Virginia Central Railroad depot. Once he completed that mission, Hunter intended to advance on Charlottesville.[30]

Though Sheridan won the fight at Yellow Tavern, his raid failed to achieve its objectives: defeat the Confederate cavalry and enter Richmond. However, in spite of this failure, Sheridan earned a reputation with the Confederates as a "vicious" cavalry leader.[31] Because Sheridan did not rejoin the Army of the Potomac until May 25, Meade had only five cavalry regiments for more than two weeks of hard campaigning. The absence of the Army of the Potomac's Cavalry

---

28 Sandy Barnard, ed., *An Aide to Custer: The Civil War Letters of Lt. Edward G. Granger* (Norman: University of Oklahoma Press, 2018), 215.
29 John D. Imboden to I. Marshall McCue, October 1, 1883, John D. Imboden Papers, Archives, Museum of the Confederacy, Richmond, Virginia. For a detailed discussion of the campaign in the Shenandoah Valley, see Richard R. Duncan, *Lee's Endangered Left: The Civil War in Western Virginia, Spring of 1864* (Baton Rouge: Louisiana State University Press, 1999).
30 *OR* 37, 1:485–86.
31 Thomas Nelson Conrad, *The Rebel Scout: A Thrilling History of Scouting Life in the Southern Army* (Washington, D.C.: The National Publishing Co., 1904), 109.

Corps probably cost Grant a prime opportunity to win the war at the North Anna River and left him blindly groping for his adversary.[32]

Sheridan tried to put a positive spin on those events in his memoirs. "Our return to Chesterfield ended the first independent operation the Cavalry Corps had undertaken since coming under my command," he claimed, "and our success was commended highly by Generals Grant and Meade, both realizing that our operations in the rear of Lee had disconnected and alarmed that general so much as to aid materially in forcing his retrograde march." Sheridan also stated that "when Stuart was defeated the main purpose of my instructions had been carried out and my thoughts then turned to joining General Butler to get supplies."[33]

Despite failing to achieve their objective, the Yankee troopers considered the raid a great success because they had killed Stuart. "With regard to this expedition, now at an end, it seemed upon all hands to be taken for granted that it was a brilliant and complete success," a Federal trooper declared. "Whenever in the course of conversation any allusion to it chanced to be made, it was referred to more as a matter which spoke for itself than as one requiring illustration or admitting discussion."[34] Sheridan echoed similar sentiments, asserting that even though his horses were jaded from overwork and lack of forage, his corps was in "fine spirits with its success."[35]

Despite what Sheridan and his men claimed, the raid was ill-advised. "Serious criticism can be leveled against the broader features of Sheridan's campaign," historian Gordon C. Rhea correctly observed. "By taking his cavalry from Spotsylvania Court House, Sheridan severely handicapped Grant in his battles against Lee. The Union army was deprived of its eyes and ears during a critical juncture in the campaign. And Sheridan's decision to advance boldly to the Richmond defenses smacked of unnecessary showboating that jeopardized his command."[36] In spite of these negative effects, the morale of the Federal horse soldiers reached an all-time high as a result of the Richmond raid.

The unusually warm spring of 1864 took a further toll on Sheridan's horses. The Cavalry Corps required additional refitting before it could attempt another major raid. Despite a leisurely

---

32 For a detailed study of the lost opportunity at the North Anna, see Rhea, *To the North Anna River.*
33 Sheridan, *Personal Memoirs*, 1:390–92.
34 Charles E. Phelps, "Recollections of the Wilderness Campaign," Charles E. Phelps Papers, Archives, Maryland Historical Society, Baltimore, Maryland.
35 *OR* 36, 1:777.
36 Rhea, *To the North Anna River*, 62.

marching pace, worn-out beasts dropped by the score. Rather than allowing broken-down horses to fall into Confederate hands, where they could be nursed back to health and put into service, the animals experienced a harsher fate. As horses deteriorated on the side of the road, Yankee troopers shot them and then trudged off, the saddles and equipment slung over their shoulders.[37] Despite these losses, the Cavalry Bureau provided sufficient remounts and reinforcements to keep a large, effective force in the field.

The Overland campaign marked a change in the mission of the Army of the Potomac's Cavalry Corps. Severe tests awaited the blue-clad troopers in the coming days.

---

37 Carpenter, "Sheridan's Expedition around Richmond," 321.

CHAPTER THREE

Wade Hampton and His Cavaliers

Although the first two years of the war were difficult for the Army of the Potomac's Cavalry Corps, by the summer of 1863, the Yankee cavalry had grown into a formidable adversary. Stuart began suffering defeats at the hands of an enemy that he had laughed off only months earlier. Federal tactics and leadership caught up to Stuart's command, and Northern technology gave the Yankee troopers an advantage in firepower and logistics. Further, much of Stuart's command was understrength and widely scattered during the winter of 1863-1864, and it did not reunite until the Overland campaign had nearly completed. As a result, Maj. Gen. William H. F. "Rooney" Lee's division had only one brigade until late spring 1864. Although reinforcements were forthcoming from the Deep South, Stuart and his Cavalry Corps paid dearly that spring.

Heavy casualties in the officer cadre of the Army of Northern Virginia's Cavalry Corps forced a major reorganization in the fall of 1863. Until September 1863, Stuart commanded an oversized and unwieldy division of seven brigades, as he was the only major general of cavalry assigned to the Army of Northern Virginia. The new command structure established two divisions under major generals Fitzhugh Lee and Wade Hampton. In March 1864, Rooney Lee, who was captured in June 1863 while recuperating from combat wounds received at the June 9 battle of Brandy Station, was exchanged and returned to the Army of Northern Virginia. After receiving a promotion to major general, he needed troops to command. Stuart assigned a brigade each from the other two divisions to form Rooney Lee's division.

General Robert E. Lee was dealing with far-reaching ramifications after the 31-year-old Stuart's death on May 12, 1864. Now left without his eyes and ears, General Lee reportedly wept upon hearing news of Stuart's death, lamenting, "He never brought me a piece of false information."[1] Trooper William L. Watson of the 12th Virginia Cavalry rued the dashing cavalier's passing. "The Cavalry corps has

---

1 Emory N. Thomas, *Bold Dragoon: The Life of J. E. B. Stuart* (New York: Random House, 1986), 297.

lost its great leader the unequalled Stuart," he wrote. "We miss him much. Hampton is a good officer but Stuart's equal does not exist."[2]

As a result of Stuart's passing, General Lee faced a difficult situation. A rivalry smoldered between his nephew Fitzhugh Lee and Wade Hampton. One of Fitz Lee's troopers staked his hero's claim to command of the Cavalry Corps: "The mantle of Stuart finally came to Fitzhugh Lee," he asserted. "This was but natural. Stuart and Fitz Lee fought side by side, and planned cavalry campaigns together, and Fitz was Stuart's trusted officer to carry out the boldest maneuvers. The cavalry of the Army of Northern Virginia wanted no other leader than Fitz Lee after Stuart's death."[3]

However, Hampton was senior in rank to Fitz Lee, which presented problems. "Hampton's seniority in rank was based upon his commission as brigadier two months ahead of Fitz, and the listing of his name immediately above Fitz's in the recommendations for promotion to major-general," one of Hampton's biographers asserted. "This was a margin so narrow as perhaps to seem no margin at all to Fitz and his friends."[4] Hampton and one of Fitz Lee's brigade commanders, Brig. Gen. Williams C. Wickham, also had bad blood, as Hampton blamed Wickham for the death of his brother, Lt. Col. Frank Hampton, at the June 1863 battle of Brandy Station.[5] Because of this conflict and tension, General Lee elected not to appoint a new corps commander but instead maintained the three divisions as independent commands, with each division commander reporting directly to him.[6] While this was a wise political move, it created its own problems by not having a clear chain of command in the field.

---

2 Festus P. Summers, ed., *A Borderland Confederate* (Pittsburgh, PA: University of Pittsburgh Press, 1962), 80; Tracy Power, *Lee's Miserables: Life in the Army of Northern Virginia from the Wilderness to Appomattox* (Chapel Hill: University of North Carolina Press, 1998), 57.

3 G. T. Cralle, "The Bold Horsemen," *Richmond Dispatch*, January 7, 1900.

4 Manly Wade Wellman, *Giant in Gray: A Biography of Wade Hampton of South Carolina* (New York: Charles Scribner's Sons, 1949), 140.

5 Ibid., 109. The courtly Hampton, who was almost invariably diplomatic in his dealings with his fellow officers, publicly criticized Wickham. "But for one fact," he said, "that the Fourth Virginia Cavalry, under the Command of Colonel Wickham, broke and ran, my brother, Frank Hampton, would not have been killed that day."

6 *OR* 36, 2:1001. ("[U]ntil further orders, the three Divisions of Cavalry serving with this Army will constitute separate commands and will report directly to and receive orders from this headquarters."); Lloyd Halliburton, ed., *Saddle Soldiers: The Civil War Correspondence of General William Stokes of the 4th South Carolina Cavalry* (Orangeburg, SC: Sandlapper Publishing Co., 1993), 193 ("Since Stuart has been killed I hear there will be no more Cavalry Corps, but that each of the major generals will have a division and report direct to General Lee.")

When Fitz Lee chose to act on his own, as he often did, it only exacerbated these issues.

Short in height and prone to obesity, Fitzhugh Lee, whom Douglas Southall Freeman dubbed "The Laughing Cavalier" for his goofy nature, was a member of the West Point class of 1856. Fond of good food and fine whiskey, Fitz graduated near the bottom of his class, 45th out of 49 cadets, and accumulated numerous demerits for pranks and shenanigans. Fitz was commissioned into the 2nd U.S. Cavalry (later redesignated as the 5th U.S. Cavalry) and fought Comanche Indians in Texas. In 1859, while chasing Comanches in Kansas, Fitz led his troopers in a dismounted attack and took an arrow to the chest, which badly wounded him.[7] He

Maj. Gen. Fitzhugh Lee, commander, Fitz Lee's Division, Cavalry Corps, Army of Northern Virginia.

(Library of Congress)

eventually recovered from the injury and returned to duty in 1860. Again pursuing Indians, Fitz found himself in hand-to-hand combat with a hostile brave. Using his ample bulk, he wrestled the warrior to the ground before dispatching him with two revolver shots.[8]

When the Civil War broke out, Fitz Lee was teaching tactics at West Point. He resigned his commission in the U.S. army, accepted a commission in the Provisional Army of the Confederate States of America, and joined Gen. Joseph E. Johnston's staff. After serving on Brig. Gen. Richard S. Ewell's staff at the First Battle of Bull Run in July 1861, he was appointed lieutenant colonel of the 1st Virginia Cavalry, serving under Col. Jeb Stuart. After Stuart's promotion in April 1862, Fitz Lee was elected colonel of the 1st Virginia. He received promotion to brigadier general three months later in recognition of his service during the Peninsula campaign.[9]

---

7 James R. Arnold, *Jeff Davis's Own: Cavalry, Comanches, and the Battle for the Texas Frontier* (New York: John Wiley & Sons, 2007), 243–44.
8 Ibid., 282–84.
9 Warner, *Generals in Gray*, 178.

Brig. Gen. Williams C. Wickham, commander, Wickham's Brigade, Fitz Lee's Division, Cavalry Corps, Army of Northern Virginia.

(Library of Congress)

To date, Fitz's service had been a mixed bag. He and Stuart were close friends, sharing the same sense of humor, the same love of frivolity, and the same enjoyment for pomp and circumstance. Lieutenant General James Longstreet thought Fitz Lee "was anything but an efficient cavalryman," a sentiment others shared.[10] Sometimes, such as at Chancellorsville, Virginia, when his scouts discovered the Union flank was unprotected and vulnerable to attack, he was brilliant; other times he seemed slow and stupid. Fitz was plagued with the early stages of arthritis that kept him from actively participating in the battle of Brandy Station.[11] In September 1863, though, he was promoted to major general and assumed command of a division.

Fitz Lee's division consisted of Wickham's and Brig. Gen. Lunsford Lomax's veteran brigades. Williams Carter Wickham, an influential Virginia lawyer, planter, and politician, was 44 years old. He was directly descended from Robert "King" Carter, who owned 300,000 acres and 42 plantations in Virginia, and his mother was a first cousin of Robert E. Lee. He also became Rooney Lee's father-in-law. He attended the University of Virginia and was admitted to the bar in 1842. After practicing law for five years, he opted for the genteel life of a Virginia planter, judge of the county court, and politician, serving in the House of Delegates and the state senate in the years before the Civil War. He had strongly opposed Virginia seceding, voting against it at the secession convention, but once the Ordinance of Secession

10 James Longstreet to Thomas T. Munford, September 9, 1894, Munford-Ellis Family Papers, Perkins Library, Duke University, Durham, NC.
11 Edward G. Longacre, *Lee's Cavalrymen: A History of the Mounted Forces of the Army of Northern Virginia, 1861–1865* (Mechanicsburg, PA: Stackpole Books, 2002), 190.

passed, Wickham cast his lot with his state, believing he was duty-bound to protect his fellow citizens. Brave in the fight, Wickham suffered a severe wound at the May 1862 battle of Williamsburg. He continuously commanded a brigade of cavalry under Fitz Lee until resigning his commission to take a seat in the Confederate States of America Congress in November 1864.[12]

Fortunately, Wickham had a very competent senior colonel—Thomas T. Munford of the 2nd Virginia Cavalry. Munford, a 33-year-old graduate of the Virginia Military Institute, was long overdue for promotion to brigadier general. One biographer stated that Munford's "career as a cavalry officer was brilliant and notable," despite failing to achieve the high rank he deserved. Wickham's brigade

Brig. Gen. Lunsford L. Lomax, commander, Lomax's Brigade, Fitz Lee's Division, Cavalry Corps, Army of Northern Virginia.

(USAHEC)

contained some of the finest mounted units in either army: Stuart's and Fitz Lee's former command, the 1st Virginia Cavalry; Munford's 2nd Virginia Cavalry; the 3rd Virginia Cavalry; and Wickham's own 4th Virginia Cavalry—all hard-fighting, veteran units.[13]

---

12 Benjamin E. Snellgrove, "Williams Carter Wickham," included in William C. Davis and Julie Hoffman, eds., *The Confederate General*, 6 vols. (New York: National Historical Society, 1991), 6:134–35 (hereafter, "The Confederate General").

13 Both men were experienced commanders. Munford commanded Fitz Lee's brigade at Brandy Station and at the June 17, 1863, battle of Aldie, and Wickham commanded Fitz's division in the Shenandoah Valley in the fall of 1864, when Lee assumed command of all of the Army of the Valley's cavalry. Lee was severely wounded at the September 19, 1864, Third Battle of Winchester, missing much of the rest of the war. Wickham helped block Alfred Torbert's advance in the Luray Valley, thwarting Sheridan's chances for an even greater victory at Fisher's Hill. Then, after Wickham left the army to take his seat in Congress, Munford assumed command of the division.

Maj. Gen. Wade Hampton, commander, Hampton's Division, Cavalry Corps, Army of Northern Virginia.

(Library of Congress)

Lomax, also a member of a prominent, multigenerational Virginia family, commanded Fitz Lee's other brigade. The 29-year-old Lomax was once Fitz's West Point classmate. He served on the frontier in the Regular Army before resigning his commission in the spring of 1861, after which he immediately received a captain's commission in the Confederate army. After staff assignments in both major theaters of the war, Lomax was appointed colonel of the 11th Virginia Cavalry in the spring of 1863, and he served competently in the Gettysburg campaign. In August 1863, he received a promotion to brigadier general and was assigned to command a brigade.[14] Capable and steady, Lomax's brigade consisted of the 5th, 6th, and 15th Virginia Cavalry, as well as Col. Bradley T. Johnson's 1st Maryland Cavalry Battalion and the Baltimore Light Artillery, each part of the Maryland Line, which operated as an independent command despite being attached to Lomax's brigade. These veteran units had seen intense fighting and marching throughout the war.

Wade Hampton, the second division commander, was one of the unsung heroes of the Civil War. "Hampton I think is superior to Stuart in prudence, judgment, and military affairs," Col. Richard H. Dulany of the 7th Virginia Cavalry opined, "not the extreme dash and perseverance for which Genl. Stuart was remarkable."[15] Major G. Moxley Sorrell, who served on Lt. Gen. James Longstreet's staff, recalled of Hampton, "This officer had served from the very beginning of the war with high distinction, had proved himself a careful, vigilant,

14 Jeffry D. Wert, "Lunsford Lindsay Lomax," included in *The Confederate General*, 4:85.
15 Margaret Ann Vogtsberger, *The Dulanys of Welbourne: A Family in Mosby's Confederacy* (Lexington, VA: Rockbridge Publishing, 1995), 219.

as well as enterprising cavalry leader, and possessed the confidence of the cavalry troops ... General Hampton was of fine presence, a bold horseman, a swordsman, and of the most undaunted courage."[16] An admiring trooper in the 6th South Carolina Cavalry declared Hampton "the grandest man South Carolina ever produced, grand in war and grand in peace."[17]

Reputedly the wealthiest man in the South, Hampton was named after his father and grandfather, both American generals; however, he had no formal military training. Even though he opposed secession, Hampton personally raised, funded, and equipped a combined-arms unit called the Hampton Legion when his native South Carolina seceded in the spring of 1861. Slightly wounded at the First Battle of Bull Run in July 1861 and badly hurt during the Peninsula campaign at the battle of Fair Oaks in May 1862, Hampton proved brave and extremely competent. At 46, he was 14 years older than Stuart and not considered part of the Virginia "in crowd." Stuart and his fellow Virginians treated Hampton as an outsider, although nobody disputed his courage or competence. Perhaps as a result of many years spent hunting bears, the utterly fearless Hampton preferred to lead pell-mell charges himself.[18]

In July 1862, the brigadier general led a brigade of Georgians, Mississippians, and North Carolinians. He was severely wounded in combat on East Cavalry Field at Gettysburg on July 3, 1863, while leading his brigade in a saber charge. In September 1863, while recuperating from his battle wound, he received promotion to major general and command of a large veteran division. Big, handsome, and amiable, "his lack of ... military training would prove an impediment at first, until practical experience in the field, developing the natural bent, had supplied its place."[19] One Northern officer suggested that although Hampton was an unschooled soldier who had probably never read a book on tactics, he "knew how to maneuver the units of his command so as to occupy for offensive or defensive action the strongest points of the battlefield, and that is about all there is in tactics." To be considered a successful strategist, an officer needed a broader field for the employment of his military talents. A Yankee

16 G. Moxley Sorrell, *Recollections of a Confederate Staff Officer* (New York: Neale Publishing Co., 1905), 249.

17 Charles M. Calhoun, *Liberty Dethroned* (n.p., 1903), 127.

18 James G. Holmes, "The Fighting Qualities of Generals Hampton, Butler, and Others Related by Adjutant-General Holmes of Charleston," *The Sunny South*, June 13, 1896.

19 Wells, *Hampton and His Cavalry*, 76. For the best full-length biography of Hampton, see Rod Andrew, *Wade Hampton: Confederate Warrior to Southern Redeemer* (Chapel Hill: University of North Carolina Press, 2008).

Col. Gilbert J. Wright,
commander, Young's Brigade,
Hampton's Division, Cavalry
Corps, Army of Northern
Virginia.

(Georgia Historical Soceity)

officer said Hampton "appeared possessed of almost an instinctive topographical talent. He could take in the strong strategic points in the field of his operations with an accuracy of judgment that was surprising to his comrades ... He would hunt his antagonist as he would hunt big game in the forest." The officer continued, "The celerity and audacity of his movements against the front, sometimes on the flank then again in the rear, kept his enemies in a constant state of uncertainty and anxiety as to where and when they might expect him." Concluding, he stated, "With his wonderful powers of physical endurance, his alert, vigilant mind, his matchless horsemanship, no obstacles seemed to baffle his audacity or thwart his purpose."[20]

Hampton's division consisted of two veteran brigades and a very green brigade that was just joining the Army of Northern Virginia. In April 1864, proud of his division, Hampton proclaimed, "They have done their duty in the fullest sense, and deserved the praise of their country. I have seen [them] sleeping upon the frozen ground without tents, shoes, overshoes, or blankets, only waiting for the morning's light to attack the enemy, whose fires lighted our own bivouac, and I have not yet heard a murmur" of complaint or protest.[21] These tough veterans had proven their mettle on every field and were the flower of the Army of Northern Virginia's praised Cavalry Corps.

Brigadier General Pierce M. B. Young, a member of the West Point class of 1861, normally commanded one of the two veteran brigades.[22]

---

20 Rodenbough, "Some Cavalry Leaders," 275–76.
21 *Supplement to the Columbia South Carolinian*, April 23, 1864.
22 Young and George Custer were good friends from their days as cadets at West Point. For a full-length biography of Young, see Lynwood Mathis Holland, *Pierce M. B. Young: The Warwick of the South* (Athens: University of Georgia Press, 1964).

However, as described more fully below, Young was temporarily commanding one of Rooney Lee's brigades, leaving Col. Gilbert J. "Gib" Wright of the Cobb Legion Cavalry in command of Young's brigade. Gib Wright, a tall 39-year-old Georgian, was a walking paradox. While a practicing attorney, Wright killed a close friend in a drunken brawl prior to the Civil War. This combat veteran of the Mexican–American War had also served as a judge and mayor of Albany, Georgia. His "unique personality ... vigorous intellect and ... untiring energy made a remarkable impression upon all with whom he came into contact."[23] While not a professionally trained soldier, Wright possessed a "bulldog courage" and "stentorian voice" that were conspicuous in battle, and "he was seriously wounded several times, but before his wounds ever healed

Brig. Gen. Thomas L. Rosser, commander, Laurel Brigade, Hampton's Division, Cavalry Corps, Army of Northern Virginia.

(Library of Congress)

he would be back again on the field of battle."[24] He rose through the ranks of the Cobb Legion from lieutenant to colonel, ultimately commanding the regiment.[25] The brigade included the Cobb Legion Cavalry, the Jeff Davis Legion Cavalry, the Phillips Legion Cavalry, and the 20th Battalion of Georgia Cavalry (Partisan Rangers Battalion), which had just joined the Cavalry Corps.

Brigadier General Thomas L. Rosser, at 28 years old, commanded Hampton's other brigade. Also a member of the West Point class of 1861, he and George Custer were friends. The burly Texan also found favor with Stuart. Rosser resigned from West Point only two weeks

23 William J. Northern, ed., *Men of Mark in Georgia*, 3 vols. (Atlanta: A. B. Chapman, 1907–1912), 3:352–53.

24 Ibid., 353; *Atlanta Constitution*, June 4, 1895.

25 Robert K. Krick, *Lee's Colonels: A Biographical Register of the Field Officers of the Army of Northern Virginia* (Dayton, OH: Morningside, 1992), 409.

before graduation to cast his lot with the Confederacy. He accepted a commission in the artillery, and after serving as commander of a battery at the First Battle of Bull Run, he was promoted to colonel of the 5th Virginia Cavalry in the spring of 1862. He was wounded at Mechanicsville during the June 1862 Seven Days Battles and again at the March 17, 1863, battle of Kelly's Ford. Despite the wounds, Rosser led his regiment with great success until his promotion to brigadier general in September 1863. When he had been passed over for promotion in the summer of 1863, he had turned on his patron, Stuart, believing that Stuart had deceived him. Although Stuart probably never imagined the depth of Rosser's loathing, the two men were never close again.[26]

"Tall, broad-shouldered and muscular, with black hair and mustache, dark brown eyes, strong jaw, and a countenance denoting self-confidence, a good horseman and always superbly mounted, the men of the brigade recognized in their new commander the typical soldier," one of Rosser's soldiers remembered.[27] Another Confederate recalled, "[T]here were few officers in the service who had as much military genius as he had. Instinctively, he seemed to know what was best to do, and how to do it. It appeared almost impossible to tire him, or to break him down."[28] Nonetheless, Rosser was apparently prone to periodic drinking binges, earning him notoriety in the army.[29]

In the winter of 1863 to 1864, Rosser dubbed his unit the "Laurel Brigade." Perhaps the finest cavalry brigade in Confederate service, the Laurel Brigade consisted of hard-fighting and hard-riding veterans accustomed to the vicissitudes of cavalry service. A large percentage of the brigade's men came from the Shenandoah Valley. The Laurel Brigade consisted of the 7th, 11th, and 12th Virginia Cavalry and the 35th Battalion of Virginia Cavalry, and it took on the bulk of the fighting during the 1863 campaigns. Raised by the legendary Brig. Gen. Turner Ashby and trained by Brig. Gen. William E. "Grumble" Jones,

---

26 Robert K. Krick, "Thomas Lafayette Rosser," *The Confederate General,* 5:112–15. For a full-length biography of Rosser, see Sheridan R. Barringer, *Custer's Gray Rival: The Life of Confederate Major General Thomas Lafayette Rosser* (Burlington, NC: Fox Run, 2019). In fact, Stuart's support of Rosser stirred up a great deal of controversy. Lieutenant Colonel Henry Clay Pate felt that he was entitled to command the 5th Virginia Cavalry, not Rosser. Pate ended up a defendant in a general court-martial. He was convicted and cashiered from the army. See Thomas, *Bold Dragoon,* 202.

27 William N. McDonald, *A History of the Laurel Brigade* (Baltimore, MD: Sun Job Printing Office, 1907), 196–97.

28 Francis W. Dawson, *Reminiscences of Confederate Service, 1861–1865* (Baton Rouge: Louisiana State University Press, 1980), 139.

29 Thomas, *Bold Dragoon,* 202.

who died during battle in June 1864, these troopers had won nearly every engagement in which they had participated.[30]

As Sheridan's Richmond raid wound down, Hampton learned that a large, inexperienced brigade of South Carolinians, sent north from Charleston at Hampton's behest, would soon reinforce his division. Brigadier General Matthew C. Butler, a 27-year-old lawyer with no formal military training, commanded this untested brigade. Despite his lack of training, Butler nevertheless had a fine military pedigree: he was a nephew of the War of 1812 naval hero Commodore Oliver Hazard Perry, and his father was a naval surgeon. Married to the daughter of South Carolina Governor Francis W. Pickens,

Brig. Gen. Matthew C. Butler, commander Butler's Brigade, Hampton's Division, Cavalry Corps, Army of Northern Virginia.

(Library of Congress)

Butler's future in Palmetto State politics seemed bright.[31]

Butler, then a colonel and protégé of his fellow South Carolinian Wade Hampton, was seriously wounded at the June 9, 1863, battle of Brandy Station when Pennington's battery carried away his right foot with a solid artillery shot. One of Butler's troopers described his

30 A member of the West Point class of 1848 and a classmate of John Buford, Jones was unable to get along with Stuart. The two men loathed each other. Their hatred finally bubbled over in September 1863 when Stuart brought court-martial charges against Jones for insubordination. Robert E. Lee realized the Confederate service could not spare Jones, so he transferred Jones, whose nickname "Grumble" clearly suited him, to command of the Confederate troops assigned to the Shenandoah Valley. Jones was killed in combat while leading a mounted charge at the June 5, 1864, battle of Piedmont. For a full-length biography of Jones, see James Buchanan Ballard, *William Edmonson "Grumble" Jones: The Life of a Cantankerous Confederate* (Jefferson, NC: McFarland & Co., 2017).

31 Lawrence L. Hewitt, "Matthew Calbraith Butler," in *The Confederate General*, 1:150–53. For a full-length biography of Butler, see Samuel J. Martin, *Southern Hero: Matthew Calbraith Butler, Confederate General, Hampton Red Shirt, and U.S. Senator* (Mechanicsburg, PA: Stackpole, 2001).

demeanor: "It used to be said his skin glanced bullets, and that it required a twelve-pounder to carry it away."[32]

J. Russell Wright of the 6th South Carolina Cavalry noted that Butler showed "no emotion as he scanned the field" of battle, calmly taking in the situation and carefully planning a response.[33] One historian remarked of Butler, "[S]o fine was his courage, so unshaken his nerve, that, if he realized danger, he scorned it and his chiseled face never so handsome as when cold-set for battle, never showed if or not his soul was in tumult." He was the sort of leader who sat on his horse quietly while shot and shell stormed around him and other men ran for shelter.[34] At the height of his fame, he led his men with only a riding whip clasped in hand during battle.[35]

Butler returned to duty on crutches in the fall of 1863, when he was promoted to brigadier general and assumed command of a brigade consisting of the 4th, 5th, and 6th South Carolina Cavalry. These regiments spent the first two years of the war performing coastal defense duty and saw no combat before transferring to Virginia. Numbering 1,300 troopers, it was the largest cavalry brigade assigned to the Army of Northern Virginia.[36] The men carried muzzle-loading Enfield rifles, not conventional cavalry weapons, and acted more like mounted infantry than cavalry.[37] These soldiers made an immediate impact when they joined the Army of Northern Virginia.

Major General William Henry Fitzhugh Lee, known to his friends as "Rooney" and to his family as "Fitzhugh," was Robert E. Lee's second son and commanded the third division of cavalry. Very tall for a cavalryman, standing at six feet, four inches, and tending toward corpulence, Rooney was a big man. "Though carrying more weight than was suitable to the saddle and the quick movements of cavalry service, he was, nevertheless, a good horseman and an excellent judge

32 Edward Laight Wells, "A Morning Call on Kilpatrick," *Southern Historical Society Papers* 12 (March 1884), 127.

33 J. Russell Wright, "Battle of Trevilian," *Recollections and Reminiscences 1861–1865*, 12 vols. (Charleston: South Carolina Division of the United Daughters of the Confederacy, 1995), 6:372.

34 Holmes, "The Fighting Qualities."

35 Walbrook D. Swank, *The Battle of Trevilian Station: The Civil War's Greatest and Bloodiest All Cavalry Battle* (Shippensburg, PA: Burd Street Press, 1994), 43.

36 Matthew C. Butler to Edward Laight Wells, June 7, 1888, Edward Laight Wells Correspondence, Archives, Charleston Library Society, Charleston, South Carolina.

37 Butler himself observed, "[m]y brigade . . . was armed with long-range Enfield rifles, and was, in fact, mounted infantry, but for our sabres." Matthew C. Butler, "The Cavalry Fight at Trevilian Station," in *B&L*, 4:237.

38 George W. Beale, *A Lieutenant of Cavalry in Lee's Army* (Boston: Gorham, 1918), 220.

of horses," one of his officers recalled. "So well and wisely, did he select them, that when mounted there seemed an admirable harmony between his own massive form and the heavy build and muscular power of his steed."[38]

Rooney Lee was not a West Pointer; his brother George Washington Custis Lee graduated from the military academy, and War Department policy forbade two sons of the same family from receiving a free education at West Point. Instead, Rooney attended Harvard University, where he was a star oarsman and the campus bare knuckles boxing champion. In 1857, after three years at Harvard,

Maj. Gen. William H. F. "Rooney" Lee, commander, Rooney Lee's Division, Cavalry Corps, Army of Northern Virginia.

(USAHEC)

Rooney abandoned academics to accept a commission as lieutenant in an infantry regiment of the U.S. army. He resigned after two years, determined to become a gentleman farmer at White House, a plantation on the Pamunkey River that he had inherited from the Custis family.[39] "Lee is ... a heavy set but well-proportioned man, somewhat inclined to boast, not overly profound and thoroughly impregnated with the idea that he is a Virginian and a Lee withal," Union officer John Beatty sniffed, clearly not impressed with Rooney.[40]

After Virginia seceded, Rooney Lee received a commission as captain in the 9th Virginia Cavalry and in April 1862 was elected colonel of the regiment, receiving a promotion to brigadier general five months later. He was solid and competent, if not spectacular, and well respected within the Confederate cavalry ranks. Stuart soon came to depend on his good judgment and unflappable demeanor.[41] Rooney

39 Warner, *Generals in Gray*, 184. For a full-length biography of Rooney Lee, see Mary Daughtry, *Gray Cavalier: The Life and Wars General William H. F. "Rooney" Lee* (New York: Da Capo, 2002).
40 John Beatty, *The Citizen Soldier: The Memoirs of a Civil War Volunteer* (Cincinnati: Wilstach, Baldwin & Co., 1879), 470.
41 Longacre, *Lee's Cavalrymen*, 33.

*Brig. Gen. John R. Chambliss, Jr.,
commander Chambliss' Brigade,
Rooney Lee's Division, Cavalry
Corps, Army of Northern Virginia.*

(USAHEC)

Lee was wounded at the battle of Brandy Station, on June 9, 1863, and was taken to his father-in-law Williams C. Wickham's plantation in Hanover County to recuperate. Union cavalry captured him there, and Rooney was imprisoned at Fortress Monroe until he was exchanged for Brig. Gen. Neal Dow in the winter of 1864. Rooney was promoted to major general while in prison, and upon his release, he assumed command of the third division of cavalry, consisting of two brigades.

Brigadier General John R. Chambliss Jr. was born on January 13, 1833, at Hicksford, in Greenville County, Virginia. In 1849, he enrolled at West Point, where he was best friends with David M. Gregg. Chambliss graduated in the same class with Sheridan, ranking 31st out of 53 cadets. He was breveted a second lieutenant in the Regiment of Mounted Rifles and received an assignment to the Cavalry School of Practice at the Carlisle Barracks in Pennsylvania.[42] He resigned from the army on March 4, 1854, and returned home, where he ran a plantation. From 1856 to 1861, while ranked a major, he served as an aide-de-camp to governors Henry Wise and John Letcher; then he commanded a militia regiment as a colonel from 1858 to 1861. For years, he served as brigade inspector.

After Virginia seceded in 1861, Chambliss was commissioned colonel of the 41st Virginia Infantry. In late July 1862, he became colonel of the 13th Virginia Cavalry, serving in that capacity until January 1864. As the senior colonel of Rooney Lee's brigade, Chambliss took command of the unit after Rooney was wounded. He was promoted to brigadier general on January 27, 1864, to rank from

---

42 The Cavalry School of Practice was where raw recruits into the U.S. army's mounted service learned how to become cavalrymen.

December 19, 1863. After Rooney Lee's exchange and promotion to major general in April 1864, Chambliss officially assumed command of Rooney Lee's former brigade. He was a capable officer whom his comrades admired.[43] Chambliss' brigade consisted of the 9th, 10th, and 13th Virginia Cavalry regiments.

Brigadier General James B. Gordon commanded the North Carolina cavalry brigade assigned to Rooney Lee's division until he was mortally wounded at Meadow Bridges on May 12, 1864. After Gordon's death, Young temporarily assumed command of the brigade, which consisted of the 1st, 2nd, 3rd, and 5th North Carolina regiments. In early June 1864, Lt. Col. Rufus Barringer, 1st North Carolina Cavalry, was promoted to brigadier general as a permanent replacement for the lamented Gordon.

In addition, Maj. Roger P. Chew commanded the horse artillery assigned to the Army of Northern Virginia's Cavalry Corps. The 12 batteries of horse artillery were divided into two battalions. Chew led one, while Maj. James Breathed commanded the other. Breathed's battalion included the renowned Stuart Horse Artillery, formerly Breathed's own command. While West Point-trained Regulars typically did not lead Confederate batteries, they nevertheless were extremely effective and played an important role on several battlefields during the Civil War.

The Confederate cavalry was not as well armed as its Union counterpart. The command's only repeating weapons were those captured from Union soldiers, as Southern-made copies of the Sharps carbine were not as reliable or as effective as the real thing. Some Confederates carried two-band muzzle-loading Enfield rifles, which could not be reloaded quickly. With the evolution of cavalry tactics resulting from technological advances, the Army of Northern Virginia's Cavalry Corps could not produce the same quantity or quality of firepower as its Northern foe.[44]

Further, since Confederate cavalrymen rode their own mounts into battle and not government-supplied horses as did Union troopers, their mounts were in various states of health. There was no uniformity in accouterments, and many Confederates used captured saddles, bridles, and halters. If a trooper lost his mount, he had to either arrange for a replacement or join the dreaded ranks of "Company Q,"

---

43 Arthur W. Bergeron Jr., "John Randolph Chambliss, Jr.", included in *The Confederate General*, 1:172–73.

44 In fact, many Confederate cavalrymen were armed with captured weapons. Some of Rosser's Virginians carried captured Spencers, while numerous Southerners relied upon captured Sharps and other similar single-shot breech-loading carbines.

dismounted cavalrymen assigned to intermediate duties or subject to transfer to the infantry, a fate any Confederate horse soldier dreaded.[45] Harsh service in the field had likewise taken its toll on the Confederates' horses. The dismounted men's inability to obtain adequate replacements for the ranks greatly reduced the strength and effectiveness of Robert E. Lee's cavalry.

Although Union cavalry's star was ascendant, the Army of Northern Virginia's Cavalry Corps remained a force to be reckoned with, and its formidable leader was on the brink of leading it to even greater accomplishments.

---

45 Samuel Carter III, *The Last Cavaliers: Confederate and Union Cavalry in the Civil War* (New York: St. Martin's Press, 1979), 10. Stuart formally did away with Company Q in the fall of 1863, but the hardships of service in the field led to more and more men being dismounted. Although Company Q technically no longer existed, it was still a factor to be overcome and a fate to be dreaded.

CHAPTER FOUR

Across the Pamunkey:
The Battle of Hanovertown

With the Cavalry Corps returned to the Army of the Potomac, and with his attempt to storm the North Anna River stymied, Grant decided to try yet another move around the Army of Northern Virginia's right flank, a tactic that had served him well throughout the Overland campaign. This time Grant intended to shift the army's base of operations to the Pamunkey River. Beginning on May 26, one of Sheridan's divisions would feint west while the other two divisions spearheaded the army's movement by riding east, deploying pickets along the Pamunkey's northern bank and securing Dabney's Ferry at Hanovertown. If all of the pieces fell into place, the entire army would steal a march on Lee.[1]

The Pamunkey, formed by the confluence of the North and South Anna rivers five miles northeast of the town of Ashland, "is an extremely crooked stream," Brig. Gen. Wilson later recalled, "with many bends, swamps, and small tributaries."[2] It forms the boundary of Hanover and Caroline counties, generally flowing southeasterly to the town of West Point, where it merges with the Mattaponi River to form the York River. In 1862, newspaper correspondent George A. Townsend described it as "a beautiful stream, densely wooded, and occasional vistas opened up along its borders of wheatfields, and meadows, with Virginia farmhouses and negro quarters on the hilltops." He believed "[f]ew of the northern navigable rivers were so picturesque and varied."[3] Grant intended to make White House Landing on the Pamunkey the primary supply depot for his operations toward Richmond. The Pamunkey was a formidable obstacle with considerable strategic significance.

It rained hard on May 26, making life miserable for the men of both armies. Despite his failure in the Wilderness, Wilson's Third Cavalry Division drew the task of demonstrating to the west. Sheridan apparently did not trust Wilson after the Wilderness debacle and had relegated him to only minor roles in the campaign.

---

1 *OR* 36, 3:207–10.
2 Wilson, *Under the Old Flag*, 1:423.
3 George Alfred Townsend, *Campaigns of a Non-Combatant, and His Remaunt Abroad During the War* (New York: Blelock & Co., 1866), 71.

Wilson's troopers swung into their saddles, moving out at 6:00 A.M. Their route carried them past Grant's headquarters at Quarles' Mill, where Wilson stopped to pay his respects to the lieutenant general, who warmly greeted the young brigadier. Grant's staff officers told Wilson that Sheridan's adjutant, Lt. Col. Charles Kingsbury Jr., had criticized his performance in reports. Outraged, Wilson fired off a letter to Sheridan demanding Kingsbury's removal.[4] After a pleasant lunch with Grant, Wilson continued on to Jericho Mills, crossed the North Anna River on pontoon bridges, and passed behind Maj. Gen. Horatio G. Wright's VI Corps on the way to Little River. Colonel John Hammond's 5th New York Cavalry had been screening Wright's flank and rejoined Wilson's division for this expedition.

"I examined the country for means of crossing Little River, so as to strike well in toward Hanover Junction," Wilson reported, "but I found the bridges all destroyed and the streams so much swollen that the fords were impracticable." The Federal horse soldiers engaged elements of the Cobb Legion Cavalry near Little River. "Our boys are skirmishing with the Reb pickets, the river between them," Samuel Gilpin, 3rd Indiana Cavalry, noted in his diary. "The infantry have all moved to the left and probably the most of them are beyond the Pamunkey ere this."[5] Hindered by heavy rains, Wilson demonstrated instead by directing his horse artillery to open fire and by sending troopers across the Little River on a rickety bridge made from a fallen tree.[6] "To complete the deception," one of Wilson's horsemen recalled, "fences, boards, and everything flammable within our reach were set fire to give the appearance of a vast force, just rebuilding its bivouac fires."[7]

In the meantime, the remainder of the Army of the Potomac broke its camps and headed toward the Pamunkey River crossings. All of this activity drew Lee's attention, and he ordered skirmishers to advance to determine whether Grant was retreating. Fitz Lee's cavalry division screened the Army of Northern Virginia's right flank toward Hanover Court House, so Fitz sent scouting parties east to Hanovertown along the Pamunkey's south bank. When Fitz's main body failed to locate the Union cavalry, it returned to Hanover Court House, where his

4 James H. Wilson diary, entry for May 26, 1864, James H. Wilson Papers, Manuscripts Division, Library of Congress, Washington, D.C. Wilson had served on Grant's staff in the Western Theater, and the two had a close relationship.
5 Samuel L. Gilpin diary, entry for May 27, 1864, Manuscripts Division, Library of Congress, Washington, D.C.
6 *OR* 36, 1:880.
7 Louis N. Boudrye, *Historic Records of the Fifth New York Cavalry, First Ira Harris Guard* (Albany, NY: J. Munsell, 1868), 134.

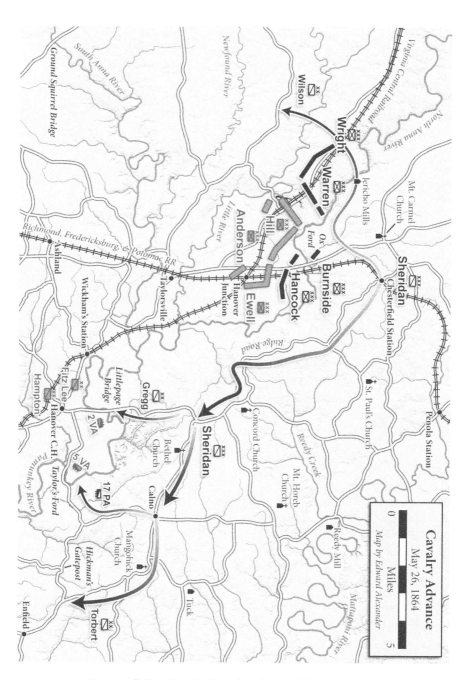

Route of Sheridan's Cavalry Corps, May 26, 1864

division united with Hampton's division. General Lee then awaited Grant's next move.[8]

Meanwhile Confederate infantry skirmished with the Union infantry along its front, looking for signs of Grant's intentions. The unmistakable sounds of wagon trains moving behind the Army of the Potomac's II Corps persuaded Lee that the enemy were marching—but to where? Lee took the bait, believing Wilson's movement toward Little River strongly suggested that Grant intended to move around the Army of Northern Virginia's left, prompting him to advise Richmond that Grant's "present indications seems to contemplate a movement on our left flank."[9] The Federal ruse worked. Once again, as he had done so many times during the Overland campaign, Lee misread Grant's intentions.

Meanwhile, late on the afternoon of May 26, the Union Cavalry Corps' First and Second divisions, accompanied by two pontoon trains, started south from Chesterfield Station to seize the Pamunkey River crossing at Dabney's Ferry and to establish a bridgehead at Hanovertown. With Sheridan and his staff at the head of the column, the blue horsemen marched south along Ridge Road until they turned east toward Concord Church, heading through the narrow strip of land separating the Mattaponi and Pamunkey rivers. After passing Concord Church, the Federal cavalry turned onto the road to Littlepage Bridge, which had been destroyed earlier in the war. However, this route offered the Confederates an opportunity to interdict the Union marching path, so Sheridan sent elements of Gregg's Second Cavalry Division to hold Littlepage Bridge while the rest of the column continued east.[10] "I thought it was nothing more than a raid," a Northern trooper declared, "but it has turned out a grand flank movement."[11]

The road to Taylor's Ford on the Pamunkey was a few miles farther down Ridge Road. Sheridan detailed Lt. Col. James Q. Anderson's 17th Pennsylvania Cavalry of Devin's Second Brigade, First Cavalry Division, to hold the crossing. The rest of Torbert's division, with Custer's Michigan Cavalry Brigade leading the way, continued east on Ridge Road to Mangohick Church, where they then turned south to Dabney's Ferry and Hanovertown.[12]

---

8 Memorandum of Maj. James D. Ferguson, entry for May 27, 1864, Jedediah Hotchkiss Papers, Manuscripts Division, Library of Congress, Washington, D.C.

9 *OR* 36, 3:834.

10 Gordon C. Rhea, *Cold Harbor: Grant and Lee May 26–June 3, 1864* (Baton Rouge: Louisiana State University Press, 2002), 32.

11 Delos S. Burton, "Spotsylvania: Letters From the Field: An Eyewitness," *Civil War Times* 22 (1983), 26.

12 Rhea, *Cold Harbor,* 32.

Confederate cavalrymen picketed the Pamunkey River crossings. Troopers of Lomax's brigade of Fitz Lee's division operated out of Hanover Court House. Colonel Bradley T. Johnson's Maryland Line—the 1st Maryland Cavalry and the Baltimore Light Artillery—operated with Lomax's brigade. The North Carolina cavalry brigade, with Col. John A. Baker temporarily leading, also served with Lomax's troopers. Members of the 5th Virginia Cavalry picketed the river near Hanover Court House on the night of May 26, while troopers of the 5th North Carolina Cavalry picketed the crossings near Hanovertown, about eight miles downstream.

The 17th Pennsylvania arrived at Taylor's Ford as darkness fell. About 50 men of the 5th Virginia Cavalry had established their bivouac on the Pamunkey's south bank, and they mistook the approaching Pennsylvanians for scouts of another Confederate regiment reconnoitering the north bank. "Is that you, 9th Virginia?" they called out. "Camp in that side," one of Anderson's men replied, "and lay low till morning." After tangling with the Virginians at Yellow Tavern and at Meadow Bridges the next day, the Pennsylvanians felt a degree of camaraderie with their enemy, and when Anderson ordered his men to open fire, one yelled out a warning: "Look out, rebels, we are going to fire on you," as he and his fellow troopers fired a harmless volley over their heads. With the river separating them, both sides "soon became intimate, and the rascals made merry with their defeats and losses," calling across the water about their recent encounters. Anderson left a squadron behind to watch the ford while he spurred off with the rest of his regiment to rejoin the column after determining that these Confederates posed no threat.[13]

Troopers of Gregg's Second Cavalry Division had a similar experience at Littlepage Bridge, where they found a small detachment of Company I of the 2nd Virginia Cavalry picketing. These Virginians stayed on the south bank of the river, so Gregg left a few troopers to keep an eye on them and rode off. Both sides put up earthworks.[14] "Crossing the Pamunkey River on the twenty-seventh, we halted, and soon a thousand camp fires were brightly gleaming in the valleys and along the hillsides," a member of the 6th Ohio Cavalry recollected.[15]

That night, the Army of the Potomac abandoned its works at Ox Ford and moved out, following the same route as the cavalry. Grant's ruse succeeded, and the Northerners stole a march on Robert E. Lee,

13 Dispatch of R. H. McBride of May 30, 1864, *Daily Morning Chronicle*, June 2, 1864.
14 John J. Woodall diary, entry for May 26, 1864, Archives, Richmond National Battlefield Park, Richmond, Virginia.
15 Alphonso D. Rockwell, *Rambling Recollections: An Autobiography* (New York: P. B. Hoeber, 1920), 147.

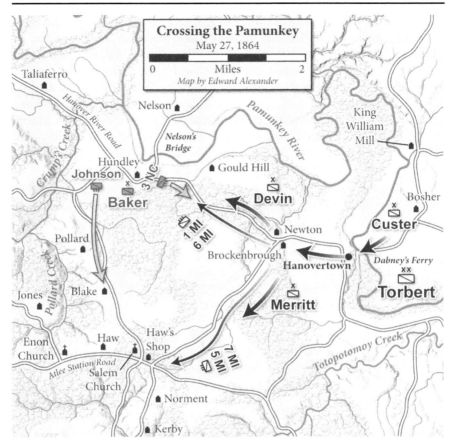

who remained befuddled about Grant's intentions. The infantry had about 30 miles to cover to reach the Pamunkey River crossings at Hanovertown.

Thick fog rolled in during the night of May 26. Early the next morning, Custer's Wolverines led the First Division's advance toward the Pamunkey. Sheridan, Torbert, and Custer led the way. When Custer rode down to the riverbank alone to reconnoiter, Southern pickets dispatched a few bullets his way, prompting his staff to encourage the general to seek shelter, which he did immediately.[16] When Torbert reached the riverbank, Sheridan instructed him to secure both flanks so the Army of the Potomac's engineers could construct pontoon bridges. Custer soon joined them, contemplating the swollen river's rapid current. With no enemy in sight, Custer decided to swim his horse across. His mount splashed into the swift

---

16 Paul Davis, ed., *I Rode with Custer: The Civil War Diary of Charles H. Safford, Bvt. Major, 5th Michigan Cavalry* (Detroit: Ashton Z Publishing, 2014), 104.

current, spooking the animal. The horse began bucking, so Custer grabbed the reins and pulled hard, flipping backwards into the river. The horse, suddenly free of its burden, climbed back onto the bank, leaving Custer bobbing in the water, his fancy velvet uniform completely drenched. The general made for the shore and climbed out of the river, looking "like a drowned rat." Chuckling, Sheridan asked the bedraggled cavalryman if he had enjoyed his bath. "I always take a bath in the morning when convenient," Custer cracked in response, "and have paid a quarter for many not so good as this."[17]

The 1st Michigan Cavalry led Custer's column that day. Custer instructed Lt. Col. Peter Stagg, the regiment's commander, to gather his men on the north bank to prepare to cross the river. As they assembled, a detachment of about 60 troopers from the 5th North Carolina Cavalry opened fire on them from the south bank, which an officer of the 5th Michigan Cavalry describing as "formidable."[18] The 50th New York Engineers, traveling with the pontoon trains, followed closely behind the cavalry. "They had marched all night as fast as the cavalry," a weary officer of the 50th New York recalled.[19]

The troopers of the 1st Michigan Cavalry's Company C returned fire with their Burnside carbines, scattering the Carolinians, while some of the engineers started assembling a pontoon bridge, laying the pontoon boats in place under the firing cover of Stagg's men. The members of Company C rowed two pontoon boats across the river, cleared the far side of Confederates, and established a bridgehead on the south bank. Working diligently under the Tar Heels' long-range fire, the engineers pushed the pontoon bridge across the wide river, losing a sergeant to sniper fire and prompting Capt. Charles Safford of the 5th Michigan to declare: "[T]he affair was most gallantly done."[20]

It took about an hour for the engineers to assemble the pontoon bridge. Once the flooring was nailed to the 180-foot span, the rest of the 1st Michigan trotted across, along with the remaining Michigan Cavalry Brigade and Torbert's other two brigades, commanded by Devin and Merritt. With a full division of horsemen across the river, the engineers set about building a second span a few yards up the river.[21] "I now occupy Hanovertown," Sheridan reported at 9:00 a.m.

17 Burton, "Spotsylvania: Letters From the Field," 26–27.
18 Davis, *I Rode with Custer*, 104.
19 Dale E. Floyd, ed., "Dear Friends at Home…": *The Letters and Diary of Thomas James Owen, Fiftieth New York Volunteer Engineer Regiment, During the Civil War, U.S. Army Corps of Engineers Historical Studies*, No. 4 (Washington, D.C.: U.S. Government Printing Office, 1985), 42.
20 Ibid.
21 *OR* 36, 1:312 and 804; Dexter Macomber diary, entry for May 27, 1864, Clarke Historical Library, Central Michigan University, Mt. Pleasant, Michigan; McBride dispatch.

"The crossing was taken with little opposition, a small picket of cavalry being the only force found at this point."[22]

"We had but little difficulty crossing the river there being no Rebs here, except about 70 cavalry that were guarding the ferry," one of Torbert's troopers said. "Those could have done us considerable mischief had they been as determined as some of those fellows are."[23]

By getting his entire division across the Pamunkey, Torbert secured Hanovertown for the Army of the Potomac's passage later that day. Only a handful of decrepit houses dotted the floodplain and the neighboring hills, prompting Maj. Howard M. Smith of the 1st New York Dragoons to describe the area as "one of the most desolate parts of Virginia I have yet been in." The local citizenry did not impress Smith. "The inhabitants, what few there are, show signs of the most wretched poverty and ignorance."[24]

Torbert ordered Custer to seize and hold the hills so that the army could assemble in the floodplain after crossing. As the Wolverines advanced, they drove the annoying Tar Heel troopers west along Hanover River Road, and Custer established his headquarters in the yard of "Westwood," the handsome residence of Dr. William S. R. Brockenbrough. Custer watched from his horse, which he had recovered after the botched river crossing. "Give it to them boys," he called, "give them hell! See them run, the Secesh sons of b___h!"[25]

The Hanover River Road jogged to the right at Brockenbrough's house, passed through about a mile of woods, and emerged into the cleared farm fields of the Hundley family. Another road ran a quarter of a mile north to the river crossing at Nelson's Bridge. Realizing Nelson's Bridge provided the Army of the Potomac with another crossing via a shorter marching route from the North Anna River, Torbert ordered Custer to send Stagg's 1st Michigan Cavalry and Maj. James H. Kidd's 6th Michigan Cavalry west along the river road to clear the Hundley property of any lingering Confederates. They were also commanded to open the road to Nelson's Bridge, making it available for the Army of the Potomac to access.[26]

Another road forked to the left at Brockenbrough's house and traversed two-and-a-half miles to the settlement of Haw's Shop, the location of a machine shop that manufactured quality farming and milling machinery. After the Army of the Potomac occupied the area

22 *OR* 36, 3:258.
23 Burton, "Spotsylvania: Letters From the Field," 26.
24 Howard M. Smith diary, entry for May 27, 1864, Howard Malcolm Smith
   Papers, Manuscripts Division, Library of Congress, Washington, D.C.
25 Burton, "Spotsylvania: Letters From the Field," 27.
26 *OR* 36, 1:804.

in 1862, John Haw III, the machine shop's owner, sold his equipment to Works in Richmond. By 1864, the area had been largely abandoned and had fallen into ruins, leaving only Salem Presbyterian Church and a few houses standing, including the Haw homestead, an attractive two-story house known as "Oak Grove." John Haw lived with his wife and their 24-year-old daughter at Oak Grove; his three sons were serving in the Confederate army. Enon Methodist Church was half a mile farther west. With stout wooden fences and dense woods lining both sides, the Atlee Station Road

Lt. Col. Peter Stagg, commander, 1st Michigan Cavalry.

(USAHEC)

passed by Oak Grove. Five roads converged there, including two that led directly to Richmond via Atlee Station.[27] Torbert instructed Custer to send his other two regiments, the 5th and 7th Michigan cavalries, to secure the crucial intersection. He also ordered the rest of his division to support Custer's divided brigade, with Devin's brigade following Stagg and Kidd along the river road, while Merritt's Reserve Brigade headed toward Haw's Shop.[28]

On a scorching hot day, the Army of the Potomac's main body followed Sheridan's route to the Pamunkey River. The Union soldiers had a long, unpleasant march, but they had slipped away from the Army of Northern Virginia at the North Anna and were in the process of turning General Lee's right flank. Wilson's Third Cavalry Division brought up the army's rear.

By mid-day on May 27, General Lee realized the Army of the Potomac was on the move, but he still could not ascertain Grant's intentions. He ordered the Army of Northern Virginia to shift about

---

27 Joseph R. Haw, "Haw's Shop Community of Virginia," *Confederate Veteran* 33 (1925), 340.
28 *OR* 36, 1:804.

Union pontoon bridges at Hanovertown Ferry.

(Library of Congress)

15 miles southeast of the North Anna to a spot near Atlee's Station on the Virginia Central Railroad, where it could move to block Grant no matter which direction he marched.[29]

At 9:00 a.m., Sheridan reported to General Meade that he had established two pontoon bridges across the Pamunkey; Torbert was clearing the roads from Hanovertown; Gregg was preparing to cross the river; and Brig. Gen. David Russell's VI Corps was not far behind Gregg.[30] Custer, with the 5th and 7th Michigan, headed toward Haw's Shop. The 1st and 6th Michigan, led by Lieutenant Colonel Stagg of the 1st Michigan, neared the Hundley farm, located about a mile from Hanovertown. There Confederate resistance stiffened. After learning that a large Union cavalry force had arrived at Hanovertown, Fitz Lee

---

29 Ibid., 3:836; *OR* 51, 2:962. At 8:30 that morning, Col. Walter Taylor, one of General Lee's military secretaries, advised the Army of Northern Virginia's II Corps commander, Lt. Gen. Richard S. Ewell: "the enemy's infantry and cavalry as having crossed at Hanovertown, on the Pamunkey. The general commanding desires you to begin to withdraw your troops quietly and so as not to be seen, and to move back to the south side of the North Anna." Ibid., *OR* 51, 2:962.
30 Ibid., *OR* 36, 2:257.

had ordered the rest of the North Carolina cavalry brigade to block the Federals.

Colonel John A. Baker of the 3rd North Carolina Cavalry, the brigade's senior colonel, now commanded the North Carolina brigade, consisting of the 1st, 2nd, 3rd, and 5th North Carolina Cavalry regiments. Baker's 3rd North Carolina Cavalry had spent the war guarding outposts on the Pamunkey and Blackwater rivers, so Baker had no experience commanding men in battle. A diarist called Baker "notoriously unfit ... confessedly ignorant [and] incompetent [and] inefficient" as a colonel, to the point that his officers eventually asked him to resign. His debut as a brigade commander did not go well.[31]

Col. John A. Baker of the 3rd North Carolina Cavalry, temporary commander of the North Carolina Cavalry Brigade.

(Author's collection)

31 Bruce S. Allardice, *Confederate Colonels: A Biographical Register* (Columbia: University of Missouri Press, 2008), 50. John Algernon Baker was born on September 19, 1830, in Brunswick County, North Carolina. He attended South Carolina College (now the University of South Carolina) and Harvard Law School, practicing law in Wilmington before the war. One subordinate noted Baker was "the finest-looking man I ever saw," which helps to explain why he was married six times in his life. With the coming of war, he was commissioned first lieutenant in Battery E, 1st North Carolina Artillery, on May 16, 1861. He was promoted to captain in 1862 and served as aide-de-camp to Gen. Samuel G. French. On September 3, 1862, he was appointed colonel of the 3rd North Carolina Cavalry, even though he had no experience commanding horse soldiers. He was captured near Petersburg, Virginia, on June 21, 1864, and became one of the Immortal 600—a group of captured Confederate officers who were exposed to artillery fire on a prison ship in Charleston Harbor and who were only fed starvation rations. These men were called the Immortal 600 because most of them refused to take the oath of allegiance to the United States; had they done so, they would have been freed. Baker took the oath of allegiance in March 1865, earning the enmity of his fellow Confederates. He lived in Wilmington, North Carolina; Charleston, South Carolina; and the West Indies after the war, before settling in Roanoke, Virginia, to practice law. He died in Galveston, Texas, on March 15, 1903, and was buried in Galveston's Calvary Cemetery. Ibid.

Baker dismounted three regiments, posting them behind improvised log and dirt barricades in the woods east of the Hundley farm. Baker's 3rd North Carolina Cavalry, Lt. Col. Alfred M. Waddell in command, stayed mounted and went scouting east along Hanover River Road until it collided with Stagg's two regiments. A stiff fight ensued as Waddell resisted the Union advance, conducting a fighting withdrawal to Baker's main battle line. The Michiganders followed them until volleys from the makeshift works in the woods halted their pursuit. Major Kidd dismounted his 6th Michigan Cavalry and formed his men on the north side of the road, while Stagg deployed his dismounted men to the south, extending the Union line perpendicular to the road. Kidd ordered his men to attack, but severe fire from the Tar Heels quickly halted them. When he heard a band playing behind the Confederates, Kidd realized he faced not just the 3rd North Carolina but an entire brigade attempting to outflank him.[32]

Recognizing he was outnumbered, Kidd sent a staff officer for reinforcements. The officer found Devin's brigade, which was not far behind. Torbert, who was riding with Devin, exploded in anger when he overheard the staff officer's report that Kidd was in danger of being flanked. "Who in [the] hell is this who is talking about being flanked?" Torbert demanded. Devin ordered his lead regiment to hurry ahead while the staff officer dug his spurs into his horse's sides and galloped off to inform Kidd that reinforcements were on the way. The staffer also recounted Torbert's outburst to the major. "I was mortified at this," Kidd acknowledged, "and resolved never again to admit to a superior officer that the idea of being flanked had any terrors."[33]

Torbert was new to division command; he had missed most of the Overland campaign while on medical leave, and he was eager to prove himself. Knowing the other half of the Michigan Cavalry Brigade was nearby, Torbert thought he saw an opportunity to capture Baker's entire unit. He knew that Custer, with the 5th and 7th Michigan, had reached Haw's Shop and that a road from there cut across Dr. George W. Pollard's farm, known as "Williamsville," and intersected the Hanover River Road a bit west of the Hundley farm. Torbert instructed Custer to take the two regiments past Williamsville, come out behind Baker's position, and capture the whole bunch. [34]

Fitz Lee realized that the Baker's North Carolina brigade needed help and ordered Col. Bradley T. Johnson and the 1st Maryland

---

32 Kidd, *Personal Recollections*, 319
33 Ibid. This incident may have triggered the contentious relationship between Kidd and Torbert. In the fall of 1864, Kidd briefly commanded the Michigan Cavalry Brigade after Custer's promotion to division command, and Torbert relieved Kidd of command after a clash.
34 *OR* 36, 1:804.

Cavalry, about 250 men in total, and the Baltimore Light Artillery to reinforce Baker.[35] Leading his Marylanders across the Hundley farm fields, Johnson extended Baker's line. Not realizing that the rest of the Michigan Cavalry Brigade and Devin's brigade were on the way, Johnson and Baker decided to attempt capturing the 1st and 6th Michigan. His plan was for Baker to hold the Wolverines in place while Johnson took the 1st Maryland and a squadron of the 5th North Carolina southeast past Williamsville to Haw's Shop, where they would turn north and dash into the enemy's rear at Brockenbrough's house.[36] "After a conference Johnson agreed that if Baker could hold the Federals while he, Johnson, could get at them, the two would capture the whole party," Henry C. Mettam of the 1st Maryland observed. Unfortunately for Baker and Johnson, their scheme mirrored Torbert's movement, meaning the two forces were destined to collide.[37]

Col. Bradley T. Johnson, commander, Maryland Line Cavalry, Rooney Lee's Division, Cavalry Corps, Army of Northern Virginia.

(Library of Congress)

35 Bradley Tyler Johnson was born in Frederick, Maryland, on September 29, 1829. He graduated from Princeton University in 1849, and became a prominent state's attorney, orator, and chairman of the Maryland Democratic Party in the 1850s. He backed John C. Breckinridge for president in 1860, and when the Civil War broke out in 1861, he supported the Confederate cause. Virginia Governor John Letcher offered him a commission as lieutenant colonel, but Johnson declined in order to assist in organizing Maryland units for the Confederacy. After helping recruit and organize the 1st Maryland, Johnson was commissioned a major in June 1861. He fought at the First Bull Run and assumed command of the 1st Maryland when the colonel and lieutenant colonel were both wounded. When Col. Arnold Elzey received a promotion to brigadier general and George H. Steuart a promotion to colonel, Johnson was promoted to lieutenant colonel. In the spring of 1862, when Steuart was promoted to brigadier general, Johnson became colonel of the regiment, fighting in the Seven Days Battles in June 1862. When the 1st Maryland was disbanded, Johnson temporarily commanded a brigade at Second Bull Run and again at Gettysburg. Johnson was then assigned to

Just as Johnson turned down the farm road toward Haw's Shop, the 17th Pennsylvania and 9th New York—Devin's lead regiments—arrived on Hanover River Road to reinforce Stagg and Kidd. The Federals could hear Baker's men chopping down trees to barricade the road, which steeled them for a fight. Devin sent the Pennsylvanians and a squadron of New Yorkers north, beyond Kidd's flank, and also deployed a two-gun section of Lt. Edward Heaton's combined batteries B and L, 2nd U.S. Artillery, to cover the road. A number of the New Yorkers got tangled up in the dense timber as they tried to find the enemy, leaving only 18 troopers in the road.[38] Realizing the tide had turned, Baker conducted a fighting withdrawal westward across the Hundley farm, resisting every step. The 17th Pennsylvania pushed the retreating Tar Heels hard, capturing two officers and 20 men as they pursued.[39]

In the meantime, Johnson sent the 5th North Carolina squadron ahead to scout the road to Haw's Shop. After about a mile, the Tar Heels ran into Custer's 5th and 7th Michigan approaching from the opposite direction. The North Carolinians hastily retreated, galloping back to tell Johnson that a large force of Yankee horse soldiers was headed straight for him. The Marylanders found themselves hemmed into a narrow road with swampy ground on their left and a stout wooden fence on their right. Johnson ordered his men to tear down part of the fence and escape through the opening into Pollard's fields. Johnson's adjutant, Capt. George W. Booth, prepared the command to

command the Maryland Line Cavalry, consisting of the 1st Maryland Cavalry and the Baltimore Light Artillery, in 1863. He was finally promoted to brigadier general in June 1864, after Stonewall Jackson had recommended him for promotion twice. He assumed command of a brigade of cavalry in the summer of 1864. That November he was assigned to command the prisoner of war camp at Salisbury, North Carolina, a position he held until the end of the war. Once the war was over, he settled in Richmond, opened a law office, and served in the Senate of Virginia from 1875 to 1879. He then returned to Baltimore, where he spent his final years writing historical and legal papers. He died in Amelia, Virginia, on October 5, 1903, and was buried in Loudoun Park Cemetery in Baltimore. See Jeffry D. Wert, "Bradley Tyler Johnson," included in William C. Davis and Julie Hoffman, eds., *The Confederate General*, 6 vols. (New York: National Historical Society, 1991), 3:172–79.

36 William W. Goldsborough, *The Maryland Line in the Confederate Army 1861–1865* (Baltimore: Guggenheimer, Weil, and Co., 1900), 198.

37 Samuel H. Miller, ed., "The Civil War Memoirs of the First Maryland Cavalry, C.S.A., by Henry Clay Mettam," *Maryland Historical Magazine* 58 (1963), 153.

38 Newel Cheney, *History of the Ninth Regiment, New York Volunteer Cavalry, War of 1861 to 1865* (Poland Center, NY: Martin Mere & Son, 1901), 175.

39 *OR* 36, 1:837; Henry P. Moyer, *History of the Seventeenth Regiment Pennsylvania Volunteer Cavalry* (Lebanon, PA: n.p., 1911), 271 and 340.

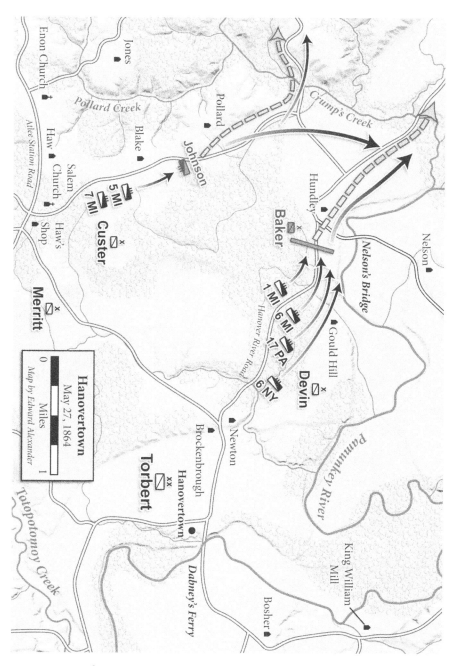

The Battle of Hanovertown Ferry, May 27, 1864

fight while the horse artillery headed back to the Hundley farm to avoid being captured.[40]

"I saw Baker's pickets coming full tilt, with Custer's men at their heels, pressing us so close that they knocked some of our men off their horses, and hardly giving us time to leave the narrow road and get into the open field, but tearing this wattling [sic] fence down we soon formed into line, and as Custer's men came up they had the brush fence to protect them, as the first volley they fired killed Colonel Johnson's horse and shot his saber clean from his side," Mettam recalled.[41]

"Before the regiment could complete the formation in the field, we were under heavy fire," Booth recounted, "but for some twenty minutes or more held our ground, suffering considerable loss." Booth headed for nearby high ground to the right, which a company of Marylanders held, in order to have a good view of the entire field. "It did not take long to comprehend the situation; we had in front of us not less than full brigade of federal cavalry, who were now advancing on our devoted command, which was holding its position with great tenacity." Johnson, recognizing the danger he faced, ordered the Marylanders to withdraw.[42]

Custer ordered the 7th Michigan to make a mounted charge. Harry Pollard, the six-year-old son of the farm's owner, observed Custer. "I never saw a more striking figure than George Custer," Harry wrote many years later. "I thought he was a very young looking man for a general. He was faultlessly dressed in a uniform covered with gold embroidery. He had long yellow hair, yellow mustache, a long thin nose, and deep blue eyes." The appearance of the "Boy General" stayed with Harry throughout the years. "The memory of him lingered in my mind more than that of any other general," he reminisced.[43]

Due to a misunderstanding, Custer's order was not obeyed as quickly as he might have liked, permitting the Maryland men to begin retreating.[44] The Wolverines formed a single-rank line of battle and drew their sabers. "Charge!" Custer thundered, and the Michigan men dug their spurs into the flanks of their steeds and surged forward. "Their dense masses came toward us as if to swallow up the little

40 George W. Booth, *Personal Reminiscences of a Maryland Soldier in the War Between the States, 1861–1865* (Baltimore: Fleet, McGinley & Co., 1898), 114.

41 Miller, "The Civil War Memoirs of the First Maryland Cavalry," 153.

42 Booth, *Personal Reminiscences*, 114.

43 Harry T. Pollard, "Some War Events in Hanover County," *Hanover County Historical Society Bulletin* 52 (1995), 2.

44 Davis, *I Rode with Custer*, 104.

command," Booth shuddered. "It was soon perceived that the enemy were wrapping around the little battalion, and threatening it with destruction when the order was given to retreat."[45]

"We're flanked!" the Marylanders cried as they broke and ran.[46] Lieutenant Colonel Ridgely Brown, second-in-command of the 1st Maryland, stopped at a gate, which he struggled to hold open so the Maryland troopers could escape. "A dreadful hand-to-hand fight ensued," a Maryland man recounted. Brown stayed at the gate as long as he could, fencing with Custer's men. After taking a serious sabre slash to his head, the badly wounded Brown escaped. Johnson also made it out, riding a mount a trooper relinquished.[47]

Lt. Col. Ridgely Brown, commander, 1st Maryland Cavalry, killed in action, Battle of Ashland.

(*The Maryland Line in the Confederate Army 1861-1865*)

"By this time a column of Federal cavalry was going by our left flank and into our rear, so we attempted to withdraw decently and in order, and as we found this impossible we were ordered to get out the best we could, and [Company E] lost some [10 or] more killed, wounded or missing," trooper Mettam of Company E stated. "The command then struck a gallop, and the retreat was made with rapidity, the order being passed down the line to the men to scatter and take care of themselves," one of Johnson's men noted.[48]

A few days earlier, George Booth had purchased an expensive gilt-corded plumed hat in Richmond. During the fighting, a ball struck

---

45 Booth, *Personal Reminiscences*, 115; Miller, "Civil War Memoirs of the First Maryland Cavalry," 153; Goldsborough, *The Maryland Line in the Confederate Army*, 198.

46 Barnard, *An Aide to Custer*, 238.

47 Booth, *Personal Reminiscences*, 115; Miller, "Civil War Memoirs of the First Maryland Cavalry," 153; Bradley T. Johnson to his wife, June 2, 1864, Bradley T. Johnson Papers, Perkins Library, Duke University, Durham, North Carolina.

48 Miller, "Civil War Memoirs of the First Maryland Cavalry," 153.

him in the shoulder—it did not break skin, but damaged his shell jacket and nearly knocked him from his saddle and the fancy hat off his head. "I could not afford to lose that hat," he remembered, "and yet riding rapidly toward me were some six or eight federals, whom, under the circumstances, I did not particularly care to meet." Booth glanced at the hat and then at the oncoming Wolverines, debating his options, and decided to make a grab for it. He hurriedly dismounted, snatching the hat while his horse grew restless nearby and swinging back into the saddle as the Wolverines closed in, revolvers blazing. Realizing he was alone with the enemy and that the rest of the 1st Maryland was retreating through the next field, Booth galloped off to join them.[49]

A lane forked off northwest of Pollard's farm, running roughly parallel to Hanover River Road and about half a mile south of it. The 1st Maryland used this road to make its escape, then crossed Crump's Creek, which flowed north into the Pamunkey River. Johnson tried to rally his command behind the creek, but the 7th Michigan pounced before they could get into position, routing them. "We had a race of several miles, in which several men were lost on weak horses," Johnson penned to his wife a few days later. The Wolverines pursued for about three miles, capturing 36 prisoners before Custer called for a halt. "My diminished numbers and exhaustion of both men and horses prevented me from making a vigorous attack on the enemy's rear," Custer reported.[50]

The Boy General was not finished, however. After routing the Marylanders, Custer realized he was in position to carry out Torbert's original plan to bag Baker's Tar Heels. He let Johnson escape and hurried his Michiganders northwest toward the Hundley farm. With the band still blaring behind them, Baker and the North Carolinians had fallen back to a stand of woods along Hanover River Road, west of the Hundley farm. "The last note of the 'Bonnie Blue Flag' had scarcely died on the air," Major Kidd described, "when far to the left and front were heard the cheery strains of 'Yankee Doodle'" announcing Custer's and the 5th and 7th Michigan's approach along the Pollard farm road.[51]

Learning of Johnson's rout, Baker ordered Maj. William H. H. Cowles to deflect the threat to the Confederate flank with detachments of the 1st and 3rd North Carolina. It was a wasted effort, however. The 1st Maryland's rout uncovered Baker's flank, leaving it exposed and open to attack. Left with no choice, Baker and the Tar Heels retreated as quickly as possible with Wolverines pushing them from two

49 Booth, *Personal Reminiscences*, 116.
50 *OR* 36, 1:820–21; Johnson to his wife, June 2, 1864.
51 Kidd, *Personal Recollections*, 320.

directions—their front and right. Lieutenant Edward Granger, who served on Custer's staff, heard the general declare he had never seen a more perfect rout in any battle of the war. Granger observed, "If the [general] had had another [regiment] to send in at that moment, he would have cut them off [and] captured a large number of prisoners, but our men were all busy." Granger was slightly wounded in the scrape.[52]

The broken North Carolinians galloped west along Hanover River Road, fleeing toward Hanover Court House where Lomax's brigade could cover them. "We were forced to fall back [and] came well nigh being stampeded," Lt. Col. Rufus Barringer of the 1st North Carolina Cavalry recalled; he would soon be promoted to brigadier general to replace the fallen Gordon. "Even the best officers and men seemed to be demoralized," Barringer admitted.[53] "Such a chase I never saw before," an amused 7th Michigan Cavalry trooper declared.[54]

Now joined by Devin's brigade, Kidd and Stagg pursued the fleeing North Carolinians who tried to make a stand where Hanover River Road crossed Crump's Creek. However, Capt. Raymond L. Wright, inspector general for Devin's brigade, led a charge of part of the 9th New York Cavalry that shattered the Confederate line and drove the rebels from the bridge back onto high ground beyond. The charge resulted in 41 prisoners captured and 4 men lost.[55]

Lieutenant John T. Rutherford of Company L, 9th New York Cavalry, led a charging column. Rutherford and his men forded Crump's Creek and pitched into the rebel cavalrymen, driving them back on their reserves and their wagon train. Rutherford demanded the surrender of the entire brigade, but a Confederate officer called on his men not to be cowards and to form a line. Rutherford's pistol cracked, killing the brave Southerner's horse. When the Confederate picked himself up off the ground, Rutherford struck at him with his empty pistol, which the Confederate parried with his sabre. However, Rutherford landed a blow, dazing the North Carolinian, who then surrendered.

The New Yorkers captured nearly 100 prisoners. "Did you intend to take the whole brigade?" a pleased Devin asked. "I would, if I had enough men to guard them," Rutherford quipped. "I believe it," an

52 Barnard, *An Aide to Custer*, 238.
53 Rufus Barringer to V. C. Barringer, January 27, 1866, Rufus Barringer Papers, Southern Historical Collection, Wilson Library, University of North Carolina, Chapel Hill, North Carolina.
54 Quoted in Edward G. Longacre, *Custer and His Wolverines: The Michigan Cavalry Brigade 1861–1865* (Conshohocken, PA: Combined Books, 1997), 223.
55 *OR* 36, 1:836–37.

amused Devin, who ordered the pursuit, chuckled. Rutherford later received the Medal of Honor for this feat.[56] The appearance of the Rebel prisoners impressed the Union cavalrymen. "The prisoners were fine looking fellows, well dressed and clean," one of Devin's New Yorkers remarked, "such an unusual thing that it was noticeable."[57]

However, Torbert countermanded the order, preferring to consolidate his position along Crump's Creek, which was consistent with Sheridan's instruction to secure the Pamunkey River crossings for the Army of the Potomac's use. Devin's 9th New York deployed at the bridge over Crump's Creek while the 17th Pennsylvania and the 6th New York, joined by Heaton's horse artillery, formed in a field north of the road. Custer then deployed his tired brigade along Crump's Creek south of Devin's position. The Pamunkey River crossings had been secured.[58]

Captain William L. Heermance served in the 6th New York Cavalry. After the fighting ended, he recognized a prisoner from the 2nd North Carolina Cavalry, a captain whom he had captured in the spring of 1863. Heermance himself was captured later in 1863 and spent some time at Richmond's Libby Prison before being exchanged. The Tar Heel remembered Heermance and told the New Yorker that his lieutenant had charge of Heermance during the journey to Richmond. Heermance was sad to learn that the kind guard had been killed in battle.[59]

Recriminations among the Confederates began immediately. Baker and the North Carolinians blamed the Marylanders, while the Marylanders blamed the Tar Heels. "We had lost heavily in this encounter," Booth stated, "about fifty or sixty men killed and wounded and prisoners, but we undoubtedly saved [Baker's] brigade from destruction."[60] In a note, Johnson told his wife, "I have a report

56 F. F. Beyer and O. F. Keydel, *Deeds of Valor: How America's Civil War Heroes Won the Congressional Medal of Honor*, 2 vols. (Detroit: The Perrien-Keydel Co., 1907), 1:329–30. Rutherford was awarded the Medal of Honor in 1892 for valor at both Yellow Tavern and at Hanovertown. His Medal of Honor citation reads: "Made a successful charge at Yellow Tavern, Va., 11 May 1864, by which 90 prisoners were captured. On 27 May 1864, in a gallant dash on a superior force of the enemy, and in a personal encounter, captured his opponent."
57 Hillman A. Hall, ed., *History of the Sixth New York Cavalry* (Second Ira Harris Guard) (Worcester, MA: The Blanchard Press, 1908), 192.
58 *OR* 36, 1:837.
59 William L. Heermance to his wife, May 31, 1864, William L. Heermance Letters, Archives, RNMP.
60 Booth, *Personal Reminiscences*, 115–16. A modern history of the 1st Maryland Cavalry identified Lt. Edmund G. Duley of Company A as captured, Pvt. Gustavus W. Dorsey as killed, three men as wounded, and one as taken prisoner. Company B lost two men captured. Captain George W.

of one killed, 16 wounded, 28 missing, but many of the latter men wounded, but we don't know which they were." Johnson had "lost [his] horse, saddle, bridle, overcoat, oil cloth, and that elegant dressing case, but thank God I escaped with my life."[61] Another Marylander said, "If unfortunate for the Maryland battalion, however, it was fortunate for Baker, whose brigade of North Carolinians would most assuredly have been cut to pieces had the enemy not been cut to pieces had the enemy not been held in check for a full half hour, thereby enabling them to escape."[62]

Two North Carolinians discussed Baker's performance that day. An unidentified trooper whose letter was published in *The Richmond Enquirer* noted: "Throughout the day, Col. J. A. Baker commanded the brigade, directing and supervising every movement." The anonymous correspondent chatted with a comrade about the day's events. "[Colonel] Baker seems to be very brave," the comrade observed. "Yes," the correspondent agreed, "he will carry you as far into the ranks of the enemy as any other living man." His comrade responded, "I'm afraid he will lead us so far in that he cannot get us out again." The correspondent retorted, "You have only to judge his future by his past." The two separated with the comrade "left ... seemingly much pleased and relieved."[63]

Neither Baker nor his Tar Heels distinguished themselves that day; they were routed and fled in disarray. The fact that Barringer was being promoted to succeed Gordon speaks volumes about the high command's lack of confidence in Baker. Barringer was just a lieutenant colonel, and he would soon assume command of the brigade.

Fitz Lee watched the demoralized Marylanders trot by as they made their way back toward Ashland. "This is a pretty howdy-do for the Maryland cavalry—let the Yankees run you off the face of the earth," he hooted, a twinkle in his eye. Other fugitives had already informed him about what had happened to the 1st Maryland that day. "Well, General, one thing is certain," Captain Booth blurted out, "the people who have been after us were white men; we stayed long enough

Howard of Company C and two of his men were captured, while Pvt. William C. Cheseldine died of his wounds, and one man was wounded. Private Alexander A. Young of Company D was killed, and Pvt. Samuel B. Mercer was mortally wounded, while another four were wounded, and nine others were taken prisoner. Company E lost one man wounded and five captured. Company F lost four men wounded and seven captured. Robert J. Driver Jr., *First and Second Maryland Cavalry, C.S.A.* (Charlottesville, VA: Rockbridge Publishing, 1999), 79.
61 Johnson to his wife, June 2, 1864.
62 Goldsborough, *The Maryland Line in the Confederate Army*, 199.
63 "Recent Cavalry Operations," *Richmond Enquirer*, June 17, 1864 (emphasis in original).

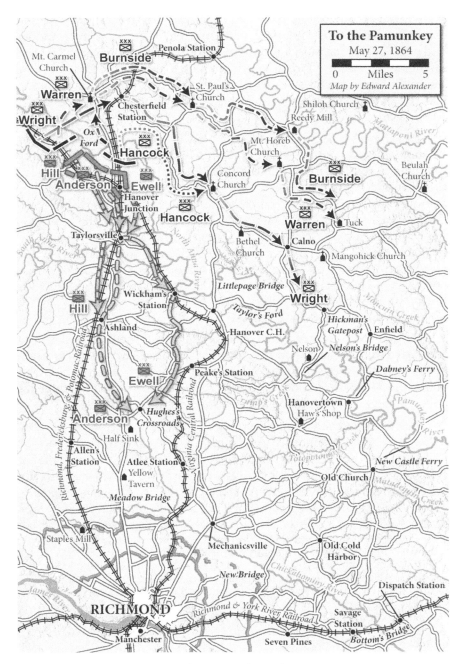

To the Pamunkey River

to find that out." Fitz Lee and the rest of the beaten Marylanders had a good laugh at Booth's impertinence.[64]

Fitz then advised his uncle: "As far as I can learn the enemy's cavalry seem to have halted at Haw's Shop and Aenon [Enon] Church. I am moving down from this place to Atlee's, where I expect to join with General Hampton, and think that we will have force enough to check any cavalry demonstration the enemy might make." He reported that he had not detected any infantry movement, but he had made sufficient arrangements to quickly learn if any occurred.[65]

The Federals, by contrast, had achieved complete surprise. As Major Kidd put it: "[T]he enemy were routed in great confusion."[66] They seized the Pamunkey River crossings and held them, thrashing the Confederate cavalry in the process. "If General Torbert's command had not been so much fatigued he would have captured the whole brigade, it was so much demoralized," Sheridan declared.[67] They suffered only negligible losses in doing so, reinforcing the widely held opinion that the Southern horse soldiers had lost their fight when Jeb Stuart was killed.[68] "Rebel cavalry is extremely demoralized, and flees before ours on every occasion," Assistant Secretary of War Charles A. Dana noted in a report to Secretary of War Edwin M. Stanton.[69] The victorious Federals camped on the field that night, weary from their 35-mile march and the fighting at Hanovertown.[70] Anticipating the next day to be a long one as well, Sheridan ordered Gregg to have his horses saddled and his artillery hitched in preparation to march at 4:00 a.m. [71]

The Army of the Potomac followed, employing the Pamunkey River crossings Sheridan's horsemen had seized. Because of the Northern cavalry's fruitful foray, Grant's plan to steal a march on Lee had succeeded. "We believe Lee is outgeneraled," a member of the 5th New York Cavalry scrawled in his diary, "and his army is soon to be whipped effectively and finally."[72] That remained to be seen, of course, but the Federals had every reason to be optimistic—Grant's plan had gone off without a hitch so far.

64 Booth, *Personal Reminiscences*, 115–16.
65 *OR* 51, 2:962.
66 *Supplement to the Official Records of the Union and Confederate Armies*,
    100 vols. (Wilmington, NC: Broadfoot Publishing, 1994), 6:620.
67 *OR* 36, 3:259.
68 Major Kidd told his parents his 6th Michigan Cavalry lost three men killed
    and one wounded on May 27. Wittenberg, *One of Custer's Wolverines*, 87.
69 *OR* 36.1:80.
70 Hall, *History of the Sixth New York Cavalry*. 192.
71 *OR* 36, 3:259.
72 Richard E. Beaudry, ed., *War Journal of Louis N. Beaudry, Fifth New York
    Cavalry* (Jefferson, NC: McFarland Publishing, 1996), 123.

Throughout the fighting, Doctor Pollard and his family cared for the wounded. "The Yankee soldiers who were brought in were fearfully wounded," young Harry Pollard recalled. "I saw two that had been shot through and through, and every time they breathed, blood would come out from front and back." Harry's sister Ellen spent the next three months caring for a Southerner shot through the hip. When he was finally well enough to leave, he thanked Ellen but proposed marriage to her sister Fanny, who had "not lifted a hand to help him," as Harry remembered.[73]

That evening Fitz Lee reported again from Atlee's Station. His scouts had sniffed out Grant's movement and he informed General Lee that the Federals were on the move. "Our cavalry is massed here now, with the intention of moving toward Hanovertown in the morning," Fitz Lee relayed.[74]

Based on news of the infantry's movement and similar intelligence, Lee concluded that the heavy concentration of Union cavalry near Haw's Shop meant Grant and the Army of the Potomac were probably going to go there as well, even though the buildup of horse soldiers could be a diversion in case Grant decided to move on Hanover Court House instead. General Lee elected to cover Atlee Station Road and the other potential destinations. He ordered his cavalry to rest until 3:00 a.m. and then march toward Atlee's Station to "get possession of the ridge between Totopotomoy and Beaver Dam Creek, upon which stands Pole Green Church."[75]

Lee directed his nephew Fitz Lee to leave Lomax's brigade at Hanover Court House to cover Hanover River Road and to then go with Wickham to Atlee's Station, where he would join Hampton's command to hold Atlee Station Road. "I think that we will have enough force to check any cavalry demonstrations the enemy might make," Fitz wrote. He told his uncle he and Hampton would advance toward Haw's Shop the next morning to ascertain Sheridan's plan. Meanwhile, the Army of Northern Virginia infantry assumed defensive positions along Totopotomoy Creek.[76]

Assistant Secretary Dana had been wrong about the Confederate cavalry. The next day at Haw's Shop would show that the Confederates remained full of fight.

---

73 Pollard, "Some War Events in Hanover County," 2–3. The soldier Ellen Pollard had nursed may have been St. George Tucker Brooke, who was actually wounded at Haw's Shop on May 28. The injury Harry Pollard described closely resembled the one Brooke had suffered. However, this remains unclear, as some discrepancies suggest Mary Jane Haw cared for Brooke.
74 *OR* 51, 2:963.
75 Ibid.
76 Ibid., 962–64.

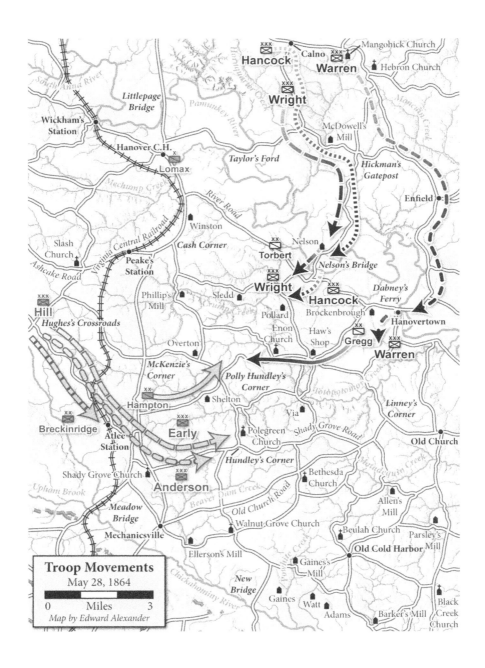

Troop Movements
May 28, 1864

0   Miles   3

Map by Edward Alexander

CHAPTER FIVE

A Heavy Engagement:
The Battle of Haw's Shop Opens

With both armies advancing toward each other on the early morning of May 28, Grant intended to move the rest of the Army of the Potomac across the Pamunkey River. Based on his nephew Fitzhugh Lee's reports, Gen. Lee concluded that Grant intended to utilize the Hanovertown crossings, push through Haw's Shop, and then head west to Atlee's Station or south to Mechanicsville. The Army of Northern Virginia marched toward Totopotomoy Creek, the first significant obstacle south of the Pamunkey, where General Lee intended to make a stand. As Lee told President Jefferson Davis early on May 28, regardless of which route Grant chose, "... I shall endeavor to engage [Grant] as soon as possible," close enough for reinforcements to reach him easily from the defenses of Richmond, which was under Brig. Gen. Arnold Elzey's command.[1] General Lee ordered Fitz Lee's and Wade Hampton's cavalry divisions to reconnoiter toward Haw's Shop, in the hope of determining Grant's plan.

James Wilson's Third Division remained north of the Pamunkey River, serving as a rear guard, while Alfred Torbert's First Division dug in along Crump's Creek, guarding against an attack from the direction of Hanover Court House. This left only David Gregg's Second Division, which was camped near Dr. William S. R. Brockenbrough's place, to scout toward Haw's Shop. The 1st New York Dragoons of Wesley Merritt's Reserve Brigade had already marched to Haw's Shop, and Sheridan had decided to use the fields near the decrepit shop as his staging area. "It was not supposed that any force of the enemy would be found there," a newspaper correspondent traveling with Sheridan's headquarters remarked.[2] About 8:00 a.m., Sheridan ordered Gregg to take his 3,500-man division to Haw's Shop and stay there in "readiness to make a reconnaissance."[3] Consequently, the opposing cavalry lay between the two armies, and the troopers soon came to blows in the fields surrounding Haw's Shop.

---

1 Clifford Dowdey, ed., *Wartime Papers of Robert E. Lee* (New York: Little, Brown, 1961), 753–54.
2 "Mr. N. Davidson's Dispatches," *New York Herald*, June 2, 1864.
3 *OR* 36, 3:273.

As senior division commander in the Army of Northern Virginia's Cavalry Corps, Hampton commanded the expedition. He had a large cavalry force at his disposal, which included the green troopers of the 4th and 5th South Carolina of Brig Gen. Matthew C. Butler's brigade and the 600 men of Lt. Col. John M. Millen's 20th Georgia Cavalry Battalion. Due to logistical challenges, it took nearly two months to transport the South Carolina regiments and their mounts to Virginia. The 5th South Carolina arrived first, followed by the 4th and then the 6th South Carolina.[4] Colonel John Dunovant's 5th South Carolina saw action at Drewry's Bluff from May 12 to 16, and then again during Fitz Lee's encounter with the United States Colored Troops at Wilson's Wharf on May 24.[5] The 4th South Carolina had not seen action yet.

Colonel Benjamin Huger Rutledge's 4th South Carolina had just arrived in Richmond on May 27. "South Carolina is a small state, but we get up big regiments," Charles M. Calhoun, who served in the 6th South Carolina Cavalry, declared.[6] Although the 4th South Carolina numbered nearly 1,000 men, only about 400 were mounted when they arrived in Richmond; nearly 600 horses were disabled with galled backs. The regiment's weapons had been shipped to Richmond by rail to lighten the horses' burden, causing considerable delay in retrieving them from the railroad. Once the weapons arrived, problems arose distributing them to the men, as their calibers were different, and certain companies required particular kinds of arms.[7]

After finally receiving its horses and arms, the 4th South Carolina marched about 20 miles to Atlee's Station and camped for the night.[8] Hampton advised Rutledge that "real serious work" would be required the next day.[9] Lieutenant Gabriel Manigault, the 4th South Carolina's

---

4 Robert E. L. Krick, "Repairing an Army: A Look at the New Troops in the Army of Northern Virginia in May and June 1864," in Gary W. Gallagher and Caroline E. Janney, eds., *Cold Harbor to the Crater: The End of the Overland Campaign* (Chapel Hill: University of North Carolina Press, 2015), 38.

5 The battle at Wilson's Wharf was a debacle for Fitz Lee. Fitz and about 2,500 men attacked 1,100 soldiers of the United States Colored Troops who were building fortifications along the James River in Charles City County. The fortifications were subsequently named Fort Pocahontas. Assisted by naval gunfire and timely reinforcements, the U.S.C.T. repulsed Lee with heavy losses—nearly 200, compared to 6 killed and 40 wounded for the Federals in the Army of Northern Virginia's first combat with African-American troops. For a detailed discussion, see Rhea, *To the North Anna River,* 362–68.

6 Calhoun, *Liberty Dethroned,* 122.

7 Benjamin H. Rutledge to Matthew C. Butler, undated, *B. H. Rutledge Letter Book,* 308, Special Collections, Addlestone Library, College of Charleston, Charleston, South Carolina ("Rutledge Letter").

8 "Orlando," "Butler's Cavalry."

9 Edward L. Wells, *A Sketch of the Charleston Light Dragoons, from the Earliest Formation of the Corps* (Charleston, SC: Lucas, Richardson & Co., 1888), 35 and 37.

adjutant, shared a small piece of cornbread with his friend Frank Middleton, observing that the Charleston Light Dragoons' exhausted troopers were "utterly out of spirits at the severe marching and the scarcity of food."[10]

Lieutenant Colonel Millen's command, which had spent the war on guard duty in the Deep South and had not seen combat, reported to Hampton at Atlee's Station on the morning of May 28. The Georgians came to Virginia without their mounts and had to wait for their horses to arrive before they could go into action. Millen expected Hampton to only inspect his troopers, not take them into battle, so he "put on his newest uniform and sash and other things calculated to make him look well."[11]

Finally, Capt. Andrew P. Love's battalion of Alabama cavalry also reinforced Hampton's command that day. Love organized his battalion in October 1863 and received orders to join the Army of Northern Virginia in the spring of 1864. The Alabamans arrived in Richmond on May 24, prompting one of the unit's troopers to state: "[T]he [w]hole world here is alive with soldiers." Love and approximately 160 troopers took the field on May 28, while fighting raged at Haw's Shop.[12]

The inexperienced South Carolinians were still adjusting to army life in the field. "In Virginia the usual daily allowance to a man was one-third of a pound of bacon and some corn meal, occasionally varied by some wheat flour, there being no coffee, tea, or other stimulant," an officer complained.[13] Oliver Middleton of the 4th South Carolina

---

10 Gabriel Manigault *Autobiography*, Archives, South Caroliniana Library, University of South Carolina, Columbia, South Carolina. Middleton was mortally wounded at Haw's Shop.

11 Charles P. Hansell, "History of the 20th Georgia Battalion of Cavalry," unpublished manuscript, Archives, Georgia Department of Archives and History, Atlanta, Georgia (hereinafter referred to as "Hansell Memoir"). John MacPherson Millen was born in Chester County, Delaware, in 1828. He served as the judge of the City Court of Savannah, Georgia, from 1856 to 1861. As a lieutenant in the Pulaski Guards, a local militia unit that became Company K of the 10th Georgia, Millen helped to organize the 20th Georgia Cavalry Battalion, which was also known as Millen's Battalion of Georgia Partisan Rangers. He was commissioned major and placed in command of the battalion on May 15, 1862. He was promoted to lieutenant colonel on September 16, 1863. Until the battalion was ordered to go to Richmond to join the Army of Northern Virginia's Cavalry Corps, it had spent its time guarding waterways around Savannah. Krick, *Lee's Colonels*, 270–71; John MacPherson Millen Find-a-Grave page, https://www.findagrave.com/memorial/8746304/john-macpherson-millen.

12 William H. Locke Letters, May 28–29, 1864, Special Collections, Alderman Library, University of Virginia, Charlottesville, Virginia. Historian Robert E. L. Krick correctly notes that virtually no accounts of the campaign include or address the presence of Love's Alabamans with Army of Northern Virginia's Cavalry Corps. Krick, "Repairing An Army," 65, n. 18.

13 Wells, *A Sketch of the Charleston Light Dragoons*, 36.

Pvt. Edward L. Wells,
Charleston Light Dragoons,
4th South Carolina Cavalry.

(South Caroliniana Library,
University of South Carolina)

sounded a similar note when he grumbled about the short rations. "They say that this is all that Lee's army gets," he told his mother, "so I suppose it is not impossible to subsist upon it, however hard it might be. We are, all of us, forever hungry and of course at first it goes rather hard with us."[14]

Edward Laight Wells of the Charleston Light Dragoons, an elite militia company that was part of the 4th South Carolina, observed that veterans wore gray jackets and usually carried breech-loading carbines captured from Federals. In stark contrast, new men tended to wear rough "homespun" uniforms and carried muzzle-loading Enfield rifles that were nearly as long as the ones the infantry carried. Veterans mocked the greenhorns and their weapons, jokingly asking how the Palmetto men would use them while mounted. "I say," a Virginian offered, "let me have your long shooter and I'll bite off the end." As an elite militia unit, the Charleston Light Dragoons wore natty uniforms and immaculate white gloves, drawing the veterans' contempt.[15]

Because Butler was still in transit, Rutledge commanded this hodgepodge detachment of new troopers as an ad hoc brigade. The 35-year-old Rutledge was from a prominent South Carolina family. His great-uncle Edward Rutledge was the youngest signer of the Declaration of Independence, and Edward's brother John was the revolutionary governor of South Carolina and one of George Washington's original nine appointees to the United States Supreme Court, briefly serving as chief justice after the first chief justice, John

14 Oliver Middleton to his mother, May 24, 1864, Middleton Family Correspondence, Special Collections, Addlestone Library, College of Charleston, Charleston, South Carolina.

15 Wells, *A Sketch of the Charleston Light Dragoons*, 38. For a detailed modern treatment of the role the Charleston Light Dragoons played in the Civil War, see W. Eric Emerson, *Sons of Privilege: The Charleston Light Dragoons in the Civil War* (Columbia: University of South Carolina Press, 2005).

Col. Benjamin H. Rutledge, commander, 4th South Carolina Cavalry.

(Author's collection)

Jay, resigned. Rutledge's grandfather Hugh was a prominent lawyer, as was Hugh's father, Benjamin Huger Rutledge Sr.[16]

Colonel Rutledge, a well-known Charleston attorney, was an ardent secessionist who signed South Carolina's Ordinance of Secession in 1860 and commanded the Charleston Light Dragoons before it became the 4th South Carolina's nucleus. He was described as "a courteous, accomplished and kindly man ... a true citizen, a true soldier, a true friend," and Gen. P. G. T. Beauregard, in urging Rutledge's promotion, stated that Rutledge had "no superior as a volunteer cavalry officer."[17] With Rutledge in command of the ad hoc

---

16 Benjamin Huger Rutledge Sr. was born on February 10, 1797. He attended South Carolina College for two years, but did not graduate. Instead, he left college in 1814 during his junior year to enlist in the army. He served as third lieutenant in the U.S. Artillery Corps from 1815 to 1817, and then attended the Litchfield Law School in Litchfield, Connecticut. He was admitted to the South Carolina bar in 1820. He married Alice Ann Weston in February 1824, and they had five children, including Benjamin Jr. Rutledge died at the young age of 35 on April 26, 1832, and was buried at Church of the Holy Cross Cemetery in Statesville, South Carolina. Benjamin Huger Rutledge Sr., Find-a-Grave page, https://www.findagrave.com/memorial/59189362/benjamin-huger-rutledge and Benjamin Huger Rutledge Sr. biography page, https://www.litchfieldhistoricalsociety.org/ledger/students/2194 (a listing of graduates of the Litchfield Law School).

17 Allardice, *Confederate Colonels*, 331 and Emerson, *Sons of Privilege*, 137. Benjamin Huger Rutledge Jr. was born on June 4, 1829, in Statesburg, South Carolina. He graduated from Yale University in 1848, and then studied law in Charleston. He served as captain of the Charleston Light Dragoons and as a delegate to the South Carolina Secession Convention. He led the Dragoons as state troops from 1861 to 1862. When the Dragoons became Company K of the 4th South Carolina Cavalry on March 25, 1862, he became its captain. He was commissioned the regiment's colonel on December 16, 1862. The 4th South Carolina served as garrison troops until it was ordered to Virginia in May 1864. After the war Rutledge resumed his legal career in Charleston and served as a member of the state legislature from 1876 to 1878. He died on April 30, 1893 and was buried in Charleston's Magnolia Cemetery. Ibid.

brigade, Lt. Col. William Stokes, who was inexperienced as Rutledge, led the 4th South Carolina.[18]

Rutledge's place in the command structure that day was unclear, and lack of clarity led to confusion on the battlefield. Butler's brigade was part of Hampton's division, but with Hampton commanding the operation, divisional commend fell to his senior brigade head Rosser, who assumed Rutledge was under his authority.[19] However, Fitz Lee, who outranked Rosser, believed Rutledge was under his command. Rutledge had no idea whose command he fell under, and he also seemed unsure about his authority over Lieutenant Colonel Millen and the Georgians, which negatively impacted their effectiveness. As Sgt. Charles Hansell of the 20th Georgia attentively noted, "[W]e seemed then and all through the fight that followed to be acting independently."[20]

Despite confusion within the chain of command, Hampton and his 4,500 troopers departed Atlee Station about 8:00 a.m. on May 28. According to Colonel Rutledge, the Confederates "marched rapidly towards Hawes Shops for the purpose of feeling Gen. Grant and developing his position."[21] As the 4th South Carolina men headed toward Haw's Shop, they learned the Army of the Potomac was on the move and realized they might see battle.[22] Wickham's brigade of Fitz Lee's division led the way, followed by Rosser's brigade and Rutledge's ad hoc brigade, with Chambliss's brigade bringing up the rear. The

---

18 William Stokes, born on October 20, 1833, was the youngest of 10 children. He was married to Eliza Jane Boulware on March 6, 1856, and they had 15 children. Stokes served as captain of a militia company of cavalry before the Civil War. He was commissioned a captain in the Confederate army on January 16, 1862 and saw action on the South Carolina coast in 1862 and 1863. On May 6, 1862, he was promoted to major of the 2nd Battalion, which was incorporated into the 4th South Carolina Cavalry in August 1862. On December 16, 1862, Stokes was promoted to lieutenant colonel. As at Haw's Shop, he periodically commanded the regiment in the field. When the war ended, he returned to South Carolina, where he entered politics and was elected to the state legislature. He then took part in the 1876 Red Shirt campaign that led to Wade Hampton's election as governor of South Carolina. Once Hampton took office, he appointed Stokes a brigadier general of militia in order to command the cavalry of the state. He died on June 30, 1905, and was buried in Hampton Cemetery at Hampton, South Carolina. Halliburton, *Saddle Soldiers*, xi–xiv.

19 Rosser claimed, "Colonel Rutledge, commanding the brigade, was directed to report to me." Thomas L. Rosser, "Annals of the War; Rosser and His Men," *Philadelphia Weekly Times*, April 19, 1884. However, during the battle of Haw's Shop, Fitz Lee gave orders to Rutledge and his men, not Rosser.

20 Hansell *Memoir*.

21 Rutledge Letter.

22 "Gills Creek," "Letter to the Editor," *The Ledger*, June 14, 1864.

men had about two-and-a-half miles to cover and were unaware they were on a collision course with David Gregg's Second Division.[23]

As ordered, Gregg's troopers moved out about 8:00 a.m. with the 380 officers and men of Maj. Matthew H. Avery's 10th New York Cavalry of Davies' brigade, which led the way. Colonel John P. Taylor's 1st Pennsylvania Cavalry followed closely behind the New Yorkers.[24] Avery's command reached Haw's Shop about 10:00 a.m. and turned west onto Atlee Station Road, while Davies established his headquarters in a stand of trees outside Oak Grove. The 10th New York dismounted near the house, leaving sufficient room in the large open field for the 1st Pennsylvania to join them.[25]

Avery ordered Capt. Martin H. Blynn and his squadron to scout toward Enon Church. Blynn and his Empire State troopers passed through John Haw's wheat field and along the Atlee Station Road before halting in thick woods beyond the church. Avery formed one company into a thin line of battle perpendicular to the road and told Lt. Truman C. White to continue west with the other company. White and his company went about half a mile farther west, posted a picket line under command of Sgt. Alfred J. Edson, and then continued toward Atlee Station with the rest of Company D. These actions ensured the two contending cavalry forces would collide, as the

---

23 Harold E. Howard Jr., ed., *"If I am Killed on this Trip, I Want My Horse Kept for My Brothers": The Diary of the Last Weeks of a Young Confederate Cavalryman* (Manassas, VA: United Daughters of the Confederacy, 1980), 14.

24 John P. Taylor was born on June 6, 1827, in Mifflin County, Pennsylvania. He lived his entire life on a family farm that he inherited. He was educated at Tuscarora Academy, and then engaged in farming and livestock trading. With the exception of his service in the Civil War, he worked in agriculture his entire life. He joined Company C of the 1st Pennsylvania Cavalry in 1861, commissioning as a first lieutenant. He was commissioned captain when the regiment reported for duty in Harrisburg. In September 1862 he was promoted to lieutenant colonel and then to colonel on January 30, 1863. On August 5, 1864, he received a brevet to brigadier general of volunteers. He took his discharge upon his term of service ending in September 1864, and returned to his farm. After the war, he was active in the local Republican Party politics, the Grand Army of the Republic, and the Military Order of the Loyal Legion of the United States. He died on June 27, 1914, and was buried in Church Hill Cemetery, near Reedsville, Pennsylvania. Ellis Franklin and Austin N. Hungerford, comps., *History of that Part of the Susquehanna and Juniata Valleys Embraced in the Counties of Mifflin, Juniata, Perry, Union, and Snyder, in the Commonwealth of Pennsylvania*, 2 vols. (Philadelphia: Everts, Peck & Richards, 1886), 1:198a–198b and Roger D. Hunt and Jack R. Brown, *Brevet Brigadier Generals in Blue* (Gaithersburg, MD: Olde Soldier Books, 1990), 606.

25 Noble D. Preston, *History of the Tenth Regiment of Cavalry, New York State Volunteers* (New York: D. Appleton & Co., 1892), 188; Noble D. Preston, "Hawes's Shop," *National Tribune*, April 21, 1887.

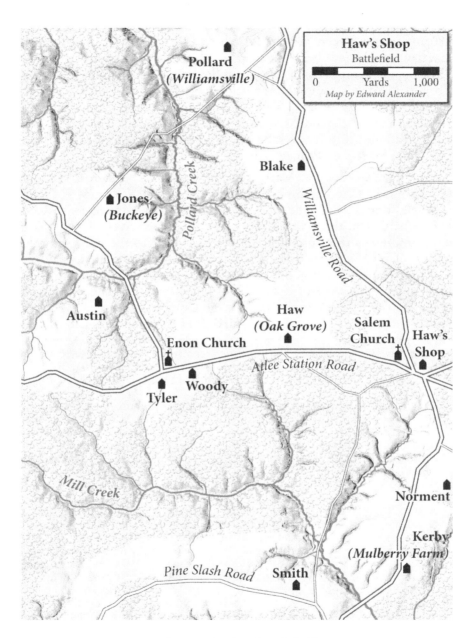

The Haw's Shop battlefield

Confederate cavalry was approaching quickly from the opposite direction on the same road.[26]

Wickham's Virginians led the advance of Hampton's column, with the 2nd Virginia Cavalry in front. Colonel Thomas T. Munford, commanding the 2nd Virginia, ordered Lt. Robert C. Wilson to scout ahead with the regiment's First Squadron, which consisted of only about 20 men. Wilson formed his men in a tight formation, and they headed east to see what they could find.[27]

Edson, leading his New Yorkers, spotted Wilson's approaching troopers. After firing a few shots, Edson put spurs to his horse to find Lieutenant White to report that enemy horsemen were

Col. Thomas T. Munford, commander, 2nd Virginia Cavalry.

(Library of Congress)

---

26 Preston, *History of the Tenth Regiment,* 188.

27 St. George Tucker Brooke autobiography, 46, Archives, Virginia State Library, Richmond, Virginia. Thomas Taylor Munford was born in Richmond, Virginia, on March 28, 1831. He was a member of one of the so-called "First Families of Virginia," the elites of antebellum Virginia society. He enrolled at the Virginia Military Institute in 1849, graduating 14th out of 24 in the class of 1852. Prior to the Civil War, he was a cotton planter in Mississippi and a farmer in Bedford County, Virginia. With the coming of the war, he was commissioned lieutenant colonel of the 2nd Virginia Cavalry on May 8, 1861, and then colonel of the regiment on April 25, 1862. He often led Fitz Lee's brigade in Lee's absence and was wounded in battle twice (at Second Bull Run and Cold Harbor). Despite having a difficult personality and a deep-seated enmity with Rosser and an inability to get along with Jeb Stuart, he was a competent soldier who deserved promotion to brigadier general long before it actually occurred. He was apparently appointed brigadier general in April 1865, and commanded Fitz Lee's division during the Appomattox campaign. He was paroled at Lynchburg on April 20, 1865, becoming a cotton planter thereafter. Munford served as vice president of the Lynchburg Iron and Mining Co. and as secretary of the Southern Historical Society. He contributed many papers to various historical publications. He died on February 27, 1918 and was buried in Spring Hill Cemetery at Lynchburg. Jubal Early described him as "a nice gentleman, but not remarkably brilliant intellectually." Allardice, *Confederate Colonels,* 285–86.

Col. John P. Taylor, commander,
1st Pennsylvania Cavalry.

(USAHEC)

Maj. Richard Falls,
commander, First
Battalion, 1st
Pennsylvania Cavalry.

(Michael Block)

approaching from the west. They then deployed across the road at the edge of the woods to try to halt the Southerners' advance, opening fire when Wilson and his men came into range. The Rebel yell quavered as the Virginians charged the Federal picket line. Uncertain about the size of the force attacking him and reluctant to bring on a full-scale fight without reinforcements nearby, White ordered his men to fall back to Blynn's line at Enon Church.[28]

Seeing the New Yorkers retiring, Wilson pursued them to Blynn's battle line, where they pulled up short at the sight of more Yankee horsemen. Munford and the rest of the 2nd Virginia soon followed—the Southerners now outnumbered the New Yorkers. Munford ordered his regiment to charge, driving the Federals back toward Davies' headquarters at Oak Grove.[29]

The sight of Blynn's men fleeing with Confederate cavalry hot on their trail spurred Davies to action. Taylor and the 1st Pennsylvania Cavalry were just arriving, so Davies ordered Taylor to meet Munford's troopers. "Draw saber!" Colonel Taylor cried as he deployed his first battalion, Maj. Richard J. Falls commanding, to the

28 Ibid.; Preston, *History of the Tenth Regiment*, 189.
29 Brooke autobiography, 46.

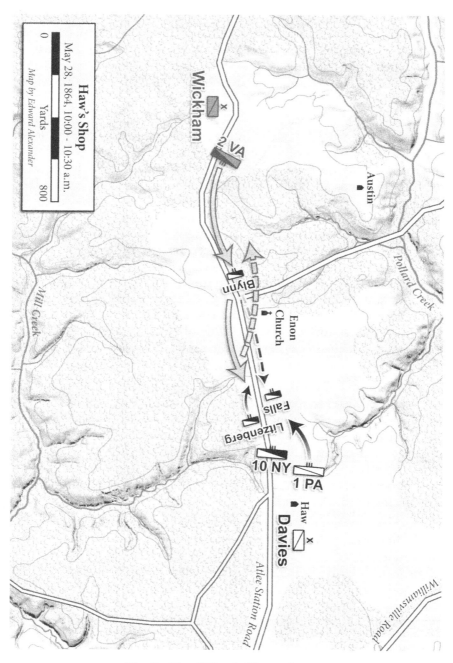

The Battle of Haw's Shop, phase 1

right of the road and his third battalion, Capt. William Litzenberg leading, to Atlee Station Road, supported by the 10th New York's sharpshooters. Taylor ordered his two battalions to charge just as the remnants of Blynn's little force galloped past. The Pennsylvanians surged forward as the 10th New York's carbineers opened fire, tearing holes in charging Virginians' line. Litzenberg's battalion crashed into the Virginians, and hand-to-hand combat, "spirited in the extreme," ensued.[30]

The size and ferocity of Taylor's determined counterattack surprised Munford. The stout rail fences lining the Atlee Station Road funneled the Virginians into a confide formation that was the width of the road, leaving no room to maneuver. "Our men, with cheers, were dashing forward, their sabers glinting in the sunlight," a Federal remembered. Taylor's charging mass crashed into the head of Munford's column, forcing it back on those coming from behind and prompting the desperate Virginians to attempt tearing down the fences. In a flash, the 1st Pennsylvania pounced on the 2nd Virginia, sabers slashing. "The 1st Pennsylvania never wielded the saber with better effect," a Pennsylvanian claimed. Overpowered, Munford's men broke and ran, scattering into the dense woods surrounding Enon Church, where they rallied, dismounted, and stacked fence rails and tree limbs into crude breastworks. Forming a line of battle across the road, they waited for Wickham's other three regiments to arrive and support them.[31]

St. George T. Brooke served in the 2nd Virginia Cavalry and was with the detachment south of the Atlee Station Road. "I was on the skirmish line when I did not realize that the rest had fallen back into the woods ... the enemy was barely 150 yards away," he wrote about his experiences that day. "I was shot and maimed for life, but managed to work my way back to my horse, which was soon after shot from under me." Brooke was fortunate to escape from the trap that Munford's men were facing in the deep woods.[32]

Davies dismounted the two regiments, ordering them to form a battle line facing the Virginians, perpendicular to the Atlee Station Road. The 10th New York deployed north of the road, its left at Enon Church, and the 1st Pennsylvania extended the 10th New York's left to the south, with Litzenberg's troopers holding the road and the rest of the regiment stringing leftward. The Union troopers took heavy fire

30 Ibid.; William P. Lloyd, *History of the First Regiment Pennsylvania Reserve Cavalry, From Its Organization, August 1861, to September 1864* (Philadelphia: King & Baird, 1864), 95.
31 Lloyd, *History of the First Pennsylvania Reserve Cavalry*, 95.
32 St. George T. Brooke memoir, Archives, Virginia Historical Society, Richmond, Virginia.

Confederate monument at Enon Church, Haw's Shop battlefield

(Author's photo)

from Wickham's men as they deployed, costing Davies several casualties.[33]

At that moment, Wade Hampton, Fitz Lee, and the rest of Wickham's brigade arrived. Hampton took a moment to assess the battlefield, determining whether it was fit for fighting; he decided to make a stand. The rest of Wickham's brigade—the 1st, 3rd, and 4th Virginia—joined Munford's 2nd Virginia, extending the Confederate line in both directions to overlap the Union line. "The woods were thick and we were tolerably well protected, but our line was not straight, there being one considerable angle," Lt. Robert T. Hubard Jr. of the 3rd Virginia recalled. "In consequence of this, we were exposed to a cross fire. The fire was most incessant and tremendous." Hubard and two of his regiment's company commanders, captains John A. Chapell and William Collins, found themselves in the middle of the angle, and "the balls from our battery and the enemy's both passed directly over us three as we were exactly in the line between them." A Union artillery shell smashed into a tree that Chapell stood behind, only four feet above the captain's head. Remarkably, the shell stuck between a splinter and the body of the tree without exploding.[34]

33 Lloyd, *History of the First Pennsylvania Reserve Cavalry*, 95; Preston, *History of the Tenth Regiment*, 189.
34 Thomas P. Nanzig, ed., *The Civil War Memoirs of a Virginia Cavalryman: Lt. Robert T. Hubard, Jr.* (Tuscaloosa, AL: University of Alabama Press, 2007), 166–67.

Oak Grove, the John Haw house on the Haw's Shop battlefield.

(Author's photo)

As Wickham's Virginians deployed, Rosser and his brigade arrived, dismounted, and marched northwest on a farm lane that extended past Wickham's left flank. Rosser told Col. Richard H. Dulany to place his 7th Virginia Cavalry and the 11th Virginia Cavalry, the next regiment in line, to extend Wickham's line farther to the north. He then placed his other two units—the 12th Virginia and the 35th Battalion of Virginia Cavalry—in a clearing at the northern end of Wickham's line. Rosser also placed in his line Capt. William M. McGregor's and Capt. Philip P. Johnston's batteries of horse artillery and a section of Capt. John J. Shoemaker's battery, which meant Davies' two regiments now faced 10 guns and two full cavalry brigades.[35]

35 Frank M. Myers, *The Comanches: A History of White's Battalion, Virginia Cavalry, Laurel Brigade, Hampton's Division, A.N.V., C.S.A.* (Baltimore, MD: Kelly, Piet & Co., 1871), 290; George Baylor, *Bull Run to Bull Run: Four Years in the Army of Northern Virginia* (Richmond: B. F. Johnson Publishing Co., 1900); Report of Roger Preston Chew, Lewis Leigh Collection, Archives, United States Army History and Education Center ("USAHEC"), Carlisle, Pennsylvania; John J. Shoemaker's report, in William Black diary, Special Collections, Virginia Military History Institute Library, Lexington, Virginia; James Breathed's report, Southern Historical Collections, Wilson Library, University of North Carolina, Chapel Hill, North Carolina. Major Roger P. Chew's battery also arrived on the field and deployed, but "did no firing, as the lay of the field and the peculiar conformation of the lines were

Enon Church, Haw's Shop battlefield.

(*Author's photo*)

The Confederates held a strong defensive position perpendicular to Atlee Station Road, near Enon Church. The road ran along the spine of a ridgeline, dividing Crump's Creek from Totopotomoy Creek. Hampton's left flank, which Rosser's regiments and 10 guns were holding, was about half a mile north of the road, anchored on a tributary of Crump's Creek that ran parallel to the road until it turned right and flowed into Haw's mill pond, which protected Hampton's right flank. Wickham's men held Hampton's right, which rested on Mill Creek, a tributary of Totopotomoy Creek, half a mile south of the road. Heavy timber and secondary brush covered the banks of both streams. The Confederates held a compact, mile-long line, with dense woods behind them.[36]

The Southerners quickly constructed crude breastworks and dug hasty rifle pits. Always spoiling for a fight, Hampton invited the Federal cavalry to attack his reinforced position—much of his line

unfavorable for artillery firing," as a member of the battery noted. George M. Neese, *Three Years in the Confederate Horse Artillery* (New York: Neale Publishing Co., 1911), 278.

36 Joseph R. Haw, "The Battle of Haw's Shop," *Confederate Veteran* 33 (1925), 374.

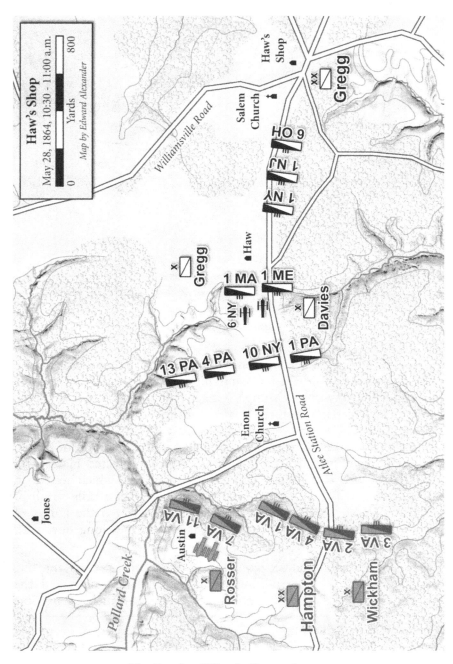

The Battle of Haw's Shop, phase 2

rested in the deep woods, and both flanks were anchored on streams, so they could not be easily turned.[37] "The Confederates had the advantage of the forest almost the entire length of the battle line," John Haw's son Joseph wrote years later, "while the Yankees had forest on the right of the road, but field and small pines on the left."[38] Hampton, pleased with his position, rode up to Lt. Col. Elijah V. White, commanding the 35th Battalion of Rosser's brigade, and confidently declared, "Good morning, Colonel. We've got the Yankees where we want them now."[39]

However, as Capt. Frank Myers of the 35th Battalion keenly noted, "in about fifteen minutes the battalion concluded that the boot was on the other foot, for the Yankees certainly had them where they didn't want to be. The storm of shot and shell that howled madly over and around them was terrific." Two members of the 35th Battalion, Lt. Harrison Strickler of Company E and Pvt. Jack Howard of Company A, who Myers described as "two splendid men," both fell wounded after just a few moments on the field—Strickler was injured on the knee, and Howard took an unexploded shell to the face when it came bouncing along and struck him.[40]

While this drama played out, Davies deployed his two remaining regiments, the 4th and 13th Pennsylvania, on the northern end of his line, which now consisted of the 13th Pennsylvania, the 4th Pennsylvania, and the 10th New York north of Atlee Station Road and the 1st Pennsylvania south of the road. Gregg also called for Capt. Joseph Martin's 6th New York Independent Battery to deploy its four guns north of the road, about 250 yards west of Oak Grove, with the 1st Massachusetts Cavalry in support. Private George Perkins, who served in Martin's battery, recalled a "smart fire going on in the woods in front." He considered this "the hottest musketry fire I have ever been under. It is wonderful some of us were not hit by them."

Martin instructed his cannoneers to fire over the 10th New York troopers deployed in their front. The first shell exploded over the Federals' heads, prompting Perkins to remark, "The shell was good for nothing and not to be trusted. The fuse ought to have carried three times as far." The errant shell wounded one New York trooper and several horses. "The men of that reg[iment] talked hard against us," he

---

37 Gilbert Thompson memoirs, entry for May 31, 1864, Manuscripts Division, Library of Congress, Washington, D.C.
38 Haw, "The Battle of Haw's Shop," 374.
39 Myers, *The Comanches*, 290.
40 Ibid.

concluded.[41] With the 1st Maine Cavalry supporting, Gregg deployed a second battery to Martin's left, near an abandoned brick kiln, reducing the Confederate artillery advantage to two guns.[42]

Martin then advanced his guns to within 50 yards of the woods. "As we took this new position the mini bullets whistled thick around us, one struck the limber wheel right in front of me," Richard Griffin remembered. "The musketry was terrific only about a hundred [yards] in front of us." Because the battery was short on ammunition, its guns fired slowly, and some of Hampton's guns answered with counterbattery fire. "By the way their first shot came right over our gun and struck in the ground only 20 feet in advance of us," Griffin added. Martin's guns kept firing until they ran out of ammunition, then withdrew, allowing another battery to replace them. One of Martin's men was killed, two lost legs to amputation, and the heavy musketry fire wounded three. Several horses were killed, including that of Lt. J. Wade Wilson, which died while Wilson was riding it.[43]

Davies ordered his dismounted troopers to attack, but Wickham's and Rosser's Virginians quickly repulsed them. Gray-clad soldiers came out from behind breastworks to pursue, but concentrated Union Spencer carbine fire drove them back. This sort of dismounted slugging continued back and forth across Haw's farm fields. "It was clearly an unequal contest, so far as numbers were concerned, but never did the regiment display better staying qualities or exhibit more gallantry than on this occasion," a New Yorker declared.[44] "The fighting at once assumed the most desperate character," William P. Lloyd of the 1st Pennsylvania Cavalry recalled, and raged "at point-blank range, neither able to carry the other's position, but each determined to hold its own." Although only about 200 1st Pennsylvania troopers were involved, they expended nearly 18,000 rounds of ammunition, prompting Lloyd to observe, "Many of our carbines, also, became so heated as to render them for a time entirely useless."[45]

---

41 Richard N. Griffin, ed., *Three Years a Soldier: The Diary and Newspaper Correspondence of Private George Perkins, Sixth New York Independent Battery, 1861–1864* (Knoxville: University of Tennessee Press, 2006), 234. A trooper of the 10th New York noted in his diary that the horses of the regiment were "under severe fire" that day. He may not have known it was friendly fire. Diary of John R. Maybury, entry for May 28, 1864, http://digitalsc.lib.vt.edu/CivilWar/Ms2008-044.

42 "Mr. N. Davidson's Dispatches"; Tobie, *History of the First Maine Cavalry*, 276; Benjamin W. Crowninshield, *A History of the First Regiment of Massachusetts Cavalry Volunteers* (Boston: Houghton, Mifflin & Co., 1891), 218.

43 Griffin, *Three Years a Soldier*, 234–35.

44 Preston, *History of the Tenth Regiment*, 189–90.

45 Lloyd, *History of the First Pennsylvania Reserve Cavalry*, 95.

Maj. Delos Northway of the 6th Ohio Cavalry, killed in action at Haw's Shop.

(Ken Lawrence)

Pvt. Henry Miller of the 6th Ohio Cavalry, captured at Haw's Shop.

(Ken Lawrence)

Davies now committed the 6th Ohio Cavalry to the fray, hoping it would break the deadlock. These reinforcements dismounted "under a storm of shot and shell, which killed two men and wounded several others," Capt. N. A. Barrett of the 6th Ohio recounted.[46] Major Delos R. Northway, just promoted two weeks earlier, rode to another company commander and said, "Captain, I had expected to turn the command of the squadron over to you this morning, but Colonel Steadman does not seem disposed to place me in command of my battalion until I am mustered." The Buckeyes formed north of the road, between the 10th New York and 4th Pennsylvania, and charged dismounted through the woods. They crashed into the 7th Virginia Cavalry, and Major Northway fell, shot through the heart while leading his squadron. He landed "flat on his back, his feet to the foe, straight as an Indian." His older brother, Sgt. George R. Northway, and another man rushed forward to rescue the mortally wounded major, but they also fell, badly injured—a bullet struck Sergeant Northway in the head, staggering him, and he was then shot in his side and leg. Five other Buckeyes, including Lt. Josiah E. Wood, tried to climb a fence but were hit while crossing it. A brave soldier dodged the heavy Confederate fire to drag Wood to safety. When he opened Wood's tunic, he noticed the ball had struck the lieutenant's breastbone and glanced away, causing only a minor wound.[47]

The advancing Buckeyes had to contend with a deep ravine, which they tried to cross on a large fallen tree. "Some of our men were very shaky in the knees and tumbled off into the ravine, but of course they were on hand for the fight," Sgt. Truman Reeves, 6th Ohio, noted. "About fifteen rods from the ravine we met the enemy in the wood [which] were quite open and much dead timber was lying on the ground. With this we fortified ourselves the best we could." Reeves recalled that "[a]fter we had been engaged about 15 or 20 minutes, it became so hot that I was sure that every man in the Company [G] would go down, and I found out afterwards that it was equally hot all along the line." Before long, Reeves suffered a severe wound. "I was just pumping out the old cartridge and was putting a new one in my carbine, when a minnie [sic] ball passed through my left arm near the

46 N. A. Barrett, "Sixth Ohio Cavalry," *Western Reserve Chronicle*, June 22, 1864.

47 Wells A. Bushnell memoir, in Palmer Regimental Papers, Archives, Western Reserve Historical Society, Cleveland, Ohio; J. N. Roberts to C. F. Wolcott, September 28, 1905, included in Fortieth Annual Reunion of the Sixth Ohio Volunteer Veteran Cavalry (n.p., 1905). Major Northway was cited for bravery many times during the war, and the men of his unit badly missed him.

48 Edwin C. Bearss, ed., *Campaigning with Sgt. Truman Reeves and Company*

shoulder," he recounted. Handing his carbine to a friend, he made his way to safety.[48]

Sheridan sent a staff officer to find the 6th Ohio's Col. William Stedman. "General Sheridan wishes to know, Colonel, how you are getting along," the staff officer inquired. The plain-spoken Stedman responded, "You tell the general that we are licking the bile out of them." Stedman's odd reply amused Sheridan so much that the general still chuckled about it years afterwards.[49]

Concerned about his northern (left) flank, Rosser sent a staff officer to find Lt. Col. Thomas C.

Sgt. Truman Reeves of the 6th Ohio Cavalry, wounded in action at Haw's Shop.

(Ken Lawrence)

Marshall of the 7th Virginia Cavalry. The staffer found Marshall on the firing line and asked how long he thought he could hold. "Until my last man falls," Marshall grimly declared.[50] "These Virginians fell

---

G, Sixth Ohio Volunteer Cavalry: From Orwell to Haw's Shop (Privately published, n.d.), 227–28. Reeves' arm had to be amputated. He spent seven months at a military hospital before he was discharged for his disability. His war was over.

49 Rockwell, *Rambling Recollections*, 149.

50 Rosser, "Annals of the War." Thomas C. Marshall was born in Oak Hill, Fauquier County, Virginia, on January 17, 1826. He was the grandson of the great Chief Justice of the United States Supreme Court John Marshall. Not surprisingly, he studied law in Winchester, and was practicing there when the war kicked off. Marshall was commissioned as a captain and served as a volunteer aide to Stonewall Jackson at the First Battle of Bull Run in July 1861. He was appointed major of the 7th Virginia Cavalry on June 20, 1862. After he was captured at Orange Court House and later exchanged, he was promoted to lieutenant colonel on October 30, 1862. He fought at the battle of Trevilian Station, and suffered wounds at the battles of Ream's Station and Petersburg. He had six horses shot out from under him during the war. He was killed at Nineveh in the Shenandoah Valley on November 10, 1864, and was buried in Stonewall Cemetery at Winchester, Virginia. See Krick, *Lee's Colonels*, 263–64; Richard L. Armstrong, *7th Virginia Cavalry* (Lynchburg, VA: H. E. Howard Co., 1992), 191.

Lt. Col. Thomas C. Marshall,
commander, 7th Virginia Cavalry.

(History of the Laurel Brigade)

back, refilled their cartridge boxes and returned to the front without hesitation," an admiring captain of the 4th South Carolina Cavalry recalled.[51]

By this time the battle had deteriorated into a dismounted slugging match, with both sides blasting away at each other at short range across a narrow no-man's land. "I stood in the midst of the dead and dying while the little missiles battered against the trees and logs and cut the twigs on every side," Capt. Noble D. Preston, 10th New York Cavalry, stated.[52] The opposing horse artillerists engaged in intense counterbattery duels, featuring heavy, accurate fire. The "storm of shot and shell that howled madly over and around was terrific," a 35th Battalion of Virginia Cavalry trooper, assigned to guard the Confederate guns, shuddered.[53] Hoping to break the tension, 12th Virginia Cavalry Capt. George Baylor decided to have some fun by tossing a shell fragment onto one of his men, who lay terrified on the ground. Thinking he was wounded, the man, "[w]ith a cry of anguish[,] ... leaped up, left his horse, ran back through the pines, and all my efforts to stop his retreat were futile," Baylor recalled.[54]

A Confederate artillery shell struck the color bearer of the 1st Massachusetts Cavalry, killing him instantly. The Bay State men did not enjoy acting as support for the horse artillery. "To sit on one's horse behind artillery in action, without any possibility of protection, to be a mark for the enemy's guns and at the same time to be powerless to deal a blow in return, is the hardest duty a cavalry soldier can perform," an officer of the 1st Massachusetts remarked. "An infantryman can lie down under fire, but a cavalry soldier is obliged to

51 Thomas L. Pinckney diary, entry for May 28, 1864, Special Collections, Addlestone Library, College of Charleston, Charleston, South Carolina.
52 Preston, "Hawes's Shop."
53 Myers, *The Comanches*, 290.
54 Baylor, *Bull Run to Bull Run*, 212.

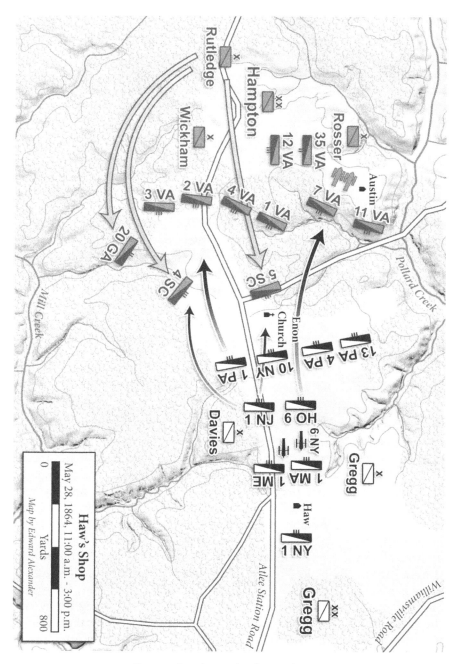

The Battle of Haw's Shop, phase 3

remain upon his horse, and frequently to see his enemy point his gun at him, and the artilleryman pull the lanyard which fires it, knowing all the time that he is the mark at which it is aimed."[55]

Troopers of the 1st Maine Cavalry, taking shelter by the abandoned brick kiln, watched Southern projectiles whizz by, threatening to strike the chimney and shower them with brick fragments. "Shells never scream so fiercely or sound so wickedly as under those circumstances," a Maine man reflected. "Men can only think and hope, and their nerves are sorely tried."[56]

Twenty-six-year-old Cpl. Thomas W. Colley served in the 1st Virginia Cavalry of Wickham's brigade. Colley had suffered two combat wounds earlier in the war and was still recuperating from his most recent injury. Originally detailed as a horse holder because of his weakened condition, Colley decided to trade places with his cousin, positioning himself on the battle line. "We could not see or be seen until we came right up to the line, which was formed at a fence or rather two fences with a small space between them—hardly big enough for a hog or sheep to pass between them." As they took their place in line, two Yankee sharpshooters popped up from between the fences, exclaiming, "Don't shoot us we are your men," prompting officers and men to shout out not to shoot. They stared each other down, and then the Federals raised their rifles, drew a bead, and opened fire. "They both sprang over the fence as we all fired at them, and disappeared in the dense forest and bushes." Colley realized a Southerner had left his saber belt behind and wondered if a bullet had cut the belt.

Colley and his fellow Virginians took their places in line, engaging in dismounted combat for about two hours. One of his comrades fired a shot from behind him, nearly striking Colley in the head. While turning to yell out a warning, a ball struck the end of a rail and threw dust and splinters all over Colley's face. He turned again, asking his comrades not to shoot over him, when a ball struck him half an inch in front of his boot heel, passed through the sole of his foot, and traveled to his ankle bone, wrecking the joint. Because the wound was not painful at first, Colley continued firing from a prone position. "I began to feel a stinging sensation on my ankle bone and the blood was running up my boot leg," he recalled. Out of ammunition, he rose to see whether he could walk. With the damage to his joint, he would have fallen had his comrades not come to his aid. Drawing heavy fire the entire way, the two men carried Colley to safety. Medical personnel put him in an ambulance, taking him to a field hospital almost three-

---

55 Crowninshield, *A History of the First Regiment*, 218.
56 Tobie, *History of the First Maine Cavalry*, 276–77.

quarters of a mile away. A field surgeon amputated Colley's foot, ending the war for him.[57]

As John Haw, his elderly wife, and their daughter Mary hid in the cellar, Gregg commandeered Oak Grove as a field hospital, and the yard filled with dead and injured Union cavalrymen and a single wounded trooper of the 2nd Virginia Cavalry, who went down early in the battle. Doctor Alphonso D. Rockwell served as surgeon for the 6th Ohio Cavalry. When he reported to the field hospital at the Haw homestead, he saw "an old house filled and a yard strewn with wounded men who had either been operated upon or were patiently waiting their turn to be placed on repulsive-looking tables."[58]

Before long, the Confederate horse artillerists zeroed in on the Haw house. A well-aimed cannonball tore through three horses tethered to a fence, and another sheared an officer's leg clean off and eviscerated his horse, dumping both rider and beast on the ground. "The officer caught hold of the stump of his leg and called to the men to take him to the surgeons," a horrified witness described. "Blood spurted in large streams from the stump for a distance of three or four feet."[59]

"Can I ever forget that shell?" Doctor Rockwell trembled decades later. "I heard it coming from behind, shrieking like a thousand devils. I remember thinking that I was done for. Another surgeon was riding by my side, our knees nearly touching, yet the shell fell between our two horses, exploding as it touched the ground." He continued, "The horse of my fellow surgeon was literally disemboweled, while my own horse was untouched, but the shock was terrible." The sight of the mortally wounded horse, rearing and spraying arterial blood, lingered with those who saw it.[60]

Doctor H. K. Clarke served as a surgeon in the 10th New York Cavalry and established a treatment ward in one of Haw's outbuildings. There he treated a Sergeant Reynolds, whose leg a Confederate artillery shell had mangled. As Clarke began amputating the sergeant's leg, a shell crashed through the door, ricocheted into one of the roof beams, dropped to the floor, and rolled under Clarke's

57 Michael K. Shaffer, ed., *In Memory of Self and Comrades: Thomas Wallace Colley's Recollections of Civil War Service in the 1st Virginia Cavalry* (Knoxville: University of Tennessee Press, 2018), 95–97. Colley's memoir of his life addresses the ordeals he faced as a crippled veteran in the years after the Civil War. Editor Michael K. Shaffer suggests Colley probably suffered from post-traumatic stress disorder, which would not be surprising given the circumstances.
58 Alphonso D. Rockwell, *Rambling Recollections: An Autobiography* (New York: P. B. Hoeber, 1920), 148.
59 Brooke autobiography, 50–51.
60 Rockwell, *Rambling Recollections*, 148–49.

operating table. Everyone tensed, waiting for the explosion. Frozen in place expecting a detonation, Clarke held a severed artery. Fortunately, the shell's fuse had burned out, and the shell did not explode. Heaving a great sigh of relief, Clarke barked, "Take that shell out!" As orderlies removed it, Clarke resumed his amputation procedure. Shortly thereafter, medical providers determined the Haw house and outbuildings were too exposed, and had the wounded Union men carried back to Salem Church, which became the new field hospital. The wounded Confederate cavalryman was left behind, exposed to further fire.[61]

An hour into what was already an intense fight, Hampton decided to deploy Rutledge's brigade, which he had been holding in reserve on Atlee Station Road behind Wickham's line of battle. Captain Rawlins Lowndes of Hampton's staff galloped up to Rutledge, extended Hampton's compliments, and asked him "to be kind enough" to order his regiment to mount and hurry to the front.[62] Lieutenant Colonel William Stokes' 4th South Carolina Cavalry was closest to the firing line, with Lieutenant Colonel Millen's 20th Georgia and Colonel Dunovant's 5th South Carolina waiting behind them. This was the first time most of the rookies had seen combat, and the sight of wounded men horrified them. Seeing a dead lieutenant, with his body draped over a horse, particularly struck them. Fortunately, a moment of comic relief followed when a bursting shell catapulted a nearby courier into the air. "Getting on his feet in a somewhat dazed condition, the man looked furtively first on one side and then on the other, as a rabbit might do before springing up, and then bolted back in the direction from which he had ridden, with incredible swiftness, his sabre trailing out behind him almost horizontally," Edward Wells of the 4th South Carolina laughed.[63]

Sergeant Charles P. Hansell commanded a platoon of the 20th Georgia Battalion. Looking up to see a cannonball whizzing directly at him, he ordered his men to hug the ground, awaiting the inevitable impact. Luckily for him, the shell crashed into a nearby horse, almost severing the hand of the trooper holding its bridle.[64]

Wickham's men had been taking a pounding, so some of them began abandoning the line. Worried, Wickham persuaded them to resume their positions, but Fitz Lee was concerned that if Sheridan launched a determined attack, he might shatter the Confederate line. Fitz Lee asked Hampton for permission to commit the 4th South Carolina to the fight, and Hampton agreed, so Fitz ordered Stokes to

---

61 Preston, History of the Tenth Regiment, 207.
62 Wells, *History of the Charleston Light Dragoons*, 38.
63 Ibid., 40.
64 Hansell Memoir.

march his men across Wickham's rear and form on the Confederate right, further extending the line.[65] Dismounting had reduced the the 4th South Carolina's effective strength to 300 officers and men—every fourth man had to be detailed to hold his horse and those of three comrades, thereby reducing effective combat strength by one-quarter—but the rookies headed off in "good style, giving a splendid Confederate battle yell" as they went into combat for the first time. They drew fire immediately as they crossed a clearing, and three fell, including Percival Porcher, who lay writhing in agony as the rest of the regiment stepped over him on their way into battle.[66]

Lieutenant Colonel Stokes told his men to stay low to avoid drawing fire. "They had just reached the center of the line when they were ordered to halt and await orders, and in the midst of a most terrific fire from the enemy's forces," a South Carolinian stated. "They were kept in this position for upwards of an hour, during which time several fell killed and wounded."[67] Finally, Hampton determined the crisis was over and ordered Stokes to return to Atlee Station Road. The South Carolinians drew heavy fire as they made their way back to rejoin Millen's and Dunovant's troopers. "We lay down behind a few scattered rails—not enough to be called a rail pile," Hansell recalled. "Here [Lieutenant Colonel Millen] walked up and down the line and encouraged the men to keep cool and be ready to receive the enemy warmly."[68]

In the meantime, Gregg faced a tough fight at Haw's Shop. Wickham's troopers were pushing hard against the center of the Union line, so Gregg committed his only reserve, the 1st New Jersey Cavalry. Now, all of his troopers were engaged. Worried about the enemy's strength, Gregg asked Sheridan for reinforcements. "I sent him word as to how we stood," Gregg later reported, "and stated that with some additional force I could destroy the equilibrium and go forward."[69]

Plenty of Union infantry on standby could have been brought to bear, but Sheridan refused to use them, preferring to give his cavalry the honor of carrying the day. He declined to ask for infantry reinforcements, leaving Gregg to make do with available elements of Davies' brigade. Wilson's Third Division remained north of the Pamunkey River, too far away to be of assistance. At Crump's Creek, the VI Corps infantry was relieving Brigadier General Torbert's command, so Torbert would be of no help. Consequently, Gregg elected to take the fight to Hampton.

65 Hampton, *Connected Narrative*, 38.
66 Wells, *History of the Charleston Light Dragoons*, 41–42.
67 "Orlando," "Butler's Cavalry."
68 Hansell Memoir.
69 "The Battle of Haw's Shop," *Philadelphia Inquirer*, June 3, 1864.

Gregg directed Col. John W. Kester, commanding the 1st New Jersey, to send a company to each end of the Union battle line as videttes, and then split the rest of his regiment into two wings.[70] Captain Walter R. Robbins led four companies north of Atlee Station Road to reinforce the 10th New York, while Maj. Hugh H. Janeway led the rest of the regiment south of the road to reinforce the 1st Pennsylvania.[71]

"I stood in the midst of the dead and dying while the little missiles battered against the trees and logs and cut the twigs on every side," Capt. Noble D. Preston, 10th New York Cavalry, recalled. Preston was distinctly unenthusiastic about attacking the Confederate breastworks. "An aide arrived from General Gregg, saying the line must be advanced. He ducked his head while the bullets whistled past, and shrugged his shoulders as he started for the rear, stating, 'Those are the orders.'"[72] Enthusiastic or not, orders were orders, so the blue-clad horse soldiers obeyed.

As Captain Robbins and his troopers prepared to attack, Capt. Henry C. Weir, the staff officer Gregg had sent, rode over to Robbins and stated, "The General instructs me to say to you that you are to take command of the Tenth New York Cavalry." They advanced into the teeth of heavy small arms and artillery fire, discovering the Confederates had forced the 10th New York to bend its right flank back a few hundred yards, creating a gap between the Empire State

---

70 Colonel Kester's story is a sad one. John Wood Kester was born in Frankford, Pennsylvania, in 1842. He attended Allegheny College in Meadville, Pennsylvania, and the University of Pennsylvania, dropping out of the class of 1863 to go to war. He had worked as a wholesale druggist before the war. He was commissioned a second lieutenant in the Commonwealth Artillery of Pennsylvania on April 24, 1861, and honorably mustered out on August 5, 1861. He was commissioned captain of Company E of the 1st New Jersey Cavalry on August 9, 1861 and served as a staff officer on Gregg's staff from May 13 to November 2, 1863. He was commissioned lieutenant colonel of the 1st New Jersey on September 21, 1863, and then an artillery shell badly contused his head and neck at the battle of Jack's Shop that day. He was promoted to colonel of the 1st New Jersey Cavalry on July 6, 1864 and mustered out due to disability on September 25, 1864. He engaged in several unprofitable business ventures after the war, and his mental capacity deteriorated, apparently as a result of his combat wound in 1863. Finally, he had to be confined in a Philadelphia insane asylum in1882. He spent the rest of his life committed, and died on March 1, 1904. He was buried in the St. Luke's Episcopal Graveyard, located in the Germantown section of Philadelphia. See Roger D. Hunt, *Colonels in Blue: Union Colonels of the Civil War, Pennsylvania, New Jersey, Maryland, Delaware and the District of Columbia* (Mechanicsburg, PA: Stackpole, 2007), 205. For a full-length biography of Kester's tragic life, see Donald E. Kester, *Cavalryman in Blue: Colonel John Wood Kester of the First New Jersey Cavalry in the Civil War* (Hightstown, NJ: Longstreet House, 1997).

71 *OR* 36, 1:861.

72 Preston, "Hawes's Shop."

men and the 4th Pennsylvania to the north. If the Confederates could exploit that gap, then they could split the Union line in two.

Robbins recognized the threat and sent his men straight into the gap. Heavy black powder smoke combined with thick woods hid the Confederates, but the attentive Robbins estimated the Rebels' position from the sound of their gunfire. He rode through the woods and found an officer of the 10th New York, which surprised him. "Where is your command?" Robbins inquired. "Over there," the officer replied "in a tremulous, agitated voice, pointing to the right." Robbins told the officer he had been ordered to take charge of the line and sent him to his company, using "a peremptory tone." Relentlessly, Robbins struck anyone sulking with the flat of his sword, venting his "towering rage" on whoever fell behind, and berated the troopers for cowardice.[73]

Capt. Walter R. Robbins, 1st New Jersey Cavalry, wounded at Haw's Shop.

(Library of Congress)

A "tremendous volley" erupted in Robbins' front, and Capt. Garrett V. Beekman, one of Robbins' company commanders, turned, appearing to prepare for a retreat. "Back to your place, Captain," Robbins thundered, and the Jerseymen charged, shoving the Confederates back over a fence and across a gully toward another fence line, along the farm road that ran northwest from Enon Church. "It was every man for himself," a 1st New Jersey trooper declared, "and from behind trees, stumps and the fence we poured a heavy fire upon the rebels behind a fence scarcely 30 yards away." Looking for a chance to redeem himself with Robbins, Beekman led a detachment into the

---

73 Lillian Rea, ed., *War Record and Personal Experiences of Walter Raleigh Robbins from April 22, 1861, to August 4, 1865* (n.p., n.d.), 86–87.

Lt. Col. William Stokes, 4th South Carolina Cavalry.

(Author's Collection)

gully fronting the enemy position. Firing rapidly, they broke the initial Confederate line and crashed into Wickham's main line. The Virginians' heavy fire took the starch out of their attack, and the Jerseymen fell back across the gully, rallying at a fence in front of the Union line. "Thus the time passed on," 1st New Jersey chaplain, Henry Pyne, wrote, "both parties holding their own, and neither gaining ground upon the other."[74]

Responding to Robbins' attack, Fitz Lee turned to Stokes of the 4th South Carolina Cavalry and instructed him to "relieve that Virginia brigade and hold that wood."[75] By giving orders directly to Stokes, Lee usurped Rutledge, commander of the makeshift brigade of South Carolinians and Georgians, of any authority, leaving Rutledge to gripe that he was "literally left without command except of the horses." Rutledge and his adjutant, Lt. Gabriel Manigault, spent the battle in the rear, playing no active role.[76]

Stokes again led his South Carolinians behind Wickham's line of battle. "Where we fought was tolerably thick undergrowth and a good many trees about twelve inches thick in diameter," Stokes recounted the next day, "which we took shelter behind."[77] At their jumping-off point, they unloosed a Rebel yell and charged. Stokes and part of the regiment stayed on Wickham's right, adjacent to the 3rd Virginia Cavalry, while Capt. Thomas Pinckney and the rest of the 4th South Carolina—consisting of the 2nd Squadron and the Charleston Light Dragoons—went into a branch of the ravine south of Stokes' position, where his men took heavy fire. "I experienced here for the first time

---

74 Ibid.; Henry R. Pyne, *Ride to War: The History of the First New Jersey Cavalry* (Trenton, NJ: J. A. Beecher, 1871), 210.
75 Halliburton, *Saddle Soldiers*, 140.
76 Rutledge Letter.
77 Halliburton, *Saddle Soldiers*, 140.

what is meant by a 'hail storm of bullets,' as they whistled by and in close proximity above our heads for some two hours," Pinckney recollected.[78] A 4th South Carolina trooper, assigned to horse-holding duty, distinctly heard his regiment's cheers as it went into battle. "Now the battle seemed to redouble its fury," he proclaimed.[79]

Stokes' men immediately opened fire on the 1st Pennsylvania, and the fighting soon devolved into a confused scene, with South Carolinians and Virginians intermixed and thick smoke and dense woods concealing both sides. "Most of the shots had to be snaps, fired at faces only for a second thrust from behind a tree, or peering round a bush, or at the rifle flashes, which were sending the lead zipping and singing through the air like devil's bumblebees," a member of the Charleston Light Dragoons reported. "Then came in play practice had by many a boy in the forests and fields of Carolina with his rifle at the squirrels, or with gun among the birds."[80]

Stokes' rookies performed well in their first combat against the Yankee veterans, "giving them volley after volley, which was so terrific that that the enemy wavered and gave back," another Palmetto trooper observed. "This continued for three quarters of an hour, the battle raging at its highest pitch conceivable, without intermission or cessation, but one continual roar of musketry, it seeming impossible that a man could escape."[81] Another member of the 4th South Carolina said, "Now it was that death was poured into our ranks and there the 4th stood and held her position until they had shot from eight to fifteen rounds."[82]

Edwards Wells recalled that four dismounted Yankees had snuck up quite near the position of the Charleston Light Dragoons, hidden by the dense undergrowth. One of the Dragoons touched two of his comrades on the shoulder and pointed at the bushes. "Three rifles deliberately aimed, cracked, and there was then only one live man left behind that bush." Realizing he was in trouble, the surviving Yankee decided to make a run for safety, but "those three rifles had been reloaded and cracked again, and 'subsequent proceedings interested him no more.'"[83]

Captain Henry McIver, commanding Company A of the 4th South Carolina, was shot from his horse and crashed to the ground, his right arm and leg broken. Private James Harris Stanton served in McIver's company and saw his captain tumble from the saddle. Stanton, who

78 Pinckney diary, entry for May 28, 1864.
79 "Gills Creek," "Letter to the Editor."
80 Wells, *Charleston Light Dragoons*, 42–43.
81 "Orlando," "Butler's Cavalry."
82 "Gills Creek," "Letter to the Editor."
83 Wells, *Charleston Light Dragoons*, 43.

was very fond of his commander, dismounted and dashed to rescue McIver, even though the air was thick with rounds. Dodging heavy fire, he grabbed McIver, placed him on his shoulders, and carried him to safety.[84]

The valor of the inexperienced South Carolinians impressed the Federals. "The men opposed to us at this crisis, though the most desperate fighters that we encountered among the Southern cavalry, were, nonetheless, evidently new to their business, and not handled with remarkable skill," a Northern officer observed. "As the colonel remarked to a staff officer, they showed their inexperience by continually half-rising to fire or to look at our line, thus giving our line an opportunity of which our marksmen took instant and fatal advantage. Their line was thus converted into a perfect slaughter house, preventing them from making a dash on our weaker front."[85] Because the South Carolinians had to stand up to load their Enfield rifles, they offered conspicuous targets, prompting one of Wickham's men to remark that he "never saw so many men wounded in the arm as in this fight."[86]

Hampton decided to commit Col. John Dunovant's 5th South Carolina to "the bloody contest" north of Atlee Station Road.[87] Between the dense woods and thick pall of smoke hanging over the battlefield, Dunovant's men resorted to firing at patches of blue uniforms that became visible from time to time. Lieutenant Amos O. Banks, Company F of the 5th South Carolina, described as "one of the

---

84 "Died at Post of Duty: Policeman Stanton, Gallant Veteran who Saved Life of Justice McIver at Haw's Shop Dead," *The Herald and News*, August 27, 1909. McIver, who had served as a delegate to the South Carolina Secession Convention, was taken first to Jackson Hospital in Richmond, Virginia, and then to the field hospital in Florence, South Carolina, where he recovered from his wound. He served as president of the Cheraw and Darlington Railroad, and then served on the South Carolina Supreme Court for 26 years, including 12 years as chief justice from 1891 to 1903.

85 Rodenbough, "Sheridan's Richmond Raid," 193.

86 Haw, "The Battle of Hawes's Shop," 374.

87 "Orlando," "Butler's Cavalry." John Dunovant was born in Chester, South Carolina, on March 5, 1825. He served in the Mexican-American War as a sergeant in the Palmetto Regiment in 1847. He was commissioned as captain of Company A, 10th U.S. Infantry Regiment, serving from 1855 to 1860. An ardent secessionist, "saturated with the war fever," Dunovant resigned his U.S. army commission on December 20, 1860. He was commissioned major of the 1st South Carolina Regular Infantry Regiment and became its colonel on January 19, 1861. He ran afoul of two superior officers, Roswell Ripley and Nathan G. Evans, and was transferred to the Stono River in May 1862. At the battle of Secessionville, he was accused of being drunk in combat, and was arrested, court-martialed, and convicted. He was to be dismissed from the service, but President Jefferson Davis relented, appointing him colonel of the 5th South Carolina Cavalry on July 25, 1863. He commanded his

best soldiers in Butler's Cavalry—brave and true to the last," was wounded twice during this fighting, shot in the thigh and in the hand. Banks recovered and served honorably for the rest of the war.[88]

"The storm of lead became terrible," a soldier in the 10th New York remembered. "It was at times the hottest place I ever was in. I had participated in engagements of greater magnitude, but never did I encounter in so short a space of time so much desperate fighting."[89] The dense under-growth "served as a screen but not as a shelter," as Edward Wells of the 4th South Carolina described.[90] While the intense firing raged, Colonel

Col. John Dunovant, commander, 5th South Carolina Cavalry, wounded at Haw's Shop.

(Author's collection)

Dunovant received a painful wound to his left hand.[91] While Dunovant sought treatment, Lt. Col. Robert J. Jeffords took command of the 5th South Carolina.[92]

regiment during the siege of Charleston in the summer of 1863. On March 18, 1864, the regiment was ordered to report to Virginia, but it did not leave until April 25. It arrived in time to participate as infantry in the Bermuda Hundred campaign and in the severe cavalry battle at Haw's Shop. Dunovant was wounded on May 28. He did not return to duty until July 8, 1864, missing numerous engagements during that time, including the battle of Trevilian Station. Hampton recommended him for promotion to brigadier general on July 18, which Butler and other officers supported. On August 22, he was promoted and assumed command of the South Carolina Cavalry Brigade, after Butler was promoted to divisional command. He was killed in battle on September 30, 1864, and buried in the family's cemetery in Chester, South Carolina. See Richard J. Sommers, "John Dunovant," included in William C. Davis and Julie Hoffman, eds., *The Confederate General*, 6 vols. (New York: National Historical Society, 1991), 2:86–87; see also, Adelia A. Dunovant, "Gen. John Dunovant, Houston, Tex.," *Confederate Veteran* 16 (1908): 183–84.

88 "Amos O. Banks," *Lexington Dispatch*, May 10, 1911.
89 Preston, "Hawes's Shop."
90 Wells, *History of the Charleston Light Dragoons*, 47.
91 "Orlando," "Butler's Cavalry."
92 Lewis K. Knudsen Jr., *A History of the 5th South Carolina Cavalry, 1861–1865* (Wilmington, NC: Broadfoot Publishing, 2016), 158.

To meet Dunovant's threat, Col. John W. Kester reacted by shifting Maj. Hugh Janeway's battalion north of the Atlee Station Road. The Jerseymen emptied their carbines as quickly as they could fire and reload the weapons, causing them to run low on ammunition and send for more. The accurate fire of the South Carolinians' Enfield rifles took a heavy toll on the 1st New Jersey's officers. Captain Beekman was dispensing cartridges along the front line when a bullet carried off two fingers from his right hand.[93] Lieutenants John W. Bellis and Alexander Stewart received mortal wounds.[94]

Captain Walter Robbins took friendly fire. "There had been another lull in the firing and I concluded to make a charge and get to the far side of the road in front of us," he recalled. "We had just reached the near edge in front of us, however, when I received a bullet through my right shoulder; it turned me half around. As the bullet struck me the sound was like two boards coming together." A disgruntled member of the 1st New Jersey, nursing a grudge against Robbins for accusing him of cowardice, squeezed off that shot. Another New Jersey trooper who witnessed it claimed he and the soldier who fired it "had a hearty laugh at seeing the Captain dancing from the pain of the shot." The hit staggered Robbins. "My first impulse was to go on," he wrote, "then a feeling of faintness followed, and I was carried off the field to a field hospital."[95]

A Confederate bullet grazed Major Janeway's forehead. Lieutenant Joseph Brooks, whose 1st New Jersey squadron was positioned north of the Atlee Station Road, rose to lead an attack when a ball tore through his abdomen, knocking him back almost 30 feet. Despite the awful wound to his midsection, Brooks staggered to his feet long enough to order his men to advance, then stumbled and collapsed. The unrelenting, fierce fire lasted for hours, causing heavy casualties on both sides.[96] Capt. Garrett Beekman was shot through both hands as he reached to distribute additional information to his men, who burned through bullets quickly.[97]

At the other end of the Union line, the men of the 1st Pennsylvania took a pounding from Wickham and Stokes. When they began to falter, Kester and three companies of the 1st New Jersey,

---

93 Rea, *Henry Raleigh Robbins*, 88.
94 Pyne, *Ride to War*, 210.
95 Warren C. Hursh, "Battle of Hawes's Shop," *National Tribune*, November 11, 1886; Rea, *Henry Raleigh Robbins*, 88. Robbins recovered, returned to duty, and eventually achieved the rank of colonel. He was brevetted to brigadier general of volunteers for his service throughout the war.
96 Pyne, *Ride to War*, 210–12.
97 John Y. Foster, *New Jersey and the Rebellion: A History of the Service of the Troops and People of New Jersey in Aid of the Union Cause* (Newark, NJ: M. R. Dennis, 1868), 461.

commanded by Captain Moses M. Maulsbury, arrived to reinforce them. The Pennsylvanians and Jerseymen charged, breaking a portion of Wickham's line. A witness reported the Virginians headed for the rear, "so fast as to be almost a run."[98] A South Carolinian recalled, "The battle was raging with unremitting severity when it was perceived when the left wing of the line was fast giving way and they were about being surrounded."[99]

Reacting quickly, Fitz Lee ordered Lieutenant Colonel Millen to commit his Georgia rookies to the fight south of the road, where they got mixed up with the Virginians and South Carolinians. "I had a fine opportunity of looking around and noting the effect of this first taste of battle on the men," Sgt. Charles Hansell stated, regarding the 20th Georgia. "Most of them stood it all right, but some few were so badly rattled that they had no idea where they were going or what they were doing." He observed, "[I]n one or two instances no attention was paid to the calls, commands, or curses of their officers." The green Georgians took heavy fire from the 1st Pennsylvania and 1st New Jersey, but not knowing any better, stood their ground. "Our line did not give way," Hansell proudly declared, "but halted to face the fire and took advantage of every shelter they could."[100] The stubborn Georgians inflicted heavy losses on the 1st New Jersey and mortally wounded Captain Maulsbury. His successor, Lieutenant Vorhees Dye, was killed, so command of the squadron devolved on Sgt. Thomas S. Cox, who remained in place despite suffering a serious wound to his back.[101]

General Davies and his staff rode up and down his lines, "animating the men and so disposing the forces as to strengthen the weakest portions of the line," when a Confederate ball cut his saber in half and another sliced off part of his horse's tail, but Davies somehow remained unscathed. Lieutenant W. W. Wardell of Davies' staff died instantly at the general's side, and two other staffers fell wounded in the same well-aimed volley.

Wardell's tent mate, Lt. Frederick L. Tremain of the 10th New York Cavalry, who served on Davies' staff, barely avoided the same fate. "The General was riding a white horse, and went up on the skirmish line with two staff officers, two orderlies and one bugler," Tremain told his father. "One staff officer was killed instantly, the other had his horse killed, and the bugler was also killed. The General's horse was shot through the tail, and a bullet broke his

---

98 Pyne, *Ride to War*, 211.
99 "Orlando," "Butler's Cavalry."
100 Hansell Memoir, 7.
101 Pyne, *Ride to War*, 211.

scabbard. It is my duty to be with the General always, unless sent away specially, and fortunately for me, I was so sent to another part of the field, and was looking for the General when this occurred, and in one minute more would have been in the same place, had I not met him coming out when he stopped me." Tremain's horse was slightly wounded during the intense fighting.[102]

Colonel Gregg, tall and conspicuous on his horse, also tried to encourage his men. A Confederate artillery shell struck the ground under his mount. "The musketry was very heavy," an observer reported, "and as incessant for a time as the volleys between infantry in regular line of battle."[103]

The repeated Union attacks failed to break Hampton's battle line and met with "sickening failure." The already intense fighting would soon grow even fiercer.[104]

102 Henry Lyman Tremain to his father, May 30, 1864, included in Lyman
    Tremain, *Memorial of Frederick Lyman Tremain, Late Lieut. Col. of the 10th
    N. Y. Cavalry, Who was Mortally Wounded at the Battle of Hatcher's Run,
    Va., February 6th, and Died at City Point Hospital, February 8th, 1865*
    (Albany: Van Benthuysen's Steam Printing House, 1865), 30.
103 "Mr. N. Davidson's Dispatches."
104 Preston, "Hawes's Shop."

CHAPTER SIX

The Climax of the Battle of Haw's Shop

While the slugging match at Haw's Shop dragged on, the Army of the Potomac's infantry began crossing the Pamunkey River on two pontoon bridges at Nelson's Bridge. Before long, large bodies of Union foot soldiers had massed between the river and Salem Church, not far from where the cavalrymen were fighting. Lee rightly feared that Grant might be gathering his infantry behind Sheridan's cavalry at Haw's Shop. If so, they would extend beyond Lee's flank and head straight for Richmond via Mechanicsville. Lee directed Lt. Gen. Jubal A. Early to deploy his II Corps south, across the nearby Old Church Road.[1]

Hampton soon learned that Early's troops were close by and could easily cross Totopotomoy Creek and assist him at Haw's Shop. "Whilst the fight was going on, I suggested to General Early, who was stationed at Pole Green Church, to move down in the direction of Old Church [east] and there by turning to his left to gain the rear of the force opposed to me," Hampton recorded. However, Early refused out of concern that if he crossed Totopotomoy Creek, he would be on the same side of the creek as the Federals and cut off from the rest of the Army of Northern Virginia. Early had no interest in being defeated in detail if Hampton's troopers did not hold.[2]

Meanwhile, the fighting raged at Haw's Shop, and reinforcements reached both sides. Because most of the Army of the Potomac was across the Pamunkey, Torbert's First Division no longer had to hold the defensive line at Crump's Creek. When elements of the VI Corps relieved Torbert's horsemen, Sheridan immediately ordered Torbert to head to Haw's Shop to reinforce Gregg. Torbert's division passed Dr. George Pollard's farm on its way to the Haw's Shop intersection, where it turned right on Atlee Station Road. Wesley Merritt's Reserve Brigade formed behind Gregg's right flank. Colonel Thomas C. Devin ordered the 17th Pennsylvania to go to Gregg's right as well and positioned the balance of his brigade as reserves at Haw's Shop. About 4:00 p.m., six hours after the brutal slugging match began, Custer and

---

1 Jubal A. Early, *Autobiographical Sketch and Narrative of the War Between the States* (Philadelphia: J. B. Lippincott, 1912), 361.
2 Hampton Connected Narrative, 39.

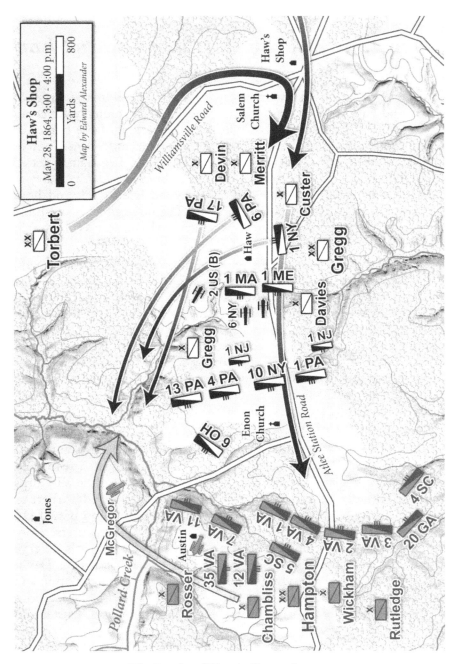

The Battle of Haw's Shop, phase 4

his Wolverines arrived at Haw's Shop. Sheridan now had two full cavalry divisions at his disposal, numbering about 9,000 sabers.[3]

Hampton also received reinforcements. About the same time, Rooney Lee arrived, with Brig. Gen. John R. Chambliss' veteran brigade of Virginians in tow. Hampton ordered Rooney Lee to dismount the Virginians, march them to the Confederate far left (northern) flank, deploy skirmishers, and "turn the right flank of the enemy if he could do so." Accompanied by Capt. McGregor's battery of horse artillery, Chambliss' men formed on Rosser's left, north of the tributary of Crump's Creek, facing east.[4] Chambliss' troopers "halted in the road as though we might be needed in a mounted charge," Lt. George Beale of the 9th Virginia Cavalry recounted.[5] Lee was heard crying out to his men: "We must hold on here! I cannot give up any more ground!"[6] A disgusted Maj. James D. Ferguson of Fitz Lee's staff observed that while Rooney Lee's command had been ordered to join the fight, it did so "very feebly."[7]

While awaiting orders, Lieutenant Beale rode to where the body of Maj. William G. Thomson of the 20th Georgia lay. Thomson's head rested at the roots of a tree, and Beale could see from the corps' upturned face that a bullet had penetrated his forehead just above his eyes. "He was rather small in stature, but his face was intellectual and his brow noble," Beale detailed, "and it seemed a pity indeed that the death-dealing missile had found so splendid a mark."[8]

In deploying, Chambliss' troopers met Merritt's Reserve Brigade as it moved onto the Union right. Dismounted horsemen of the 6th Pennsylvania Cavalry drove in Chambliss' skirmishers, but McGregor's guns checked the Pennsylvanians' advance, giving Chambliss' men time to throw up crude breastworks.[9] Merritt deployed Williston's Battery B, 2nd U.S. Artillery, and a severe counterbattery duel broke out immediately.[10] Rooney Lee mistook the dismounted Pennsylvanians for infantry and reported to Hampton that a heavy force of foot soldiers had attacked him. He requested

3 James C. Mohr, ed., *The Cormany Diaries: A Northern Family in the Civil War* (Pittsburgh, PA: University of Pittsburgh Press, 1982), 429; Theophilus F. Rodenbough, ed., *From Everglade to Cañon with the Second Dragoons* (New York: D. van Nostrand, 1875), 309 and OR 36, 1:837.
4 Hampton Connected Narrative, 38.
5 Beale, *A Lieutenant of Cavalry in Lee's Army*, 158.
6 David W. Lowe, ed., *Meade's Army: The Private Notebooks of Lt. Col. Theodore Lyman* (Kent, OH: Kent State University Press, 2007), 180.
7 Ferguson Memorandum, entry for May 28, 1864.
8 Beale, *A Lieutenant of Cavalry in Lee's Army*, 158.
9 Samuel L. Gracey, *Annals of the Sixth Pennsylvania Cavalry* (Philadelphia: E. H. Butler & Co., 1868), 251; OR 36, 1:848.
10 Beale, *A Lieutenant of Cavalry in Lee's Army*, 158.

*Lt. Robert C. Wallace, 5th
Michigan Cavalry.*

(USAHEC)

permission to withdraw, advising that he was in no shape to fight infantry and that the Federals might turn his flank.[11]

While Chambliss conferred with Hampton, Custer and his Wolverines drew artillery fire as they turned west on Atlee Station Road. "Owing to the thick woods and dense underbrush [in front of the enemy's position] it was impossible to maneuver the command mounted," Custer reported. "The entire brigade was therefore dismounted and formed in line."[12] The Wolverines halted and dismounted behind Gregg's troopers, forming two lines of battle across the road. Sheridan then appeared, pointed out Gregg's predicament, and instructed Custer to "fight it for all it was worth."[13]

Lieutenant Colonel Peter Stagg's 1st Michigan and Maj. James H. Kidd's 6th Michigan deployed north of the road, while Capt. William T. Magoffin, temporarily commanding the 5th Michigan, and Maj. Alexander Walker's 7th Michigan deployed south of the road. Custer's men stood so close to the enemy that "we could hear the commands of the rebel officers, and presume they could also hear ours," Lt. Robert C. Wallace of the 5th Michigan recalled.[14] With the Wolverines preparing to attack, Custer rode ahead of the line, doffed his hat, and called for three cheers. As the brigade's band played "Yankee Doodle," Kidd remembered, "[t]he cheers were given and we went in."[15]

As the Wolverines were deploying, Col. John W. Kester and his Jerseymen swung back to the right of their line to open a gap for the Michigan men to pass through. Thinking the New Jersey men were retreating, a detachment of Lt. Col. John M. Millen's rookies cried the Rebel yell and attacked east along the road, taking cover behind fences

11 Hampton Connected Narrative, 38.
12 *OR* 36, 1:821.
13 Barnard, *An Aide to Custer,* 239.
14 Robert C. Wallace, *A Few Memories of a Long Life* (Fairfield, WA: Ye Galleon Press, 1988), 57.
15 Wittenberg, *One of Custer's Wolverines,* 88.

while firing into Kester's flank.[16] The Georgians' fire also dropped troopers of the 5th and 7th Michigan, and Custer's attack bogged down in a stand of pine trees. "A perfect hell of fire and smoke broke from the rebel works," the 5th Michigan's Sgt. James Henry Avery remembered. "Even the air we breathed seemed thick with lead and sulphur [sic]. It did not seem possible for balls to fly thicker. The boughs were dropping constantly from the pines." He continued, "The leaden messengers splished and spat and chuckled as they passed or struck the mark, burying themselves in a human target, when fell all sides, some to rise no more some to get up and stagger off to the rear, while others started for the rear with arms dangling helplessly, and then were overtaken and brought down again, perhaps forever." Avery concluded, "I never saw men fall so fast, and still the storm increased, and the surging lines wavered."[17]

"The woods through which we drove them were so full of fallen trees [and] under brush as to make it very hard work to get through them, even without any opposing enemy," one of Custer's staffers observed. "But our Spencer Rifles are terrible weapons," and indeed they were.[18]

Captain David Oliphant of the 5th Michigan was mortally wounded during the fighting. Oliphant was popular with the men; 5th Michigan Cavalry commander, Col. Russell A. Alger, remembered him as "[a]lways ready to do his duty, fearless of self in danger, generous and kind to all, he had won the highest esteem from all who knew him."[19] Oliphant and Lt. Robert C. Wallace sat on a log smoking until it came time for the captain's operation. Wallace held chloroform to Oliphant's face, rendering him unconscious, Wallace patted him on the head, bidding his friend a last goodbye. Oliphant died on the way to Fredericksburg. "He was one of the best officers in the regiment and his loss was sorely felt," Wallace lamented. "It was rather discouraging to see one's friends and companions shot down one by one and yet no end of the war in sight. That's what jars a fellow's nerves."[20]

The 5th Michigan suffered 50 casualties in just a few minutes to the Georgians' intense fire, including Sgt. John A. Huff of Company E, whom Alger credited with firing the shot that mortally wounded Jeb Stuart at Yellow Tavern.[21] While the heavy fire inflicted significant

---

16 Pyne, *Ride to War*, 212–13.
17 Karla Jean Husby, comp. and Eric J. Wittenberg, ed., *Under Custer's Command: The Civil War Journal of James Henry Avery* (Washington, D.C.: Brassey's, 2000), 79.
18 Barnard, *An Aide to Custer*, 240.
19 *OR* 36, 1:831.
20 Wallace, *A Few Memories of a Long Life*, 57.
21 *OR* 36, 1:829. Historian Robert E. L. Krick wrote an extremely persuasive essay demonstrating that Huff could not have been the one to fire the fatal

Maj. Charles Safford,
5th Michigan Cavalry.

(Author's collection)

losses on the Michigan men, Custer's legendary good luck held. Even though Custer's horse was shot out from under him, the Boy General survived the ordeal unscathed, the seventh time in the war. Custer's close friend and aide, Lt. James I. Christiancy, fell severely wounded, losing the end of his thumb to a ball and taking a severe flesh wound to his thigh from another. A spent ball struck the head of Custer's acting assistant adjutant general, Capt. James L. Green.[22] "At one time it seemed as if the whole staff must be killed or wounded," Maj. Charles H. Safford, 5th Michigan Cavalry, bleakly observed.[23]

The cheering Wolverines dashed to within about 10 yards of the 4th South Carolina, Millen's Georgians, and some of Wickham's men, who unleashed a deadly volley. "We had only one thin line and they just swarmed right upon and through the line," Lt. Robert Hubard, 3rd Virginia, recounted. "Captain Collins and I discharged every barrel of our pistols at a batch of Yankees who got upon the line ten paces to our right and then withdrew." The Federals overwhelmed two squadrons of the 3rd Virginia, but the rebels soon received reinforcements. "Old Wickham rode around waving his saber and

shot at Stuart, and the actual identity of the Wolverine who did fire the shot will probably remain unknown. Robert E. L. Krick, "Stuart's Last Ride: A Confederate View of Sheridan's Raid," in Gary W. Gallagher, ed., *The Spotsylvania Campaign* (Chapel Hill: University of North Carolina Press, 1998), 127–69.

22 Kidd, *Personal Recollections*, 325; "General Custer," *Daily Morning Chronicle*, June 7, 1864; "The Battle of Hawes's Shop" and Barnard, *An Aide to Custer*, 239. Custer's aide, Lt. Edward Granger, reported that Christiancy "is now in Washington staying with Mrs. Custer [and] enjoying himself immensely." Ibid.

23 Davis, *I Rode with Custer*, 105.

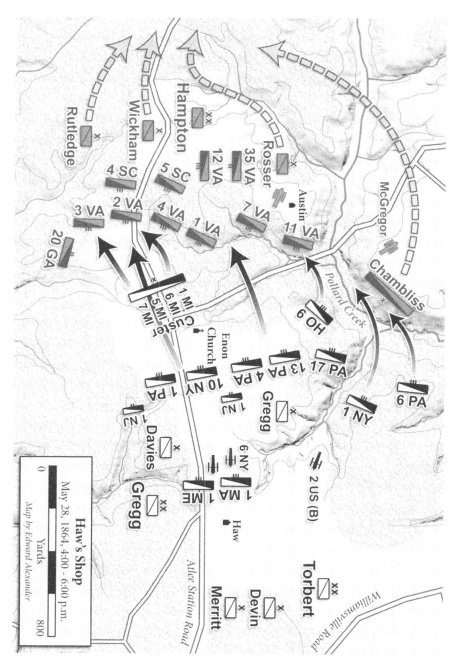

The Battle of Haw's Shop, climax

cursing 'like a trooper,'" remembered Hubard, who tried to rally men to support Millen and his Georgians.[24]

"They fought desperately but then had to give way," Kidd stated. "Many of them refused to surrender and were shot down." Kidd noted that the 4th South Carolina and 6th Michigan each had about 150 men in the fight, losing 50 and 34 men, respectively. "The ground was covered with rebel dead and wounded," he said. "One regiment alone lost 160 men. We captured a large number of prisoners."[25] Kidd also recalled, "[T]he sound of their bullets sweeping the undergrowth was like that of hot flames crackling through dry timber." Sergeant James Brown fell dead at Kidd's side, while Cpl. Seth Carey "met his fate like a soldier, his face to the foe." Another mortally wounded 6th Michigan trooper staggered toward Kidd, exclaiming, "Oh, Major!" before falling into Kidd's arms, staining the officer's uniform tunic with his blood.[26]

By now, the Wolverines were receiving heavy fire from Lt. Col. William Stokes and Wickham in their front and from Millen's Georgians in their flank, blunting their attack. Some of the Jersey men stuck between the Michiganders, and the Georgians got caught in the crossfire, causing some of the Michigan men to mistake Kester for a Confederate officer. They opened fire on him, wounding his horse and riddling his coat with bullets, but the colonel somehow managed to avoid being hit, although his coat was "so torn that his escape appeared miraculous." The 1st New Jersey's historian later claimed that all of Millen's men along the road were killed, wounded, or captured.[27]

The courage of the South Carolinians impressed the Wolverines. "Some of [them] exhibited a fool-hardy courage never seen anywhere else so far as my knowledge extends," Kidd grudgingly marveled. Kidd witnessed Sergeant Avery demand the surrender of a Palmetto man. "I have no orders to surrender, _____ you!" the South Carolinian shouted. "He surrendered, not his person, but his life," Kidd remarked. "Such a fate befell more than one of those intrepid heroes."[28]

Major Kidd found himself under fire. "Several bullets whistled so close as to convince me that they were designed for my especial benefit," he wrote in a letter home. "I sent back an officer and some men who found that a party of rebels had been left behind in the eagerness of the pursuit and these men paying their compliments to us in regular Free Pass style. They were captured." He noticed "the . . .

24 Nanzig, *The Civil War Memoirs of a Virginia Cavalryman*, 167.
25 Wittenberg, *One of Custer's Wolverines*, 88.
26 Kidd, *Personal Recollections*, 326.
27 Pyne, *Ride to War*, 212–13.
28 Kidd, *Personal Recollections*, 327.

small saplings where we fought were riddled," evidencing the Confederates' severe fire.[29]

Rooney Lee persuaded Hampton that Union infantry had arrived on the northern end of the battlefield, so Hampton authorized Chambliss to withdraw. "This we were glad to do," a relieved Lt. George Beale of the 9th Virginia Cavalry admitted, "and having gained our saddles, we withdrew without being pressured."[30] As Chambliss' Virginians began withdrawing, troopers of the 6th Pennsylvania Cavalry and 1st New York Dragoons of the Reserve Brigade advanced and took their place; a strong Union force now had a solid foothold on Rosser's left flank. When the Pennsylvanians and New Yorkers opened an enfilading fire, they forced Rosser to withdraw, which in turn exposed Wickham's left flank, compelling his Virginians to retire as well. Most of Wickham's troopers retired in good order, as did Colonel John Dunovant's 5th South Carolina and the left wing of the 4th South Carolina, under Stokes' direct command.[31]

Colonel Rutledge and his adjutant, Lt. Gabriel Manigault, had remained with the held horses for most of the fight. Wanting to participate, Rutledge sought out Hampton to ask permission to rejoin their regiment since Rutledge's role as ad hoc brigade commander "had become a sinecure." They spotted a red flag flying over a house, assumed it marked Hampton's headquarters, and sent an orderly to find the regiment's position. However, Hampton told Rutledge "the combat was over, its purposes accomplished, its troops ordered to retire." Hampton then ordered the brigade's horses brought forward so the troops could mount quickly and "prevent any confusion in that corner."[32]

Wickham sent couriers to warn the rest of the 4th South Carolina, Millen's Georgians, and elements of the 2nd Virginia of Wickham's brigade to withdraw, but none of the couriers arrived, so the troopers remained in place by themselves. Sergeant Thomas J. Brown served in Company E of the 2nd Virginia Cavalry. "Our position [fighting on foot] in the edge of a dense body of pines, an open field behind, so that the enemy could see our every movement, while we could not see them until they approached within a very few yards of us," Brown recalled. "Had to cut our way out," Pvt. John J. Woodall, 2nd Virginia Cavalry, stated.[33]

29 Wittenberg, *One of Custer's Wolverines*, 88.
30 Beale, *A Lieutenant of Cavalry in Lee's Army*, 158.
31 "Orlando," "Butler's Cavalry"; Wells, *Charleston Light Dragoons*, 44–45.
32 Rutledge Letter.
33 Woodall diary, entry for May 28, 1864.

When his company's ammunition became depleted, Capt. Edgar Whitehead of the 2nd Virginia, the company commander, sent a man back to request more ammunition. The man was shocked to find Federal troopers marching on both sides of the Virginians' position and advised Whitehead of the dire situation. Whitehead consulted with the 4th South Carolina company commander next to his own company and announced that his men were going to fight their way out. "As soon as we came out in the field the Federals on both sides of us saw us and opened fire," Brown wrote, "and while we ran the gauntlet across that field, they wounded a good many of our men, but, as I now recall, killed only one, Pitt Higginbotham. We learned afterwards, that the Federals in firing at us, fired into each other and killed and wounded more of each other than of us."[34]

A captain of the 2nd Virginia made his way to Capt. Thomas Pinckney, commanding the 4th South Carolina detachment, to reassure the South Carolinian that Wickham and the rest of the brigade remained in place, removing an "danger of our being flanked." Thus, while the northern end of the Confederate battle line withdrew, the unsuspecting men south of the Atlee Station Road remained in place, alone and nearly surrounded.[35]

Custer realized that reduced firing from the north meant Hampton was withdrawing, so he immediately ordered the 1st and 6th Michigan to attack. The Wolverines charged, overrunning the last remaining enemy troopers in their front and positioning themselves north of Millen and Pinckney. "Balls came singing by, not only from the front but from the left flank," Sgt. Charles Hansell of the 20th Georgia recollected.[36] "We were outflanked and exposed to a terrific crossfire," a South Carolinian shuddered. He continued, "I was not hurt, though in perfect hailstorm of balls—three balls struck one small tree as I stood by it."[37] Seeing an opportunity to finish off any remaining resistance, Custer ordered the rest of his brigade to charge, and the cheering dismounted troopers of the 5th and 7th Michigan smashed into the remaining isolated pockets of Confederates.

Lieutenant Edward W. Nowell of the Charleston Light Dragoons understood the precarious position in which his men found themselves when a panicked Confederate officer told him that Union cavalry was pouring past the Dragoons' left flank.[38] About the same time, Fitz Lee

---

34 Robert J. Driver Jr. and H. E. Howard, *2nd Virginia Cavalry* (Lynchburg, VA: H. E. Howard Co., 1995), 122–23.

35 Ulysses R. Brooks, *Butler and His Cavalry* (Columbia, SC: The State Co., 1909), 209.

36 Hansell Memoir.

37 Allen Edens to his family, in Walbrook D. Swank, ed., *Confederate Letters and Diaries, 1861–1865* (Mineral, VA: self-published, 1988), 146.

38 Wells, *History of the Charleston Light Dragoons*, 44.

recognized what had happened and sent Sgt. John Gill, a courier detached from the 1st Maryland Cavalry, to tell Millen and Pinckney to leave. Concerned for Gill's wellbeing, several staff officers called out farewells as he dashed off to deliver the message. Gill dodged the fusillade of bullets while riding to the Dragoons. "Right about face," he cried. "Double quick, march!" Fitz Lee later complimented Gill for the prompt manner in which he acted, and he "was also congratulated on all sides on having come out myself unscathed."[39]

As Stokes led his battered 4th South Carolina battalion off the field, Hampton rode up and told him he had done all the general had expected him to do, advising him to quickly get the men to their horses and

Lt. Col. John B. Millen, commander, 20th Battalion Georgia Cavalry, killed in action at Haw's Shop.

(Jennifer Carney)

fall back behind the second line of defense. After the battle, Rutledge generously told Hampton and Butler that Stokes deserved credit for the 4th South Carolina rookies' stout fight.[40]

Belatedly, Hampton realized he should not have given Rooney Lee permission to withdraw Chambliss. "We had a strong position and could have held it until now," he told Rosser after the war, "but Rooney Lee reported that the infantry was coming up on his flank and he could not hold his position longer, and the whole line was, therefore, ordered to withdraw."[41] Faced with that reality, Hampton rode into the dense woods to help lead his men to safety. Following his lead, they fell back into a field and rallied behind a rail fence. "The presence of Hampton, calm, cool, and reassuring, had braced everyone up," a Confederate horse soldier recalled.[42] Hampton used his words

39 John Gill, *Reminiscences of Four Years as a Private Soldier in the Confederate Army, 1861–1865* (Baltimore: Sun Printing Office, 1904), 99–100.
40 Halliburton, *Saddle Soldiers*, 140–41.
41 Haw, "The Battle of Haw's Shop," 375.
42 Wells, *Hampton and His Cavalry in '64*, 160.

sparingly: "I rode in and brought them out, but not without a heavy loss."[43]

Some of Millen's Georgia rookies unwittingly stood their ground and were captured. Others withdrew slowly, hiding behind one tree and then the next, hoping to escape detection. "We all gave back," Sergeant Hansell stated, "were rallied to the old line, but could not hold it." Millen directed a detachment of mounted soldiers into the fight to reinforce his position, but a Wolverine's accurate gunfire instantly killed the colonel. "There was a scarcity of officers at this point," Hansell continued; he could recall seeing only a single Virginia colonel passing along the line during this critical period.[44]

Custer's triumphant, cheering Wolverines pressed their advantage, firing into the retreating Confederates. As they watched the Confederates flee, Gregg's troopers joined the pursuit. Captain Charles F. Wolcott of the 6th Ohio Cavalry spotted a felt hat lying on the ground and picked it up. He noticed the left rim of the hat was looped up against the hat's crown and fastened with a metal South Carolina button featuring a palmetto tree, a coiled serpent, and Latin words. A bullet had punched a hole in the crown, and strands of dark hair filled the exit hole. The hat fit, so Wolcott wiped the former owner's hair from the bullet hole, removed the Palmetto tree button, and pursued the fleeing Confederates with his new chapeau perched squarely atop his head.[45]

What began as an orderly retreat quickly turned into a complete rout. "On their hands and knees, afraid to stand upright, [Confederates] scrambled with wonderful rapidity through the grass and underbrush," the 1st New Jersey Cavalry's chaplain noted.[46] "Had to cut our way out," a soldier of the 2nd Virginia Cavalry admitted.[47] "We [h]ad just the [h]eardest [sic] time I ever had," Lt. George Engle,

---

43 Hampton Connected Narrative, 39.
44 Hansell Memoir. Lieutenant Colonel Millen's remains were taken to Richmond, and he was buried in the Confederate officers' section of Hollywood Cemetery. Although his command preferred to be called Millen's Battalion in his memory, that did not last long. The 20th Battalion of Georgia Cavalry ceased to exist as an independent command when it was ordered to disband in July 1864. Three of its companies joined the 8th Georgia Cavalry, three more joined the 10th Georgia Cavalry, and one company joined the Jeff Davis Legion Cavalry of Mississippi. See the Compiled Service Records of the 20th Battalion of Georgia Cavalry, M266, Carded Records Showing Military Service of Soldiers Who Fought in Confederate Organizations, Compiled March 19, 1927, Documenting the Period 1861–1865, National Archives and Records Administration, Washington, D.C.
45 Charles F. Wolcott, "Army Stories," in *Report of the Proceedings of the Sixth Ohio Cavalry* (Privately published, 1911), 40–41.
46 Pyne, *Ride to War*, 213.
47 Woodall diary, entry for May 28, 1864.

Company D, 12th Virginia Cavalry, told his wife, "for we [h]ad to [r]un about 2 miles under the fire of small [b]alls [and] canister."[48] Sergeant Hansell watched trooper Lee Bacon, who served in Hansell's platoon of the 20th Georgia, staggering through the thick woods, bleeding heavily from a severe chest wound. Bacon's brother tried to rescue the wounded trooper, pleading with Hansell to "make a stand" to gain sufficient time for them to escape, an idea that struck the sergeant as strange. "The idea of one man making a stand when the whole Battalion had been unable to do so struck me as so ridiculous that I could hardly keep from laughing," a flabbergasted Hansell remembered years later.[49]

While trying to lead some of his South Carolinians to safety, Captain Pinckney found himself at the mercy of two officers and a private from the 7th Michigan Cavalry. Pinckney surrendered to Lt. James H. Ingersoll, who demanded Pinckney's sword, a family heirloom that had belonged to Pinckney's grandfather, Charles C. Pinckney, a signer of the Declaration of Independence and Revolutionary War hero. When Pinckney refused to surrender the sword, Ingersoll drew the sword from its scabbard and closely examined it. Ingersoll told Pinckney that he preferred a straight blade compared to the curved one he carried, and handed his own sword to the South Carolinian. Ingersoll declared that he would keep the heirloom and return it after the war, prompting Pinckney to quip that he hoped to meet Ingersoll before then and win his blade back. "It must have afforded an interesting sight to lookers on," Pinckney reflected, "to observe us during this parley, brandishing each other's sabers."[50]

Captain Andrew P. Love's small battalion of Alabama cavalry arrived too late to help Hampton. Love's green troopers arrived just as Hampton's line collapsed, so they never got a chance to fire a shot. Their horses had not been trained for cavalry duty, so the dismounted fighting at Haw's Shop would have better suited their abilities and training, but they never got the opportunity to show what they could do, other than to dismount and form a skirmish line to help cover the

---

48 Dennis E. Frye, *12th Virginia Cavalry* (Lynchburg, VA: H. E. Howard Co., 1988), 66.
49 Hansell Memoir.
50 Pinckney diary, entry for May 29, 1864. Pinckney later alleged that he wrote to Ingersoll after the war to request the return of the sword, but Ingersoll did not reply. Undaunted, Pinckney communicated through the offices of a good friend in the United States Senate. Ingersoll refused to return the sword, claiming that it was his by right of capture, but he indicated that he might be willing to sell it back. Pinckney refused the offer, as he did not want Ingersoll to "have the satisfaction of getting money from me for it."

withdrawal of the rest of Hampton's troopers. Even so, one rookie noted, "The balls flew thick and fast at least I thought so."[51]

While Hampton's line collapsed, Gen. Lee urgently told Maj. Gen. John C. Breckinridge, former vice president of the United States who now commanded an infantry division, "I wish you would place your troops on the road from [Atlee's Station] to Haw's Shop [or Salem Church] to guard that road. The enemy is at Haw's Shop, and may take our troops in reverse."[52] Responding quickly, Breckinridge set his column in motion on Atlee Station Road and deployed across it at Totopotomoy Creek, where his men dug in. "There were few, if any spades or shovels," one of the Kentuckian's men recalled, "but the men split their canteens, making scoops of them, and, together with the bayonets and their hands, for the soil was light and sandy, soon had a very respectful earthwork thrown up." Although Hampton's line had been broken, Breckinridge's infantry provided him solid support if the victorious Federals tried to pursue his beaten troopers.[53]

By 6:00 p.m., it was all over. Hampton's defeated troopers withdrew across Totopotomoy Creek and passed through Breckinridge's line. Brigadier General Lunsford Lomax's brigade joined the rest of Hampton's command at its campsite, bringing fresh troops to bear should they be needed.[54] "General Breckinridge's forces . . . won't go very far before they will bump up against some lively game in the shape of Yankee infantry," Sgt. George M. Neese, of Maj. Roger P. Chew's battery, observed.[55] Breckinridge's strong position accomplished the intended goal: it deterred Sheridan's troopers from further pursuit, although periodic firing lit up the dark night—a sight that reminded a lieutenant of Chambliss' 9th Virginian Cavalry of fireflies.[56]

That night, Brig. Gen. Matthew C. Butler arrived and assumed command of his South Carolina cavalry brigade, thus Rutledge's short

---

51 Krick, "Repairing an Army," 51; William H. Locke to his wife, May 29, 1864, William H. Locke Letters, Special Collections, Alderman Library, University of Virginia, Charlottesville, Virginia. As historian Robert E. L. Krick correctly notes in his essay, "Repairing an Army: A Look at the New Troops in the Army of Northern Virginia in May and June 1864," no other account of the battle of Haw's Shop has ever mentioned Love's battalion, let alone placing it on the battlefield, before his important and well-documented 2015 essay.
52 *OR* 36, 3:844.
53 T. C. Morton, "Incidents of the Skirmish at Totopotomoy Creek, Hanover County, Virginia, May 30, 1864," Southern Historical Society Papers 16 (1908), 47.
54 Ferguson Memorandum, entry for May 28, 1864.
55 Neese, *Three Years in the Confederate Horse Artillery*, 278.
56 Beale, *A Lieutenant of Cavalry*, 158.

and inconsequential tenure in command.[57] Butler met with colonels Rutledge and Dunovant and the newly arrived Col. Hugh Aiken, 6th South Carolina Cavalry, to understanding the situation.[58] Furthermore, 75 troopers of the 5th South Carolina Cavalry who had gone to Richmond to have their horses shod rejoined the regiment.[59]

Lieutenant Lewis McMakin served as the 13th Pennsylvania Cavalry's adjutant. He had the opportunity to visit with one of the South Carolinians who had been captured during the attack of the Michigan Cavalry Brigade. He asked the Palmetto man whether the firing had been hot where he was, and the man replied, "Yes." Responding, McMakin observed, "You fellows were too stubborn, you held on too long." The prisoner grimly concluded, "They told us if we-uns would stick, you-uns would get up and git."[60]

Union artillerist Frank Wilkeson visited the battlefield as dusk fell. The number of dead cavalrymen strewn abundantly about struck him. "The poverty of the south was plainly shown by the clothing and equipment of the dead," he noted. "There were ancient and ferocious-looking horse pistols, such as used to grace the Bowery stage, lying by the dead Confederates." After dark, Wilkeson searched for water in the woods and found more corpses. "I struck a match so as to see one of these men plainly, and was greatly shocked to see large black beetles eating the corpse," he shuddered. "I looked at no more dead men that night."[61]

"In passing over the ground of the fight of the 28th, we found it covered as with a carpet with the leaves and twigs which had been cut

57 Wells, *Hampton and His Cavalry in '64*, 170–71.
58 Richard Kevin Dietrich, *To Virginia and Back with Rutledge's Cavalry: A History of the 4th South Carolina Cavalry Regiment* (Wilmington, NC: Broadfoot Publishing, 2015), 74. Hugh Kerr Aiken was born in Winnsboro, South Carolina, on July 5, 1822. He attended South Carolina College and became a planter in Winnsboro after graduating. In 1856, he moved to Charleston, where he married the daughter of a former governor of Alabama. He served in the militia, achieving the rank of major general in the state service. He was commissioned lieutenant colonel of the 16th South Carolina Cavalry Battalion on July 21, 1862. The 16th battalion provided the nucleus for the 6th South Carolina Cavalry, which was also sometimes called Aiken's Partisan Rangers. Aiken was commissioned colonel of the 6th South Carolina on November 1, 1862. He was severely wounded at Trevilian Station on June 11, 1864 and returned to duty that fall. He commanded Butler's brigade through part of the 1865 Carolinas campaign, until he was killed in action on February 27, 1865, in a skirmish near Darlington, South Carolina. He was buried at Sion Presbyterian Church in Winnsboro. Allardice, *Confederate Colonels*, 39.
59 Knudsen, *Fifth South Carolina Cavalry*, 160.
60 Lewis McMakin, "Custer in Action," *National Tribune*, September 8, 1910.
61 Frank Wilkeson, *Recollections of a Private Soldier in the Army of the Potomac* (New York: G. P. Putnam's Sons, 1887), 125–26.

off by the musketry during the engagement," Capt. Charles McK. Loeser, 2nd U.S. Cavalry, remembered after the war.[62] Lieutenant Edward Granger, of Custer's staff, simply said, "I never saw dead [and] wounded men so thick as they were laying in those woods."[63] Lieutenant Frederick Tremain of Davies' staff sounded a similar note. "We found on the field, after we had driven them from it, 166 dead rebels and 40 wounded men," he told his father, "and as there are usually eight or ten wounded to one killed, their loss must have been immense."[64] Captain Hampton S. Thomas, 1st Pennsylvania Cavalry, who served on Gregg's division staff, observed, "In this engagement, I think we piled up more dead rebels than in any other of our fights. A few days afterwards General Grant made his headquarters on our battle-ground, but was forced to move them on account of the stench arising from the dead bodies which were still unburied."[65]

Sergeant Henry Avery of the 5th Michigan assisted in collecting the wounded after the fighting ended. "The ground was covered with guns, revolvers, and other arms; the dead lay thickly around, and in the rear, close to the field, the wounded were gathered together, and the surgeons and their assistants, were busy over them, here probing a gunshot wound in the leg, and if necessary, off it comes, there dropping off an arm," Avery described with a shudder, "yonder, under a tree is a man whose deep drawn breath, accompanied by a suppressed groan as the surgeon examines a puncture in the breast, tells you of death soon to follow; others with slight wounds are awaiting to be treated."[66]

Private John Brown served in Company K, 6th Ohio Cavalry, alongside his son Daniel. After the battle, John was helping to remove wounded men. As he laid a desperately injured man on the ground, he realized that it was his son. Brown "sat upon the ground holding the head of his dear boy for two hours until he breathed his last," another Buckeye recalled. Dan "did not know his father; he was unconscious; he was shot through the head." One can only imagine a father's pain watching his son die in his arms.[67]

---

62 Charles McK. Loeser, "Personal Recollections—A Ride to Richmond in
    1864," in Rodenbough, *From Everglade to Cañon*, 309.
63 Barnard, *An Aide to Custer*, 240.
64 Tremain to his father, May 30, 1864, in Tremain, *Memorial of Frederick
    Lyman Tremain*, 31.
65 Hampton S. Thomas, *Some Personal Reminiscences of Service in the
    Cavalry of the Army of the Potomac* (Philadelphia: R. Hamersly & Co.,
    1889), 18.
66 Husby and Wittenberg, *Under Custer's Command*, 79–81.
67 *Report of the Thirty-Third Annual Reunion, Sixth Ohio Veteran Volunteer
    Cavalry Association, Held at Warren, Ohio, October 4th, 1898* (Garrettville,
    OH: The Journal Printing Co., 1898), 7.
68 *OR* 36, 1:793.

Past dark, and after the dead of both sides were buried, foot soldiers of the V Corps relieved Gregg's weary troopers, who fell back to Hanovertown Ferry and bivouacked at midnight.[68] "Had a rather quiet night," noted a soldier of the 16th Pennsylvania Cavalry.[69] "In the evening, after having established a secure line of pickets, the main body of the corps retired and went into camp," an officer of the 4th Pennsylvania Cavalry recalled. "About this time the forage gave out, and the horses of the whole corps had to subsist on the poorest kind of grazing."[70]

Pvt. John Brown of the 6th Ohio Cavalry. His son was mortally wounded in combat at Haw's Shop and died in John Brown's arms.

(Ken Lawrence)

"I fired over 50 rounds at the [Rebels] yesterday," Cpl. Kimball Pearsons, 10th New York, wrote to his family the next day. "Twas [sic] as hard a days work as I have ever done. I was completely tired out long before night but stayed on the skirmish line till after dark when we were withdrawn and moved back a few miles leaving our Infantry in front of us." Pearsons had a close call in the woods surrounding Haw's Shop that warm day. "I am all right only being hit with a spent ball on my hat which did no damage."[71]

By contrast, the troopers of the Michigan Cavalry Brigade marched back to the Pamunkey River crossings, bivouacking near where Totopotomoy Creek empties into the river, supposedly to negate the presence of Rooney Lee's division. They did not arrive at their bivouac until 2:30 a.m.[72]

69 Mohr, *The Cormany Diaries*, 429–30.
70 William Hyndman, *History of a Cavalry Company: A Complete Record of Company "A", 4th Pennsylvania Cavalry* (Philadelphia: J. B. Rodgers Co., 1870), 199.
71 David B. Russell, ed., *Tough & Hearty: Kimball Pearsons, Civil War Cavalryman, Co. L, 10th Regiment of Cavalry, New York State Volunteers* (Bowie, MD: Heritage Books, 2012), 239–40.
72 Barnard, *An Aide to Custer*, 241; Asa B. Isham, *An Historical Sketch of the Seventh Regiment Michigan Volunteer Cavalry from Its Organization, in*

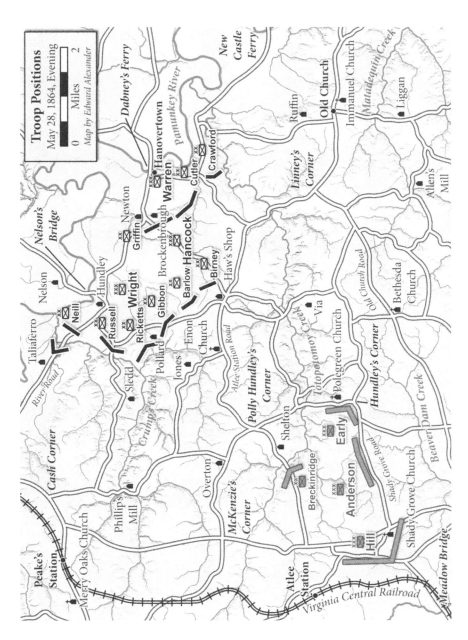

Troop positions, evening of May 28, 1864

For seven long hours, Federal and Confederate dismounted troopers slugged it out at Haw's Shop in one of the most severe cavalry engagements yet, prompting a newspaper correspondent to claim: "This was unquestionably the sharpest cavalry fight of the war—the hottest fire of musketry and shell."[73] The severity of the fight had few equals during the course of the war, perhaps matched only by the two-day bloodletting at Trevilian Station that began a mere 14 days later. "Not much advantage gained on either side," Jasper Hawes of the 11th Virginia Cavalry reported.[74] "The trouble was, the confounded rebels would not vacate the place when we Yanks wanted it," a trooper of the 6th Ohio Cavalry complained, "and they persisted in staying there when they ought in all fairness and vacate and let us Yanks alone."[75] Sheridan correctly labeled it as "a hard contested engagement, with heavy loss, for the number of troops engaged, to both sides."[76]

Researcher Alfred C. Young III has done groundbreaking work on Confederate losses in the Overland campaign of 1864, and his analysis indicates that Rosser lost 33 men at Haw's Shop, and Chambliss lost 25, while Wickham reported 12 killed, 64 wounded, and 10 missing, totaling 86 losses in his brigade. The green units under Rutledge's command greatly suffered for their courage under fire. The 4th South Carolina lost 127 out of 300 men engaged, including, as Lieutenant Colonel Stokes lamented, "some of our most valuable and gallant officers and men." In particular, the Charleston Light Dragoons—Company K of the 4th South Carolina—took terrible losses; out of 47 men engaged, the Dragoons suffered 10 killed or mortally wounded, 8 more wounded, and one man captured, for losses of 40 percent of their manpower engaged.[77] The 5th South Carolina suffered 31 casualties. The 20th Georgia lost Lieutenant Colonel Millen and Maj. William G. Thomson, both killed, as well as a captain, two lieutenants, and about 80 enlisted men.[78] "Most of our loss is attributable to the fact that nearly all the force engaged on our part were new men," a Richmond reporter inaccurately claimed, "whose only idea was to go in and fight, which they [did] most gallantly and credibly."[79]

1862, to Its Muster Out, in 1865 (New York: Town Topics Publishing Co., 1893), 53; OR 36, 1:804–5.

73 "Mr. N. Davidson's Dispatches."
74 Jasper Hawes diary, entry for May 28, 1864, Archives, Virginia Historical Society, Richmond, Virginia.
75 Charles F. Wolcott, "The Cavalry Arm," *National Tribune,* September 8, 1910.
76 *OR* 36, 1:793.
77 Wells, *History of the Charleston Light Dragoons,* 46.
78 Alfred C. Young III, *Lee's Army During the Overland Campaign: A Numerical Study* (Baton Rouge: Louisiana State University Press, 2013), 315, 316, 318, 320, and 322; Halliburton, *Saddle Soldiers,* 140.
79 "From the Army of Northern Virginia," *Richmond Enquirer,* May 31, 1864.

The South Carolinians, in particular, earned the praise and respect of the men of both sides. Davies acknowledged their "desperate courage," concluding that they were "too inexperienced to know when they had suffered defeat, and continued to resist long after it was apparent that the position they held was turned and efforts to maintain it were hopeless."[80] One of Gregg's New Jersey men called them "the most desperate fighters that we had encountered among the Southern cavalry."[81] Major Kidd, 6th Michigan, said the South Carolinians "exhibited a foolhardy courage never seen anywhere else for far as my knowledge extends," and believed they were "the most stubborn foe Michigan had ever met in battle."[82]

Hampton's veterans agreed. Just a day before, they had laughed at the fancy uniforms and white gloves of the Charleston Light Dragoons, but these bluebloods proved their mettle beyond any doubt at Haw's Shop. "No more was heard about that 'kid-gloved company,'" a Confederate admitted, "and often delicate little compliments were paid in yielding to the 'Drags' particularly hot spots and lonely picket posts."[83] A South Carolinians proudly stated, "Nobody ever behaved with more coolness under such a fearful and terrific fire, and being the first general engagement that a majority of them had ever been into, it was generally acknowledged by those who saw the 4th [South Carolina] go into action that they never saw men go in better or behaved more gallantly."[84]

Doctor Brockenbrough, whose farm at Hanovertown Ferry saw fighting on May 27, chatted with a Union cavalryman who mentioned the performance of the South Carolinians. The trooper surmised that the Palmetto men took such heavy losses because "they were then fresh troops full of enthusiasm but had not learned to take care of themselves like the older [and] more experienced troops," which made for an entirely plausible explanation.[85]

Captain Alfred B. Mulligan commanded Company B of the 5th South Carolina Cavalry. "The enemys forces were entirely to [sic] strong for us," he proudly wrote home, "but we kept him in check all day." Mulligan continued, "My men all have acted firmly so far. I lost one man killed yesterday."[86] Lieutenant Allen Edens of Company E,

80 Davies, *General Sheridan*, 117.

81 Hursh, "Battle of Hawes's Shop."

82 Kidd, *Personal Recollections*, 325–28.

83 Wells, *Charleston Light Dragoons*, 46–47.

84 "Orlando," "Butler's Cavalry."

85 William S. R. Brockenbrough letter of September 16, 1864, Middleton Family Correspondence.

86 Olin Fulmer Hutchinson Jr., ed., *"My Dear Mother & Sisters": Civil War Letters of Capt. A. B. Mulligan, Co. B 5th South Carolina Cavalry—Butler's Division—Hampton's Corps 1861–1865* (Spartanburg, SC: The Reprint Co., 1992), 121.

4th South Carolina, said, "We fought no doubt 20 to one ... we had nothing engaged on our side but Cavalry, South Carolina and [Virginia] but they fought like soldiers and died like men." Edens noted that he came through his first battle unscathed, and "we have any quantity of troops here this morning and are all anxious for [the Yankees] to try again."[87]

Unfortunately, Colonel Rutledge did not share in the praise heaped upon his command. By staying with the held horses, he failed to control his brigade, keeping him from the events that unfolded. While the fighting had raged, Brig. Gen. Young had detoured to the battlefield while on his way to assume temporary command of the North Carolina Cavalry Brigade. He had come upon Rutledge and Manigault while they waited with the brigade's horse holders near a small house in the rear of the Confederate position. Young later reported to Fitz Lee that he had found Rutledge and his adjutant "seeking protection behind a house." Manigault felt that it was "spiteful" of Young to report that sort of conduct, because it did "much injury" to the reputations of the two men, especially Rutledge's, who was "anxious for promotion." That promotion never came, perhaps as a consequence of his failure at Haw's Shop.[88]

Lieutenant Colonel Stokes said, "I held my line in perfect order until we were ordered to fall back, which we did firing on the enemy. I held my line perfect order until we were nearly surrounded and were ordered to fall back." He proudly concluded, "We were beaten back from our position by overwhelming force but not routed." He also reported that a Virginian "told me that it was the hottest fight they had ever been in. We were under fire for three hours, but were only actively engaged for about one half hour, and you see our loss in that little time."[89]

Sheridan's command suffered similar losses. Gregg's division, which did most of the fighting that day, reported the loss of 30 officers and 220 enlisted men, prompting a New York newspaper correspondent to proclaim: "General Gregg has, if possible, won new laurels in his management of this action."[90] Custer's Michigan Cavalry Brigade reported the loss of 6 officers and 109 enlisted men. In only 20 minutes of combat, the 5th Michigan Cavalry lost 5 killed and 50 wounded out of 150 engaged.[91] "Our loss in this battle," Custer reflected, "was greater than in any other engagement of the

87 Swank, *Confederate Letters and Diaries*, 146–47.
88 Manigault Autobiography.
89 Halliburton, *Saddle Soldiers*, 140–41.
90 "Mr. N. Davidson's Dispatches."
91 J. K. Lowden, "A Gallant Record: Michigan's 5th Cav. in the Latter Period of the War," *National Tribune*, July 30, 1896.

campaign"—including the vicious slugging match at Trevilian Station just two weeks later—even though the Michigan Brigade only participated in the final phases of the fighting at Haw's Shop.[92]

Both sides claimed victory. Sheridan rightfully claimed that his troopers broke Hampton's battle line and drove the Southern cavalry off the field.[93] It was a "very hard fight," a trooper of the 10th New York Cavalry recorded in his diary that night.[94] "The Mich. Brigade turned the tide (as usual)," Custer bragged in a letter to his wife.[95] A correspondent from the *Philadelphia Inquirer* declared of Sheridan: "He appears to keep himself so thoroughly informed as to know just how many men to send in to win a fight, or else he is endowed with intuitive judgment in this respect, for he always wins."[96]

In contrast, Hampton also claimed victory. His mission that day was to prevent Sheridan and his cavalry from finding the main body of General Lee's army while determining the whereabouts of the Army of the Potomac, and Hampton successfully did both. His Iron Scouts nabbed a number of prisoners from the Army of the Potomac's V and VI corps, confirming General Lee's suspicion that Grant had crossed the Pamunkey River in force. The brutal fight at Haw's Shop "resulting in unmasking and locating the enemy's infantry at a very critical period of the campaign," claimed a member of the 4th South Carolina, "inflicted severe losses upon [Sheridan's] cavalry, which materially checked them for the future, and above all had convinced friend and foe that dismounted Confederate troopers would fight against vastly superior numbers with the stubborn tenacity of infantry."[97] A Richmond newspaper sounded a similar note, claiming, "The object of the enemy's cavalry was probably to mask the movements of Grant's infantry behind them, but the manner in which they were defeated and driven by our cavalrymen compelled Grant to show his other force."[98]

Perhaps most importantly, Haw's Shop marked Wade Hampton's coming-out party as commander of the Army of Northern Virginia's Cavalry Corps. It was the first time he led the corps in battle, and he gave a mixed performance. Hampton had "put in the troops magnificently," a North Carolina newspaper declared,[99] and his troopers appreciated that he stood up to Sheridan and only broke off

---

92 *OR* 36, 1:821.
93 Ibid., 793.
94 John R. Maybury diary, entry for May 28, 1864, Special Collections,
    Virginia Polytechic Institute, Blacksburg, Virginia.
95 Merington, *The Custer Story*, 100.
96 *Philadelphia Inquirer*, June 3, 1864.
97 Wells, *Charleston Light Dragoons*, 46–47.
98 "A Cavalry Fight," *Charleston Daily Courier*, June 3, 1864.
99 "Cavalry Engagement," *The Weekly Confederate*, June 8, 1864.

and withdrew when compelled to do so. "The importance of the engagement has never been fully appreciated," a Confederate horse artillerist stated. "Had Hampton failed, Richmond would have fallen."[100]

Hampton also demonstrated an understanding of the benefits of earthworks. His performance at Haw's Shop strongly suggested he would prove to be a highly capable commander and successor to Jeb Stuart. "The men of his corps soon had the same unwavering confidence in him that the 'Stonewall Brigade' entertained for their general," one of Rosser's men claimed.[101] Two weeks later, he would prove just how well he had learned the lessons of Haw's Shop when he and Sheridan met again at Trevilian Station.

At the same time, Hampton made errors and seemed uncertain in command. By choosing to stand and fight north of Totopotomoy Creek, far from reinforcements or infantry support, Hampton risked his entire corps, which could have been cut off, destroyed, or captured. Hampton only had a portion of his command with him; if Sheridan had committed his entire corps to the fight, instead of a division and a portion of another, he would have greatly outnumbered the Confederates, particularly after the Army of the Potomac's infantry crossed the Pamunkey and moved into position to support Sheridan's cavalry. This would have left Hampton's entire command vastly outnumbered and in dire peril.

Fortunately for Hampton, Sheridan did not press his advantage—a critical error on the Union commander's part. One of Millen's Georgians claimed that Butler, who was not present at Haw's Shop, later "cursed Fitzhugh Lee, who commanded the fight in person, for everything he could think of—told him he was a fool for making the fight with so few men."[102] Butler may not have been present, but Hampton was, and the criticism remained valid. "I did not then and do not now see that there was any point in pushing the attack as our cavalry did," the Army of Northern Virginia's chief engineer, Martin Smith, observed the next day, "as all that is required of them is to warn of the enemy's approach or movements."[103]

Hampton's inexperience as commander of a large force was also apparent. He seemed uncertain, and his tactics were unsophisticated,

100 "Record of Hart's Battery from Its Organization to the End of the War," in Ulysses R. Brooks, *Stories of the Confederacy* (Columbia, SC: The State Co., 1912), 267.

101 Myers, *The Comanches*, 291.

102 J. M. Reynolds to William J. Dickey, June 1, 1864, Dickey Family Papers, Georgia Department of Archives and History, Atlanta, Georgia.

103 Martin L. Smith to his wife, May 29, 1864, James S. Schoff Collection, William L. Clements Library, University of Michigan, Ann Arbor, Michigan.

amounting to little more than a protracted slugging match at short range. Also, rather than taking the offensive, Hampton stayed on the defense all day. He forfeited opportunities to attack or turn Davies' flanks early on, when the Confederates enjoyed a significant numeric advantage. Further, granting Rooney Lee's poorly considered request for permission to break off and withdraw ultimately cost Hampton the battle, as the move uncovered the flanks of one brigade after another, forcing them to disengage and retreat. "We had a strong position and could have held it until now," Tom Rosser claimed years later, "but 'Rooney' Lee reported that the infantry was coming up on his flank and he could not hold his position longer, and the whole line was, therefore, ordered to withdraw."[104]

For his part, Hampton blamed his line's collapse on the "too sudden withdrawal of Wickham's Brigade, by which a gap was left in the center of the line and the flank brigades were thus exposed."[105] Regardless, as the overall Confederate commander, Hampton bore the ultimate responsibility for the collapse of his battle line that day—he gave permission for Chambliss to pull out, leading to the rolling up of his entire line of battle. "We feel depressed at the loss of General Stuart," an artillerist of Captain McGregor's battery lamented in his diary on May 28, "while Hampton is a good fighter, we have not that confidence in him like we had in Stuart."[106] Fortunately for the Army of Northern Virginia, Hampton was a keen student and quick learner, and he did not make the same mistakes again for the rest of his tenure in command of Lee's mounted arm, an evolution that changed his men's sentiments dramatically.

Lieutenant Gabriel Manigault, adjutant of the 4th South Carolina, left a detailed analysis of the tactics employed at Haw's Shop. "The Battle of Haw's Shop made a great impression, for it was the turning point in the management of the cavalry encounters. Under Stuart the men had fought partly from their horses, and when they dismounted, as soon as the fighting became brisk, they would 'haul out' of the fight, and leave the heavy work to be done by the infantry," he wrote. "This had become so common that the cavalry of Lee's army was generally looked down upon, and it was a common saying among the infantry, when the cavalry were seen retiring from an engagement which they had begun—'there's work ahead for the cavalry are coming back.'" He continued, "In this affair however the entire cavalry were dismounted

---

104 Haw, "Battle of Hawes's Shop," 375.
105 Hampton Connected Narrative, 38.
106 George W. Shreve, "Reminiscences in the History of the Stuart Horse Artillery, C.S.A.," in Robert J. Trout, ed., *Memoirs of the Stuart Horse Artillery Battalion*, Vol. 2 (Knoxville: University of Tennessee Press, 2010), 304.

and made to stand their ground, and the fresh troops from South Carolina and Georgia, who had been carefully drilled as infantry, fought so pertinaciously that the enemy said of us that we were not cavalry but mounted infantry."

Referring to his own unit, Manigault wrote: "The [Charleston Light Dragoons] suffered more than any other single company some of their best men having been killed. It was partly due to their inexperience, for cavalry fighting had become an imitation of Indian fighting. Every man for himself and sought protection behind any tree that was at hand. If it was a fallen one, he would lie on the ground, and, if a change of position was ... necessary, he would dart like an arrow from one protection to another. Our men should have been told this, and their ignorance of it was the cause of a most useless loss of life."[107]

Sheridan's performance also left much to be desired. Sheridan either did not realize that a significant portion of the Army of Northern Virginia's Cavalry Corps was isolated and ripe for capture for most of the day at Haw's Shop, or if he did realize it, he failed to act upon that opportunity. Sheridan neglected to send scouts to see whether he could encircle or outflank Hampton, a troubling tendency that cost him the battle at Trevilian Station two weeks later. Sheridan's lack of aggressiveness permitted Hampton's command to break off and safely withdraw from the trap in which it found itself. Even though Union infantry was less than a mile away, within earshot of the severe fighting raging at Haw's Shop, neither Grant nor Meade ever ordered anyone to support Sheridan. "I could not convince Meade that anything but the enemy's horse was fighting us," Sheridan claimed in his posthumous memoirs, "and he declined to push out the foot-troops, who were much wearied by night marches."[108] However, one must remain skeptical of the contents of Sheridan's memoirs: Sheridan was a known liar, and nothing in his contemporaneous report, or those of anyone else, corroborates his claim. The fact remains that Sheridan's lack of both diligence and aggressiveness cost his command a much larger victory at Haw's Shop.

107 Manigault Autobiography.
108 Sheridan, *Personal Memoirs*, 1:401–2.

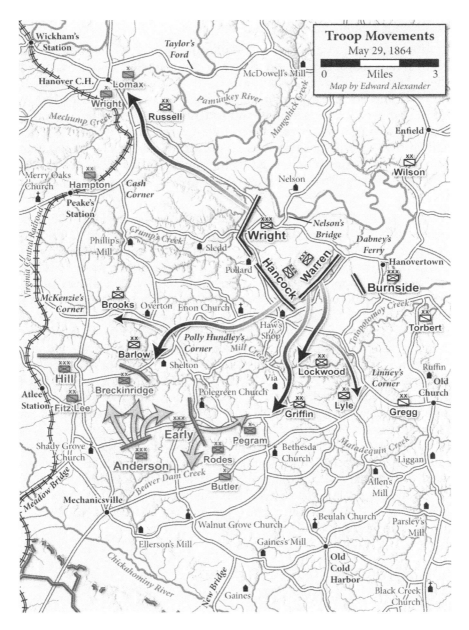

Troop movements, May 29, 1864

CHAPTER SEVEN

May 29: Opportunities Lost

May 29, 1864, was a day of lost opportunities, bungled away by the Union high command. Although the entire Union army was now across the Pamunkey River, Hampton's sortie to Haw's Shop on May 28 and the resulting brutal slugging match that occurred there stymied Sheridan's attempts to locate the Army of Northern Virginia. Because Sheridan failed to find Lee's army, Grant had no solid intelligence about the Southern army's dispositions or even its location. Pinpointing Lee's army became Grant's objective for Sunday, May 29. Hampton and his horsemen had stopped Sheridan at Haw's Shop, so Grant knew that the Confederate cavalry was present in force, and he assumed that Confederate infantry was nearby, but he did not know exactly where it was.

Understanding neither the whereabouts or nor dispositions of the Army of Northern Virginia, Meade ordered his army to deploy in a continuous north-south line from the Pamunkey River to Totopotomoy Creek, extending about three miles from the river. Wright's VI Corps already occupied earthworks along Crump's Creek, with its right anchored on the Pamunkey and its left at Dr. George Pollard's farm. Hancock's II Corps began where Wright's line ended at the Pollard farm and extended along a ridge paralleling the road that connected Pollard's farm to Haw's Shop. Major General Ambrose E. Burnside's IX Corps crossed the Pamunkey at Dabney's Ferry, and after bivouacking at Hanovertown on the night of May 28, was to push on to Haw's Shop, connecting with Hancock's left. Warren's V Corps would then connect with Burnside's left, securing its left flank on Totopotomoy Creek. Once the Army of the Potomac completed these movements, it would occupy a strong position with well-anchored flanks that could not be turned.[1]

However, Meade's well-laid plans did not materialize. Burnside claimed that his men were weary from two long days and nights of marching, so Meade ordered Hancock to extend his left all the way to Haw's Shop and for Burnside to connect with Hancock there.[2] That plan was short-lived, as Meade quickly changed his mind, ordering Burnside to mass his corps as a reserve east of Haw's Shop, with

---

1 Rhea, *Cold Harbor*, 94.
2 *OR* 36, 3:300, 301, and 309.

Warren connecting his right to Hancock's left and extending south behind Little Mill Creek. Finally, by noon on May 29, the Army of the Potomac was in position.[3]

Traveling with Grant's headquarters, Assistant Secretary of War Charles A. Dana reported: "Present indications are that the Rebels are beyond the Chickahominy."[4] Grant, however, believed that the Army of Northern Virginia was closer than the Chickahominy, perhaps even as close as Totopotomoy Creek. Uncomfortable with the uncertainty, Grant did not want to commit to any specific course of action until he knew Lee's location. "This army has been successfully crossed over the Pamunkey and occupies a front about three miles south of the river," he told Maj. Gen. Henry W. Halleck, the army's chief of staff. "Yesterday two divisions of our cavalry had a severe engagement with the enemy south of Haw's Shop, driving him about 1 mile on what appears to be his new line. We will find out all about it today."[5]

Meade shared Grant's concerns and uncertainty. "We have crossed the Pamunkey, and are now within eighteen miles of Richmond," he explained to his wife. "Lee has fallen back from the North Anna, and is somewhere between us and Richmond. We shall move forward to-day to feel for him." He told his wife that he hoped that the Army of the Potomac would continue to maneuver Lee back into the defenses of Richmond, and then bring him to battle in the war's grand decisive fight.[6]

Neither Grant nor Meade was particularly good at utilizing cavalry in its traditional roles of scouting, screening, and reconnaissance, and Sheridan actively opposed employing his corps in those roles.[7] Further, Grant had not managed his cavalry well throughout the campaign, beginning with the Wilderness. Then, by allowing Sheridan to go off on an ill-advised raid that kept the Cavalry Corps away from the Army of the Potomac for nearly three weeks, Grant almost stumbled blindly into Lee's trap along the banks of the North Anna River. He made another critical mistake on May 29: instead of having Sheridan continue searching for Lee, he sent the Army of the Potomac's Cavalry Corps away, allowing it to bivouac behind the army.

Also, and as set forth more fully in Chapter One, Sheridan firmly believed the primary role of the Cavalry Corps was as a fighting force, not meant for reconnaissance and scouting, and he downplayed those traditional roles. Consequently, he had no interest in continuing to

3 Ibid., 310.
4 Ibid., 1:81.
5 Ibid., 3:289.
6 Meade, *Life and Letters*, 2:199.
7 For further detail, see Note 54, Chapter One.

search for the Army of Northern Virginia. He had orders to keep the roads open for the arrival of Maj. Gen. William F. "Baldy" Smith's XVIII Corps of the Army of the James, which was coming up from east of Richmond to reinforce the Army of the Potomac. But there was little for the Union cavalry to do, so Sheridan took liberties with his orders, as he tended to do.

Instead, he moved his horse soldiers to the east to rest, once again removing them from the area of active operations, which meant the Army of the Potomac's infantry, rather than its cavalry, would have to serve as the army's eyes and ears. Gregg moved his Second Division near Old Church, where it camped after vigorous skirmishing.[8] "The Infantry have the job now and we lie 'round and rest,'" Samuel Cormany of the 16th Pennsylvania Cavalry of Col. Gregg's brigade noted.[9] George Perkins of Martin's battery said, "We laid abed 'til an hour after sunrise. Got a hearty breakfast and watered the horses in the Pamunkey at the bridge where we had crossed which was only about a mile from where we lay." Perkins noticed numerous contrabands near the bridge, mostly women.[10] He spent much of the day washing his filthy clothing until he and the rest of the battery saddled up and moved half a mile east about 4:00 p.m., camping in a large field on high ground.[11]

Torbert and his First Division rode down the Pamunkey, picketed for a while near Old Church, and then crossed Totopotomoy Creek where they set up camp, prompting a member of the 1st New York Dragoons to quip, "They say this is Sunday, but no one would suspect it."[12] Effectively out of the war, the Michigan Cavalry Brigade lay in camp most of the day, moving only once for a few miles.[13] The rest of Torbert's troopers left their camp about noon and marched for six hours, halting near Old Church. The 6th Pennsylvania Cavalry bivouacked "in a magnificent clover-field, the headquarters of the regiment being established under a very large and beautiful oak tree in the centre [sic] of the field."[14]

Wilson's Third Division remained on the Pamunkey's north bank, rounding up stragglers and guarding the roads back to Port Royal.[15]

8 Preston, *History of the Tenth Regiment of Cavalry*, 192–93.
9 Mohr, *The Cormany Diaries*, 430.
10 Contraband was a commonly used term to describe escaped slaves who attached themselves to Union field armies after the U.S. government decided to stop returning escape slaves to their masters in 1861.
11 Griffin, *Three Years a Soldier*, 235.
12 Loeser, "Loeser's Recollection," 309; J. R. Bowen, *Regimental History of the First New York Dragoons* (Privately published, 1910), 171.
13 Barnard, *An Aide to Custer*, 241.
14 Gracey, *Annals of the Sixth Pennsylvania Cavalry*, 251–52.
15 *OR* 36, 1:805, 822, and 3:311; James H. Wilson diary, entry for May 29, 1864, Wilson Papers.

Colonel George H. Chapman of the 3rd Indiana Cavalry commanded Wilson's Second Brigade. Referring to May 28 and 29, he observed, "No event of importance occurred to mark these days."[16] Sergeant Samuel Gilpin of the 3rd Indiana Cavalry complained in his diary about the hot and dusty weather, noting that they were camped in a grove of trees on the north bank of the Pamunkey River. "We hear nothing from Grant," he said.[17] "The enemy are in our front again, by marching fast and on interior lines," Lt. William Brooke-Rawle, 3rd Pennsylvania Cavalry, penned in his diary on May 29.[18] Wilson's division also received reinforcements that day when the troopers of the 2nd Ohio Cavalry reported to join Col. John B. McIntosh's brigade.[19]

Bored, Sheridan's troopers spent much of the day looting nearby plantations while some of Wilson's men plundered wagon trains for their provisions.[20] Some of Gregg's men paid particular attention to Marlbourne, the plantation of Edmund Ruffin, a firebrand secessionist. "I got a shell from the cabinet of Edmund Ruffin who—it was said—fired the first shot on Fort Sumter," Cormany wrote in his diary that night.[21] The Federals liberated Ruffin's livestock and foodstuffs, broke windows, and helped themselves to Ruffin's priceless paleontology collection.[22]

Instead of sending his cavalry on the mission it was best suited for, Meade sent three infantry divisions on a reconnaissance in force. Brigadier General David Russell's VI Corps division was to march northwest along the Hanover River Road, headed toward Hanover Court House; Brigadier General Francis C. Barlow's II Corps division was to proceed west along the Atlee Station Road toward Totopotomoy Creek; and Brigadier General Charles Griffin's V Corps division was to push across Totopotomoy Creek and probe west along Shady Grove Road, toward Polegreen Church and Hundley's Corner, with Burnside's corps waiting in reserve, ready to deploy wherever needed.[23] "What is to be the next move on the chess board by Genl. Grant I don't know," a colonel of a New Jersey infantry regiment wrote while watching the troops prepare for the three-pronged

---

16 *OR* 36, 1:899.
17 Gilpin diary, entry for May 29, 1864.
18 Acken, *Blue Blooded Cavalryman*, 151.
19 H. W. Chester, *Recollections of the War of the Rebellion*, Alberta R.
   Adamson, Robert I. Girardi, and Roger E. Bohn, eds. (Wheaton, IL: Wheaton
   History Center, 1996), 79. The 2nd Ohio had served mostly in the Western
   Theater to date. It had just transferred east to join the Army of the Potomac.
20 Isaac Gause, *Four Years with Five Armies* (New York: Neale Publishing Co.,
   1908), 248–49.
21 Mohr, *The Cormany Diaries*, 430.
22 Robert G. Ahearn, ed., "The Civil War Diary of John Wilson Phillips,"
   Virginia Magazine of History and Biography 62 (1954), 104.
23 *OR* 36, 3:293–94.

reconnaissance. "They can't go far to the front before they encounter the enemy."[24]

Once again, the Union high command failed to make proper use of the Army of the Potomac's Cavalry Corps, and just like before, that ill-advised choice cost the army the opportunity to find the precise location and dispositions of the Army of Northern Virginia. Instead, Grant sacrificed the advantage of massing his infantry and forced his foot soldiers to perform duties for which they were not well suited.

The Army of Northern Virginia was indeed nearby, deployed along the south bank of Totopotomoy Creek, waiting for Grant to make his move. After considering all possible approaches, Lee expected Grant to advance along Atlee Station Road. "I do not propose to move the troops today unless it becomes absolutely necessary," he told Breckinridge on the morning of May 29. "I think it probable that should the enemy intend to advance from his present position on Richmond, it will be by Haw's Shop to Atlee's Station. I have directed General [A. P.] Hill to be ready to support you. Take a position to resist his advance, acquaint yourself with the roads and country in your vicinity, and post your pickets to insure your security."[25]

Hampton gathered his widely dispersed forces and picketed all the roads toward the Union forces' known positions. He also ordered his Iron Scouts to hover near the Army of the Potomac's lines to detect and report on any movements.[26] Fitzhugh Lee's division operated between Hanover Court House and Wickham's, a point on the Virginia Central Railroad named for Brig. Gen. Williams Wickham's family. After morning church services, some of Wickham's men "moved backwards and forwards all day," as a trooper of the 2nd Virginia Cavalry noted in his diary.[27] Fitz Lee and his men covered only two miles toward Hanover Court House before word spread that enemy infantry was advancing. Fitz Lee's Virginians fell back to the south side of Totopotomoy Creek, extending the Army of Northern Virginia's left flank to counter the Federals' corresponding movements. That night they withdrew to Atlee's Station on the Virginia Central, where they camped.[28] They drew three days' rations and corn meal, receiving orders to cook it immediately. John Woodall

24 James I. Robertson, ed., *The Civil War Letters of General Robert McAllister* (New Brunswick, NJ: Rutgers University Press, 1965), 430. For a detailed discussion of the machinations of the infantry of both sides on May 29, 1864, see Rhea, *Cold Harbor*, 92–113.
25 *OR* 36, 3:848.
26 Rosser, "Annals of the War."
27 Woodall diary, entry for May 29, 1864.
28 Ferguson Memorandum, entry for May 29, 1864.

of the 2nd Virginia Cavalry complained that water was scarce at their Atlee's Station bivouac.[29]

Hampton massed his division on the Virginia Central near Peake's Station, between Atlee's Station and Hanover Court House. "We rested and the infantry came in and waited for an attack which was not made," Sgt. Charles P. Hansell of the 20th Georgia Battalion recalled.[30] Bradley Johnson's Maryland Line picketed the Confederate far left flank near Ashland.[31] Thus, the Confederate horsemen, now reinforced by the arrival of the rest of the corps, occupied positions where they could provide precisely the sort of screening and intelligence gathering that Sheridan failed to provide that day.

"We remained in camp to-day until noon, then moved in a meandering direction toward the Chickahominy," Sgt. George Neese, of Maj. Roger P. Chew's battery, noted in his diary. "I do not know where we have been today, only that we have been meandering over Hanover County." Neese concluded, "We did not encounter any Yanks today. However, we were on a very warm trail at one time and put our guns in battery, but did no firing." He did report, though, that he and the rest of Chew's gunners could hear Breckinridge's men firing near Totopotomoy Creek that afternoon.[32]

Most of Butler's brigade remained camped behind Breckinridge's men, resting and drawing rations for the first time in two days.[33] "Skirmishing is going on now with the men and our Infantry," Lt. Col. William Stokes told his wife. "We expect a big battle to come off near here as the enemy are on this side of the Pamunkey trying to make down to the Peninsula."[34] The South Carolinians had a good spot for watching the Army of Northern Virginia's infantry march by, and they were impressed by the tough appearance of the Southern foot soldiers.[35] Lieutenant Allen Edens, who served in the 4th South Carolina Cavalry, welcomed a day of rest after the previous day's ordeal at Haw's Shop. "Remember me in your prayers for this is a trying time," he wrote home on May 29. "I have gone through the first battle safe and it [was] an awful hot one."[36]

James Barr served in the 5th South Carolina Cavalry. "I think Cavalry service is the hardest service out here as we fight any way and

29 Woodall diary, entry for May 29, 1864.
30 Hansell Memoir.
31 *OR* 51, 2:297 and 36, 3:968; Booth, *Personal Reminiscences of a Maryland Soldier,* 117.
32 Neese, *Three Years in the Confederate Horse Artillery,* 279.
33 Dietrich, *To Virginia and Back with Rutledge's Cavalry,* 74.
34 Halliburton, *Saddle Soldiers,* 141.
35 Wells, *Charleston Light Dragoons,* 48.
36 Swank, *Confederate Letters and Diaries,* 147.

always on the go," he wrote his wife that day. His horse suffered from inadequate rest and nutrition. "My horse will soon be done," he reported. "He will soon go up the spout as the boys say, but many others are the same way." Unfortunately, the conditions of the horses of Butler's brigade would get much worse before they got better.[37]

Four troopers of Company D, 5th South Carolina Cavalry—N. G. B. Chafee, John Tharin, J. W. Ward, and their commander, Glenn E. Davis—were scouting through some woods and stumbled upon a camp of one of Gregg's companies. The Palmetto men wheeled their horses and dashed down a narrow road, drawing fire from the pursuing Union troopers. Mounted on better horses, the South Carolinians soon outpaced their pursuers and entered a stand of woods. Instead of following them into the woods, the Federals dispersed into groups of eight to 10 men and tried to surround the woodlot.

The South Carolinians realized that they were surrounded and would have to break through the Union troopers if they hoped to escape. After a brief conference to ensure they shared a common plan, Davis led them out of the woods at a gallop. "As soon as they struck the guarding squad dropped their reins over the pommel of their saddles and with pistols in each hand did some lively and accurate shooting, emptying four saddles," a South Carolinian described. Drawn by the sound of pistol fire, the entire Union company pursued the fleeing Palmetto men for nearly three miles, finally giving up as they neared the Confederate picket line. The troopers and their horses escaped with minor injuries. Therin suffered a slight scalp wound; Ward's horse was shot in the neck; a piece of Davis' horse's ear was shot off and a bullet severed one stirrup, and a pistol ball entered his clothing without breaking skin. Chafee had two shots pass through his hat, and he suffered a slight wound to his side. After Chafee emptied both of his pistols, he knocked a Yankee from his saddle who was about to slash at him with a saber, smashing the Northerner's front teeth in the process. "The boys of the Fifth South Carolina Cavalry had many exciting experiences," one reflected, "but perhaps the above incident was as thrilling a one as they had to tackle during the war."[38]

Accompanied by Col. Benjamin Rutledge, Butler led two squadrons from the 4th and 5th South Carolina to Cold Harbor where they "engaged in a warm skirmish for several hours with an advance party of the enemy," Rutledge recounted. "These squadrons lost on

---

37 Thomas D. Mays, ed., *Let Us Meet in Heaven: The Civil War Letters of James Michael Barr, 5th South Carolina Cavalry* (Abilene, TX: McWhiney Foundation Press, 2001), 229.
38 Ulysses R. Brooks, "Cavalry Stories from Recollections of War," *Richmond Times-Dispatch*, January 28, 1912.

this occasion five or six men each killed and wounded." This was Butler's first engagement since losing his foot at the battle of Brandy Station, nearly a year earlier, and it would not be his last.[39]

The 9th Virginia Cavalry of Maj. Gen. Rooney Lee's division camped along the road to Old Cold Harbor. Lieutenant George Beale recalled seeing at the intersection where his regiment camped a large mound of fresh earth enclosed by a tall rail fence. At the head of the mound, a board stated the name of a colonel's horse, which had been shot and buried there. "The men of the regiment thus had paid tribute to the familiar steed which they had been wont to follow on the march and in battle," Beale said. Late in the day, Beale's regiment reached Col. Edwin Shelton's historic house—the home of Patrick Henry's father-in-law. Barlow's infantry arrived about then also, and the two sides skirmished for a time.[40]

That afternoon, Lomax's cavalry detected the movement of Brigadier General Russell's VI Corps division toward Hanover Court House, and Lomax dispatched a galloper to report this critical information to General Lee. The courier arrived at Lee's headquarters about 3:30 p.m. while the general was penning a letter to his wife. Lee realized that Union infantry would reach the Virginia Central Railroad near Peake's Station if it continued on, suggesting that Grant might be doubling back toward the Pamunkey River. "The enemy is moving again this afternoon, apparently to our left on the line which they came from," Lee wrote to Mary. "I am writing in the midst of many things," he stated, abruptly closing the letter.[41] He then had his adjutant, Col. Walter Taylor, draft a note to Maj. Gen. Richard H. Anderson, who was commanding the I Corps, formerly under Lt. Gen. James Longstreet, who had been seriously wounded in the Wilderness. "General Lee directs me to inform you that the enemy appear to be moving toward [the Virginia Central Railroad]," Taylor said. "Be prepared to move in any direction."[42]

Soon, conflicting reports filtered in as Hampton's troopers detected the movement of two other Union divisions in different directions. Lee could not tell which, if any, constituted the main Union thrust, or if these were just probes. He had to remain prepared to respond promptly, shifting forces to meet the enemy as needed and looking for opportunities to exploit any Federal errors. Fortunately for him, neither Grant nor Meade intended to attack that day.

---

39 Rutledge Letter; Manigault Autobiography, 407.
40 Beale, *A Lieutenant of Cavalry*, 159–60. Patrick Henry may have been married at Colonel Shelton's home.
41 Dowdey, *Wartime Papers of Robert E. Lee*, 756.
42 *OR* 36, 3:846.

"It will be well to keep the troops that have gone in search of the enemy to the front and close up on them in morning," Grant told Meade at 4:00 p.m. "If you think their position unsafe, strengthen the front tonight." After Barlow reported meeting resistance along Totopotomoy Creek, Grant also instructed, "If the enemy is found in the position described by General Barlow, he had better be supported before making the attack. They are probably only covering whilst getting everything well ready to receive us on the south side of the creek."[43]

At 7:00 that evening, Sheridan reported to army headquarters that he had established his headquarters at New Castle Ferry on the Pamunkey River and that his pickets covered an extended area. He noted that Wilson's Third Division was camped two miles from Hanovertown, north of the Pamunkey, and reported that he had ordered Wilson to report to him in the morning. He also ordered Gregg to have his command ready to move by 4:00 a.m. the next morning and to report to Cavalry Corps headquarters. Having unwisely rested on May 29, Sheridan intended to resume moving the next day.[44]

Grant and Meade both made several crucial errors on May 29 that cost the Army of the Potomac the opportunity to locate Lee's Army of Northern Virginia before it could assume a strong defensive position along Totopotomoy Creek. Sheridan compounded those errors by refusing to deploy his horsemen where they could provide useful intelligence. Instead, he allowed them to waste a day plundering the countryside. Those errors cost the Army of the Potomac dearly in the coming days. The cavalry corps of both armies faced more hard work ahead.

43 Ibid., 290.
44 Ibid., 311.

Old Church Tavern, with cavalry horses hitched outside it. It served as Sheridan's headquarters.

(*Library of Congress*)

Chapter 8
May 30:
The Battle of Matadequin Creek

Although Maj. Gen. Philip H. Sheridan failed to perform cavalry's traditional roles on May 29, the Army of the Potomac's infantry nevertheless located the Army of Northern Virginia's position on Totopotomoy Creek. Armed with this critical information, General Grant hoped to drive Lee's army back to the defenses of Richmond. Consequently, the Army of the Potomac advanced on its entire front on May 30, aiming to bring the Army of Northern Virginia to battle.

Lee liked his position along Totopotomoy Creek, as it was firmly anchored with Confederate cavalry on both flanks. Fitz Lee's division was stationed at McKenzie's Corner, and Col. Gilbert Wright's brigade of Hampton's division was near Hanover Court House, protecting the north end of the Confederate position. Cavalry was also stationed near the southern end of Lee's line, but the protection there was thinner. Jubal Early's II Corps could defend against attacks along Shady Grove Road and Old Church Road, but four miles south of there sat a crucial intersection called Old Cold Harbor, where five roads converged. Old Cold Harbor was just four miles from Sheridan's camps at Old Church, and there was little to stop the Rebels from going there. If Union cavalry seized the Old Cold Harbor crossroads, they could pass around the Confederate right flank and head straight for downtown Richmond. The only troops available to guard this critical road network were Matthew C. Butler's two regiments of green South Carolinians, reinforced by the 7th South Carolina, an equally inexperienced, newly arrived regiment that was part of a raw brigade of Palmetto men commanded by Col. Martin W. Gary, a protégé of Wade Hampton's, known as the "Bald Eagle" for his bald pate.[1]

---

1 Rhea, *Cold Harbor*, 114. Martin Witherspoon Gary was born in Cokesbury, South Carolina, on March 25, 1831. He was educated at Cokesbury Academy, and then enrolled at South Carolina College in 1850, although he did not graduate. He graduated from Harvard University in 1854, and was admitted to the bar in South Carolina the next year. He opened a practice in Edgefield. In 1860, he was elected as a prominent secessionist state legislator. He was colonel of the 2nd South Carolina Militia Cavalry Regiment. On April 16, 1861, he was appointed as an aide to Gen. Richard Dunovant at Sullivan's Island, but he declined the appointment. Instead, he raised Company B of the Hampton Legion's Infantry Battalion and became its captain. He entered Confederate service on June 12, 1861. His troops captured Ricketts' battery at First Bull Run, and Gary assumed command of

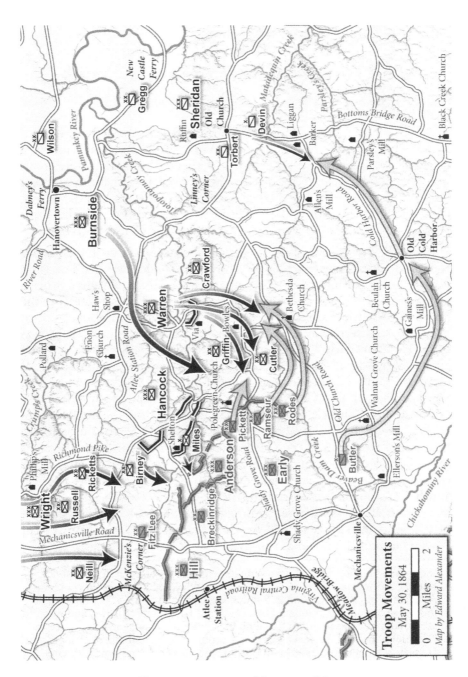

Troop movements, May 30, 1864

Grant, in turn, set the Army of the Potomac in motion that morning. Hancock's II Corps and Wright's VI Corps engaged Breckinridge's Confederates along Totopotomoy Creek, and Warren's V Corps and Burnside's IX Corps fought on the Army of the Potomac's left flank, meaning that all of the Army of the Potomac's infantry was engaged for much of May 30.[2]

About 7:00 a.m., Col. Bradley T. Johnson's Marylanders detected Brig. Gen. David Russell's VI Corps division moving. Capturing and interrogating a few prisoners, Johnson learned that Russell's division had moved "by the left flank as skirmishers over the road parallel to the railroad," aiming to cover the movement of the VI Corps near Peake's Station. Fitz Lee's men also detected the VI Corps' movement and reported their intelligence.[3] Responding to this news, General Lee sent a galloper to Butler, whose cavalry was near Mechanicsville. "The General thinks the enemy is moving around our right, and desires that you will push some bold scouting parties up the road in which your command is and endeavor to ascertain which way they are going," General Lee's adjutant, Col. Charles Marshall, wrote. "Use every

the infantry battalion by the end of the day. He fought at Eltham's Landing and Seven Pines during the Peninsula campaign. He was commissioned as the Legion's lieutenant colonel on June 16, 1862, and led the battalion at Gaines' Mill, Malvern Hill, Thoroughfare Gap, Second Bull Run, South Mountain, and Antietam. The Legion was reorganized as a full regiment and assigned to Lt. Gen. James Longstreet's I Corps, and Gary became its colonel on December 18, 1862. The Legion saw little action at Fredericksburg and Gettysburg, but it saw heavy combat with Longstreet in the Western Theater before receiving orders to report to Greenville, South Carolina, on March 17, 1864, to be mounted for service at Richmond. They departed on May 12 and arrived on May 19. He commanded the Cavalry Brigade, Department of Richmond, consisting of his own Hampton Legion, the 7th South Carolina Cavalry, the 42nd Battalion of Virginia Cavalry, and the 1st Virginia Local Defense Cavalry Battalion. The 7th Georgia Cavalry joined his brigade in the fall of 1864. Gary was promoted to brigadier general on June 14, 1864. He led his brigade with distinction for the balance of the war, but refused to surrender at Appomattox in 1865, instead escaping with a handful of troopers. He disbanded his command and never signed his parole. He was elected to the South Carolina Senate and was a leader in redeeming South Carolina from carpetbaggers in 1876. His radical policies alienated himself from his former commander, Wade Hampton. Gary died on April 9, 1881. He was buried in Cokesbury. Richard J. Sommers, "Martin Witherspoon Gary," included in in William C. Davis and Julie Hoffman, eds., *The Confederate General*, 6 vols. (New York: National Historical Society, 1991), 2:176–79.

2 The fighting on Totopotomoy Creek is also sometimes known as the battle of Bethesda Church. The specifics of the extensive infantry fighting on May 30 stray beyond the scope of this study and hence will only be touched upon in a very cursory fashion. For further detail, see Rhea, *Cold Harbor*, 114–60. For a monograph on Hancock's fight along Totopotomoy Creek, see Robert Bluford Jr., *The Battle of Totopotomoy Creek: Pole Green Church and the Prelude to Cold Harbor* (Charleston, SC: The History Press, 2014).

3 *OR* 51, 2:970 and 971.

prudent means to find out which way the enemy is going." Augmented by Gary's rookies, Butler had his command in motion toward Old Cold Harbor within the hour.[4]

Benjamin Franklin Stringfellow, a 24-year-old captain in the 4th Virginia Cavalry, was considered the most accomplished scout in the Army of Northern Virginia. Early in the war, Stringfellow's reliable intelligence reports earned Jeb Stuart's praise, and he soon became Stuart's trusted personal scout. On the morning of May 29, Stringfellow was scouting around Old Church and discovered that Union cavalry had occupied Old Church and were moving south toward Old Cold Harbor. "Judging from what I hear and see, I think that General Grant is concentrating a large force on his left, and contemplates a move in this direction very soon," he declared—precisely the development that General Lee most feared. Lee responded by putting his own infantry in motion, looking for an opportunity to strike the Federals a blow.[5]

Acting on Stringfellow's report, Lee ordered Early to attack Warren's V Corps near Bethesda Church, and a heavy engagement broke out. Warren repeatedly asked Sheridan to clear the Confederate cavalry buzzing around his troops along the Old Church Road, but the cavalryman largely ignored Warren's increasingly strident summons. Sheridan finally sent three squadrons of the 17th Pennsylvania Cavalry late in the morning, but this force was insufficient to cover Warren's flank, forcing Warren to commit infantry to duties best suited to cavalry. "There seems to be some mistake about the cavalry covering my left," he complained to Meade about 2:00 p.m. After explaining his situation, he concluded, "General Sheridan's cavalry is I believe lying in the vicinity of New Castle Ferry."[6]

For whatever reason, Sheridan disregarded Warren's entreaties. Sheridan was supposed to guard the approaches to White House Landing and New Castle Ferry—the Army of the Potomac's new supply base—and to keep the way open for the arrival of Smith's XVIII Corps. Consequently, he was simply unconcerned with protecting Warren's flank. Meade had his own issues with Sheridan and also was weary of Warren's constant carping, so he stayed out of the dispute. Grant did not get involved either, so Warren's complaints fell on deaf ears all around.

4 Marshall to Butler, 8:00 a.m., May 30, 1864, included in Brooks, *Butler and His Cavalry*, 224.

5 *OR* 36, 3:850–51. For a biography of Stringfellow, see R. Shepard Brown, *Stringfellow of the Fourth* (New York: Crown, 1960).

6 Ibid., 339–40. The brewing animosity between Sheridan and Warren, which had its roots in the opening phases of the Overland campaign at the beginning of May 1864, eventually led to Sheridan unjustly relieving Warren of command at the April 1, 1865, battle of Five Forks.

Sheridan moved his headquarters from New Castle Ferry to Edmund Ruffin's handsome plantation near Old Church. Wilson remained north of the Pamunkey, protecting the river crossings and Grant's line of retreat, Gregg's Second Division patrolled the Pamunkey's south bank to New Castle Ferry, and Torbert's troopers remained camped around Old Church, where they had spent the night. Immanuel Church and James A. Lipscomb's tumbledown inn, called the Old Church Hotel, were the only landmarks in the area, other than Ruffin's plantation house.

Torbert's men unsaddled and washed their horses, then turned them out to graze. "They were cut loose and we were taking things cool," Cpl. Nelson Taylor, 9th New York Cavalry, recalled, "but the Rebs could not let us rest."[7]

The road network at made Old Church a critical intersection. One road ran southeast to White House Landing, 12 miles away, and became the main route used to supply the Army of the Potomac. Old Church Road ran west to Bethesda Church and on to Mechanicsville, south of Warren's flank. Bottoms Bridge Road ran south toward the eponymous span across the Chickahominy River. About a mile and a half south of the Old Church intersection, Bottoms Bridge Road intersected one of the roads that led to the Old Cold Harbor intersection, providing a direct route to that crucial crossroads.[8] With all of that in mind, it is not difficult to understand why Sheridan concentrated a significant portion of his command there. "As our occupation of this point was essential to secure our lines to the White House, which was to be our base," he observed, "its possession became a matter of deep interest."[9]

Evidently tired of Warren's whining, Sheridan finally responded that afternoon. by ordering Torbert to cover Warren's left flank. Torbert, in turn, ordered Devin and his Second Brigade, camped near the Old Church intersection, to picket toward Old Cold Harbor. Warren wanted the Old Church Road patrolled in order to keep the Confederates away from his flank, but his message got garbled, so Devin rode out Bottoms Bridge Road and headed toward Old Cold Harbor. Less than a mile from the Old Church intersection, Bottoms Bridge Road crossed Matadequin Creek, "a deep, and in some places, impassable stream," as Torbert described it.[10]

7 Gray Nelson Taylor, ed., *Saddle and Saber: Civil War Letters of Corporal Nelson Taylor* (Bowie, MD: Heritage Books, 1993), 152.
8 Hanover County Historical Society, *Old Homes of Hanover County, Virginia* (Hanover, VA: Hanover County Historical Society, 1983), 39–40.
9 *OR* 36, 1:794.
10 Ibid., 805.

Devin realized the creek's high banks offered excellent defensive positions and decided to deploy part of his brigade there. He left a reserve at the creek and positioned a squadron of the 17th Pennsylvania Cavalry three-quarters of a mile south at the intersection of the Bottoms Bridge Road and the road to Old Cold Harbor. The Pennsylvanians established vidette posts on the Barker family farm, just northwest of the intersection of the Cold Harbor Road and Bottoms Bridge Road. Devin later described his mission: "My orders were, if attacked, the reserve should hold [Matadequin Creek] in any event until support arrived," and he made his dispositions accordingly.[11]

Butler left the newly arrived 6th South Carolina Cavalry at Mechanicsville to guard the Army of Northern Virginia's right flank. The one-legged general, with his three regiments of inexperienced South Carolinians, numbering about 2,000 troopers—which included Col. Benjamin H. Rutledge's 4th South Carolina, Lt. Col. Robert J. Jeffords' 5th South Carolina of Butler's own brigade, and Lt. Col. Alexander C. Haskell's 7th South Carolina Cavalry of Gary's brigade—marched toward Old Cold Harbor as General Lee had ordered to see whether Grant intended to concentrate there. "The brigade was ordered to trot for about half a mile, and then it was turned into an open field on the left, where a few squadrons were immediately dismounted and marched until the enemy was met, in an adjoining wood," Lt. Gabriel Manigault, the 4th South Carolina's regimental adjutant, reported.[12] They passed through Old Cold Harbor intersection and headed out Cold Harbor Road on a collision course with Devin's troopers.[13]

The addition of Haskell's 7th South Carolina did not sit well with Rutledge, who was still smarting from being shunted aside at Haw's Shop. Further, Early chastised him that morning for his inability to read a map of the vicinity, and the South Carolinian wanted to prove his worth.[14] The 7th South Carolina was "not a part of Butler's brigade and when Rutledge who was the senior colonel saw that he was so completely ignored he lay down near a tree not far from where his regiment remained mounted, none of its squadrons having yet been ordered into the fight," Manigault recorded. "This was the first act of

11 Ibid., 837; Moyer, *History of the Seventeenth Regiment*, 272.

12 Manigault Autobiography, 407.

13 Joseph I. Waring, ed., "The Diary of William G. Hinson During the War of Secession," *South Carolina Historical Magazine* 75 (1974), 17. Butler never explained why he left the 6th South Carolina Cavalry behind, but it was newly arrived and completely inexperienced. It makes sense that Butler would have elected to leave it behind to guard the roads rather than having two untried regiments on his excursion.

14 Brooks, *Butler and His Cavalry*, 205–6.

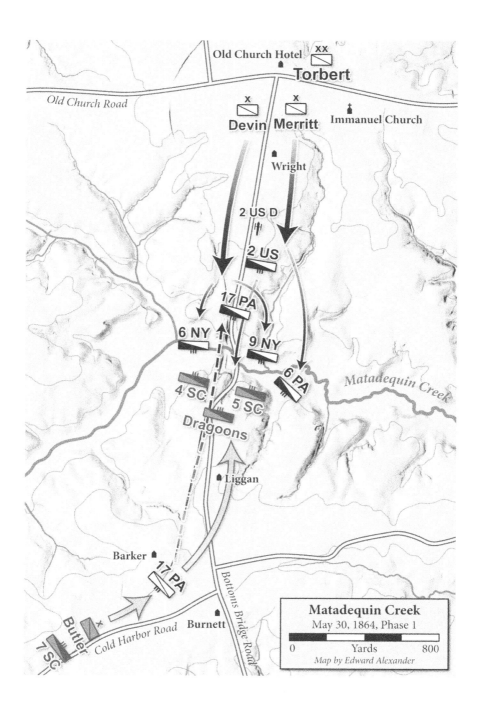

Old Church Hotel
Torbert
Old Church Road
Devin Merritt
Immanuel Church
Wright
2 US D
2 US
17 PA
6 NY
9 NY
6 PA
Matadequin Creek
4 SC
5 SC
Dragoons
Liggan
Barker
17 PA
Butler
Cold Harbor Road
Burnett
Bottoms Bridge Road
7 SC

Matadequin Creek
May 30, 1864, Phase 1
0   Yards   800
Map by Edward Alexander

hospitality by Butler towards Rutledge and it was persisted in to the end of the war." The unhappy Rutledge dismounted and lay down under a tree, sulking. Conflict among his subordinates was the last thing Butler needed as he led his brigade that day—a much bigger challenge loomed ahead.[15]

The South Carolinians approached the 17th Pennsylvania Cavalry at the Barker farm between 1:00 and 2:00 p.m. Skirmishers leading Butler's advance quickly drove the single squadron of the 17th Pennsylvania Cavalry three-quarters of a mile north, across the Barker farm fields and all the way back to Matadequin Creek. Seeing the Pennsylvanians falling back, Devin ordered two more squadrons of the 17th Pennsylvania, commanded by Maj. Coe Durland, to engage. Durland ordered his troopers to draw sabers and charge; they crashed into the lead elements of Butler's advance, driving them back across the Barker farm. The Pennsylvanians then reoccupied the original picket line at the road junction. Driving the South Carolinians off with no difficulty, Devin assumed he faced an insignificant enemy force and neglected to reinforce his picket line.[16]

Devin was mistaken. About an hour later, at 3:00 p.m., Butler attacked with overwhelming numbers. The Confederates charged west across Bottoms Bridge Road and occupied the fields of Spottswood Liggan's farmstead. Badly outnumbered and flanked, the 17th Pennsylvania troopers fell back to Matadequin Creek, where they formed along the creek's northern bank, hoping to keep the South Carolinians from crossing. Realizing he had misjudged the strength of the Confederate force, Devin ordered two more regiments—the 6th and 9th New York Cavalry—to come from Old Church to reinforce the Pennsylvanians. The New Yorkers quickly dismounted and formed along Matadequin Creek, facing south, with the 6th New York to the right of the 17th Pennsylvania, west of Bottoms Bridge Road, and the 9th New York to the left of the Pennsylvanians, east of the road.[17] "Soon our whole front was a line of fire and smoke," a member of the 6th New York stated.[18]

"In charging across a piece of swampy ground I stuck fast and before I could get out the rebels discovered me and shot at me quite lively, but I succeeded in extricating myself before I was hurt," Capt. William Heermance of the 6th New York recounted. "Charged on and the rest of the line not advancing, before I knew it I was in the rear of the enemy with thirty men. Fortunately I was not discovered by them

---

15 Manigault Autobiography, 408.
16 *OR* 36, 1:838; Moyer, *History of the Seventeenth Regiment*, 272.
17 Ibid.
18 Hall, *History of the Sixth New York Cavalry*, 193.

until I had nearly got back to our lines, or we would all have been gobbled."[19]

Another trooper of the 6th New York became separated from the rest of the command and found himself facing an entire squad of Rebels. A bullet grazed his temple, and the Empire State trooper dropped and played dead, lying motionless until a South Carolinian kicked him and "guessed he was dead." The South Carolinians diverted their attention elsewhere, and the "dead man" crawled away to safety, rejoining his regiment.[20]

Butler rode his lines, taking personal command of the developing battle.[21] He counterattacked with two of his three regiments along the axis of Bottoms Bridge Road, which ran north-south, with the 4th South Carolina on the Barker farm, west of the road, facing the 6th New York and part of the 17th Pennsylvania. Before Butler sent the 4th South Carolina into battle, he addressed the Charleston Light Dragoons. "Men, I have stood it long enough," he declared. "I wish the enemy driven from that house in the field." The house was about a quarter of a mile away, and cheering, the dismounted Dragoons went forward at the double-quick.[22] The 5th South Carolina extended the line east across the Liggan farm, facing the 9th New York and the rest of the 17th Pennsylvania. Butler and Gary ordered their men into place "by squadrons as they were needed," trooper Edward L. Wells of the 4th South Carolina later recalled. Haskell's 7th South Carolina Cavalry remained in reserve south of Matadequin Creek, perhaps covering the Cold Harbor Road.[23]

The 9th New York Cavalry, on Devin's left, drove the South Carolinians' skirmish line back across two ravines to Matadequin Creek, which had cut a deep swale east of Bottoms Bridge Road, featuring 40-foot high banks. About 100 yards back on the creek's south bank, Jeffords' 5th South Carolina waited behind fence rails. Colonel William Sackett, commanding the 9th New York, attempted to cross there, but the Enfield rifles of the South Carolinians barked, felling a number of the New Yorkers and persuading Sackett to call off his attempt to cross.[24]

19 William Heermance to his wife, May 31, 1864, William Heermance Papers, Archives, Richmond National Battlefield, Richmond, Virginia.
20 Ibid.
21 "Orlando," "Butler's Cavalry."
22 Ibid.
23 Wells, *Charleston Light Dragoons*, 50.
24 William Sackett was born on April 16, 1839, in Seneca Falls, New York. He was a lawyer in Albany, New York, in the years prior to the Civil War, after being admitted to the bar in 1859. With the coming of war, he was commissioned a major in the 9th New York Cavalry, and then as lieutenant colonel in 1862 and as the regiment's colonel in 1863. He was highly

Hearing gunfire to his south, Torbert made his way from Old Church to investigate. He quickly realized three regiments would not be enough to stop Butler, so he ordered Merritt and Custer to reinforce Devin. A courier dashed into the Reserve Brigade's camp and relayed Torbert's orders to Merritt. "Boots and Saddles" sounded, followed by the bugle call to move out, and the troopers quickly rode for the creek.[25] The Reserve Brigade arrived first, advancing "elegantly," as Merritt described it. "As we hove into sight, the Johnnies were socking it to Devin's boys at a lively rate," the historian of the 1st New York Dragoons remembered.[26] Merritt deployed Lt. Robert Williston's Battery D, 2nd U.S. Artillery, consisting of four smoothbore Napoleons, to support his position.[27]

Merritt's arrival had precisely the effect that Torbert had wanted—the Federals now held the numerical advantage. The arrival of the Reserve Brigade could not have been better timed, as the 17th Pennsylvania was nearly out of ammunition and fell back, the 2nd U.S. Cavalry Regulars replacing them along Bottoms Bridge Road. Captain Theophilus F. Rodenbough ordered his Regulars to attack, and, joined by the 6th New York, they forced their way across the creek, shoving the 4th South Carolina back and threatening to punch a hole in the Confederate line where it crossed the Liggan farm along the road. The Charleston Light Dragoons dashed forward to plug the hole, tore down a fence, and cobbled together some crude breastworks. When Private W. R. Withers of the Dragoons unwisely stood up, a Yankee ball tore through his felt hat, cutting off some of his hair, but causing no other damage. "Spoilt [sic] my hat," Withers noticed as he removed it, "but I'll never again grumble at not being taller."[28] The New Yorkers and Rodenbough's Regulars sought cover in the nearby Liggan farmhouse and outbuildings.[29]

Merritt next decided to try to outflank Jeffords' strong position and ordered Capt. Charles L. Leiper and his 6th Pennsylvania Cavalry to pass around the left flank of the 9th New York and find a place to cross the moat. Leiper's men made it over the creek but immediately got tangled up with the 5th South Carolina in a vicious hand-to-hand

respected by the men who served under him, as well as by his peers in the officer corps. Sackett was mortally wounded while leading an attack on the first day of the battle of Trevilian Station on June 11, 1864. He died on June 14. He was initially buried on the battlefield, but his body was recovered. He was taken home for burial in Restvale Cemetery at Seneca Falls, New York. Hunt and Brown, *Brevet Brigadier Generals in Blue*, 530.

25 Bowen, *History of the First New York Dragoons*, 172.

26 J. R. Bowen, *Regimental History of the First New York Dragoons* (Privately published, 1910), 173.

27 *OR* 36, 1:848.

28 Wells, *Charleston Light Dragoons*, 50.

29 *OR* 36, 1:848.

fight.[30] Leiper sustained a severe wound, and the regimental adjutant, Lt. Stephen W. Martin, was killed. "Our brave boys fought with desperation, though losing heavily," Chaplain Samuel L. Gracey of the 6th Pennsylvania recalled.[31] With Merritt's attack checked, the battle had reached stalemate.

Just then, Custer and his Wolverines arrived. "Boys, I have found a genteel place for you to go in," Custer told them.[32] Custer ordered his men to dismount, placing Col. Russell A. Alger's 5th Michigan on the right of Bottoms Bridge Road, Capt. William T. Magoffin's 1st Michigan and Maj. Alexander Walker's 7th Michigan on the left of the road, and the 6th Michigan in reserve.[33] Custer

Capt. Charles L. Leiper, commander of the 6th Pennsylvania Cavalry, wounded at Matadequin Creek.

(USAHEC)

---

30 *OR* 36, 1:848.

31 Gracey, *Annals of the Sixth Pennsylvania Cavalry*, 254.

32 Lowden, "A Gallant Record."

33 Alger had just returned to duty after being on sick leave. Russell A. Alger was born in Lafayette Township, Medina County, Ohio, on February 27, 1836. Orphaned at the age of 13, he worked on a farm to support himself and his two siblings. He attended Richland Academy in Summit County, Ohio, and then taught school for two years. He studied law in Akron for two years before he was admitted to the bar in March 1859. In 1860, he moved to Grand Rapids, Michigan, where he entered the lumber business. He enlisted in the 2nd Michigan cavalry as a private in September 1861, and then served as captain and major of that regiment. On July 11, 1862, he led a successful attack against Confederate cavalry at Boonville, Mississippi, but he was wounded and captured. He escaped the same day, however. On October 16, 1862, he was commissioned lieutenant colonel of the 6th Michigan Cavalry. On February 28, 1863, Alger was commissioned as colonel of the 5th Michigan Cavalry. He resigned his commission on September 20, 1864, and received a brevet to brigadier general of volunteers on March 13, 1865, and a brevet to major general of volunteers in 1867. After the war, he was very active in veterans' affairs and became wealthy from the lumber business. He served two years as governor of Michigan. Then, in 1897, Alger was appointed President William McKinley's secretary of war, serving through the Spanish-American War. Perhaps as a result of severe criticism of his

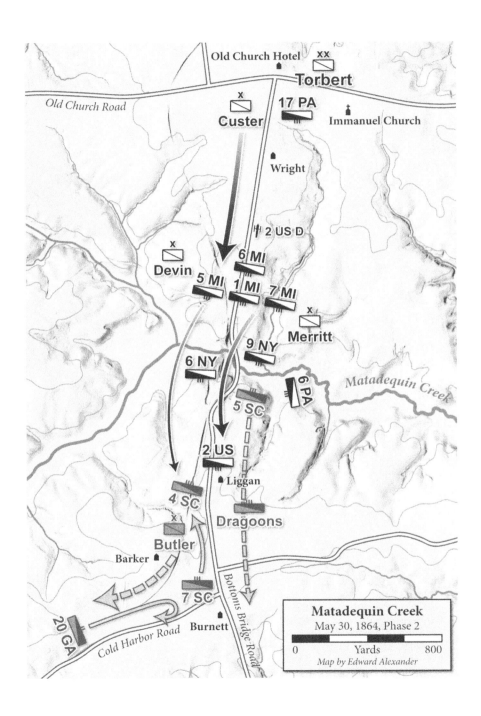

Old Church Hotel

xx
Torbert

Old Church Road

x
Custer

17 PA

Immanuel Church

Wright

2 US D

6 MI

x
Devin

5 MI 1 MI 7 MI

x
Merritt

9 NY

6 NY

6 PA

Matadequin Creek

5 SC

2 US

Liggan

4 SC

x
Butler

Dragoons

Barker

7 SC

20 GA

Burnett

Cold Harbor Road

Bottoms Bridge Road

Matadequin Creek
May 30, 1864, Phase 2

0   Yards   800

Map by Edward Alexander

wanted the 5th Michigan to outflank the western end of the Confederate line while the 1st and 7th Michigan attacked straight down the Bottoms Bridge Road. "With a rush and a yell that made the hills and woodlands resound," an admiring member of the 6th New York recalled, "the 'Wolverines' charged the 'greybacks,' pouring deadly fire from their seven-shooters, which caused the enemy to break and fall back in precipitate flight."[34]

As the 5th Michigan formed, Custer proclaimed, "I have a good place boys, under the brow of that hill, and when they come over give them hell." Custer rarely swore, and it struck the men as odd. "Jumping off our horses, we formed a line by the side of the column," Sgt. Henry Avery of the 5th Michigan recounted, "then marching by the right flank, we moved out to a field in which there was a rise of ground."[35] While the 5th Michigan threatened to turn the Confederate left, the 1st and 7th Michigan attacked south along Bottoms Bridge Road, and Custer held the 6th Michigan in reserve. Major James H. Kidd noted, "The regiment was held in reserve mounted, but for some reason was not ordered to charge as was expected."[36]

Lieutenant Edward Granger served on Custer's staff. As the Wolverines prepared to attack, Granger dismounted to adjust his saddle, which was too loose. By the time he was finished, the attack had begun. Granger rode up a hill, looking for Custer, but learned that all had advanced into some woods on his right, so the lieutenant turned to ride down to join them. "Just as I reached the edge of the woods a spent ball struck me in the breast," Granger reported. "I think the ball must have struck a tree before it reached me as I was too near the Reb. lines for a ball to have lost its force—no thanks to my good intentions, however, as I wouldn't have gone there with my eyes open." Fortunately, the ball barely broke skin, though it left a scar like a real wound. Granger spotted the distinctive white hat of Maj. Charles H. Safford of the 5th Michigan far ahead of his men as they charged into the woods. "The Rebs did not make another stand, and the field was soon our own," Granger concluded.[37]

---

management of the department, he resigned at McKinley's request on August 1, 1899. On September 27, 1902, Alger was appointed to the U.S. Senate from Michigan, and he later won re-election. He served until his death on January 24, 1907. He was buried in Detroit's Elmwood Cemetery. See Hunt and Brown, *Brevet Brigadier Generals in Blue*, 10.

34 Hall, *History of the Sixth New York Cavalry*, 193.
35 Wittenberg, *Under Custer's Command*, 81.
36 Report of Maj. James H. Kidd, December 17, 1864, *Supplement to the Official Records of the Union and Confederate Armies*, 100 vols. (Wilmington, NC: Broadfoot Publishing, 1994), 6:621.
37 Barnard, *An Aide to Custer*, 241–42.

As Safford led the 5th Michigan into the woods, a ball from one of the South Carolinians ripped through his white hat. "It spoiled the cap but did no damage to the head except removing a tuft of hair," Safford's friend Lt. Robert C. Wallace, 5th Michigan, remembered.[38] Unfazed, Safford and his Wolverines pressed on.

Flanked on their left by the 5th Michigan, Rutledge's 4th South Carolina withdrew south across the Barker farm fields, while the 1st and 7th Michigan forced their way across Matadequin Creek on Bottoms Bridge Road, turning Rutledge's right flank. Flanked on both sides, the 4th South Carolina broke and ran. Seeing them go, Sackett ordered the 9th New York, which had been facing the Palmetto men across the creek, to charge. The New Yorkers crashed into the panicked mass of Rebels. "Coming out of this Hell was a terrible matter," Pvt. Albert Elmore of the Charleston Light Dragoons shuddered. "Thicker and thicker came the bullets, and it looked as if every blade of grass and each weed in the field were being cut down as they skimmed past humming their devilish tunes."[39]

The Dragoons, in particular, found themselves in as difficult a position as the one at Haw's Shop two days earlier—Michigan cavalrymen outflanked their left, cutting them off. "Before long the bullets began to come from the left, and the fence ceased to be of much service as a protection," Wells, a Dragoon, recalled. "Then every private knew, as well as if each had been the commanding general, that the line was flanked."[40]

Private Elmore spotted another 4th South Carolina trooper squatting with his Enfield rifle to his shoulder, the gun resting on a fence rail, fully cocked. "I thought it strange that he did not pull the trigger or make any motion to run when we were all getting away as fast as we could," Elmore said. "Upon closer notice I found that he had been killed, shot through the head in the very act of firing. Death had been so instantaneous that he still retained his position and grasp on his gun, which through the rails of the fence steadied the body as it had been last in life."[41]

Private William Bell served in the 4th South Carolina Cavalry's company K and was wounded twice that day. The second wound, to his right hip, debilitated him. As Bell lay on the ground, pursuing Federal soldiers swept past him, although one of them seemed determined to finish the wounded Bell off. "One fellow stopped, and

38 Wallace, *A Few Memories of a Long Life*, 57.
39 Albert Rhett Elmore, "Incidents of Service with the Charleston Light
   Dragoons," *Confederate Veteran* 24 (1916), 541.
40 Wells, *Charleston Light Dragoons*, 50–52.
41 Elmore, "Incidents of Service," 541.

taking a rest against a tree, shot at me deliberately seven times," Bell later recalled. "I counted the shots laying perfectly still in the alley by two old corn rows where I had fallen. Some other shots passed over me and others fell short throwing the dirt over my hat or body." After the Federal emptied his gun, he approached Bell and tried to jerk him up by the collar. Bell jested, "Don't be so rough—don't you know I am wounded?" Bell then headed off to captivity.[42]

The sight of the South Carolinians' collapse prompted the Regulars who had been sheltering in the Liggan farm buildings to charge, breaking the line of the Charleston Light Dragoons. The dismounted troopers of the 2nd U.S. Cavalry drove the South Carolinians before them, armed only with pistols after their carbine ammunition gave out, with Capt. Joseph O'Keeffe of the Cavalry Corps staff leading them into action.[43]

Lieutenant Edward W. Nowell, commanding the Dragoons, tried to rally his men for a countercharge, but few responded; the rest of the company broke and ran south across the Liggan farm fields. "It is needless to say that before we knew it we were badly whipped," one remembered. Nowell was captured, and 14 of the 28 men who went into battle with him that day were killed, wounded, or captured. Between Haw's Shop and Matadequin Creek, the Charleston Light Dragoons suffered frightful losses.[44]

By contrast, the Federals attacking east of Bottoms Bridge Road had to contend with the creek's very steep, long banks. Those deep gullies provided cover for the 5th South Carolina until the blue-clad troopers carried the Liggan farm fields, exposing the flank of Jeffords' men, who had to retreat. "I had to run myself near to death to keep from being captured," trooper John M. Cummings of the 5th South Carolina, who had a ball go through his jacket but not his body, wrote.[45] Kidd was getting his 6th Michigan Cavalry ready to attack when the line of the South Carolinians crumbled, causing Custer to call off the attack.[46] The Rebels "fled precipitously on all parts of the field," a member of Merritt's 6th Pennsylvania Cavalry stated, "leaving a large number of dead and wounded and prisoners in our hands."[47]

---

42 Paul Gervais Bell, "The Battles of Hawes Shop and Cold Harbor and William Bell's Involvement in Them," Paul Gervais Bell Papers, Archives, South Carolina Historical Society. Bell survived his wound and his captivity at the notorious Federal prison camp at Elmira, New York.
43 *OR* 36, 1:805.
44 "Orlando," "Butler's Cavalry."
45 John M. Cummings to his wife, May 31, 1864, John M. Cummings Papers, Special Collections, Perkins Library, Duke University, Durham, North Carolina.
46 Kidd, *Personal Recollections*, 330.
47 Gracey, *Annals of the Sixth Pennsylvania Cavalry*, 254.

Jeffords received a severe wound to his thigh and was carried from the field as his 5th South Carolina collapsed.[48]

The 7th South Carolina Cavalry's rookies had hunkered in reserve in a depression south of the creek with a wheat field in their front. However, as the 4th and 5th South Carolina broke and ran, Lieutenant Colonel Haskell, whom famed Confederate diarist Mary Chesnut described as having "all human perfections except that he stammers fearfully in speech," ordered his eight companies to attack in an attempt to stem the overwhelming Union drive.[49] Haskell instructed them to advance and then lie down, which they did under heavy fire. Before long, Haskell gave the order to charge.[50] "Our eight companies were ordered to charge dismounted across an open wheatfield [of the Barker and Liggan farms] to try to check the advance, and give them an opportunity to withdraw," William G. Hinson, 7th South Carolina, recorded in his diary.[51]

Private Adolphus E. Fant served in Company C of the 7th South Carolina Cavalry. "The fire from the enemy was terrific and effective," Fant recalled. "So many of the men were shot down that it was necessary for the order to dress to the center so as to keep a solid front." The green South Carolinians kept closing the gaps until they were ordered to fall back.[52] Haskell and Maj. Edward M. Boykin led the 7th South Carolina from horseback, and both suffered. The Michigan men mowed down the South Carolinians—both Haskell and Boykin were seriously wounded, and six of their eight company captains fell dead or wounded.[53] Haskell and his horse were both hit seven times. A ball cut a lens off Haskell's field glasses and another broke a ring from his sword. He did not return to duty until August. Captain William Trenholm was so severely wounded that he was unable to return to duty.[54]

---

48 "Orlando," "Butler's Cavalry."

49 C. Vann Woodward, ed., *Mary Chesnut's Civil War* (New Haven, CT: Yale University Press, 1981), 139.

50 Robert Jerald L. West, ed., *Found Among the Privates, Recollections of the Holcomb's Legion 1861–1864* (Sharon, SC: privately published, 1997), 79.

51 Waring, "Diary of William G. Hinson," 18.

52 West, *Found Among the Privates*, 79–80.

53 Manigault Autobiography, 409.

54 Marc Ramsey, *The 7th South Carolina Cavalry: To the Defense of Richmond* (Wilmington, NC: Broadfoot Publishing, 2011), 51 and 55. Alexander Cheves Haskell was born in Abbeville District, South Carolina, on September 22, 1839. He graduated from South Carolina College just prior to the Civil War. He enlisted in Company D, 1st South Carolina Infantry in January 1861, and became regimental adjutant in February. He received a brevet to second lieutenant in July 1861. On December 14, 1861, he was commissioned lieutenant and appointed to serve on the staff of Gen. Maxcy Gregg. He was promoted to captain and assistant adjutant general on January 18, 1862. He

As the Federals repulsed the 7th South Carolina, the 20th Georgia Battalion arrived to reinforce Butler, just in time to get caught up in the chaotic Confederate retreat. With everyone "riding as fast [as] his horse could go," the fleeing South Carolinians nearly overwhelmed the Georgians. A bareheaded officer, "apparently frightened out of his wits," stopped long enough to tell the Georgians that he was a member of Butler's staff and to warn that Yankee infantry—probably Brig. Gen. Samuel W. Crawford's V Corps infantry located on Old Church Road to the north—was using another route to flank and cut them off.[55]

Col. Martin W. Gary, commander of the 7th South Carolina Cavalry, wounded at Matadequin Creek.

(Author's collection)

Colonel Gary's horse was killed under him, but he escaped uninjured. In Manigault's opinion, Gary "had lost his head . . . he stood near us having coming out of the fight, he announced that he had the enemy completely in a corner and with two squadrons more the day would certainly end in our favor." Gary clearly had no concept of the true state of affairs.[56]

As Butler's inexperienced men fell back, they discovered the horse holders had not only fled but had taken the horses of the men on the

---

was appointed lieutenant colonel of the 7th South Carolina Cavalry on April 20, 1864, and then to colonel in June 1864. He was wounded in action four times: Fredericksburg, Chancellorsville, Matadequin Creek, and Darbytown Road, a head wound that disabled him for six months and caused a temporary loss of memory and the ability to speak. He surrendered at Appomattox. After the war, he was a teacher and a lawyer, and then became president of two different railroads. He served in the South Carolina legislature from 1865 to 1866. He died at Columbia, South Carolina, on April 13, 1910, and was buried in Elmwood Cemetery. His brother, John Cheves Haskell, married one of Wade Hampton's daughters. Allardice, *Confederate Colonels*, 187.
55 Hansell Memoir.
56 Manigault Autobiography, 409.

firing line with them, in what Lieutenant Colonel Stokes described as "a stampede" in which the horse holders "ran off shamefully."[57] Panicked, dismounted troopers made their way south along Bottoms Bridge Road for hours, some of them walking all the way to the Chickahominy River.[58] "The retreat was made, but with some little confusion, the enemy pressing us closely," a South Carolinian reluctantly admitted. "The day was very warm and the retreat was exhausting; many gave out and could not go further, and stopped and were captured."[59]

Most of Butler's defeated troopers retreated west along Cold Harbor Road, Torbert's victorious men gleefully pursuing them. The 5th Michigan Cavalry "completely routed them," one recalled, "firing our Spencers and yelling as only Michigan men can yell, Wolverines sure."[60] As they had done at Haw's Shop two days earlier, the men of Custer's Michigan Brigade delivered the knockout blow that carried the day for the Union cavalry. The Wolverines had every reason to be proud of their performance since crossing the Pamunkey River.

Captain John C. Foster commanded a squadron consisting of companies H and I of the 4th South Carolina Cavalry. "As I was about the last to get back to our led horses, when I got there got mounted my bugler, who was my horse-holder, told me that the regiment had gone, that Colonel Stokes had gone, and unless was started right away we would not be able to overtake them," Foster recalled many years later. Foster saw Butler on the field about 50 yards away, so he told his bugler that they should wait and see whether Butler needed them. A few moments later, Butler called Foster over, telling him to place his 15 to 20 men and the other scattered troops into a column of fours facing the field they had just left, allowing the woods behind them to cover the rear of their column.

Foster did so, and he had just taken his position at the head of this makeshift rear guard when his men heard the pursuing Federals dashing toward them at a gallop, their sabers and stirrups clanking. Foster guessed a full brigade was bearing down on them. "General Butler sat there in twenty or thirty paces of us, perfectly cool, and when the Yankee brigade had cleared the woods in front of us by about two files in column of fours, gave the 'Draw saber' and afterwards, 'Show them the steel!'" Foster and his men immediately obeyed, and they heard the Federals call out: "Halt! Halt," which they did. "With our general at our head, sabre in hand, we sat there and dared them until they headed column to the rear and moved out of our sight,

---

57 Halliburton, *Saddle Soldiers*, 142.
58 Hansell Memoir.
59 "Orlando," "Butler's Cavalry."
60 Wittenberg, *Under Custer's Command*, 81.

leaving us to retire in good order at will, back to the main body of our troops at Cold Harbor," Captain Foster proudly concluded.[61]

Realizing Butler had finally rallied near the Old Cold Harbor intersection, Torbert called off the pursuit and had his men withdraw and establish camps across the route to Old Church. Devin's brigade bivouacked at the Cold Harbor Road and Bottoms Bridge Road intersection, and Custer's Wolverines bivouacked to the south at Parsley's Mill.[62] The men of the 6th Pennsylvania Cavalry camped on the same ground they had occupied two years earlier during the Seven Days' Battles of 1862. "We fastened our horses to the picket posts put up by the regiment," one of the men said.[63]

Despite breaking and running, Butler's determined but inexperienced Palmetto men earned the Union troopers' grudging respect. "They fight better than Stuart's cavalry can or at least better than they done this spring," Cpl. Nelson Taylor, 9th New York Cavalry, observed.[64] Captain Charles McK. Loeser of the 2nd U.S. Cavalry remembered the day's fighting as "the warmest action of the campaign so far."[65]

Lieutenant Granger of Custer's staff was not as impressed by the South Carolinians' performance. "It was Butler's Brig. that we fought there, but they did not do as well as they did at [Haw's Shop]," he declared. "They had learned to retreat."[66] Major Charles H. Safford of the 5th Michigan agreed with Granger. "So much for the vaunted boast of South Carolina that one of her sons was a match for five Yankees," he dismissively sniffed.[67]

Private Oliver H. Middleton Jr., the 18-year-old brother-in-law of Col. Benjamin H. Rutledge and the son of a wealthy Edisto planter, served in the Charleston Light Dragoons. He was mortally wounded that day when a ball entered his shoulder, passed through his lungs, and exited near his backbone. He lay suffering on the grounds of the Liggan farm when one of the Liggan boys and a Union trooper carried him into the farmhouse, where Mrs. Liggan did what she could to offer comfort. Although weak and in intense pain, Middleton gave his name and his family's address. "The reason we asked him those questions, we could see that he would die," the Liggan boy solemnly remembered. "Just a little while before he became delirious, he said, 'Oh! My dear mother if I could only see you once more before I die.'" When

61 Brooks, *Butler and His Cavalry*, 218–19.
62 *OR* 36, 1:809 and 822.
63 Gracey, *Annals of the Sixth Pennsylvania Cavalry*, 255.
64 Taylor, *Saddle and Saber*, 152.
65 Loeser, "Loeser's Recollections," 309.
66 Barnard, *An Aide to Custer*, 242.
67 Davis, *I Rode with Custer*, 106.

Pvt. Oliver H. Middleton, Jr.,
Charleston Light Dragoons,
4th South Carolina Cavalry,
mortally wounded at
Matadequin Creek.

(South Carolina Historical Society)

Middleton's suffering ended, the Liggans wrapped his body in a blanket and buried him in their family graveyard. An officer of the Dragoons who knew Middleton's family stuck a board at the head of the grave and carved Middleton's initials into the wood. In order to ensure the grave could be located later, the officer also carved "O. H. M." on a large apple tree near the grave.[68]

Butler's weary troopers camped at Cold Harbor that night. He told the men of the 5th South Carolina that it mortified him to call on them so much, but "it was the only regiment he could rely on."[69] Two squadrons of the 20th Georgia Battalion established vidette lines along Cold Harbor Road, not far from Torbert's picket lines.[70] It was an extremely dark night, so the Georgians rode cautiously in column of fours. Before long, shots rang out, and mounted horses began coming their way. "The afternoon's experience had made this sound very familiar to us," Sgt. Charles P. Hansell, 20th Georgia, sighed, "and every man felt he must get out of there."[71]

The panicked Georgians turned and headed back toward Old Cold Harbor "in a wild stampede," a soldier recalled, "through tree limbs, over fences, ditches, and everything in their path."[72] The stampeding

68 William S. Brockenbrough to Harriett Middleton, September 16, 1864; Henry W. Richardson to O. H. Middleton, December 19, 1864; and M. E. L. to Mrs. Middleton, August 1, 1864, Middleton Family Correspondence. Oliver Middleton's body was recovered, and he was brought home and buried in Charleston's Magnolia Cemetery. Pvt. Oliver Hering Middleton Jr. Find-a-Grave page, https://www.findagrave.com/memorial/33447334/oliver-hering-middleton.
69 Mays, *Let Us Meet in Heaven*, 232.
70 Brooks, *Butler and His Cavalry*, 227–29.
71 Hansell Memoir.
72 Ibid.

Georgians crashed into a squadron of South Carolinians who mistook them for charging Federals and opened fire. "I was wounded slightly in the left temple by a minnie [sic] ball," one of them wrote home the next day. He noted nearly every horse in his squadron was knocked down during the panicked retreat. "Then ensued a scene that battles description," a member of the Charleston Light Dragoons proclaimed. "Horses became perfectly frantic with terror, and each for himself strove madly to break through or get away." Terrified men and panicked horses crushed together in a defile where the road was a mere narrow trench.

"It was a frightening scene," the weary Dragoon recalled, "for the poor victims pulled out from beneath the horses were literally covered from head to foot with blood." One man was killed and several others were wounded in the chaos.[73] "I never saw such a thing," Pvt. John Cummings of the 5th South Carolina stated. "The Road was literally covered with dead men, Horses, Cripple men Horse saddles, Blankets, Clothing, guns and everything they had was lost."[74]

Butler feared Federal cavalry had caused the mayhem, so he ordered his staff to deploy across the road, pistols at the ready, to restore order. A loose horse tore through Butler's camp, and a pistol strapped to the horse's saddle discharged, sparking renewed panic. Several from the 4th South Carolina, including a sergeant, were trampled to death, and the rest, as Colonel Rutledge put it, "were swept along by the resistless rush of the horror stricken."[75] Only the deployment of the 5th South Carolina across the road finally ended the chaos. This sad episode horrified one of Butler's staff officers, who called it "the most inexcusable, unaccountable performance" he ever witnessed.[76] Sergeant Hansell acknowledged that the Georgians presented "a sight to behold the next morning, bloody faces, dirty clothes, no hats, etc."[77] It was a fitting ending to a bad day for Butler's green troopers.

About midnight, once things settled down, an angry Butler summoned Rutledge and his adjutant Manigault to his headquarters. Butler blamed the 4th South Carolina for the panicked stampede, while Rutledge blamed Butler for slighting him. "There was a sharp parlay between the two for a few minutes during which the colonel gave the general tit for tat," Manigault recalled. Butler declared that he longed for the days when he was with his old regiment, the 2nd South

73 Wells, *Charleston Light Dragoons*, 45–55.
74 Cummings to his wife, May 31, 1864.
75 Rutledge Letter.
76 J. M. Reynolds to William J. Dickey, June 1, 1864, Dickey Family Papers, Georgia Department of Archives and History, Atlanta, Georgia.
77 Hansell Memoir.

Carolina Cavalry, rather than having to put up with the 4th, for which he had little respect. Rutledge, who was already seething over his treatment, left soon thereafter, even more unhappy with his plight.[78] Stokes later observed, "[N]othing that Rutledge ever did was satisfactory at Brigade headquarters, and ... it was the constant effort of everyone there to belittle him," making for an extremely difficult and tense working relationship between the two men.[79]

Although his troopers were soundly beaten, Butler nevertheless obtained the intelligence Lee desired. "I do not think [the Federals] had infantry," he reported, "and from all I could learn I do not think they have infantry moving down this side of the Pamunkey River."[80] That intelligence, however, had been dearly bought. The 4th Carolina, which had been pummeled at Haw's Shop, lost another 52 men; the 5th South Carolina lost 16 men, the 7th South Carolina 82 men, and the 20th Georgia Battalion 38 men, for total losses of 188 men.[81] Butler's horse was wounded in the hip, but survived.[82]

After being mauled twice in three days, the South Carolinians were understandably demoralized. Lieutenant Manigault believed that Butler should have broken off and withdrawn when the Union horse artillery deployed. He also noted, "The truth was that our men were completely exhausted by the day's work. It had lasted from sunrise until well into the night."[83] Lieutenant Colonel Stokes agreed that Butler had dragged the battle on for longer than needed. "The fight was a very unfortunate one," he reported, "and nothing was gained by continuing it for so long." He also said, "General Butler is not popular with the Brigade. He wants to be too stiff, though he seems to find a good many things for me to do for him and gives me pretty hot places in action."[84]

Nevertheless, the South Carolinians had every reason to be proud of their performance. "Butler's Brigade has been well worked and done its full share in this campaign," one of them declared. "No body of troopers is more deserving of credit for gallantry and bravery on the field of battle than General Butler's South Carolina Cavalry Brigade."[85]

The 20th Georgia's performance did not impress Butler's weary troopers. "The 20th Georgia behaved very badly," Pvt. James Barr of the 5th South Carolina stated. "They ran, thought the enemy was after

78 Manigault Autobiography, 368-369.
79 Quoted in Emerson, *Sons of Privilege*, 84.
80 Butler to Lee, May 30, 1864 in Brooks, *Butler and His Cavalry*, 225.
81 Young, *Lee's Army During the Overland Campaign*, 322-323.
82 Mays, *Let Us Meet in Heaven*, 232.
83 Manigault Autobiography, 410.
84 Halliburton, *Saddle Soldiers*, 143.
85 "Orlando," "Butler's Cavalry."

them and their horses [and] ran away with them, killing three or four by throwing them off." The next morning, he realized the Georgians were hunting for their horses, lost hats, and missing equipment, scattered in the chaos of their panicked retreat. "They had a regular stampede," he disgustedly concluded.[86]

At the same time, though, the large concentration of Union cavalry at Old Church, extending south toward Old Cold Harbor, verified Lee's hunch: Grant intended to move his entire army toward Cold Harbor, Sheridan leading the way. Would the Confederate army be able to hold the critical road intersection?

---

86 Mays, *Let Us Meet in Heaven*, 232.

Chapter 9

Wilson vs. Rooney Lee
at Hanover Court House

With the Army of the Potomac on the move toward Cold Harbor, General Grant remained concerned about his rear, his lines of communication, and his ability to retreat, should that become necessary. Specifically, a large body of Confederate cavalry—Col. Gilbert J. Wright's brigade of Hampton's division—was located at Hanover Court House, just below the Pamunkey River. The road network there offered the Southern horsemen the chance to move south along Mechanicsville Pike into the Union rear, or they could go southeast along the Hanover River Road, following the Pamunkey's south bank, and slam straight to Grant's massive supply depot at White House Landing, where they could wreak havoc on Union logistics.

When Wright learned that Union soldiers had left Hanover Court House, he allowed his men to graze their horses, then they rode to Ashland. Upon arriving, Lt. Col. J. Frederick Waring received orders to march his Jeff Davis Legion Cavalry back to Hanover Court House, as the enemy was on its way there.[1]

Wilson's Third Cavalry Division remained north of the Pamunkey to watch the Army of the Potomac's rear and General Lee's cavalry. About noon on May 30, just as events were beginning to unfold near Old Church, General Meade ordered Wilson to cross to the south bank of the Pamunkey and deploy his two brigades of cavalry and two batteries of horse artillery on Hanover River Road at Crump's Creek, four miles southeast of Hanover Court House. Hence, Wilson and his cavalrymen were squarely positioned between the Army of the Potomac and Rooney Lee's division.[2]

Wilson saw an opportunity to do more than just protect the Army of the Potomac's rear. The Virginia Central Railroad—a critical supply line connecting Richmond to the west—passes through Hanover Court House. Not far away, and running parallel to the Virginia Central, ran the Richmond, Fredericksburg and Potomac Railroad ("RF&P"), which was also a major line of supply for the Confederacy. While the railroads themselves could be easily restored if cut, the bridges carrying

---

1 Donald A. Hopkins, *The Little Jeff: The Jeff Davis Legion, Cavalry, Army of Northern Virginia* (Shippensburg, PA: White Mane, 1999), 203.
2 *OR* 36, 3:361 and 1:880.

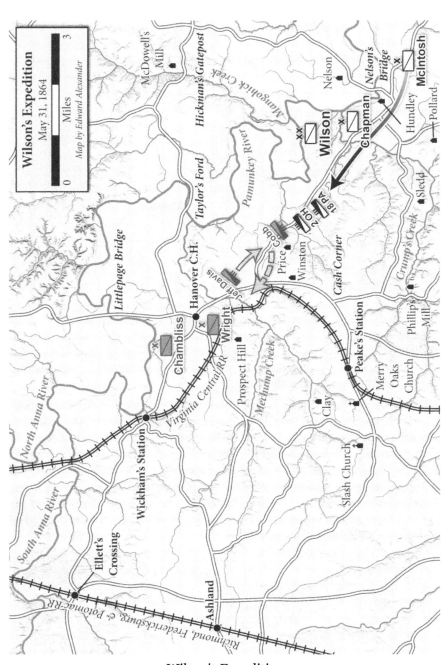

Wilson's Expedition
May 31, 1864

both rail lines across the South Anna River were not so amendable to repair. Two miles northwest of Hanover Court House, the river road crossed the Virginia Central at Wickham's Station, near Wickham's Hickory Hill plantation. The river road crossed the RF&P three miles further west at Ellett's Crossing. Both crossings were close to the South Anna bridges.[3]

When the Army of the Potomac crossed the Pamunkey, the VI Corps constructed earthworks east of Crump's Creek to protect against potential attacks from the direction of Hanover Court House, and those vacant earthworks became Wilson's staging area for his advance on Hanover Court House.[4] Meade intended for Wilson to occupy the gap between the river and the army's rear and to destroy the two railroad bridges across the South Anna. Wilson got the order to "hold the line of Crump's [Creek], between the right of the army and the river." However, he did not receive the order to destroy the railroad bridges.[5]

About noon, Wilson ordered Chapman's First Brigade to cross the Pamunkey and move to Crump's Creek. Chapman and his troopers crossed and occupied the empty earthworks. "We have been marching in dust so thick to-day that one can scarcely see one rod from him," Col. Hammond of the 5th New York groused, "and now that we have bivouacked we look more like dirty rebels than ourselves. Our immense wagon trains are nearly all across the river. I hope soon to have the satisfaction of being in front of Richmond." He continued, "We get very little sleep, which I think agrees with us. We always turn out at two or three o'clock [in the morning] and get ready to move. We look forward to the events of the coming week with a great deal of interest."[6] The men of the 1st Vermont Cavalry spent the day "doing nothing but hearing heavy firing in front," Sgt. Horace K. Ide noted.[7]

Chapman directed Patton's 3rd Indiana Cavalry to scout west along the Hanover River Road, looking for Confederate cavalry. Not far out, they encountered pickets of Colonel Wright's brigade, who skirmished with Patton's scouts for most of the afternoon. Because they were unable to reach Hanover Court House, the Hoosiers returned to Crump's Creek at dark and rejoined the rest of Chapman's brigade.[8] The 3rd Indiana pulled all-night picket duty, remaining

3 Rhea, *Cold Harbor,* 174.
4 Ibid.
5 *OR* 36, 1:872–73.
6 *John Hammond. Died May 28, 1889, at his Home, Crown Point, N.Y.* (Chicago: F. F. Pettibone & Co., 1890), 81.
7 Horace K. Ide, *History of the First Vermont Cavalry Volunteers in the War of the Great Rebellion* (Baltimore: Butternut & Blue, 2000), 172.
8 Wilson diary, entry for May 30, 1864.

"saddled and bridled and sleeping in overcoat and boots," an Indiana trooper recalled.[9]

Sometime after midnight, Wilson learned that all of the wagons had crossed the Pamunkey River, and he and Col. John B. McIntosh's Second Brigade rode off to join Chapman on the south bank. They crossed the Pamunkey at Dabney's Ferry and reached Chapman's camp at Crump's Creek about 5:00 a.m. on May 31. The entire Third Division was finally across the Pamunkey, and Wilson was eager to advance on Hanover Court House. Leaving Chapman's brigade in reserve at the Crump's Creek fortifications, Wilson and McIntosh headed west on Hanover River Road.[10]

Two miles west of the Crump's Creek position, Hanover River Road forked. The right branch continued northwest to Hanover Court House, whereas the left branch ran southeast to Cash Corner, then on to the Richmond Pike, the Mechanicsville Road, and the rear of the VI Corps' position along Totopotomoy Creek. Dundee, "a large and magnificent mansion house of brick, painted brown, embowered in a forest of oak trees," sat atop a knoll near the fork in the road.[11] Jeb Stuart had spent many a happy hour at Dundee, owned by Dr. Lucien Price, and the armies of both sides had passed by the estate during the 1862 Peninsula campaign. The Cobb Legion Cavalry, of Wright's brigade, was posted near the house to guard the fork in the road, and before long, McIntosh's two lead units, the 2nd Ohio Cavalry and the 18th Pennsylvania Cavalry, engaged the Cobb Legion in what developed into a nasty little fight. Once he realized how large of a force faced him, Wright reinforced the Cobb Legion with the Jeff Davis Legion Cavalry, and the two Southern regiments fought a delaying action in the dense woods and underbrush along the road.[12]

McIntosh deployed Lt. Charles L. Fitzhugh's combined batteries C and E of the 4th U.S. Artillery to support his attack. McIntosh's troopers drove Wright's horsemen along the Hanover River Road for nearly two miles until they reached an overgrown field, where tall grass offered the Confederates cover. "A Johnnie dropped down just ahead of me, and calling to the lieutenant to know if I should go after him, and receiving no answer, I concluded to make an effort anyway," trooper Isaac Gause, 2nd Ohio Cavalry, recounted. "On rising to my knees I discovered it was too much like attracting a nest of hornets. With the shower of lead falling about, I experienced a sudden change of mind, and concluded that we did not want any Johnnies."[13]

9 Gilpin diary, entry for May 30, 1864.
10 Wilson diary, entry for May 30, 1864; *OR* 36, 3:363.
11 Albert Barnitz's Field Notes, entry for June 2, 1864, Brinecke Barnitz Papers, Special Collections, Yale University Library, New Haven, Connecticut.
12 *OR* 36, 1:804.

The Union troopers could clearly see the town of Hanover Court House a short distance west, across Mechump Creek, a slow-moving tributary of the Pamunkey that had a wide, marshy floodplain, and which made an effective obstacle against Wilson's advance. Captain William M. McGregor's battery of horse artillery came up to support Wright's troopers and to engage Fitzhugh's Federal guns.[14] "The field was being swept with rifle bullets ... and artillery fire also," one of McGregor's men, Pvt. David Cardwell, recalled. Dragging two dead horses, McGregor's artillerists unlimbered their guns and opened fire at short range. As they went into position, troopers of the 10th Virginia Cavalry of Chambliss' brigade came to support them. Lieutenant Colonel Robert Caskie, 10th Virginia, rode a fine gray horse that suddenly went down with the colonel pinned under it. "We did not stop to help him out," Cardwell wrote. "[W]e were too busy."[15] The two batteries blasted away at each other from short range.

"I have been in a heap of fights but that was the closest place I was ever in," a member of the Cobb Legion Cavalry recounted. "The balls just plowed up the ground and skinned the trees."[16] Facing accurate artillery fire and heavy carbine fire, McIntosh elected not to cross Mechump Creek and pulled his men back to the nearby Price farm, where they began cooking rations. A detachment of Federals remained near the marshy ravine, "watching the movements of the enemy cavalry, dismounted and ready to receive us, on the hill on the opposite side," a member of the 1st Connecticut Cavalry reported.[17] Lieutenant Colonel John W. Phillips of the 18th Pennsylvania said something similar. "We lay in the little ditch behind a fence all day as skirmishers watching the enemy who was in plain sight on the hills around the village. We were annoyed occasionally by a couple of pieces of [a]rtillery which he had there."[18]

Dundee served as Wilson's headquarters, McIntosh's camp, and a field hospital for wounded troopers, so it teemed with Union soldiers, horses, and supply wagons. Bickerton L. Winston's nearby farm, across Signal Hill, also served as campsite for some of McIntosh's men. Winston's place was also familiar to the Union troopers, as elements of the Army of the Potomac camped there in May 1862.[19] Wilson detailed

13 Isaac Gause, *Four Years with Five Armies* (New York: Neale Publishing Co., 1908), 250–51.

14 Chew report; Waring diary, entry for May 31, 1864.

15 David Cardwell, "Where the Gallant Lieutenant Ford was Killed," *Confederate Veteran* 26 (1918), 207.

16 W. W. Abercrombie to his wife, June 1, 1864, Archives, Georgia Historical Society, Atlanta, Georgia.

17 "Connecticut," "The First Connecticut Cavalry," *New Haven Daily Palladium*, June 21, 1864.

18 Ahearn, "Civil War Diary of John Wilson Phillips," 104.

*Lt. Col. Erastus Blakeslee,
commander, 1st Connecticut
Cavalry, wounded at
Ashland.*

(USAHEC)

some troopers to go to Cash Corner and then on to Phillip's Mill, where they connected with infantrymen guarding the rear of the VI Corps. Chapman's First Brigade remained at Crump's Creek, watching Wilson's rear and line of retreat, as well as being available to respond, if needed. With those dispositions completed, Wilson concluded he had fulfilled his orders to plug the hole between the Union line and the Pamunkey.[20] "We lay on the line, exchanging occasional shots until about dark," Lt. Col. Erastus Blakeslee, 1st Connecticut Cavalry, recalled.[21]

Not long after Wilson had established camp at Dundee, a galloper from Meade's headquarters reined in, carrying a 10-hour old message from the Army of the Potomac's chief of staff, Maj. Gen. Andrew A. Humphreys. "The order for the destruction of the [railroad] bridges has not been countermanded," Humphreys wrote, providing Wilson with his first inkling that he had been ordered to destroy the bridges. Humphreys instructed Wilson that he was not only to cover the army's right flank, but he was also to wreck the twin railroad bridges.[22] "I have now one brigade occupying the Richmond Road in force to [Cash Corner], covering its junction with the Mechanicsville Road, with orders to patrol to the right of the army," the flabbergasted Wilson replied. "The other brigade is at the crossing of Crump's Creek, but, if you think it necessary, it might be moved to the vicinity of Enon Church." Wilson asked Humphreys to "inform me of your wishes by return courier." He also noted, "I think my present position more defensible and

19 Beaudry, *War Journal*, 124–25.
20 *OR* 36, 1:880.
21 Erastus Blakeslee, "Addenda to the History and Roster of the Connecticut Cavalry Volunteers: 1861–1865," included in *The Connecticut Cavalry Volunteers in the War of the Rebellion, 1861–1865* (Hartford, CT: Case, Lockwood & Brainard, 1889), 4.
22 Ibid.

affording better means of communication with the right of the army than the one behind the creek."[23]

Humphreys' response did not arrive until 7:00 p.m.[24] In it, Humphreys instructed Wilson to continue to Hanover Court House with his command, then to send out parties to destroy the Virginia Central and RF&P railroad bridges across the South Anna River. After wrecking the bridges, Wilson was to advance "in the direction of Richmond till [he] should encounter the enemy in such strength that [he] could no longer contend with them successfully."[25] These orders concerned the cavalryman, who believed that the destroying the twin railroad bridges would require the entire Cavalry Corps, not just two small detachments. Wilson also worried that his lone division would be cut off as it moved farther from the main body of the Army of the Potomac. Despite his concerns, Wilson complied with the orders, instructing McIntosh to "get ready to advance at once."[26]

To get to the railroad bridges, Wilson first had to capture the town of Hanover Court House. Given that Confederate cavalry and horse artillery were there in force, and he had to deal with swampy Mechump Creek to reach them, this would be no small undertaking. "Before us was a narrow belt of timber on the extreme verge of a steep bluff," a trooper of the 2nd Ohio Cavalry shuddered, "and at the foot of the bluff a narrow meadow, cut up with deep ditches full of running water, and girdled by a thick, matted growth of brush, briars, and blackberry bushes—and on the opposite of the meadow the bluffs of Hanover, on which were stationed two brigades of rebels with four pieces of artillery." There were only two ways across the marsh: one carrying the Hanover River Road, and the other carrying the Virginia Central Railroad, about a mile to the south. The two well-guarded crossings would be difficult to seize.[27]

After reconnoitering, Wilson concluded that McIntosh should attack from the west and attempt to storm the railroad bridge. McIntosh dismounted his troopers and deployed them east of Mechump Creek, perpendicular to Hanover River Road. Colonel George Purington's 2nd Ohio straddled the roadway, with Maj. Dudley Seward's 1st Battalion north of the road and Maj. A. Bayard Nettleton's 2nd and 3rd battalions extending south. Lieutenant Colonel William P. Brinton's 18th Pennsylvania Cavalry formed on Purington's right, spread across a field, while Lt. Col. Erastus

23 Ibid., 3:413.
24 Wilson diary, entry for May 31, 1864.
25 *OR* 36, 3:414 and 1:881.
26 Wilson, *Under the Old Flag*, 1:429.
27 "Old Po'Keepsie," to the editor, *Painesville Telegraph*, June 23, 1864.
28 Phillip Koempel, *Phil Koempel's Diary 1861–1865* (n.p., 1923), 8.

Brig. Gen. Pierce M. B. Young, temporary commander, North Carolina Cavalry Brigade, Rooney Lee's Division, Cavalry Corps, Army of Northern Virginia, severely wounded at Ashland.

(USAHEC)

Blakeslee's 1st Connecticut Cavalry lined up to Purington's left, extending south to the railroad tracks. "Close call on the firing line," Sgt. Phillip Koempel of the 1st Connecticut recorded. "While dismounting to advance a shell burst in the rear of my horse."[28] Colonel Otto Harhaus and his 2nd New York Cavalry remained mounted behind the 2nd Ohio, ready to support the dismounted attack on the bridge with a saber charge.[29]

In the meantime, Rooney Lee's fresh division arrived to relieve Wright's weary troopers. Exhausted after a full day of skirmishing with McIntosh's men, Wright's brigade pulled out and took up a position several miles to the west.[30] As Colonel John Baker had not performed well at Hanovertown Ferry four days earlier, and as Lt. Col. Rufus Barringer's promotion to brigadier general had not yet come through, Brig. Gen. Pierce M. B. Young assumed temporary command of the North Carolina brigade on May 30, leading it in combat for the first time at Hanover Court House.[31]

29 *OR* 36, 1:881, 888, and 894. There were three battalions per Union cavalry regiment. A battalion consisted of two squadrons of cavalry. A squadron of cavalry consisted of two companies, or troops, as they were sometimes called.

30 Waring diary, entry for May 31, 1864; "Recent Cavalry Operations," *Atlanta Daily Intelligencer*, June 14, 1864.

31 "Barringer's N.C. Brigade of Cavalry," *Raleigh Daily Confederate*, February 22, 1865. Pierce Manning Butler Young was born at Spartanburg, South Carolina, on November 15, 1836. Young's family moved to Bartow County, Georgia, when he was still a child. Young attended the Georgia Military Institute until his appointment to West Point in 1857, where he was a classmate and friend of George A. Custer. While at West Point, Young was an outspoken supporter of secession and resigned from the academy in March

Young deployed his troopers on high ground along the western bank of Mechump Creek. The 2nd North Carolina held the left of Young's line, near the county's historic courthouse complex in the middle of town; the 3rd North Carolina extended the line to the south; and the 5th North Carolina anchored the Confederate right, near the Virginia Central depot in the town.[32] The 1st North Carolina Cavalry remained mounted and spread out as skirmishers along the Confederate battle line. "The 1st, 2nd, 3rd, and 5th regiments were dismounted and double quicked in with as much élan as old veteran infantry," one of the Tar Heels recounted. "The hot rays of the last day of May seemed to be preparing a welcome for the first summer month."[33]

Chambliss' brigade of Virginians—the 9th, 10th, and 13th Virginia Cavalry—remained in reserve in fields north of the courthouse buildings. "Our [regiment] is in line of battle in the woods the men are

1861, after Georgia seceded during his senior year. On March 16, 1861, he was commissioned a second lieutenant of artillery in the Confederate army. He briefly served on the staff of Gen. Braxton Bragg at Pensacola, Florida, before returning to Georgia in July and accepting an appointment to be adjutant to Cobb's Legion. By early 1862, he was a major, but illness forced him to step aside for a time. When he returned to duty, he was promoted to lieutenant colonel and given command of the Legion's cavalry battalion. In 1862, the Cobb Legion Cavalry was assigned to Wade Hampton's brigade. Young suffered a wound in action at Burkittsville, Maryland, in August 1862, and on September 13, at Middletown, Maryland, he was wounded in the chest. He was cited for remarkable gallantry during the Maryland campaign and was promoted to colonel on November 1, 1862. He performed well during the campaigns of 1863, and his performance during the Gettysburg campaign earned him a commission as brigadier general to rank from September 28. He was assigned to command Hampton's former brigade. He was promoted to major general that fall and commanded Hampton's division for part of 1864, and in November he was ordered to Augusta, Georgia, to help defend the Confederate arsenal there. He served under Hampton's command in 1865. Young was wounded in battle four different times during the war, serving honorably and courageously. After the war, he returned to Georgia and farmed. In 1868, he was elected to the House of Representatives, serving three terms. He attended the 1872, 1876, and 1880 Democratic conventions as a delegate. In 1885, President Grover Cleveland appointed Young consul general to St. Petersburg, Russia. He remained in Russia for two years, and in 1893, he was named U.S. ambassador to Guatemala and Honduras. He was serving in this diplomatic post when he died in New York on July 6, 1896. He was buried near his plantation in Cartiersville, Georgia. Jeffry D. Wert, "Pierce Manning Butler Young," included in William C. Davis and Julie Hoffman, eds., *The Confederate General*, 6 vols. (New York: National Historical Society, 1991), 6:169–70.
32 Ibid. The county courthouse dates back to 1735 and is one of the oldest continuously operating courthouses in the country. Patrick Henry, one of Virginia's most famous orators, argued cases there. It is listed on the National Register of Historic Landmarks.
33 "The Recent Cavalry Operations." *Richmond Enquirer*, June 9, 1864.

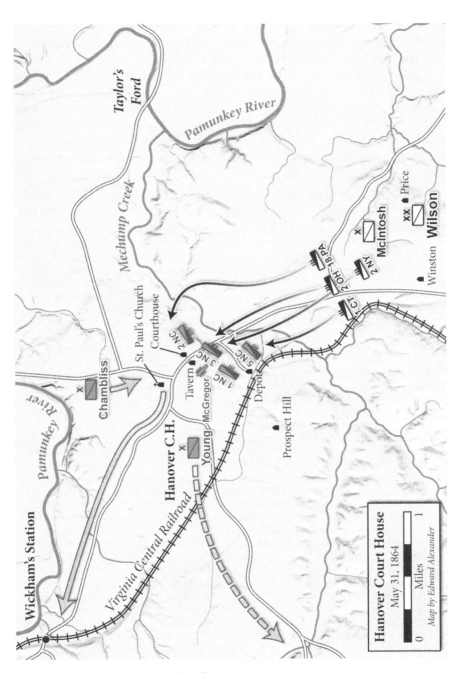

The Battle of Hanover Court House
May 31, 1864

lying around asleep (as today we have another brigade in front of us)," a Virginian wrote. "The horses standing thick around me and occasionally a shot is fired by our artilery [sic] ... at the yankees who are fortifying[.] I shall take this opportunity as it may be the only one I may have for several days."[34]

Wilson ordered McIntosh to attack at dusk. "The sun was almost down, and we could distinctly see our foes upon the opposite plain, loading and firing upon us," a trooper of the 2nd Ohio remembered. "Their artillery was in position and every movement made was plainly visible. The clear, unclouded sky placed them in such position that they resembled monuments moving about and changing places before us."[35]

Despite facing this obvious resistance, McIntosh's men did as instructed and advanced down a steep bluff to Mechump Creek, where they began making their way across. With ditches crisscrossing the floodplain and many trees downed by the Confederates, the field was wide open and bereft of cover, subjecting the attacking Federals to fire every step of the way. Tar Heels on the western edge of the ravine opened on McIntosh's dismounted troopers as soon as they spotted them approaching.[36] "By the aid of grape vines, brush and rocks, we gained the valley below and charged over the meadow, but the ditches and briars checked our progress, and after crossing each ditch were obliged to halt and reform under a heavy fire," a Connecticut man reported. McIntosh had ordered his men to hold their fire to cross the ravine as quickly as possible, and many of them were already across before the Tar Heels even realized it. "We charged right across this valley," the Connecticut trooper continued, "in the face of grape and canister, waded the creek [and] went steadily through the bushes that lined its side."[37]

"The scene was grand ... as our boys jaded and worn rushed over a hill and saw the long black lines of the enemy sweeping over a wide plain, rushing to gain the position that lay before them," a North Carolinian said. "At the same time the white clouds of smoke from our cannon gave assurances that we had help from behind [as] our boys dashed impetuously forward hardly waiting to fire."[38] From that point, Lieutenant Colonel Barringer, 1st North Carolina, recalled, "[P]retty much the entire [b]rigade was dismounted, and withstood, with undaunted spirit, a fierce and overwhelming attack of the enemy."[39]

34 Irvin Cross Wills to Dear Cousin, May 30, 1864, Irvin Cross Wills Papers, Archives, Library of Virginia, Richmond, Virginia.
35 "Old Po'Keepsie" to the editor.
36 *OR* 36, 1:881.
37 "Connecticut," "The First Connecticut Cavalry."
38 "The Recent Cavalry Operations," *Richmond Enquirer*, June 9, 1864
39 "Barringer's North Carolina Brigade of Cavalry."

Lt. Col. Rufus Barringer, commander, 1st North Carolina Cavalry (depicted as a brigadier general, June 1864).

(Library of Virginia)

The troopers of the 2nd Ohio met heavy resistance along the roadway from North Carolinians firing at them from behind crude breastworks made of fence rails. "At short range infantry were pouring small shot on us, while the artillery commenced using up their surplus grape and canister and threw it toward us," one of the Ohioans stated.[40] They pushed across Mechump Creek, both north and south of the Hanover River Road bridge, before taking cover behind a small bluff along the western bank of the creek, clinging tightly to the ground.[41] McIntosh mistook this movement as indicating that the Tar Heels had repulsed his attack and ordered his bugler to sound the recall. "Many of the officers in the other regiments thought it applied to the whole line and ordered a retreat," according to a Buckeye trooper, "which left the line with gaps in it, some going back and some advancing."[42]

Major Nettleton, who commanded the two battalions of the 2nd Ohio south of the road, recognized that it would be safer to press the attack rather than fall back and ordered anyone with at least five rounds to charge. "About one hundred were found 'not wanting,' and we moved off on the double quick," Lt. Luman Harris Tenney of the 2nd Ohio said. Tenney, who rode into battle, also noted, "Firing very hot indeed."[43] After the Buckeyes reached the far crest, the mounted men of the 2nd New York cheered loudly, drew their sabers, and charged across the bridge, heading straight for the fence and the North

40 "Old Po'Keepsie" to the editor.
41 *OR* 36, 1:894.
42 Gause, *Four Years in Five Armies*, 253.
43 Luman Harris Tenney, *War Diary of Luman Harris Tenney, 1861–1865* (Cleveland: Evangelical Publishing House, 1914), 117.

Carolinians sheltering behind it. "Our ammunition failed and in some part of the line the enemy were actually driven from their position with stones and clubs," Colonel Purington recounted.[44]

Major Seward's battalion of the 2nd Ohio had tough going north of the railroad bridge. "When we came to the top of the bank, we were met with a fresh volley reserved for our reception, but fired too soon to do any damage," Isaac Gause, 2nd Ohio, remembered. "We dropped flat between the rows of dead corn stalks, and they had a woeful sound when struck by bullets." The Buckeyes clung to the ground as Confederate bullets splatted all around them, spraying them with dirt. "It appeared to me as if every cornstalk in that field was hit," Gause shivered years later.[45]

Meanwhile, on the left end of McIntosh's attack, the 1st Connecticut charged into the creek bed under heavy fire and crashed into the 5th North Carolina. Tar Heel Major James H. McNeil hunkered down in the railroad depot, where he and his men fought savagely.[46] However, the 18th Pennsylvania, attacking on the Union right, left the protection of a fence located to the east of the creek, slogged through marshy ground, and struggled up the opposite bank, where they turned the Confederate left flank. "We charged that [half] mile under a heavy fire and under great difficulties, there being a ... swamp and there was a steep hill to go over," Maj. John W. Phillips of the 18th Pennsylvania claimed. "Our line never wavered, and in fifteen minutes from the time we left the fence the enemy were leaving the village in confusion."[47] Captains M. S. Kingsland and David Hamilton of the 18th Pennsylvania suffered severe wounds in this charge, while the regimental commander, Lt. Col. William P. Brinton, received a minor wound.[48]

Flanked, the Tar Heels broke and ran. Seeing a rout developing, Chambliss ordered his mounted Virginians to draw sabers and charge

---

44 *OR* 36, 1:894.

45 Gause, *Four Years in Five Armies*, 254.

46 "First Regiment Cavalry," in *Annual Report of the Adjutant General of the State of Connecticut for the Year Ending March 31, 1865* (New Haven, CT: A. N. Clark & Co., 1865), 412–13.

47 Ahearn, "Civil War Diary of John Wilson Phillips," 104.

48 Publication Committee of the Regiment, *History of the Eighteenth Regiment of Pennsylvania Cavalry, Pennsylvania Volunteers 1862–1865* (New York: Winkoop Hallenbeck Crawford Co., 1909), 24 and 52. The regimental history claims that Phillips suffered a severe wound that day, but Phillips' published diary makes no mention whatsoever of having been wounded, and, in fact, indicates that he did his duty in the next day's fighting. I have, therefore, chosen not to suggest that Phillips was wounded on May 31. Hamilton's hip wound was so severe that it caused partial paralysis of his legs, and he never rejoined the regiment. David Hamilton Find-a-Grave page, https://www.findagrave.com/memorial/10926204/david-hamilton.

Lt. Col. William P. Brinton, commander, 18th Pennsylvania Cavalry, wounded at Hanover Court House.

(*History of the Eighteenth Regiment of Pennsylvania Cavalry*)

in an attempt to cover the retreat of Young's men.[49] "In passing over open country to our position on the line of battle, the shells screamed and the minnie [sic] balls whistled, but passed harmlessly over our heads," Col. Richard L. T. Beale of the 9th Virginia Cavalry recalled.[50]

Captain McGregor also realized the moment of crisis had arrived. "Give 'em hell, boys!" he called out to his artillerists. "Pour it in, boys!" Lieutenant Charles E. Ford, a graduate of the Virginia Military Institute, served in McGregor's battery. He rode quietly up and down the lines behind the guns, silhouetted against the gathering darkness by muzzle flashes from the cannons. Ford offered a tempting target, and soon Union troopers drew a bead on him and the battery's other mounted officers. Private David Cardwell warned Ford that bullets were flying thickly, prompting Ford to call out to McGregor to retire the guns. McGregor did not hear him, so Ford turned in his saddle and cried: "Limber to the rear!" The gunners quickly obeyed, so they did not see Ford fall from a mortal wound, although one of the gunners caught Ford as he fell from the

49 John W. Chowning diary, entry for May 31, 1864, Special Collections, Mary Ball Washington Library, Lancaster, Virginia.
50 Richard L. T. Beale, *History of the Ninth Virginia Cavalry in the War Between the States* (Richmond. B. F. Johnson Publishing Co., 1899), 126.

saddle. Just then, Cardwell's horse was wounded, and "over we went," leaving Cardwell stunned and bruised. Ford died soon after, and by the light of a campfire, Cardwell and a few others buried him near a fence on Wickham's plantation.[51]

Having broken the Confederate line, McIntosh's men pressed on. "They finally gave way before the galling fire from the Spencer carbines and the battery," trooper Isaac Gause, 2nd Ohio, recalled, "which had a fine range on them."[52] "They were routed completely," a member of the 1st Connecticut observed. Some of the mounted men of the 2nd New York nearly captured McGregor's guns, but the Virginians spirited them away in the nick of time.[53]

By then, it was too dark to pursue the routed Confederates. McIntosh established his camp on the courthouse grounds, put out pickets, and allowed his weary men and horses to rest. "It was so dark when we were through the days work," a Buckeye remembered, "that we could not distinguish between our uniform and that of the rebels, so when we awoke at daylight we were surprised to find we had been sleeping by the side of a dead rebel."[54] Another Ohioan said, "About eleven o'clock our horses came up. Our mess had to borrow some rations to get a little supper. A detail was sent to the pack train, and brought some rations, which were issued about two o'clock with orders to get breakfast." The Ohio trooper did not get much sleep that night; a wounded Confederate lying in front of his position kept calling for water, and the kindly Buckeye made three trips to give him water. "Where did you Yanks come from?" the wounded Tar Heel inquired. "We never heard anybody yell like that, and thought it was an infantry charge." The Ohioan tartly replied, "We learned it from the Indians."[55]

Wilson left the 1st Connecticut in place on the skirmish line, directing that the "left is a very important post and I must have a regiment that I can trust; the First Connecticut must stay all night." Sergeant Phillip Koempel of Company B noted in his diary that the regiment remained in line until 4:00 in the morning.[56] This assignment did not sit well with the men. "We felt grateful for the compliment but would have liked a cup of coffee better," one complained. That night, they buried Pvt. Frank Hiller of Company D, who was killed in the

---

51 Cardwell, "Where the Gallant Lieutenant Ford was Killed," 207; Shreve, "Reminiscences in the History of the Stuart Horse Artillery, C.S.A.," 304–5.
52 Gause, *Four Years in Five Armies*, 251.
53 "Connecticut," "The First Connecticut Cavalry."
54 H. W. Chester, *Recollections of the War of the Rebellion*, Alberta R. Adamson, Robert I. Girardi, and Roger E. Bohn, eds. (Wheaton, IL: Wheaton History Center, 1996), 81.
55 Gause, *Four Years in Five Armies*, 255.
56 Koempel, *Phil Koempel's Diary*, 8.

attack, as well as a captain and four enlisted Confederates. They also did what they could to care for wounded Southerners left on the field.[57] Another trooper of the 1st Connecticut noted, "We kept our skirmish line all night, a certain portion of the men dropping down right where they had been standing and sleeping there without supper or nourishment of any kind."[58]

Chapman's brigade rode over from Crump's Creek and joined them there, meaning the Third Division was in place to fulfill the rest of its assigned mission. "After dark, our brigade was ordered to Hanover Court-House, and we spent the principal portion of the night in marching and countermarching," Sgt. Samuel L. Gilpin, 3rd Indiana Cavalry, noted in his diary, "and we spent the principal portion of the night in marching and countermarching."[59]

"Just at night we drew rations and were busily engaged in getting supper, when we received orders to move, and consequently had to drop all and go," Sgt. Horace K. Ide, 1st Vermont Cavalry, recalled. "We marched about four miles, countermarched a short distance, part of us were cut off by the 3rd Indiana Cavalry, and finally came into line and laid down about midnight."[60]

Wilson had every reason to be pleased with the day's accomplishments—his plan of battle worked perfectly. He called it a "very handsome fight," stating in his diary: "Whipped rebels easily."[61] He reported to Humphreys that his men were "fatigued from their fighting today, and ammunition exhausted. I have therefore concluded to halt for the night, recruit men and horses, get ammunition and provisions, so as to push out at the first dawn of day" for the twin railroad bridges spanning the South Anna. He indicated that he intended to leave two regiments at Hanover Court House while he went to destroy the twin bridges with the rest of his division. He also requested that Humphreys send him powder and slow matches to use destroying the bridges, because he lacked the proper equipment to do so.[62]

During this operation, Wilson was completely out of touch with Sheridan and Cavalry Corps headquarters. He had received no orders from Sheridan and had no idea where the other two divisions of the corps were located or what they were doing. He had orders to carry out a difficult mission against what proved to be stout resistance, with

57 Blakeslee, "Addenda," 4.
58 "Connecticut," "The First Connecticut Cavalry."
59 Gilpin diary, entry for May 31, 1864.
60 Ide, *History of the First Vermont Cavalry Volunteers*, 172–73.
61 Wilson diary, entry for May 31, 1864.
62 *OR* 36, 3:414 and 872–73.

no realistic prospect of reinforcements if things went badly. Wilson was alone in enemy territory, a situation which understandably made him uncomfortable. "My instructions came directly from Meade's headquarters and necessarily left me in doubt as to everything except what concerned my command," he wrote years later.[63]

The beaten Confederates finally halted near Ashland, about seven miles away.[64] "When the night was well on the regiment retired on the road to Ashland, halting to sleep only an hour or two on the road, and were in the saddle again at four o'clock [a.m.]," Colonel Beale of the 9th Virginia Cavalry said. He noted that they marched to Wickham's plantation and formed a line of battle, but when no fight occurred, they returned to Ashland.[65]

Rooney Lee's men experienced an extremely difficult day. The North Carolina brigade suffered 3 men killed, 24 men wounded, and 15 men missing, for total losses of 42. Chambliss' brigade suffered 2 killed and 15 wounded, for total losses of 17 men, which meant the two brigades of Rooney Lee's division suffered 59 casualties in the short, sharp fight at Hanover Court House.[66]

Plenty of hard work awaited them the next day.

63 Wilson, *Under the Old Flag*, 1:431.
64 *OR* 36, 3:414 and 872–73.
65 Beale, *History of the Ninth Virginia Cavalry*, 126.
66 Young, *Lee's Army During the Overland Campaign*, 324–27.

The Old Cold Harbor intersection.

(Author's photo)

Chapter 10
May 31: Cold Harbor

General Lee recognized the strategic significance of the Old Cold Harbor intersection. He worried that a Union force might dash through Cold Harbor, turn the right flank of his Totopotomoy Creek line, press on to Mechanicsville or head across the Chickahominy River, then capture Richmond. The only Confederate forces holding the crucial intersection were Matthew Butler's and Martin Gary's battered rookie South Carolina cavalrymen, who had camped there after being routed at Matadequin Creek the evening before.

Butler recognized the weakness of his force and position. At 4:00 a.m. on May 31, he requested Jubal Early to send a regiment of infantry to reinforce his command. Early declined out of concern over weakening the line facing Warren's V Corps. He estimated the right of his II Corps "cannot be more than three miles from Cold Harbor, perhaps not that," and believed his troops were in position "to protect Mechanicsville," assuring that they "will do so." Early thought that enemy campfires indicated that Grant had moved a significant portion of the Army of the Potomac below Totopotomoy Creek and onto Shady Grove and Old Church roads. He also reported seeing "considerable light farther to [the] south, perhaps on the Matadequin lower down," which was probably from the campfires of "Baldy" Smith's XVIII Corps of the Army of the James, which had come from the south to reinforce the Army of the Potomac.[1]

General Lee lacked sufficient troops to withdraw any from his stout defensive position along Totopotomoy Creek. Luckily, General Beauregard, commanding the forces defending Richmond, had ordered Maj. Gen. Robert F. Hoke's division to march from Bermuda Hundred to reinforce the Army of Northern Virginia.[2] At 2:00 a.m.,

---

1 *OR* 51, 2:974.
2 Robert F. Hoke was born in Lincolnton, North Carolina, on May 27, 1837, as the son of a successful businessman and Democratic politician. He was educated in local schools and at the Kentucky Military Institute. By age 17, he was managing the family's iron works, cotton mill, and other businesses. He entered Confederate service as a second lieutenant in 1861, joining the 1st North Carolina Infantry. He performed so well at the regiment's first engagement, the battle of Big Bethel, that he was praised for his performance. He was promoted to major of the 1st North Carolina and then to lieutenant colonel of the 33rd North Carolina. In the spring of 1862, Hoke led five companies of the 33rd in hard combat at the March 14 battle of New Bern, and he assumed command of the regiment when its colonel was captured.

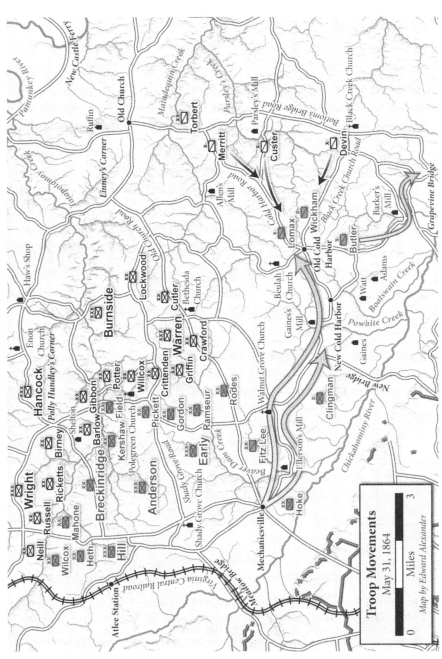

Troop Movements
May 31, 1864

Maj. Gen. Robert F. Hoke, commander, Hoke's Division, Defenses of Richmond.

(Valentine Museum)

The 33rd then joined A. P. Hill's "Light Division." Hoke led it throughout multiple engagements: Seven Days, Cedar Mountain, Second Bull Run, South Mountain, and Antietam. He was then promoted to colonel and command of the 21st North Carolina. At Fredericksburg, Virginia, he temporarily led Brig. Gen. Isaac Trimble's brigade, leading a critical counterattack that sealed a gap in the Confederate lines. He was promoted to brigadier general on April 23, 1863 and assumed permanent command of Trimble's brigade. He was wounded during the battle of Chancellorsville and returned to North Carolina. His command forced the surrender of the Union garrison at Plymouth, North Carolina, in April 1864, and he was promoted to major general on April 23. He remained with the Army of Northern Virginia through the fall of 1864. In November, he returned to North Carolina and participated in the war's final campaign. He lived for nearly 50 years after the war, and served as a director of the North Carolina Railroad Company. He died in Raleigh, North Carolina, on July 3, 1912, and was buried there. Hoke was an able division commander who was esteemed by his peers. Jeffry D. Wert, "Robert Frederick Hoke," included in William C. Davis and Julie Hoffman, eds., *The Confederate General*, 6 vols. (New York: National Historical Society, 1991), 3:114–15. For a full-length biography of Hoke, see Daniel W. Barefoot, *General Robert F. Hoke: Lee's Modest Warrior* (Winston-Salem, NC: John F. Blair Publisher, 1996).

Hoke's 6,800 men started off, Brig. Gen. Thomas L. Clingman's brigade leading the way.[3] They boarded rail cars that carried them as close to Cold Harbor as possible, then marched the rest of the way.[4]

Clingman's brigade got far ahead of Hoke's other three brigades, so Hoke ordered Clingman to halt about three miles from Cold Harbor and wait for the rest of the division to catch up. While Clingman's men waited alongside the road, the other three brigades, commanded by brigadier generals James G. Martin, Alfred Colquitt, and Johnson Hagood, struggled to catch up. "The day was exceedingly hot, the pike entirely without shade, and the men suffering for water," Hagood, whose column brought up the rear of Hoke's division, recalled. The column inched its way toward Cold Harbor in the stifling heat.[5]

The battered South Carolina cavalrymen hoped they could hold on until reinforcements arrived. They were in bad shape from the vicious fight along Matadequin Creek the day before leading Private Edward Wells of the Charleston Light Dragoons to remark that after their battlefield ordeal, his comrades "were certainly very unlike the idea given in fiction of the 'dashing Dragoon.'" They built a crude

---

3 Thomas Lanier Clingman was born in Huntersville, North Carolina, on July 27, 1812. He served as a U.S. Representative from 1843 to 1845 and as a U.S. Senator from 1847 to 1861, changing from unionist Whig to secessionist Democrat. Even after Abraham Lincoln's inauguration, he continued to attend Senate sessions, finally withdrawing without resigning on March 28, 1861. The Senate expelled him on July 11. By then he was serving as an aide to Gen. Joseph E. Johnston in Virginia. Previously, he had witnessed the fall of Fort Sumter, South Carolina, and served as North Carolina's emissary to the Confederacy. However, in September, the North Carolina assembly did not re-elect him Senator. On August 15, 1861, he was appointed colonel of the 25th North Carolina Infantry and then re-elected after its reorganization in April 1862. Although he lacked military training or experience, he was commissioned a brigadier general on May 17, 1862. He assumed command of a brigade in North Carolina and remained there for most of the war, operating in a backwater area. In the spring of 1864, his command was transferred to Virginia and assigned to Hoke's division, and he performed poorly at the job. He was severely wounded at Globe Tavern on August 19, 1864 and was disabled for more than seven months. He did not rejoin his command until after the battle of Bentonville in the final days of the war. The U.S. Senate rejected his attempt to reclaim his seat, so he practiced law, explored North Carolina's mountains, and discovered mineral resources. He died on November 3, 1897, and was buried in Asheville, North Carolina. Richard J. Sommers, "Thomas Lanier Clingman," included in William C. Davis and Julie Hoffman, eds., *The Confederate General*, 6 vols. (New York: National Historical Society, 1991), 1:202–5.

4 Thomas L. Clingman, "Second Cold Harbor," included in Walter Clark, ed., *Histories of the Several Regiments and Battalions from North Carolina in the Great War, 1861–65*, 5 vols. (Raleigh: E. M. Uzzell, 1901), 5:197.

5 Johnson Hagood, *Memoirs of the War of Secession* (Columbia, SC: The State Co., 1910), 254–55.

barricade of fence rails across Cold Harbor Road in case Sheridan decided to sortie that way from yesterday's battlefield.[6]

Worried about the inexperienced South Carolinians' ability to fend off another determined Union cavalry thrust, General Lee ordered his nephew Fitzhugh Lee to relieve them with his veteran troopers. Midmorning, while Clingman's men rested on the same road, Fitz Lee's two brigades marched to Cold Harbor from their campsite near Mechanicsville, arriving at the Cold Harbor intersection about noon. "Road strewn with cavalry equipment and hatless dragoons," Fitz Lee's adjutant Ferguson sneered upon observing the residue of the previous night's debacle.[7] While Fitz Lee's veterans deployed to defend the intersection, Butler rode south with his Palmetto men to an area near Bottoms Bridge on the Chickahominy River to rest and recuperate.[8] Fitz Lee deployed Lomax's brigade east across Cold Harbor Road to block the road from Old Church and placed Wickham's brigade across another road that angled southeast toward Black Creek Church on the Bottom's Bridge Road. Major Breathed deployed two batteries of horse artillery—those of captains John J. Shoemaker and Philip P. Johnston—to support the hasty earthworks the Virginia horse soldiers had dug.[9] Fitz Lee's cavalry and Breathed's horse artillery now stood squarely between Sheridan and the coveted road intersection.

*　　　　*　　　　*

Torbert's cavalrymen got an early start on May 31. "Reveille sounded at two in the morning," Capt. Charles McK. Loeser, 2nd U.S. Cavalry, recalled. "At half past two we were ordered on picket."[10] "We saddled up at 3 o'clock next morning, and stood to horse until 5 p.m.," Chaplain Samuel L. Gracey, the regimental historian of the 6th Pennsylvania Cavalry, recorded.[11] "The weather was very warm and the roads were many inches deep with dust," a trooper of the 6th New York Cavalry remarked.[12] The Northern horsemen had a long day ahead of them.

Brigadier generals George Custer and Wesley Merritt were concerned that the Confederate cavalry intended to resume its offensive of May 30, and so was Phil Sheridan. All wanted to seize the initiative and go on the offensive themselves. Torbert called upon his brigade commanders that morning, visiting Custer first at his

---

6 Wells, *Charleston Light Dragoons*, 56; "Orlando," "Butler's Cavalry."
7 Ferguson Memorandum.
8 "Orlando," "Butler's Cavalry."
9 Fitzhugh Lee's Report, Archives, Museum of the Confederacy, Richmond, Virginia.
10 Loeser, "Loeser's Recollections," 310.
11 Gracey, *Annals of the Sixth Pennsylvania Cavalry*, 255.
12 Hall, *History of the Sixth New York Cavalry*, 194.

headquarters near Parsley's Mill. Together, Torbert and Custer devised a two-pronged assault on the Cold Harbor intersection: Merritt, followed by Custer, would attack west along the Cold Harbor Road, while Devin would attack along Black Creek Church Road, cutting northwest into Cold Harbor. If possible, Devin would work his way around Fitz Lee's southern flank and capture his entire division's horses, which were tethered behind the Confederate battle line.[13]

Torbert took the plan to Sheridan for approval, and the corps commander ordered its "immediate execution," which he noted in his memoirs.[14] Sheridan shared the concern that "the enemy meditated an attack on the First Division of cavalry posted [one-and-a-half] miles from Cold Harbor, so I gave permission to General Torbert to attack them."[15] Sheridan also ordered Gregg's division to support Torbert, but they failed to arrive in time to join the fighting.[16] Devin questioned the wisdom of this plan, but Torbert maintained that it offered "an excellent opportunity to strike the enemy a severe blow," and ordered the attack for 3:00 that afternoon.[17]

The attack started as scheduled, Merritt and Custer heading west on the Cold Harbor Road while Devin headed northwest toward Cold Harbor on Black Creek Church Road. Before long, Merritt's vanguard encountered Fitz Lee's scouts, who scampered back to Cold Harbor to warn of the approaching Union cavalry. Fitz Lee immediately alerted his uncle that "The enemy are advancing on this place. Nothing but cavalry discovered so far." He assured General Lee that he was "prepared to dispute their progress," and reported that Clingman's brigade of Hoke's division had halted about three miles away. "Had they not better be ordered on to assist in securing this place?" Fitz Lee asked, reasonably. A galloper carried this message to General Lee, who had been expecting a Federal thrust toward Cold Harbor; he responded immediately, ordering Hoke to send Clingman's brigade on to Cold Harbor to reinforce Fitz's cavalrymen.[18]

Merritt's Reserve Brigade drove Fitz's pickets west along Cold Harbor Road. As they neared Cold Harbor, Lomax's dismounted troopers, ensconced behind their fence-rail barricades and supported by horse artillery, opened a withering fire, stopping Merritt's advance in its tracks. Merritt dismounted his troopers and deployed them facing Lomax's brigade: the 5th U.S. Cavalry on the left, the 1st New York Dragoons in the middle, and the 6th Pennsylvania Cavalry on the

13 *OR* 36, 1:794 and 805.
14 Sheridan, *Personal Memoirs*, 1:405.
15 *OR* 36, 1:783.
16 Ibid., 794.
17 Ibid., 805.
18 Ibid., 3:858.

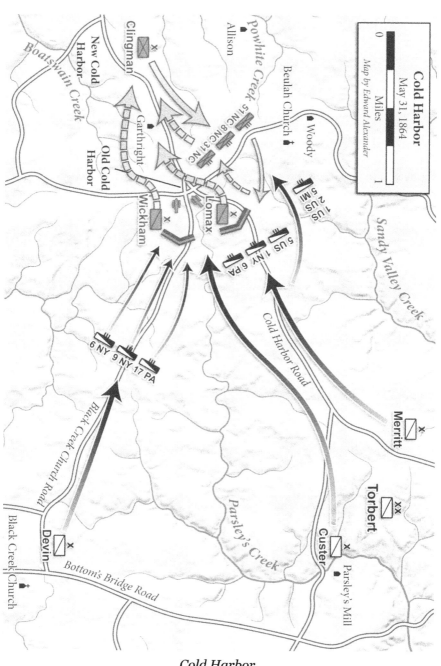

Cold Harbor
May 31, 1864

right.[19] Lomax's defenses caused the Federals to pause. "They had constructed strong breastworks of logs across each of the roads, and had artillery in a favorable position to sweep the road," one of Custer's men recounted. "Our men had to advance up a steep rise of ground entirely unprotected and attack infantry and dismounted cavalry behind works with about equal numbers."[20]

While Merritt's men tangled with Lomax's, Devin's brigade marched along the Black Creek Church Road, which angled closer to the Cold Harbor Road as it neared Cold Harbor, enabling Devin to communicate with Custer. Custer deployed Major Kidd's 6th Michigan Cavalry to repel the Confederate pickets and then seal the gap between the two roads.[21] About two miles from Cold Harbor, Devin's scouts made contact with Kidd's pickets, and pressed on. They spotted what appeared to be Confederate pickets, so the troopers halted. A reconnaissance, however, revealed that they had encountered, not Confederates, but rather members of the 5th Michigan Cavalry. Devin ordered Col. Russell A. Alger, commanding the 5th Michigan, to clear the road and move to the right. They did so, and Devin's column resumed its advance.[22]

About a mile farther on, the New Yorkers began skirmishing with Wickham's pickets, discovering the Virginians were ensconced behind works.[23] The advance guard of Wickham's brigade awaited them behind barricades of logs and brush across Black Creek Church Road. Devin's troopers heard the fighting between Lomax's and Merritt's men to the north, so they knew a fight was underway. Devin dismounted the 17th Pennsylvania Cavalry, sending it off to the right to try to flank the advance barricade. After a short firefight, the Pennsylvanians enfiladed Wickham's position, forced the Virginians back, and opened a hole in the barricade to allow the rest of the brigade to pass through.[24]

Devin soon reached Wickham's main barricade, where the dismounted troopers of the 17th Pennsylvania and 9th New York had a heavy fight with Wickham's Virginians, who had the advantage of holding terrain that allowed for a good defensive position. "This engagement was one of the most hotly contested fights we ever had," a

19 Ibid., 1:805; Bowen, *First New York Dragoons*, 174–77.
20 "Custer's Cavalry Brigade," *Detroit Advertiser and Tribune*, June 16, 1864.
21 *OR* Supplement, 6:621–22.
22 *OR* 36, 1:839.
23 Kidd, *Personal Recollections*, 331.
24 *OR* 36, 1:839. Devin mistakenly claimed that he connected with the 5th Michigan Cavalry, but those pickets were Kidd's, not Alger's.

Pennsylvanian recalled, "the command losing heavily."[25] Sergeant Joseph McCabe of the 17th Pennsylvania stated, "We had to cross an open field, and in doing so the regiment lost a number in killed and wounded. I made a very narrow escape myself; had quite a large hole shot through my hat while crossing the field."[26]

Keeping to Torbert's plan, Devin ordered the 6th New York to pass around the lower end of Wickham's line to attempt capturing Fitz Lee's horses, but the New Yorkers quickly discovered that the position was strongly defended.[27] Captain William Heermance's men of the 6th New York held the end of Devin's line. Heermance went into a nearby house and helped

Capt. William Heermance of the 6th New York Cavalry. Heermance was a Medal of Honor recipient.

(USAHEC)

himself to a chair, which he then brought out to the line. Almost as soon as he put the chair down, a hail of bullets rained down, prompting Heermance to seek shelter. No sooner had he left the chair than a bullet passed through it. Heermance's luck had held again—he had not yet been wounded in battle, despite many close calls.[28]

"The dust was suffocating and blinding whilst the whispering ball and whizzing shell were not at all soothing," Lt. Robert T. Hubard Jr., 3rd Virginia Cavalry, remarked. While Hubard sat on his horse to the right of the 3rd Virginia and the left of the 4th Virginia, watching the fighting unfold, a half-spent cannonball came bounding along, striking and breaking the hind leg of a horse belonging to a 4th Virginia trooper, before soaring high in the air near Hubard.[29]

25 Moyer, *Seventeenth Regiment Pennsylvania Volunteer Cavalry*, 341. Devin reported that the 17th Pennsylvania lost 30 men in just half an hour. *OR* 36, 1:839.
26 Ibid.
27 *OR* 36, 1:839. Torbert was displeased with Devin's performance on May 31, stating in his after-action report, "[I]t does not appear that a very serious effort was made to carry out my designs." Ibid., 822.
28 Heermance to his wife, June 5, 1864.
29 Nanzig, *The Civil War Memoirs of a Virginia Cavalryman*, 168.

Brig. Gen. Thomas L Clingman, commander, Clingman's Brigade, Hoke's Division, Defenses of Richmond.

(Medford Historical Society, Medford, MA)

About this time, Major General Hoke arrived at the Cold Harbor intersection and quickly surveyed the situation before ordering Clingman and his North Carolinians to the battlefield. As the Tar Heels arrived, Hoke ordered them to deploy on Fitz Lee's left, extending his line north toward Beulah Church. Lieutenant Colonel Charles W. Knight's 31st North Carolina Infantry formed on Lomax's flank, Lieutenant Colonel John R. Murchison's 8th North Carolina Infantry connected to Knight's left, and Col. Hector McKethan's 51st North Carolina deployed to Murchison's left. After approving the deployments, Hoke ordered Clingman to advance the 51st North Carolina 500 yards to the front and left of the Confederate main battle line to support a detachment of Lomax's dismounted cavalry.

Although very brave and patriotic, Clingman was not known for his military brilliance. A historian of his home county painted an unflattering picture of him, calling Clingman "an intrepid man of most arrogant and aggressive character, greatest self-confidence, unlimited assurance, prodigious conceit, stupendous aspiration, immense claims, more than common ability, no considerable attainments or culture, great boastfulness and much curiosity."[30] Clingman remained with the 51st North Carolina because he was concerned that being so far out in front of the main line of battle left McKethan's regiment dangerously exposed.[31]

Custer and his Wolverines arrived about that time, bringing the entire First Cavalry Division on the field. The Wolverines connected Merritt's line to Devin's. Clingman's foot soldiers held the left of the Confederate position, facing Merritt, Lomax's dismounted troopers

---

30 Forster A. Sondley, *A History of Buncombe County*, 2 vols. (Asheville, NC: Advocate Print Co., 1930), 2:406.
31 Clingman, "Second Cold Harbor," 197–98.

held the center, facing Merritt and some of Custer's men, and Wickham's brigade occupied the Confederate right, facing the rest of the Wolverines and Devin. Merritt and Custer made several unsuccessful attempts to dislodge Lomax and Clingman.[32] "The fire from this barricade was about as hot as any I ever was under," Lt. Edward Granger of Custer's staff reported, "[and] it was hard work to get the men up."[33] The 1st New York Dragoons pushed into the field across from the Confederates, and heavy volleys delivered at close range repulsed them. "It has always seemed a marvel how any of us survived," one of the Dragoons observed, "for the shower of lead was simply terrific."[34]

Meanwhile, a battalion of Custer's 1st Michigan attempted a mounted charge that also failed. "No sooner had they come within range," a New Yorker who witnessed the attack said, "than the rebels poured volley after volley into them, and unable to withstand it, they broke." Because the Confederates held a strong position on high ground, they "had decidedly the advantage, and could shoot us down like turkeys in a pen, which our shots were ineffective," a member of the 1st New York Dragoons admitted.[35] After these attacks failed, Merritt concluded he could not overrun Lomax and Clingman "without great loss, if at all."[36] Devin, who was supposed to turn the Confederate right, faced a similar situation in front of Wickham's barricades.

With this plan stymied, Torbert came up with a new scheme. While most of his men pinned the Southerners in place, a detachment would try to pass around the northern end of the Confederate army's line and turn its flank. Once they turned their flank and forced the Rebels to withdraw, the main Union force would attack. Torbert chose Merritt to lead the flank attack, which would consist of the 1st and 2nd U.S. cavalries of the Reserve Brigade and the 5th Michigan of Custer's brigade. The remaining regiments of those two brigades—the 1st New York Dragoons, the 6th Pennsylvania Cavalry of the Reserve Brigade, and the 1st, 6th, and 7th Michigan of Custer's brigade—were to demonstrate loudly, in order to pin the Confederates in place.[37]

The plan worked perfectly. While the 6th Pennsylvania and 1st New York Dragoons kept the enemy pinned down in front, the Regulars made their flanking movement. Captain Samuel McKee, 29

32 *OR* 36, 1:848.
33 Barnard, *An Aide to Custer*, 243.
34 Bowen, *First New York Dragoons*, 176–77.
35 Ibid.
36 *OR* 36, 1:848.
37 Ibid., 805, 822, and 848–49.

years old and a West Point graduate, commanded a battalion of the 1st U.S. Cavalry that day.[38] McKee, whom Merritt described as a "gallant" and "accomplished soldier," and his battalion, along with the 2nd U.S. Cavalry, turned the enemy flank, and while "advancing under a galling fire from infantry and cavalry" the Regulars captured nearly 100 prisoners. Captain George B. Sanford of the 1st U.S. Cavalry served on Torbert's staff and was McKee's close friend. Sanford was standing next to McKee when McKee when a bullet struck McKee just above the elbow, breaking his arm. McKee did not fall, "and I supposed for a moment that the injury though serious and painful in the extreme would be confined to the loss of his arm," Sanford recalled. "When however he told me that the ball had gone through the arm and into his side, I knew it all over with him."[39] The wound—a shot through the

---

38 Samuel McKee was born in St Louis, Missouri, in 1835. In 1854, 19-year-old McKee was appointed to the United States Military Academy while living in Utah and graduated 13th in the class of 1858. Upon graduation, he was initially appointed as a brevet second lieutenant of mounted rifles and served his first assignment at the Cavalry School for Practice at Carlisle Barracks, Pennsylvania. He was transferred to the 1st Dragoons on June 22, 1859; he was promoted to second lieutenant in the 1st Dragoons on January 9, 1860 and served with the parts of the regiment at Fort Tejon, California. McKee was promoted to first lieutenant on May 7, and he was appointed regimental adjutant on August 7th. He was relieved as adjutant when he was promoted to captain on November 14, with McKee in command of Company B. He participated in the spring's fighting on the Peninsula, distinguishing himself in the skirmish at Williamsburg on May 4. The following month, he departed on a leave of absence to serve as lieutenant colonel for the 77th New York Volunteer Infantry, but he rejoined the 1st Cavalry in September, in time for the Antietam campaign. He participated in the 1863 Stoneman's Raid and the Gettysburg campaign. He served prominently at Todd's Tavern and during the fighting in Sheridan's May 1864 Richmond Raid. McKee was buried with his wife in Los Angeles, California. He was well remembered by peers and superiors alike. Captain George Sanford, 1st U.S. Cavalry, said that McKee's death "cut short a most promising career and deprived the regiment of one of the finest and best loved officers who ever followed its colors." His brigade commander, Brig. Gen. Wesley Merritt, called him "a pure, unaffected, moderate man, a chivalrous, educated, accomplished soldier." Brigadier General Alfred T. A. Torbert, McKee's division commander, wrote, "[A] more gallant and accomplished soldier has not given his life for his bleeding country." George W. Cullum, *Biographical Register of the Officers and Graduates of the U.S. Military Academy at West Point, N.Y., from Its Establishment, in 1802, to 1890*, 3rd ed., 3 vols. (Boston: Houghton Mifflin, 1891), 3:704–5; F. A. Jordan, "A Forgotten Captain," *Los Angeles Herald*, April 3, 1910; Hageman. *Fighting Rebels and Redskins*, 239; *OR* 36, 1:806, 814, and 849.

39 Hagemann, *Fighting Rebels and Redskins*, 239. Sanford and another officer visited McKee at the hospital that night. The surgeons had amputated the shattered arm, but it was clear that the captain would not survive. He was too sedated to recognize the two officers. McKee died that night. Ibid.

40 *OR* 36, 1:849. Lieutenant Charles H. Veil of the 1st U.S. Cavalry recalled that McKee "had taken a fancy to me. Whenever we started out in a fight,

lungs—was indeed mortal. Merritt described the loss of McKee as "incalculable."[40]

Merritt proudly declared, "Here was accomplished a work of which everyone connected with the brigade is justly proud—a success by cavalry which has no parallel in the war—a single brigade contending with and taking from the enemy at least three times its numbers, one-third infantry, a naturally strong position, made doubly strong by artificial means."[41]

The Regulars made their way around the far left of Clingman's brigade, the exposed 51st North Carolina, which was well out in front of the main line of battle. As the flank attack kicked off, Confederate cavalry to the left of the 51st North Carolina pulled out, exposing the Tar Heels' left flank. Clingman directed two companies to reinforce the 51st North Carolina, but the officer in charge of this little force "acted badly," according to Clingman, and "kept his men lying down." Before long, Lomax's line began to crumble, and his troopers fled by squads, "alleging that their ammunition had given out," leaving Clingman to pull the 51st North Carolina back from its exposed position and attempt to reform his brigade along a fence.[42]

Clingman himself had a close call. "As I was retiring to point out the several positions each regiment was to occupy, a portion of a shell took away the front of my hat and slightly wounded my forehead," he declared. "Though somewhat stunned for an instant, I was not disabled at all, but observed that all the cavalry in reserve on my right had likewise retired."[43]

The Wolverines of the 5th Michigan also advanced, with Custer riding behind the line as they went. "As our men reached the crest of the slope, the rebels poured in a destructive fire from the front." Staff officers steadied the dismounted Michigan men, who pressed on. Custer then ordered Maj. Melvin Brewer, commanding a battalion of the 1st Michigan Cavalry, to draw sabers and charge across the field in front, hoping to drive the enemy through the woods on the far side.[44] Putting spurs to their horses, the Wolverines surged forward. "This charge produced the desired effect," Custer reported. "The enemy,

Sam would say, 'Come on, Veil.' We had a habit of always humming some tune or another whenever an engagement was on and today, as he was doing so while we were fighting on foot, he was shot through the lungs." Herman J. Viola, ed., *The Memoirs of Charles Henry Veil: A Soldier's Recollections of the Civil War and the Arizona Territories* (New York: Orion Books, 1993), 44.
41 Ibid.
42 Clingman, "Second Cold Harbor," 198; *OR* 36, 1:805, 822, and 848–49.
43 Clingman, "Second Cold Harbor," 198.
44 Davis, *I Rode with Custer*, 106.

without waiting to receive it, threw down their arms and fled, leaving their dead and wounded on the field."[45] The Wolverines wedged in between the 8th and 51st North Carolina, hitting the 8th North Carolina hardest.[46]

As the flank attack succeeded, Lt. Col. Thomas J. Thorp and Maj. Rufus Scott of the 1st New York Dragoons told their men that the hill had to be taken and led the advance. "It has always seemed a marvel how any of us escaped alive, for the shower of lead was simply terrific," the Dragoons' historian recalled. "But we went up the hill and up to the breastworks, pouring an irresistible fire into their ranks," routing the defenders. A Dragoon watched "many hand to hand struggles" play out as the dismounted Northern cavalrymen jumped over Lomax's breastworks and into the now-panicked defenders. Major Scott was wounded while leading this assault.[47]

"We drove the enemy from his works by a determined charge," the 6th Pennsylvania Cavalry historian recounted. "As we were ordered to hold this position, our fight was even more desperate than [at Matadequin Creek]." Lieutenant Arthur Murphy, regimental adjutant of the 6th Pennsylvania, was killed while encouraging the men on the skirmish line.[48]

The 6th Virginia Cavalry of Lomax's brigade "was on picket at the time, and that the enemy, succeeding in getting in its rear by a flank movement, delivered their fire at a distance of ten yards," a Richmond newspaper reported. "Our men maintained their fire until their ammunition was exhausted, and then cut their way through, bringing off their wounded," which included brash, fearless, hard-drinking, and hard-fighting 23-year-old Maj. Cabell E. Flournoy, the commander of the 6th Virginia Cavalry, who was killed in this fighting. Despite his derring-do, Flournoy had somehow avoided being wounded before this point—his luck finally ran out on May 31, 1864.[49]

45 *OR* 36, 1:822; "The Michigan Cavalry Brigade"; "The Michigan Cavalry Brigade," *Detroit Free Press*, June 15, 1864.
46 Clingman, "Second Cold Harbor," 199.
47 Bowen, *First New York Dragoons*, 177 and 179.
48 Gracey, *Annals of the Sixth Pennsylvania Cavalry*, 255.
49 Fitzhugh Lee's report; "The War News," *Richmond Daily Dispatch*, June 2, 1864; William R. Carter to his father, June 1, 1864, Carter Family Papers, Archives, Library of Virginia, Richmond, Virginia. Cabell Edward Flournoy was born on June 30, 1840, in Halifax County, the son of Thomas Stanhope Flournoy, a prominent attorney and one-term Congressman who later became the colonel of the 6th Virginia Cavalry. He attended Washington College, and then resided in Pittsylvania County. He was appointed captain of Company E, 6th Virginia Cavalry on May 27, 1861, and major on July 15, 1862. Flournoy was buried in the family cemetery in Halifax County. Krick, Lee's Colonels, 142. It is unclear what Flournoy's rank was at this time. Some primary source accounts indicate that he was a major, but others indicate that he was a

Clingman's and Lomax's collapse in turn exposed Wickham's flank. Seeing an opportunity, Devin ordered his brigade to attack, which broke Wickham's line and sent it flying. Clingman and Fitz Lee retired to high ground about a mile west of Cold Harbor, where they began cobbling together a new line, running generally north to south across the Cold Harbor Road. The pursuing Federal cavalry cut off some of Clingman's panicked infantry, capturing about 100 men.[50]

Fitz Lee lost about 80 men in the day's fighting. After a hard, intense day of combat, more work remained for the weary, famished Virginians of Fitz's division. "Fought till dark, hardest kind of fighting," John Woodall of the 2nd Virginia Cavalry complained in his diary that night. "Nothing for ourselves or our horses to eat. So ends the month of May. Most active month we have had."[51]

With night setting in, Torbert decided to end the pursuit and had his men dig in and prepare their positions at Cold Harbor. His tired troopers occupied the breastworks constructed by Fitz Lee's men, which they reversed so that they faced the opposite direction to defend against a Confederate counterattack. They were isolated and exposed, far from the main body of the Army of the Potomac. "Sheridan's cavalry were now holding Cold Harbor without support, Meade's infantry being nine miles away," a member of the 9th New York Cavalry observed.[52] They risked being cut off and captured if the Confederates became aggressive.

A mile west, Fitz Lee's troopers and Clingman's North Carolina infantrymen dug new works on their low ridge. Fortunately, more of Hoke's infantry arrived from Mechanicsville to extend their line of battle. As darkness fell, Clingman's 61st North Carolina arrived, as did Brigadier General Colquitt's brigade of Georgia infantry, and both formed in line next to Clingman's right. "We dug and shoveled dirt all night finishing our fortifications," trooper Rufus H. Peck of Company C, 2nd Virginia Cavalry stated. "Some would work while others slept and then they would wake up the sleepers and they'd go to work while the others slept."[53]

Fitz Lee wanted to counterattack before Torbert could prepare his position at Cold Harbor, but darkness forced Fitz to call off his

---

colonel, such as the Richmond Daily Dispatch article cited above. Fitz Lee's adjutant, Maj. James D. Ferguson, gave Flournoy's rank as major in his memorandum of the summer's campaigns, so I have elected to indicate that Flournoy was a major at the time of his death.

50 Clingman, "Second Cold Harbor," 198–99.

51 Woodall diary, entry for May 31, 1864.

52 Cheney, *History of the Ninth Regiment*, 179.

53 Rufus H. Peck, *Reminiscences of a Confederate Soldier of Company C, 2nd Virginia Cavalry* (Fincastle, VA: privately published, 1913), 50.

planned attack. Instead, his horse soldiers spent an unhappy night bivouacking south of Cold Harbor Road, just off the end of the Confederates' new line of battle.[54]

After dark, Sheridan reported that he had seized Cold Harbor, but that he did not know what to do next. He pointed out that his men had captured about 60 of Clingman's men, which meant that his troopers fought more than just cavalry that day. His scouts reported that Colquitt's brigade had arrived and was digging in alongside Clingman, and other prisoners told him that Maj. Gen. Joseph Kershaw's division of the Army of Northern Virginia was moving between the V Corps at Bethesda Church and Sheridan's right. "I do not feel able to hold this place, and have directed General Torbert to resume his position of this morning," Little Phil informed headquarters. "Lee's line of battle is in front of Mechanicsville, and, with the heavy odds against me here, I do not think it prudent to hold on," because the Confederate line extended south across the Chickahominy to protect the bridges over it.[55]

After conferring with Grant, Meade ordered infantry to go to Cold Harbor. He decided to also to send the VI Corps, which would take time, and Grant also directed Baldy Smith to march for Cold Harbor with the XVIII Corps, meaning two Union infantry corps would be there by morning. Recognizing the significance of the road intersection, Meade scribbled an order for Sheridan to hold Cold Harbor at all costs and sent a galloper to find the cavalry chief.

However, Sheridan had other ideas. His isolated command was nine miles from the nearest Union infantry, and Grant had not expected the cavalry to capture and hold Cold Harbor.[56] Having gotten no response to his dispatch, and with no idea that Cold Harbor had taken on great significance to army headquarters, Sheridan saw no point in telling Torbert to hold the place against enemy infantry to protect an insignificant road intersection. About 10:00 p.m., Torbert's troopers swung into their saddles and moved off to the east, headed back toward the previous night's camps.

Just as the end of Torbert's column rode off, Meade's galloper arrived with the order to hold Cold Harbor at all hazards. Sheridan immediately ordered Torbert to turn his command around and head

---

54 Fitzhugh Lee's report; Ferguson Memorandum; Clingman, "Second Cold Harbor," 198–99.
55 *OR* 36, 3:411.
56 Charles D. Rhodes, *History of the Cavalry of the Army of the Potomac, Including that of the Army of Virginia (Pope's), and also the History of the Operations of the Federal Cavalry in West Virginia During the War* (Kansas City, MO: Hudson-Kimberly Publishing Co., 1900), 118.

back to Cold Harbor.[57] Captain Charles Mck. Loeser, 2nd U.S. Cavalry, sniffed at the danger. "There seemed to me no great hazard about the matter, inasmuch as the march, which occupied all night, owing to the condition of the road and the darkness, was accomplished without meeting any opposition."[58]

Torbert dispatched Lt. Robert C. Wallace of the 5th Michigan Cavalry to find Devin and tell him to return to Cold Harbor. "It was a lonesome ride on a dark night and over the ground where the fighting took place, with the dead lying about where they had fallen," Wallace remembered with a shudder. "In passing the little schoolhouse that had been used as a hospital, where I had seen a pile of arms and legs that reached almost up to the window, a sort of chill crept up my spine and the surrounding were not cheerful." While that was unnerving, Wallace worried that Devin's men might mistake him for a Confederate and open fire. Fortunately, that concern was unfounded. "I finally came upon the outer vidette sitting his horse under a tree and sound asleep," Wallace said, relieved. "The road was soft and muddy and I had come upon him quietly and had to touch him before he awoke. Men were almost worn out and there was some excuse for the man being asleep on his post."[59]

Sometime after midnight, the weary blue-clad horsemen arrived at the Old Cold Harbor intersection, hid their horses in the shelter of the woods, filed back into Fitz Lee's works, and finished preparing them to receive an attack from the other direction.[60] Some of the breastworks had to be reconstructed in order to suit the features of the terrain.[61] "It was done so quietly," Torbert proudly claimed, "that I do not believe the enemy knew that I had, for a time, withdrawn from their front."[62] Major Kidd of the 6th Michigan reported, "[D]uring that night, we were engaged in throwing up breastworks, having received notice that the cavalry were ordered to hold [Cold Harbor] until the infantry could come up."[63]

"The first thing General Sheridan did was to dismount the command and send the horses to the rear," Lt. Charles H. Veil, 1st U.S. Cavalry, recalled. "Then we occupied the line of breastworks the enemy had held, distributed boxes of ammunition along our line, and lay waiting for daylight."[64]

57 Ibid., 794.
58 Loeser, "Loeser's Recollections," 310.
59 Wallace, *A Few Memories of a Long Life*, 58.
60 Hagemann, *Fighting Rebels and Redskins*, 240.
61 Cheney, *History of the Ninth Regiment*, 180.
62 *OR* 36, 1:806.
63 *OR Supplement*, 6:622.
64 Viola, *The Memoirs of Charles Henry Veil*, 44.

"Why the infantry should not have been put at this we could not see," Captain Sanford declared, "more especially as they had not done anything for several days, but there was no mercy for the cavalry as long as Gen. Meade controlled matters." The weary, hungry horse soldiers spent a long night marching and constructing barricades.[65]

Sheridan watched as his played-out men did their work. "The troops, without reserves, were then placed behind our cover dismounted, boxes of ammunition distributed along the line, and the order passed along that the place must be held," he stated. "All this was done in the darkness, and while we were working away at our cover the enemy could be distinctly heard from our skirmish line giving commands and making preparations to attack."[66] Exhausted men fell asleep still grasping their bridle reins.[67] Knowing they faced a large force of enemy infantry that had spent the night preparing to assault the Union cavalry's position, would they be able to hang on long enough for infantry reinforcements to arrive?

In the meantime, General Lee remained worried that Grant could turn the flank of his Totopotomoy Creek line from Cold Harbor. He had already sent two divisions there, but he now also ordered Maj. Gen. Richard H. Anderson's I Corps to withdraw from Totopotomoy Creek and march to Cold Harbor, concentrating sufficient troops to cover the Army of Northern Virginia's flank. Colonel Edward Porter Alexander, the I Corps' artillery chief, believed that General Lee's hope "was that our corps should move by night to the vicinity of Cold Harbor, where it was to unite with Hoke's division and crush Sheridan's cavalry. Then it was to wheel around to the left and come down on the flank and rear of Grant's fortified line. Once fairly started, success might mean the driving of Grant back to the Pamunkey."[68] This was a lot to hope for, and there does not appear to be any corroborating evidence supporting Alexander's claim.

Nevertheless, Sheridan's movement on Cold Harbor, triggered by his fear that the Confederates were going to attack him, meant this obscure road intersection was about to become the primary focus of both armies.

---

65 Hagemann, *Fighting Rebels and Redskins*, 240.
66 Sheridan, *Personal Memoirs*, 1:407–8.
67 *Regimental History of the First New York Dragoons*, 12.
68 Gary W. Gallagher, ed., *Fighting for the Confederacy: The Personal Recollections of General Edward Porter Alexander* (Chapel Hill: University of North Carolina Press, 1989), 398.

Chapter 11
June 1: The Battle of Ashland

Before daylight on June 1, Lt. Col. Erastus Blakeslee of the 1st Connecticut Cavalry detailed a work party to procure ammunition for his regiment.[1] Hours later, they returned empty-handed, so Blakeslee dispatched another detail. When they too returned empty-handed, he called for Lt. Henry T. Phillips of Company A to go on the same mission, insisting, "Do not return without ammunition." Phillips and a few other men rode away, and returned with sufficient ammunition to supply each of the regiment's troopers with 40 rounds. They would need all 40.[2]

Brigadier General Wilson had his Third Cavalry Division saddled and moving early on the morning of July 1. His orders were to destroy the twin railroad bridges over the South Anna River, and he was determined to do so. He decided to send Chapman with the 18th Pennsylvania and 2nd New York northwest along the Hanover River Road to destroy the bridges. However, this route exposed Chapman's men to attack because three brigades of Confederate cavalry—both of Rooney Lee's brigades, as well as Col. Wright's brigade of Hampton's division—stood between them and the bridges.

---

1 Erastus Blakeslee was born in Plymouth, Connecticut, on September 2, 1838. He decided to enter the ministry and prepared for college at Williston Seminary at Westhampton, Massachusetts. He entered Yale University in 1863, graduating the following year. He enlisted as a private in Company A of the 1st Connecticut Cavalry on October 9, 1861. He rapidly received promotions, commanding the regiment as a lieutenant colonel by the spring of 1864. Blakeslee was promoted to colonel before receiving a brevet to brigadier general of volunteers in 1865 for his gallant conduct on June 1, 1864. He was also an accomplished inventor, inventing and patenting a cartridge box for the Spencer carbine known as the Blakeslee Cartridge Box, which became standard issue. From 1865 to 1876, he was in business in New Haven and Boston. He then enrolled in the Theological Seminary at Andover, Massachusetts, and graduated in 1879. He was ordained in February 1880, whereupon he spent the rest of his life tending to congregations and publishing bible lessons that were widely translated and disseminated. Blakeslee died in Brookline, Massachusetts, on July 12, 1908, and was buried in Brookline's Walnut Hill Cemetery. He was widely known as "an able speaker, a strong and positive character, and a gentle and lovable personality." Hunt and Brown, *Brevet Brigadier Generals in Blue*, 60 and "Erastus Blakeslee," https://prabook.com/web/erastus.blakeslee/1080478.
2 William A. Croffut and John M. Morris, *The Military and Civil History of Connecticut During the Recent War of 1861* (New York: Ledyard Bill, 1868), 581.

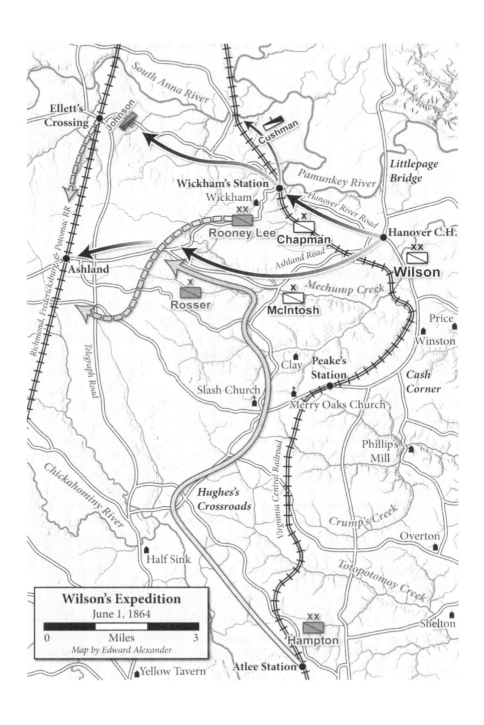

Wilson's Expedition
June 1, 1864

0   Miles   3

Map by Edward Alexander

Chapman's troopers fell back toward Ashland, about seven miles west of Hanover Court House, after the previous night's rout. To prevent the Confederates from flocking to the burning railroad trestles, Wilson sent McIntosh west along the Ashland Road to cover Chapman's left flank from Rooney Lee's troopers and from any other Confederate horsemen who might be lurking nearby. McIntosh took the 5th New York, 2nd Ohio, and 1st Connecticut, leaving the rest of Wilson's division—the 1st Vermont, 3rd Indiana, 3rd New Jersey, and 8th New York—at Hanover Court House, ready to come to the aid of either column if needed.[3]

Rooney Lee's two brigades formed a mounted line of battle on the high ground immediately south of Wickham's plantation, in an excellent position to meet the advancing Federals. "Their long blue lines, both mounted and dismounted stretched entirely across the level meadows and wheat fields of Wickham's fine plantation," Capt. Theodore S. Garnett of Rooney Lee's staff remembered. "Anticipating their attack on our front with every advantage in our favor I was hopeful of an easy repulse. They seemed to be in no hurry to begin the fight and we waited patiently for them to open the ball." Garnett sat on his horse near Rooney Lee, watching "the splendid pageant of ever-increasing numbers of blue horsemen, fully displayed to our view in the plains below." However, a galloper brought alarming news that a heavy enemy column was moving around Rooney Lee's exposed and easily turned right flank. Rooney Lee promptly ordered his command to pull back along the road to Ashland, positioning the men out of McIntosh's sight near the village.[4]

The two columns departed at about the same time. Colonel Bradley T. Johnson and the 1st Maryland Cavalry and the Baltimore Light Artillery, perhaps 150 men total, were camped along the Hanover River Road on Chapman's marching route. Johnson's Marylanders resisted as best they could, but Chapman's troopers slowly drove them back. Recognizing he was badly outnumbered, Johnson asked Rooney Lee for reinforcements. However, Rooney Lee's two brigades were already contending with McIntosh on the Ashland Road, and Lee could not afford to spare any troopers to help Johnson. Rooney Lee sent a galloper to Johnson to advise the Marylander that he was also being driven back. He promised to watch Johnson's southern flank and directed him to conduct at least a "little fight for the bridges." Offended, Johnson replied that his 150 troopers

---

3 *OR* 36, 1:881, 888, and 890; Wilson diary, entry for June 1, 1864.
4 Robert J. Trout, ed., *Riding with Stuart: Reminiscences of an Aide-de-Camp, by Captain Theodore S. Garnett* (Shippensburg, PA: White Mane, 1994), 77.

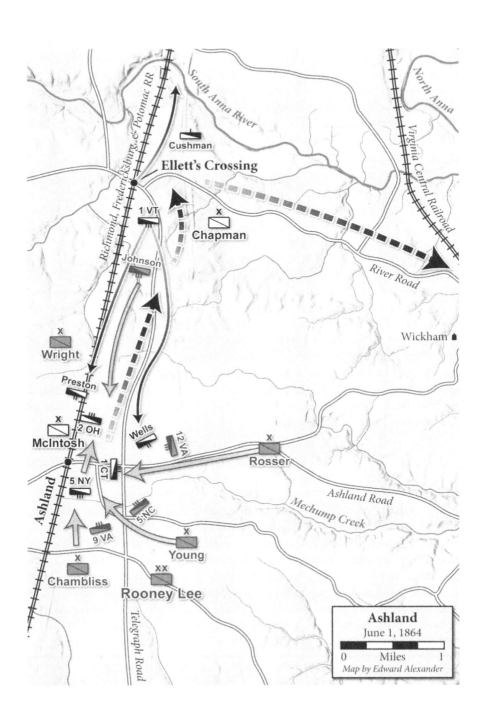

Cushman

Ellett's Crossing

1 VT

x
Chapman

Johnson

South Anna River

North Anna

Virginia Central Railroad

Richmond, Fredericksburg, & Potomac RR

River Road

Wickham

x
Wright

Preston

x
McIntosh

2 OH

Wells

1 CT

12 VA

x
Rosser

5 NY

5 NC

Ashland Road

Mechump Creek

9 VA

x
Young

x
Chambliss

xx
Rooney Lee

Ashland

Telegraph Road

Ashland
June 1, 1864

0   Miles   1
Map by Edward Alexander

"couldn't do [what Lee's] division of cavalry couldn't," and he "was going back too."[5]

Concerned that Chapman might not have a sufficient force, Wilson dispatched the 1st Vermont and 3rd Indiana as reinforcements. A squadron of the 1st Vermont under 23-year-old Capt. Oliver T. Cushman turned north at Wickham's Station and destroyed the Virginia Central's bridge over the South Anna while the rest of Chapman's command shoved Johnson's small force back to Ellett's Crossing on the RF&P.[6] "We fought the enemy from point to point in hopes that reinforcements would be sent to us, and thus save the bridges," Pvt. Henry Mettam of the 1st Maryland said.[7] Johnson had to make do with what he had—Rooney Lee had made it clear that no reinforce-

Capt. Oliver W. Cushman, 1st Vermont Cavalry. Note the visible scar under Cushman's eye from his Gettysburg wound.

(Author's collection)

ments were available. Johnson deployed his little command at Ellett's Crossing, knowing that the disparity in numbers would limit him at best to slowing Chapman down. Johnson left Ridgely Brown—who shook off the injuries he had sustained at Hanovertown Ferry on May

5 Johnson to his wife, June 2, 1864.
6 *OR* 36, 1:900. Cushman dropped out of Dartmouth College to enlist during his sophomore year. He left Vermont as a sergeant and was eventually promoted to captain. He was severely wounded—shot in the face—riding at the side of Brig. Gen. Elon J. Farnsworth during the latter's ill-fated charge on the third day of the battle of Gettysburg, and he was left for dead on the field. He fell into enemy hands but was considered too badly injured to parole. He returned to duty with an obvious scar under his eye from the Gettysburg wound. "Ordinarily quiet, modest, unassuming—in battle the lion aroused in him, and he was bravest of the brave," a comrade and friend from the 1st Vermont remembered. Cushman was killed in battle on June 3, 1864. Richard A. Hanks, ed., *Vermont's Proper Son: The Letters of Soldier and Scholar Edwin Hall Higley, 1861–1871* (Riverside, CA: Coyote Hill Press, 2014), 160.
7 Miller, "Civil War Memoirs of the First Maryland Cavalry," 154.

27—in command at Ellett's Crossing and headed west to search for a spot to fall back upon.[8]

Chapman's command reached Ellett's Crossing about 2:00 p.m. Brown assessed the situation and realized he was severely outnumbered, so he did the unexpected and ordered his men to attack. The Maryland horse soldiers drew their sabers, and, with Brown leading, put spurs to their mounts and charged. The popular Brown—"one of the best rounded and perfected characters I have ever known," according to Brown's adjutant Lt. George Booth, offered too tempting of a target for the Union carbineers, and they opened on him. A bullet passed through his right eye and out the back of his head. His demoralized troopers retreated, carrying the mortally wounded Brown off the field.[9]

Hearing the firing, Johnson dashed back to Ellett's Crossing, arriving just as Chapman prepared to lead a charge of his own. Johnson took in the situation as Chapman made "disposition for an advance which it was apparent we could not withstand with our small command," Booth recalled. "It became necessary to call in our skirmishers and retire in the direction of Ashland, which movement was made in good order, the Federals closely following and pressing our rear."[10] Rooney Lee was true to his word—when he realized that Johnson's little command was in danger, he ordered the 3rd North Carolina Cavalry to reinforce the Maryland men. Johnson, distraught over Brown's death, an officer of great promise, declined the help. "I don't want your squadron," he informed Rooney Lee's staff officer, Capt. Theodore S. Garnett, who led the detachment of Tar Heels. "Colonel Brown has just been killed. I cannot stop the enemy here. I

8 Johnson to his wife, June 2, 1864; Goldsborough, Maryland Line, 81; and Booth, *Personal Reminiscences*, 118. Ridgely Brown was born in Montgomery County, Maryland, on November 12, 1833. He was farming in Montgomery County when war came. He enlisted in Company K of the 1st Virginia Cavalry on May 14, 1861. He was then elected as lieutenant in Company K on August 1, 1861, and then appointed captain of Company A when the 1st Maryland Cavalry Battalion was split off. Brown was promoted to major on November 12, 1862, and to lieutenant colonel on August 20, 1863. On April 25, 1863, Brown had been wounded at Greenland Gap during the Jones-Imboden Raid, and he had returned to duty that summer. He was killed on the third anniversary of his enlistment in the Confederate service. Initially buried on the field, his body was exhumed and then moved to Richmond's Hollywood Cemetery four days later. Brown's family retrieved his body in 1866, and he was buried at Elton, the family farm, in eastern Montgomery County, Maryland. Krick, *Lee's Colonels*, 72 and Driver, *First and Second Maryland Cavalry, C.S.A.*, 206.
9 Booth, *Reminiscences*, 117–18; Miller, "Civil War Memoirs of the First Maryland Cavalry," 154; George S. Woolley manuscript, quoted in Driver, *First and Second Maryland Cavalry*, 81.
10 Booth, *Reminiscences*, 117.

am now falling back along the railroad." Johnson then led his men south along the RF&P toward Ashland.[11]

Shocked, Captain Garnett turned to Maj. Roger Moore, commanding the 3rd North Carolina Cavalry detachment, and said, "Major, we must get back to Gen. Lee as quickly as possible—Go at a gallop." The two officers spurred their horses, dashing off to find Rooney Lee to advise him that Johnson had retreated. As they rode, they crossed in front of some of Captain Cushman's Vermonters, but not a shot was fired. They soon entered their own lines, where they found Lee.[12]

Capt. Theodore S. Garnett, Rooney Lee's staff.

(Library of Congress)

Chapman watched as the Confederates retreated, realizing the road to the bridge was open. He seized Ellett's Crossing and then sent Cushman to destroy the RF&P bridge, which he demolished just as effectively as the other one. "Both of these bridges were most effectually destroyed by fire, including trestle work as well as superstructure, as also the water tanks, and the road was further damaged by the destruction of small bridges and cattle guards at different points," Chapman reported .[13]

The town of Ashland was 15 miles north of Richmond. The RF&P committee developed the town in the 1840s as a mineral spring resort with a racetrack for horses. It was named for Henry Clay's estate in Kentucky; Clay had been born at the nearby "Slashes of Hanover." It was officially incorporated on February 19, 1858, and featured a spa, casinos, horse racetrack, and guest cottages. It was a destination for people looking to escape the humidity of Richmond in the summer.[14]

Ashland's proximity to Richmond and its location on the railroad and on Telegraph Road—the major north-south artery for wagon

11 Trout, *Riding with Stuart*, 77.
12 Ibid.
13 *OR* 36, 1:900.
14 "Hanover's History," https://www.hanovercounty.gov/684/Hanovers-History.

Col. John Hammond,
commander, 5th New
York Cavalry,
wounded at Ashland.

(USAHEC)

traffic passing half a mile east of town—had brought the hard hand of war to Ashland several times already. Union raiders had visited it on multiple occasions, and now Wilson's troopers were driving the Confederate cavalry back on the town. War would soon visit the quaint resort once again.

The Union cavalrymen pressed Rooney Lee's beleaguered troopers hard. Leaving a small detachment on the Ashland Road near town to delay McIntosh's progress, Lee marched the rest of his division south on farm roads and turned west on Telegraph Road, deploying his troopers across McIntosh's direct route to Richmond. Colonel John Hammond's 5th New York Cavalry led McIntosh's way.[15]

The New Yorkers easily shouldered aside the detachment left on the Ashland Road, crossed the Telegraph Road, and then headed to the RF&P depot in the center of town. Upon arriving there, they set a blacksmith shop ablaze and

15 John Hammond was born on August 17, 1827, at his family's estate in Crown Point, New York. He attended Resselaer Polytechnic Institute, and then traveled to California as part of the Gold Rush. He came home to take over management of the family's iron works in Crown Point and was doing so when war came in 1861. He assisted in raising and equipping what became Company H of the 34th New York Volunteer Infantry. He then raised and became captain of Company H of the 5th New York Cavalry. Hammond was promoted to major and then to colonel of the 5th New York after Col. Othniel DeForest resigned his commission in the summer of 1863. He was wounded twice in battle, and the men of his regiment held him in high esteem. He received a brevet to brigadier general of volunteers on March 13, 1865, for his faithful and meritorious service in the war. After the war, he returned home to run the family ironworks, a farm, and a railroad. He was then elected to Congress, serving two terms from 1879 to 1883. He was active in the Grand Army of the Republic and the Military Order of the Loyal Legion of the United States. Hammond was known for his philanthropy and civic leadership. He died at Crown Point on May 28, 1889 and was buried in Forest Dale Cemetery. Hunt and Brown, *Brevet Brigadier Generals in Blue*, 258.

moved on to the other nearby buildings.[16] The 2nd Ohio followed, soon joining Hammond's men in tearing up tracks and demolishing the depot. The 1st Connecticut remained several miles behind on the Ashland Road.[17]

Wade Hampton had established his headquarters several miles away at Atlee's Station on the Virginia Central Railroad. About noon, gallopers from Rooney Lee arrived with the unwelcome news of McIntosh's movements. Hampton found Rosser and three of Rosser's Virginia regiments and set off for Ashland, intending to attack McIntosh from the rear on the Ashland Road, where he could surprise the Union troopers.[18]

Hampton and Rosser arrived at the Ashland Road shortly after the rear of McIntosh's column passed by. "The road was narrow and obstructed by a thick, bushy forest," Rosser recalled, "and when the enemy was not in sight, so recently had the rear of his column passed that the water from a branch was still running into the tracks made by his horses in the mud on its bank, not having had time to fill." Hampton rode off to find Rooney Lee to coordinate their efforts while Rosser's troopers went in search of McIntosh's rear.[19] They rode west along the Ashland Road and soon discovered that portions of the 1st Connecticut Cavalry had wandered off onto a side road, leaving McIntosh's wagon train unguarded. "Our regiment was marching quietly in the rear with our pack train and headquarters dog[,] Cash," a Connecticut man said, oblivious that a large force of Confederate cavalry was nearby and ready to pounce.[20]

Colonel Thomas Massie and the 12th Virginia Cavalry led Rosser's advance. Massie "received orders to move forward, charge the enemy as soon as they appeared in sight, and ride them down." About a mile from Ashland, the Virginians spotted "the enemy, without rear-guard, with a regiment of led horses, occupying the rear of the column, the men having gone forward," Capt. George Baylor of the 12th Virginia recalled. "The task was an easy one."[21]

On Rosser's signal, Massie's troopers crashed into the 1st Connecticut.[22] The Virginians "came down upon them like lice in Egypt," Col. George Purington of the 2nd Ohio related.[23] "The

16 "The War News."
17 *OR* 36, 1:881.
18 Chowning diary, entry for June 1, 1864.
19 Thomas L. Rosser, "Promotion for Extraordinary Valor and Skill," *Lost Cause: A Confederate War Record* 1 (1898), 53.
20 "Connecticut," "The First Connecticut Cavalry."
21 Baylor, *Bull Run to Bull Run*, 214.
22 Ibid.
23 *OR* 36, 1:895.

servants, who were riding and leading pack animals, of course were terribly scared and dashed right down the road through the center of our regiment, throwing it, for the time being, into some confusion," another recounted. Lieutenant Colonel Blakeslee, commanding the 1st Connecticut, stated, "A panic ensued, the led horses rushing through the ranks and making great confusion."[24] Blakeslee told his troopers to open their ranks to allow the horses to pass through, then tried to rally his men along both sides of the Ashland Road.[25]

Unable to resist the temptation, Rosser's men pounced on the unguarded wagons, grabbing delicacies and capturing McIntosh's spare mounts. Some of them spotted a trail of beans and followed it to an overturned mule cart. "Don't kill me," the cart driver begged, but quickly realized the Confederates were far more interested in his provisions than in him.[26] "The effect of this rear attack was to scatter the enemy in every direction through the woods, breaking up his organization," Rosser said, "but in doing so, I encumbered my men with prisoners, horses and wagons."[27]

Lieutenant George Baylor, commanding the 12th Virginia Cavalry's lead squadron, drove Blakeslee's troopers in ferocious hand-to-hand fighting. "The woods were very thick, so that I could get but few men in action at a time," Blakeslee reported, "and the woods were filled with [R]ebels, so that a saber charge in the road was impracticable." He later guessed that he reformed his ranks seven times during the nasty fight.[28]

Blakeslee found himself riding with a Virginian at his side. "He was a little in advance of his men and we met about midway between the opposing troops," Blakeslee remembered. "He was so near that I could have laid my hand on his shoulder when he thrust the muzzle of his pistol three or four inches from my right side and snapped the cap. It missed." Reacting quickly, Blakeslee raised his own pistol to the foeman's left side and pulled the trigger. The Confederate fell from his saddle, dead. "I saw his pistol drop from his grasp to the ground; and I did what in a cooler moment I should not have done," Blakeslee continued. Leaping from his horse, with bullets whizzing all around, Blakeslee grabbed the pistol and climbed back on his horse to lead the dead man's mount to the rear. He gave the animal to Sgt. Stephen N. Hinman, who had lost two mounts in two days—his horse had been shot out from under him at Hanover Court House and replaced with a

24 Blakeslee, "Addenda," 4.
25 "Connecticut," "The First Connecticut Cavalry."
26 "The Recent Cavalry Operations," *Atlanta Daily Intelligencer,* June 14, 1864.
27 Rosser, "Promotion for Extraordinary Valor and Skill," 53.
28 "First Regiment of Cavalry," 413–14.
29 Croffut and Morris, *Military and Civil History,* 582; Blakeslee, "Addenda," 4.

mule. The mule suffered a shot to the leg during Rosser's attack, leaving it lame and Hinman without a mount. Blakelsee kept the revolver as a trophy.[29] Soon, a severe hand wound disabled Blakeslee, forcing him to relinquish command to Maj. George O. Marcy.[30]

"Almost as soon as I entered the woods I turned and looked out to see what could be seen," Sergeant Hinman noted, "the dust was so dense that I could not distinguish the blue from the grey." Hinman saw two men come together a few feet away and cocked his Spencer, ready to pull the trigger. "The wonder is to me ... that I should not in the excitement have tried to fire anyway but at that instant one of them fell and I saw that the other was [Blakeslee]."[31]

Maj. Holmes Conrad, Hampton's staff.

(History of the Laurel Brigade)

Twenty-four-year-old Sgt. Phillip Koempel served in Company B of the 1st Connecticut. The German immigrant had just been promoted on May 21, and he had had a close call the day before at Hanover Court House. This day, he had just handed his canteen to his friend Cpl. Michael Flanigan when Flanigan suddenly dropped, shot through the head. "In falling he nearly threw me from my horse," Koempel penned in his diary that night. "Our Color Sergeant, [Samuel S.] Whipple [of Company G], killed, [Pvt. Charles] Taylor and myself saving the flag." Koemple also reported that three other members of Company B—Sgt. Wilbur Warren, Cpl. George Eagan, and Pvt. Edward F. Tisdale—were captured, but escaped. Company B lost 4 men killed and 10 wounded that day.[32]

30 "First Regiment of Cavalry," 413–14.
31 Blakeslee, "Addenda," 4.
32 Koempel, *Phil Koempel's Diary*, 8.

The men of Purington's 2nd Ohio Cavalry were busy tearing up railroad tracks in Ashland when the colonel heard desperate firing in his rear and he ordered his Squadron D, led by Lt. Melancthon C. Cowdery, to reinforce Blakeslee's beleaguered New Englanders. The arrival of these men caught Tom Rosser off guard. "I had kept only two squadrons in the saddle unencumbered," he later wrote. His other troopers, guarding prisoners and captured wagons, were spread out more than a mile along the Ashland Road, unprepared to receive an attack. The Buckeyes slammed into Rosser's troopers, and a brutal hand-to-hand melee ensued. "Everything was about to break when Private [Holmes] Conrad, who was [at] my side, rushed to [the 11th Virginia] and seized its colors and called to his old comrades to save their flag that had waved triumphantly upon so many glorious fields, and rush with it into the ranks of the enemy," Rosser recounted.[33]

The Virginians' determined attack tipped the balance. "Following up his success," Hampton claimed years later, "Rosser pressed the enemy vigorously and in a series of brilliant charges—some of which were over dismounted men—he drove [the rest of the Union cavalrymen] into Ashland."[34] Union sharpshooters hiding in houses opened a "galling fire," finally halting Rosser's momentum.[35] Colonel Richard H. Dulany of the 7th Virginia Cavalry had two horses shot out from under him during the fighting.[36]

While Rosser and his Virginians harassed McIntosh's rear, Rooney Lee deployed his two brigades in line perpendicular to the railroad and the Telegraph Road, blocking the direct route to Ashland. Hampton, who had command of these operations, thought he could capture McIntosh's entire detachment. Hampton had three brigades—Rosser's, Young's North Carolinians, and Chambliss' Virginians—to throw against McIntosh's three regiments. Rosser's troopers blocked the Ashland Road, barricading McIntosh's route of retreat to Hanover Court House, while Young and Chambliss, deployed south of the town, cut off McIntosh's road to Richmond. The Telegraph Road and RF&P led to Ellett's Crossing north of town, but Johnson and his Maryland men, with troopers of Wright's brigade as reinforcement, blocked those routes. McIntosh was isolated, and Chapman's troopers remained at Ellett's Crossing, tearing up the railroad and oblivious to

---

33 Rosser, "Promotion for Extraordinary Valor and Skill," 53. Conrad's bravery so impressed Rosser that he told Hampton about the young man that very day and recommended him for promotion. As a result, Conrad was commissioned as a major. Rosser letter of January 2, 1865, included in Holmes Conrad Combined Service Record, Roll 61, NARA.
34 Hampton, Connected Narrative, 40.
35 McDonald, *History of the Laurel Brigade*, 245–48.
36 Ibid., 247.

the danger McIntosh and his men now faced. Surrounded on three sides, McIntosh had only one available escape route—to the west. Hampton believed that an escape to the west would only take McIntosh farther away from the main body of the Union army, doing little more than postponing his capture.

As Hampton finalized his impromptu plan, Maj. James F. Hart's South Carolina battery of horse artillery arrived. "The battery charged through Ashland with the advance line of our troops as lovely women rushed from their residences to cheer us on," Hart remembered. "No troops were ever martialed in battle could have resisted our advance under such circumstances."[37] Hart deployed his guns, trapping McIntosh in Ashland and outnumbering him about three-to-one. The Federals now faced Confederate artillery. "Attack at once," Hampton cried, seeing the opportunity to bag McIntosh and his troopers.[38]

McIntosh spotted the Rebels forming for the charge and prepared to receive them to the best of his ability. He unlimbered his horse artillery in town, positioning his men in houses along the railroad bed and behind breastworks hastily erected in nearby woods and fields. McIntosh's men formed a semicircle with the arc's center facing east along the Ashland Road and with its flanks resting on the railroad north and south of town. Purington's 2nd Ohio faced north to cover the railroad and Telegraph Road in the direction of Johnson's and the Marylanders' location. The 1st Connecticut faced east across the Ashland Road, toward Rosser, while the 5th New York looked south toward Rooney Lee's two brigades. McIntosh had prepared as best as he could. Would it be enough?

Hampton directed Young and his Tar Heels to attack dismounted with the intention of breaking the Union line between Telegraph Road and Ashland Road. Captain Theodore S. Garnett, of Rooney Lee's staff, called out to Rosser: "Where shall we go in?" Rosser pointed to the right, and yelled, "There, in there!" The Tar Heels let loose the Rebel yell and went in as directed with Captain Garnett at their head.[39]

Hammond's New Yorkers and Marcy's New Englanders stood to meet the attack, and a severe firefight erupted.[40] Young received a severe chest wound while leading the dismounted attack and had to be carried from the field. Young's adjutant, Maj. W. L. Church, and his

---

37 James F. Hart, Levi C. Stephens, Louis Sherfesee, and Charles H. Schwing, "The History of Hart's Battery," included in Robert J. Trout, ed., *Memoirs of the Stuart Horse Artillery Battalion: Moorman's and Hart's Batteries* (Knoxville: University of Tennessee Press, 1998), 231.
38 Hampton, Connected Narrative, 40; Chew's report.
39 Garnett, *Riding with Stuart*, 78.
40 D. B. R., "Barringer's North Carolina Brigade of Cavalry"; *Wilson, Under the Old Flag*, 1:430.

assistant adjutant, Capt. Robert Aldrich, both thought the wound was fatal and arranged for their general to be taken to the rear. Fortunately, Young survived, returning to duty in the fall of 1864 after an extended convalescence. This was his fourth combat wound of the war and his second serious chest wound. Although he had only led the North Carolina brigade for a few days, Young was popular with the men. "He was the beau ideal of a cavalry leader," Maj. John M. Galloway, 5th North Carolina Cavalry, remarked.[41] With Young incapacitated, command of the North Carolina Brigade temporarily devolved upon Colonel Baker again.[42] "Deprived of the direction of [Young], the brigade failed to dislodge Wilson in the first assault," Hampton recounted.[43]

As the determined Tar Heels ran low on ammunition, they "fought the enemy with stones and brick-bats," Rufus Barringer of the 1st North Carolina recalled.[44] Hammond's Empire State men, armed with seven-shot Spencer carbines, inflicted more than 70 casualties among the North Carolinians. "Several times our boys were partially surrounded," one of Hammond's troopers wrote, "but the ceaseless fire of their carbines and the grape and canister of the artillery mowed fearful gaps in the enemy's lines, and strewed the ground with slain."[45]

The New Yorkers "fought like demons," Hammond oberved. "We were completely surrounded, and it was a matter of life and liberty, or death." Major Amos H. White of the 5th New York Cavalry was severely wounded during the fighting as he rode up and down the lines, directing operations and encouraging the men to stand and fight. Hammond also had a close call. "I had my leg bruised by a spent ball," Hammond told his wife. "The ball first struck my scabbard which broke its force and saved my leg. It made me limp a little but I kept on

41 John M. Galloway, "Sixty-Third Regiment (Fifth Cavalry)," in Walter Clark, ed., *Histories of the Several Regiments and Battalions from North Carolina in the Great War, 1861–1865*, 5 vols. (Raleigh: E. M. Uzzell, 1901), 537–38.
42 "The Recent Cavalry Operations," *Richmond Enquirer*, June 9, 1864; Jack D. Welsh, *Medical Histories of Confederate Generals* (Kent, OH: Kent State University Press, 1995), 242. Young's only published biography, 1964's *Pierce M. B. Young: The Warwick of the South*, by Lynwood M. Holland, mistakenly states that Young was wounded on May 30. However, and as set forth in Chapter 9, the North Carolina Brigade was not involved in the skirmishing that occurred that day. See p. 83. Contemporary accounts, including the newspaper article cited in this note, indicate that Young sustained his wound on June 1. Unfortunately, numerous other accounts of Manning's wounding have picked up and perpetuated that error.
43 McDonald, *History of the Laurel Brigade*, 246.
44 Barringer to Barringer, January 27, 1866. As the fighting raged in Ashland on June 1, the Confederate Senate approved Barringer's promotion to brigadier general, and he took command of the brigade on June 3.
45 Boudrye, *Historic Records of the Fifth New York Cavalry*, 137.

duty and shall be entirely well of it in a week." Unfortunately, Hammond was wrong—the injury caused him pain for the rest of his life.[46]

Desperate, McIntosh sent a galloper to Ellett's Crossing to summon Chapman and his command to reinforce him. The courier evaded Johnson's Maryland men along the road and dashed into Chapman's camp. Fortunately, General Wilson happened to be visiting Ellett's Crossing to check on Chapman's progress and heard the courier's report himself. Wilson immediately ordered Maj. William Wells and his battalion of the 1st Vermont Cavalry to ride south along the Telegraph Road to McIntosh's aid. Wells, who earned the Medal of Honor for his

Maj. William Wells, 1st Vermont Cavalry, Medal of Honor recipient.

(Library of Congress)

gallantry during Brig. Gen. Elon J. Farnsworth's charge at Gettysburg on July 3, 1863, led some of the finest horse soldiers in all of the Northern service, and they were up to the challenge.

Putting spurs to their horses, the Vermonters pushed through the thin screen of Marylanders and entered Ashland. A relieved McIntosh sent them east to assist the 1st Connecticut in its fight with Rosser's Virginians near the intersection of the Ashland and Telegraph roads.[47] "The Rebs were charging our men and driving pell mell," Wells wrote. "My [c]ommand was formed and I put them in, we drove the Rebs back and held them for [half an] hour, perhaps it saved great many men from 1st Brig."[48]

46 John Hammond, 81–82. White recovered from what was feared to be a mortal wound, returned to duty, and became the final colonel of the 5th New York.

47 George G. Benedict, *Vermont in the Civil War: A History of the Part Taken by the Vermont Soldiers and Sailors in the War for the Union*, 2 vols. (Burlington, VT: Free Press Association, 1882), 2:642–43; Ide, *History of the First Vermont Cavalry Volunteers*, 173.

48 Elliott W. Hoffman, ed., *A Vermont Cavalryman in War & Love: The Civil War Letters of Brevet Major General William Wells and Anna Richardson* (Lynchburg, VA: Schroeder Publications, 2007), 264.

While the Vermonters deployed, Purington ordered eight dismounted companies of his 2nd Ohio under Major A. Bayard Nettleton to take position behind a ditch, where they had a severe fight with Johnson's Marylanders and the 5th North Carolina Cavalry.[49]

Dismounted fighting at close range filled the streets of Ashland. "It was strange but true to see [R]ebel and Union soldiers firing from opposite sides of the same tree," a Buckeye observed. "The [R]ebels were so thick that we could scarcely miss them if we fired at random, and but few shots went astray." McIntosh's brigade was "in serious confusion and in imminent danger of being roughly handled."[50] The Southerners also suffered heavy losses. Sergeant James Wyche Tillett led 12 men of his 5th North Carolina Cavalry north on the Telegraph Road to shoot the artillerists of McIntosh's horse battery. Tillett and his men crept through the bushes until they were able to fire into the gunners at point-blank range. Only Tillett escaped.[51] "In the space of forty feet I counted 22 dead rebels, and there was a large number wounded," a Buckeye reported.[52]

Colonel Richard L. T. Beale's 9th Virginia Cavalry of Chambliss' brigade attacked and drove 1st Connecticut troopers from woods south of town. "Beside a fence, at the edge of the timber, as we hurried forward, lay the body of a soldier who had received a death shot as our first line of skirmishers had approached the fence before us," Lt. George W. Beale, son of the regimental commander, stated. As the Virginians advanced, they heard firing all around them, but no volleys in front of them. "It presently became evident that not a Confederate was in our front," Lieutenant Beale observed, "the regiment which was supposed to be there having borne to one side or the other and left only the Federals before us, well protected in the ditch." The Virginians raised the Rebel yell and dashed for the ditch, "while its occupants, leaping over the bank, beat a hasty retreat."[53]

Captain Addison G. Warner, 1st Connecticut, shouted: "Stand fast, [b]oys! Give it to them!" When the Virginians drove the Connecticut troopers back and Blakeslee rallied them again, Sgt. Alexander McDonald spotted Warner standing about a dozen yards in front of the regiment. McDonald rode over to the captain, asking what was wrong. "Mac, I'm wounded in the shoulder," Warner replied. McDonald urged him to go to the rear, but Warner refused. He held his ground as the

---

49 "Army Correspondence," *Painesville Telegraph*, June 23, 1864; Barnitz Field Notes, entry for June 1, 1864.
50 "Army Correspondence."
51 Trout, *Riding with Stuart*, 78.
52 "Army Correspondence."
53 Beale, *A Lieutenant of Cavalry in Lee's Army*, 152–53.

melee whirled around him, briefly separating Warner and McDonald. Another soldier called out: "Mac, Captain's wounded."

McDonald made his way to Warner and saw that a ball had broken Warner's leg, and he was swaying in the saddle. The two soldiers caught Warner and turned him around, as Warner insisted on facing the enemy. Just then, yet another ball struck him in the thigh, severing an artery. "A moment more and a ball passed through his head but even this did not cause instant death," McDonald, who tried to guide the desperately wounded man to safety, wrote. They struck a tree, and Warner fell from the saddle. With his foot tangled in the stirrup, the horse dragged him for some distance, until finally kicking itself free. "We rallied, drove the [R]ebels back and brought the captain off," McDonald remembered. "When we dug the grave to bury our heroic commander, the bullets flew like hail."[54]

When a Union bullet tore through a Confederate's mouth, "[T]he contact of the ball with his teeth sounded to me very much as if it had struck and shattered a china plate or cup," Lieutenant Beale said, describing the spine-tingling sound. Beale also watched Captain Warner fall. One of his men, Tom Jett, called to the lieutenant: "See me knock that officer off;" whereupon he raised his carbine and pulled the trigger. Beale watched as the officer—probably Warner—reeled in the saddle.[55]

"June 1st, I think, the hardest day's work I ever did," Pvt. James F. Bryant, Company A of the 13th Virginia, recalled. He noted that Chambliss' brigade came within 40 yards of Federal artillery, nearly capturing it, but that the Tar Heels on their left gave way before they could do so. He complained, "We had to double-quick a great deal and marched altogether several miles. The day was intensely hot in addition." He continued, "In all of these engagements we fought dismounted as infantry, being armed with carbines, and we had no breast works as shelter to fight behind, as infantry generally have, but are in the open field."[56]

McIntosh sought out Maj. Wells of the 1st Vermont and asked him to send a message to Wilson. "[McIntosh's] whole brigade was on the skirmish line," Wells advised Sgt. Horace K. Ide, chosen to transmit the message to Wilson, "and if he should withdraw, the enemy might make a rush and capture his artillery, but if General Wilson could

---

54 Croffut and Morris, *Civil and Military History*, 585; *Windham County Transcript*, June 16, 1864.
55 Beale, *A Lieutenant of Cavalry in Lee's Army*, 153.
56 Quoted in Driver, *10th Virginia Cavalry*, 55–56 and in Balfour, *13th Virginia Cavalry*, 32.

Lt. Col. Addison W. Preston, commander of the 1st Vermont Cavalry.

(Library of Congress)

attack with his other brigade, he thought they could drive the [R]ebels."[57]

Ide found Wilson and gave him the message. Wilson replied that all of his artillery had gone to the rear but that he had sent the rest of the 1st Vermont up to attack on the flank. Wilson then scribbled a hasty message to McIntosh, directing Ide to destroy the note if he was captured. Ide rode down the railroad, where he met the brigade artillery retreating, and the officer in command told Ide that he was glad the guns could get through to Wilson safely. A bit beyond, he found McIntosh and the rest of the brigade in full retreat. Ide handed him the message, and just as he delivered it, "a shell from the enemy threw dirt all over us."

Unimpeded, McIntosh continued and soon found Wilson. Relieved, McIntosh pumped Wilson's hand, declaring that he "was damned glad to see him." Wilson then ordered McIntosh to "[d]eploy the 5th New York and open fire to bring out the 1st Vermont who were getting all cut to hell."[58]

Lieutenant Colonel Addison W. Preston and the rest of the 1st Vermont dashed along the RF&P, shoved Johnson's Marylanders aside, and cut their way through to McIntosh's beleaguered troopers to establish an escape route. "Our [regiment] was put in dismounted and not supported," Major Wells complained. "We were attacked by three [b]rigades therefore we were obliged to fall back, in doing so some of our men were cut off."[59] The Vermonters arrived just in time, as McIntosh's men were nearly exhausted from the heavy fighting. "We got away as best we could," a 1st Connecticut trooper admitted, and they made their way toward Ellett's Crossing, where the rest of Chapman's brigade awaited them.[60]

57 Ide, *History of the First Vermont Cavalry Volunteers*, 174–75.
58 Ibid.
59 Hoffman, *A Vermont Cavalryman in War & Love*, 264.
60 "Connecticut," "The First Connecticut Cavalry."

Much to his disgust, Sgt. Henry W. Chester of the 2nd Ohio had been assigned to watch the horses of the regiment's dismounted men. He soon realized that even though he was not on the firing line, it was still an important duty. "Just before sundown we were ordered to retire down the railroad tracks as all the wagon roads were in possession of the enemy," he recalled. "I had the horses ready for our men to mount as soon as they came from the woods, but we had to leave all our killed and most of our wounded" to the tender mercies of the Confederates.[61] Captain Albert Barnitz of the 2nd Ohio received a severe wound to his right thigh and had his horse shot out from under him during the retreat.[62] Some men of the 1st Connecticut stayed long enough to bury Captain Warner's body in a yard next to the train depot before joining the retreat.[63]

Chambliss ordered his troopers to march toward their held horses for the purpose of making a mounted charge to try to capture the Union cavalry. However, when they reached the horses, instead of mounting, they hurried forward on foot into the woods to their right, while Lt. Thomas J. Christian led a squadron of the 9th Virginia in a charge down the road, "only to find the road barricaded and in possession of a fresh Federal brigade which had come to the rescue of the men whom we had been fighting," Lieutenant Beale said.[64]

The swarming Confederate horsemen nearly overwhelmed Preston's men, but the 5th New York, who carried Spencer repeating carbines, came to their aid, spraying heavy fire to help cover the Vermonters. "As our men were between them and the advancing tide of the enemy," a Vermont man recalled, "they did about as much damage to us as to the [R]ebels, except perhaps the noise of the volleys convinced the [R]ebels that there was a reserve."[65] The New Yorkers established a rear guard to cover the Vermonters' retreat, holding the pursuing Confederates at bay. "In getting [McIntosh] out of the scrape we got into one and had to leave on the double quick," another Vermonter remembered.[66] Eri Woodbury of the 1st Vermont said, "Soon the road was filled with the debris of several regiments drifting to the rear, which tide General Wilson and his staff vainly endeavored to check."[67] Wilson noted that his division was low on ammunition

61 Chester, *Recollections of the War of the Rebellion*, 81.
62 Barnitz field notes, entry for June 1, 1864.
63 "Connecticut," "The First Connecticut Cavalry."
64 Beale, *A Lieutenant of Cavalry in Lee's Army*, 153–54.
65 J. L. Sperry to his sister, June 5, 1864, J. L. Sperry Papers, Perkins Library, Duke University, Durham, North Carolina.
66 Eri Davidson Woodbury to his family, June 5, 1864, Eri Davidson Woodbury Papers, Special Collections, Dartmouth University Library, Hanover, New Hampshire.
67 Ide, *History of the First Vermont Cavalry Volunteers*, 175.

after 36 hours of nearly nonstop fighting and could do little more unless resupplied.[68]

"Then the bullets began to whistle by, and the whole command, from General on down, moved back, not in very good order to that indefinite, but often sought after place, the 'rear,' going back the same road we came up," Sergeant Ide recounted. "Some efforts were made on the march to bring 'order out of chaos,' but many men were missing, besides those killed and wounded."[69]

After the Federals retired from Ashland, the Confederates reentered the town. Captain Garnett rode alongside Lt. Col. Robert A. Caskie of the 10th Virginia Cavalry. Caskie pointed at three dead Yankees who were lying at considerable distances apart but in the same general direction on the level greensward stretching east of town. An admiring Caskie declared, "Those are the three best shots I have seen during the whole war; one of my men killed those three Yankees while they were running, without missing a shot." The Confederates followed as the Union rear guard retired along the railroad, "and they were soon out of our sight, retreating rapidly until they reached the road to Wickham's," Garnett observed, noticing that the Federals had taken the same road he had used to get to Ashland. Thus, the "whole of Wilson's Cavalry Division here made good their retreat towards Wickham's and the Court House, having succeeded in burning the Railroad Bridge over the South Anna River after driving [Colonel] Johnson's and the Maryland Cavalry from their front," a thoroughly frustrated Garnett concluded.[70]

McIntosh and his weary refugees reached Ellett's Crossing about nightfall. The tired horsemen made their way back to their camps at Hanover Court House. "Command all extricated after much hard fighting," Wilson noted in his diary.[71] "That night we returned to Hanover Court House, after marching fifteen miles to make eight, not being able to return the way we came," a Buckeye complained. "As we drank our coffee that night our souls were full of bitterness, and we fully expressed our sentiments as our conversation turned to the good men who had fallen and the good men who will fall."[72] Purington's command reached its camp about midnight, "tired and worn out, having had nothing to eat in twenty-four hours."[73]

About 11:00 p.m., Wilson sent a dispatch to army headquarters. "After nineteen hours' marching and fighting we bivouacked at eleven

68 *OR* 36, 1:881–82.
69 Ide, *History of the First Vermont Cavalry Volunteers*, 175.
70 Garnett, *Riding with Stuart*, 78–79.
71 Wilson diary, entry for June 1, 1864.
72 "Army Correspondence."
73 *OR* 36, 1:895.

o'clock that night in our old position at Hanover Court House," Wilson observed.[74] He described his command as having been "hotly engaged." After briefly describing the day's actions, he stated, "The whole command is now safely in camp, having been almost constantly engaged for thirty-six hours with rebel cavalry."[75]

Thus ended Wilson's expedition, which achieved mixed results. On one hand, he successfully maintained the interval between the Army of the Potomac and the Pamunkey River and destroyed the twin railroad bridges across the South Anna as ordered. "A cursory examination of the maps will show that the operations . . . were of a character to severely test the quality of the troops engaged in them," Wilson wrote in his after-action report. "An impassable stream in rear and a force of [R]ebels twice as large as in front, without over half the distance to march that we were from the main army in order to strike us in flank."[76]

At the same time, his decision to split his force nearly caused the destruction of McIntosh's brigade.[77] "We fought him nearly all day and fighting largely superior numbers and did not make much," Lt. Col. John W. Phillips, 18th Pennsylvania Cavalry, grumbled in his diary.[78] The severe fight at Ashland was unplanned, and it came with the heavy loss of 183 men. McIntosh's brigade suffered the most with 145 killed, along with 33 from the 1st Connecticut, 24 from the 5th New York, 65 from the 2nd Ohio, and 33 from Chapman's 1st Vermont.[79] Sergeant Samuel Gilpin of the 3rd Indiana observed that McIntosh's brigade and the 1st Vermont "of our brigade lost heavily in the fight on the left. A hard day on us."[80] At least some of the Federals thought they had faced Confederate infantry, not just dismounted cavalry.[81] In addition, Wilson lost precious horses and mules. A Southern newspaper

74 Wilson, *Under the Old Flag*, 1:431.
75 *OR* 36, 1:874.
76 Ibid., 882.
77 Despite the heavy losses, McIntosh received a brevet to lieutenant colonel in the Regular Army for his meritorious service that day. *Journal of the Executive Proceedings of the Senate of the United States of America from February 13, 1866 to July 28, 1866, Inclusive*, Vol. XIV, in two parts (Washington, DC: U.S. Govt. Printing Office, 1866), Part 1, 742.
78 Athearn, "The Civil War Diary of John Wilson Phillips," 105.
79 On June 2, Wilson, concerned for his wounded, asked for Meade's guidance. "I was compelled to leave 30 or 40 wounded at Ashland, two officers, for the lack of ambulances. Would it be proper to send a flag of truce, with a train of ambulances, for permission to bring them in?" *OR* 36, 3:510.
80 Gilpin diary, entry for June 1, 1864.
81 A correspondent of the 1st Vermont reported that "our division drove a force of infantry and cavalry from Hanover Court House to Ashland." "From the Vermont Cavalry," *Rutland Weekly Herald*, June 21, 1864.

correspondent reported, "A considerable amount of spoils was captured, including 300 horses and 30 pack mules."[82]

The bridges were back in service within a few days, resulting in the expedition having no lasting impact on the outcome of the campaign, which did nothing to bolster Wilson's reputation with his men, who already disliked him. "We had a hot time at Ashland, where we ran up against a heavy force and got rather the worst of it," a man of the 2nd Ohio said.[83] "Our division and brigade commanders I think did not handle their commands very well," Major Wells keenly observed.[84]

Wilson had a legitimate complaint. Years later, he griped that "the proper tactical use of cavalry under the circumstances was to send the entire corps to assist in the work committed to. This would have enabled it to destroy the bridges and railroads effectively in a few hours and would have given us, besides, an opportunity to crush or drive Hampton into the fortifications of Richmond or compel him to take refuge behind Lee's army."[85] Gregg's division, for example, was not engaged but could have been sent to Wilson's aid, evening the odds against his two isolated brigades.

Confederate losses roughly matched Wilson's. In the two days of fighting, Young's Tar Heels lost about 100 men, Rosser lost 20, and Johnson lost another 20, for total losses of approximately 190.[86] Ridgely Brown's death and Pierce Young's severe chest wound cost the Southern cavalry heavily. Some Confederate horsemen complained about Hampton's management of the two days of fighting, arguing that they should have captured McIntosh's entire brigade. "The whole affair was badly managed on our part," Capt. Garnett, Rooney Lee's staffer, declared, "and what should have been a great victory for us must be numbered among the 'lost opportunities.'"[87] By contrast, others praised Hampton's management of the battle. "In the cavalry fight yesterday, Rosser pitched into Wilson's rear whilst Rooney Lee was amusing him in front," Lt. Col. J. Frederick Waring of the Jeff Davis Legion Cavalry said. "The Yankees were badly stampeded."[88] Major James F. Hart, who commanded the Confederate horse artillery at Ashland, correctly remarked that "little damage had been done to

---

82 "Progress of the War," The Daily Progress, June 6, 1864. The same correspondent speculated, "The mules were laden with ten days' rations, showing that it was contemplated to have extended the raid beyond Ashland, probably to the canal and the Danville Railroad."

83 Robert W. Hatton, ed., "Just a Little Bit of The Civil War, as Seen by W. J. Smith, Company M, 2nd Ohio Cavalry," *Ohio History* 84 (1975), 115.

84 Hoffman, *A Vermont Cavalryman in War & Love*, 271.

85 Wilson, *Under the Old Flag*, 1:429–30.

86 Young, *Lee's Army During the Overland Campaign*, 318–27.

87 Trout, *Riding with Stuart*, 78–79.

88 Waring diary, entry for June 3, 1864.

the railroad owing to Hampton's prompt attack."[89] One of the Richmond newspapers described the engagement as "a brilliant cavalry victory."[90]

The fact remained that Hampton was still learning how to command a corps. He successfully improvised a plan to manage the threat that Wilson posed and nearly destroyed an entire brigade in the process. And while the Union cavalry got away, that was not Hampton's fault. He managed his troopers well, and his subordinates—Rosser in particular—performed effectively and efficiently.[91] Perhaps most tellingly, General Lee sent a note to Hampton declaring his "gratification at the handsome defeat of the enemy."[92] Hampton and his men also captured much needed fodder and between 300 and 500 horses, which Rosser seized, for the army's use.

However, more work remained for the Union cavalry. Torbert's First Cavalry Division still held the critical road intersection at Cold Harbor, and the men would soon be tested.

89 Hart, Stephens, Sherfessee, and Schwing, "History of Hart's Battery," 231.
90 "The Recent Cavalry Operations," *Richmond Enquirer*, June 9, 1864.
91 "Progress of the Campaign in Virginia," *Charleston Mercury*, June 4, 1864.
92 Included in Hampton, Connected Narrative, 41.

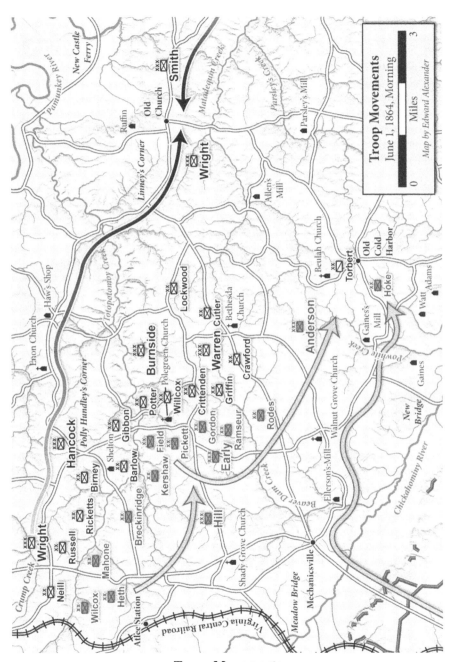

Troop Movements
June 1, 1864, Morning

Chapter 12
June 1: Cold Harbor

While Wilson's men grappled with the Confederate cavalry at Ashland on June 1, 1864, Torbert's weary troopers prepared to resume the struggle to hold the critical Cold Harbor Road intersection. At 1:00 that morning, a determined Phil Sheridan told headquarters that he was "in receipt of your dispatch to hold on to Cold Harbor, and will do so if possible."[1] The Union horse soldiers hurried back to Cold Harbor, fully expecting to fight it out there that morning. Devin's brigade, reinforced by portions of Davies' brigade of Gregg's Second Cavalry Division, occupied the intersection. Custer's Michigan Cavalry Brigade extended north along the road to Beulah Church, while Merritt's Reserve Brigade deployed on the Wolverines' right flank, extending to the church and the house of David Woody. They completed turning Fitzhugh Lee's works by facing west and erecting new works, "made of a dismantled rail fence and a few inches of earth," along the Beulah Church Road, according to a member of the 1st New York Dragoons.[2]

When the works were finished, the Northern horse soldiers lined up one rank deep behind. "By the side of each man was a pile of cartridges that he might load and fire with great rapidity," a man in the 1st New York Dragoons noticed, ensuring those units armed with Spencer carbines that they would have plenty of ammunition once the fighting got hot.[3] Williston's consolidated Battery D, 2nd U.S. Artillery, which included 12 guns, rolled up and unlimbered. "I do not remember any other engagement in which so many pieces of artillery were posted directly on a skirmish line with no line of battle behind it and not reserves," Major Kidd of the 6th Michigan observed.[4] "Devin had a great deal of difficulty in keeping his pipe lighted," Lt. Edward P. McKinney, 6th New York Cavalry, quipped, downplaying the role of the veteran brigade commander that day.[5]

---

1 *OR* 36, 3:469.
2 Bowen, *First New York Dragoons*, 180.
3 Ibid. The 1st New York Dragoons of the Reserve Brigade and the four regiments of the Michigan Cavalry Brigade all carried Spencer carbines. The rest of the units of Torbert's command carried Sharps or other similar single-shot breechloading carbines.
4 Kidd, *Personal Recollections*, 333.
5 E. P. McKinney, *Life in Tent and Field 1861–1865* (Boston: The Gorham Press, 1922), 117.

Davies' men had actually been dispatched the previous night, but they did not arrive in time to participate in the fighting on May 31. They spent the night lying on their arms and then moved up behind Torbert's troopers, comprising a rear line in support. "We also formed in a ditch, dismounted, and with our spades and the adjoining fences had in the course of an half hour a respectable line of defenses," Lt. Thomas Lucas of the 1st Pennsylvania Cavalry recounted.[6]

While Sheridan's troopers prepared to receive a Confederate onslaught, Hoke's division of North Carolinians dug in along a gentle ridge a mile west of the Cold Harbor intersection. Johnson Hagood's South Carolina brigade deployed behind the Tar Heels, and Anderson's I Corps of the Army of Northern Virginia was on its way to reinforce Hoke, as General Lee had directed.

"Before the first streaks of dawn began to appear in the east, their bugles sounded the reveille, and there was immediate commotion in the Confederate camps," Kidd recalled. "So close to us were they that the commands of the officers could be heard distinctly."[7] The blue-clad cavalrymen hunkered down, preparing to receive the attack that seemed inevitable in light of the activity across the way.

General Meade, commanding the Army of the Potomac, knew that Hoke's division remained near Cold Harbor and that Anderson's corps was on its way to reinforce Hoke, so he ordered the VI Corps to disengage from its position along Totopotomoy Creek and march 15 miles to Cold Harbor, reaching the intersection as near to dawn as possible.[8] However, Horatio Wright, heading the VI Corps, did not get his troops marching as quickly as Meade had wanted; Brig. Gen. Thomas Neill's Second Division did not march until almost 4:30 a.m., which made it impossible for the VI Corps to reach Cold Harbor by first light. Sheridan remained on his own, isolated and within earshot of the Confederates. Concerned about his isolated position, he bombarded Wright with messages urging him to move expeditiously to his aid.

However, the VI Corps' men were worn out from the exertions of the campaign. "The night was sultry and oppressive," Lt. Col. Martin T. McMahon of Wright's staff remembered. "Many of our horses and mules were dying of thirst, yet they had to be forced through streams without halting to drink."[9] The head of Wright's column was still an

---

6 Donna Bayard Sauerburger and Thomas Lucas Bayard, eds., *I Seat Myself to Write You a Few Lines: Civil War and Homestead Letters from Thomas Lucas and Family* (Bowie, MD: Heritage Books, 2002), 226.

7 Kidd, *Personal Recollections*, 333.

8 *OR* 36, 1:671, 688, and 726.

9 Ibid.; Martin T. McMahon, "Cold Harbor," included in Robert U. Johnson and Clarence C. Buel, eds., *Battles and Leaders of the Civil War*, 4 vols. (New York: Century Publishing Co., 1884–1888), 4:214–15.

hour's march away, and Smith's XVIII Corps was heading toward the Cold Harbor intersection by the same road, which promised to cause an epic traffic jam. Sheridan and his beleaguered troopers would have to go it alone, despite Meade's best intentions to provide reinforcements.

Colonel Laurence M. Keitt commanded Kershaw's lead brigade—formerly Kershaw's own brigade of South Carolinians—marching toward Beulah Church and the Woody house.[10] Keitt—the "quintessence of efflorescence," as the famous South Carolina diarist Mary Chesnut described Keitt, who had assumed command of the brigade only the day before and was unknown to his new command. His first day commanding a brigade quickly became his last.[11] "When nearing the old battlefield at

Col. Laurence Keitt, brigade commander who was mortally wounded in the fighting at Cold Harbor on June 1, 1864.

(Library of Congress)

---

10 Laurence Massillon Keitt was born in Orangeburg District, South Carolina, on October 4, 1824. He graduated from South Carolina College and became a lawyer in Orangeburg. He served in the South Carolina state legislature and then was elected to the U.S. House of Representatives, serving from 1853 to 1860, when he resigned. The fiery orator was a prominent secessionist and served as a delegate to the South Carolina Secession Convention. Keitt also served a year in the Confederate Congress. Despite having no prior military experience or training, he was commissioned colonel of the 20th South Carolina Infantry on January 11, 1862. He and his regiment served on the South Carolina coast from 1862 until the spring of 1864, when his command was ordered to join the Army of Northern Virginia. Arriving in Richmond on May 29, Keitt called on President Jefferson Davis the next day and asked to be assigned to Kershaw's brigade. Davis agreed, and so did Robert E. Lee, who was looking for a new permanent commander for the brigade. Confederate diarist Mary Chesnut described Keitt as "immensely clever and original." Allardice, *Confederate Colonels*, 224; Krick, *Lee's Colonels*, 220; Isabella D. Martin and Myrta Lockett Avary, eds., *A Diary from Dixie, as Written by Mary Boykin Chesnut* (New York. D. Appleton, 1906), 68.

11 Woodward, *Mary Chesnut's Civil War*, 204.

Cold Harbor the men began to snuff the scent of battle," one of Keitt's soldiers stated. "Cartridge boxes were examined, guns unslung, and bayonets fixed, while the ranks were being rapidly closed up." Keitt had never managed such a large body of troops before, which only complicated matters.[12]

As the head of his column neared the church, his skirmishers began trading "desultory fire" with Torbert's pickets. Mounted on a horse that Kershaw had lent him, Keitt halted his troops and ordered them to form along Allison's Road to prepare to charge. The rest of Kershaw's division also waited, expecting to resume the march soon. "Colonel Keitt had never before handled such a body of troops in open field, and his pressing orders to find the enemy only added perplexity to his other difficulties," his brigade's historian recorded. "Every man in ranks knew that he was being led by one of the most gifted and gallant men in the South, but every old soldier felt and saw at a glance his inexperience and want of self-control. Colonel Keitt showed no want of aggressiveness and boldness, but he was preparing for battle like in the days of Alva or Turenne, and to cut his way through like a storm center."[13]

The inexperienced Keitt formed his brigade in a mass, his own 20th South Carolina in front. Brigadier General Goode Bryan's brigade of Georgians, hearing the firing, moved at the double-quick to the front and took position behind Keitt. "As we advanced on the run the sharpshooters of the enemy were pouring hot fire into our ranks and killing and wounding a great many of our men," Capt. A. J. McBride of the 10th Georgia recalled. Cheering his troops, McBride mounted a breastwork and promptly received a shrapnel wound.[14]

The road passed through a stand of dense woods just before reaching Beulah Church. Unsure of what lay in front of him, Keitt decided not to launch a frontal attack there. Instead, he decided to attack through an open field that angled southeast toward the Old Cold Harbor road intersection, so he oriented his men to march across the clearing, a decision that horrified Kershaw's battle-hardened veterans because it exposed them to enfilading fire the whole way. They could see a dense stand of oak trees bristling with dismounted Union cavalrymen awaiting them.[15] But orders were orders. "The order of advance was given with never so much as a skirmish line in front," one of Keitt's officers reflected. "Keitt led his men like a knight of

---

12 D. Augustus Dickert, *History of Kershaw's Brigade* (Newberry, SC: E. H. Aull Co., 1899), 369.
13 Dickert, *History of Kershaw's Brigade*, 369.
14 A. J. McBride, "Some War Experiences," Archives, Richmond National Battlefield Park, Richmond, Virginia.
15 Dickert, *Kershaw's Brigade*, 369–70.

Beulah Church on the Cold Harbor battlefield.

(Author's photo)

old—mounted upon his superb iron-gray, and looked the embodiment of the true chevalier that he was." A member of the brigade noted that this was the first time the brigade's commander had ever led them into battle while mounted, perplexing many of the men.[16]

Many of Torbert's weary troopers had gone to the rear to rest and graze their tired horses. Merritt's line consisted of the 1st and 2nd U.S. Cavalry, the 6th Pennsylvania, and the 1st New York Dragoons. Captain Theophilus F. Rodenbough, commander of the 2nd U.S., was enjoying the morning's fourth cup of coffee when shots from the picket line alerted him that the Confederates were attacking. Runners carried reports from the Reserve Brigade's picket posts that a "compact mass of infantry, marching steadily and silently, company front," was advancing through the woods toward Torbert's line.[17]

The 20th South Carolina led Keitt's attack. Keitt positioned sharpshooters on the left to cover his brigade's flank and then angled toward Beulah Church Road. Torbert's pickets increased their rate of fire while the main line awaited its chance. "'Hold your fire until they are close upon us,' was the order passed along the Union line," an officer of the 1st New York Dragoons recalled. The South Carolinians gave the Rebel yell. "When they came within point blank range of the

16 James A. Milling, "Recollections," *Confederate Veteran* 6 (1897), 9.
17 Rodenbough, "Sheridan's Richmond Raid," 193.

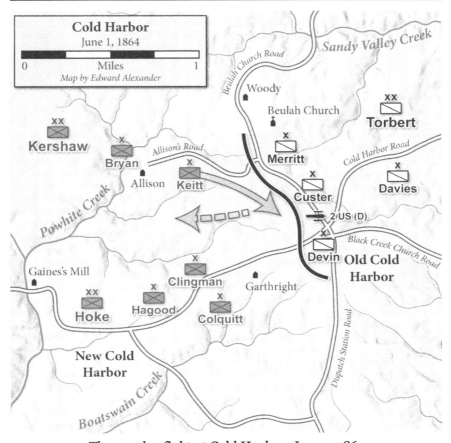

The cavalry fight at Cold Harbor, June 1, 1864

Union works, there was a crash of musketry, and the redoubt was hidden in yellow smoke," the same New Yorker recounted. Cries of agony rose from wounded Southerners.[18]

"For a moment the skirmishers redoubled their fire, the enemy took the double-quick, and as they charged us the [R]ebel yell rang through the forest. Then a sheet of flame came from the cavalry line, and for three or four minutes the din was deafening," Captain Rodenbough said.[19] Lieutenant William T. Pennock of the 1st U.S. Cavalry was shot through both eyes and blinded, two other troopers of the 1st U.S. were killed, and four were wounded.[20] Merritt later praised

18 Bowen, *First New York Dragoons*, 180.
19 Rodenbough, "Sheridan's Richmond Raid," 4:193.
20 R. P. Page Wainwright, "First Regiment of Cavalry," in Theophilus F. Rodenbough and William L. Haskin, eds., *The Army of the U. S.: Historical Sketches of Staff and Line with Portraits of Generals in Chief* (New York: Merrill, Maynard & Co., 1896), 161. Pennock came up through ranks. He enlisted as a private in the 1st Dragoons on October 23, 1857 and received

the 1st New York Dragoons' steady performance and the 2nd U.S. Cavalry in repulsing Keitt's attack that day.[21]

"The action became general in less than five minutes," Lieutenant Lucas, who had a bird's eye view of the events as they played out, reported. "The whole front line seemed a belt of fire belching forth death and destruction to the enemy and raged incessantly." Lucas noted, "Our regiment did not fire a gun being . . . in the rear or reserve line." Despite this fact, Capt. William Litzenberg, who had avoided being wounded in the ferocious fighting at Haw's Shop, suffered a wound, and so did a private.[22]

An officer of the 2nd U.S. Cavalry observed the Confederates approaching the Reserve Brigade's earthworks "with the intention of changing places with the Yankees. Between the seven-shooters of the dragoons and our carbines, however, we induced those of them that were left over to change their minds." The Yankee asked a desperately wounded South Carolinian, "without any top to his head" and whom he had saved from burning alive, why Keitt's men had done so foolhardy a thing as to try to carry that position. "Oh!" the Palmetto man responded with his last breath, "[W]e thought there were only a few cavalry up here."[23]

Meanwhile, the Wolverines on the left of the Reserve Brigade opened fire, inflicting casualties on the South Carolinians from both front and flank. "The repeating carbines [of the Wolverines] raked the flank of the hostile column while the Sharps single-loaders kept up a steady rattle," Rodenbough recounted.[24] Lieutenant Colonel Peter Stagg of the 1st Michigan spotted a gap between the Wolverines and Merritt's Reserve Brigade and moved to close the gap, arriving just in time to block the Palmetto men from exploiting the gap by turning Merritt's left. "Our men were behind breast works, but the Rebs could get pretty close to the works, in the woods, [and] the firing was at very close quarters," Granger of Custer's staff reported. Custer—the only mounted man along the firing line—rode up and down encouraging his men, all the while drawing heavy fire. "It is almost impossible to keep him from exposing himself needlessly," Granger complained, "but it can hardly be called needless exposure either, as it only incites the men

promotions to corporal and sergeant. He served as an acting second lieutenant for most of 1862, and received a commission as second lieutenant on July 17, 1862. He was promoted to first lieutenant on September 1, 1863 and received a brevet to captain for gallantry at the May 7, 1864, battle of Todd's Tavern. Due to his wound, he retired on July 1, 1865. Pennock died on August 21, 1887. Heitman, *Historical Register*, 782.
21 *OR* 36, 1:849.
22 Sauerburger and Bayard, *I Seat Myself to Write You a Few Lines*, 226.
23 Loeser, "Loeser's Recollections," 310.
24 Rodenbough, "Sheridan's Richmond Raid," 4:193.

Capt. Frank Furness,
6th Pennsylvania Cavalry.

(Theodore Green)

to 'do noble deeds of daring,' but it also keeps him posted on the exact position of his men." Granger declared that he often wished other officers did the same thing, because they would then have a better grasp of the enemy's precise dispositions.[25]

The Union horse artillery also opened, spewing death among the advancing Confederates. Keitt was shot from his saddle, and "the regiment went to pieces and threatened to overwhelm the rest of the brigade," Confederate artillerist Robert Stiles wrote, unable to repress his snarky remark. "I have never seen any body of troops in such a condition of utter demoralization," he said. "They actually groveled upon the ground and attempted to burrow under each other in holes and depressions." Major James M. Goggin unsuccessfully tried to rally the panicked Palmetto men. Thoroughly disgusted, Stiles recalled, "We actually spurred our horses upon them, and seemed to hear their very bones crack, but it did no good; if compelled to wriggle out of one hole, they wriggled into another."[26]

The South Carolinians reformed and made a second charge, which the Federals repulsed as easily as they had the first one. The 1st Michigan Cavalry, on Merritt's immediate left, drew fire, and Captain William M. Brevoort of the 1st Michigan, "one of the bravest and best officers of the brigade," according to Major Kidd, was killed instantly when a bullet blew through his head. Captains William M. Heazlett and Andrew W. Duggan, both of the 1st Michigan, also fell wounded.[27]

25 Barnard, *An Aide to Custer,* 244.
26 Robert Stiles, *Four Years Under Marse Robert* (New York: Neale, 1903), 274.
27 Kidd, *Personal Recollections,* 333–34.

A severely wounded South Carolinian lay in front of the Federal works, shot in the thigh and bleeding badly. Captain Robert W. Mitchell, 6th Pennsylvania Cavalry, spotted the desperately injured man and pointed him out to his friend Capt. Frank Furness, saying, "My God, look at that one." Furness realized the man would quickly bleed to death if steps were not taken to save him. Proclaiming, "I can't see him suffer," Furness clambered over the barricade and went to assist the wounded man. "What moved my pity more than in the countless other cases in which we almost daily witnessed was that when the poor fellow was struck, believing himself near death, he tried to struggle to his knees and clasped his upright hands in prayer," Furness remembered, years later. "What man with memories of bedtime and his mother's gentle hand would see that sight unmoved?"

Furness scrambled to the man's side, noting that his blood-soaked pants resembled "a dark alligator hide." The Confederate required an immediate tourniquet if he were to survive. Furness asked whether the soldier had a handkerchief and was told, "[I]nside pocket." The Pennsylvanian tightly wrapped the makeshift tourniquet and made the man as comfortable as possible, giving him his canteen and wishing him luck. As Furness crawled back to his own line, the Rebel called out, "You may be a Yankee, but, by Gad, you are a gentleman."

After returning to safety, Furness realized that the Confederates had held their fire while he tended to the wounded man. "Captain Mitchell, I don't believe those gentlemen fired a single shot in my direction while I was out there," he said. Furness never learned his patient's fate, but the episode haunted him for the rest of his life.[28]

---

28 Michael J. Lewis, *Frank Furness: Architecture and the Violent Mind* (New York: W. W. Norton, 2001), 47–48. Born on November 11, 1839, Frank Furness was the son of a prominent Philadelphia clergyman and abolitionist, Rev. William Henry Furness. Frank took up the study of architecture, apprenticing in New York with the famed architect Richard Morris Hunt. Instead of doing what most of his peers did, 22-year-old Frank Furness did not flee to Europe to avoid military service. Instead, he enlisted in Company I of the 6th Pennsylvania Cavalry and was quickly commissioned lieutenant. After a successful stint as a staff officer, on January 11, 1864, he was promoted to captain and assigned to command Company F. Furness was awarded the Medal of Honor for his valor in resupplying his regiment on the second day of the battle of Trevilian Station on June 12, 1864—the only major American architect to be awarded the prestigious decoration. Furness served out his term of enlistment and was discharged from the 6th Pennsylvania in the fall of 1864. Returning home to Philadelphia, he resumed his architecture career, designing nearly 650 buildings and becoming one of the highest paid architects of the time. Employing an approach based on the theory that architecture was more than just building, Furness employed a heavy Gothic style that was quite unique. In a Victorian Age noted for its aggressive architecture, Furness's buildings were certainly among the most boisterous and challenging. Working mostly between 1870 and 1895, his

During this carnage, Union regimental bands played loudly. "We at once struck up 'Yankee Doodle,'" Sgt. Walter H. Jackson of the 1st New York Dragoons' brass band recorded. "After their first repulse, and when they had fallen back to reform, we gave them 'Dixie;' and when they advanced the second time, we gave them 'Hail Columbia' on the horns while the boys put in the variations with their carbines, smashing their ranks worse than before." While the Northern carbine fire took its toll, so did the accurate fire of the Union horse artillery, which ripped holes in the ranks of Keitt's men. "To add to the horror of the scene," Lt. Joseph N. Flint of the Dragoons shuddered, "the woods took fire from exploding shells from [Lieutenant] Williston's battery, and the shrieks of the [R]ebel wounded were first heightened, then stifled, by the flames."[29]

Witnessing the carnage and watching two separate attacks fail, Kershaw called off any further attacks. "I am on the hill in front of Beulah," he wrote to Major General Anderson at 8:45 that morning. "I attacked them with two brigades. Got very near their works then stopped." He knew that Sheridan's troopers held Beulah Church, which prevented any further advance. "Colonel Keitt is killed or wounded," he added. "I am trying to get his body."[30] A Confederate artillerist blamed Keitt's repulse on the "magazine guns" that some of the Union cavalrymen carried, which acted as a force multiplier, giving

designs include some of Philadelphia's most prominent structures, such as the Philadelphia Zoo Gatehouses, the Pennsylvania Academy of Fine Arts, and the Merion Cricket Club. He cofounded the Philadelphia chapter of the American Institute of Architects and is known as the founder of the so-called "Philadelphia School" of architecture. One of his most interesting designs is the handsome monument dedicated to the 6th Pennsylvania Cavalry that graces the battlefield at Gettysburg, and which features full-scale replicas of the lances carried by the men of the regiment for the first year and a half of the war. Although he is considered the first "All-American" architect, Furness eventually fell from favor. When he died in 1912, his work was largely forgotten. He was buried at Philadelphia's Laurel Hill Cemetery. Throughout his long career in architecture, Furness was known for his daring and innovative designs. Accordingly, Furness' work attracted attention, as well as other eager young architects. Furness' most famous student was Louis Henry Sullivan, best known as one of the leading architects in late nineteenth-century Chicago and as the teacher of a young Frank Lloyd Wright, the greatest American architect. A review of Wright's early work shows a clear link to the groundbreaking work of Frank Furness, Philadelphia's soldier-architect. For a detailed biography, see Lewis, *Frank Furness*.

29 Bowen, *First New York Dragoons*, 181–82.
30 Kershaw to G. Moxley Sorrell, 8:45 a.m., June 1, 1864, Edward Porter Alexander Papers, Southern Historical Collections, Wilson Library, University of North Carolina, Chapel Hill, North Carolina.

the impression that more than just dismounted cavalry faced the Southern infantry.[31]

Despite having no reserves to commit to the fight, Sheridan and his troopers had held. The 20th South Carolina suffered about 80 casualties in this fighting. The rest of Kershaw's division, trailing Keitt's brigade, began digging earthworks along the road without firing a shot. Colonel Alexander, heading the Army of Northern Virginia's I Corps, wrote, "Without any general instructions, men here and there began to dig dirt with their bayonets and pile it with their tin cups to get a little cover." Before long, all of the gray infantrymen were digging knee-deep trenches with protective mounds of dirt in front. "As the country was generally flat," Alexander continued, "orders were given to close up the column and adapt its line as the line of battle, distributing our guns upon it at suitable point." A particularly grizzly sight left an impression on Alexander, who watched as a Confederate soldier suddenly fell to his hands and knees, gasping. "A hole in the back of his soiled gray shirt showed where a stray bullet had gone in his lungs," the artillerist remembered. "I had never before realized exactly what knocking the breath out of one means, and it made an impression on me."[32]

The rest of Kershaw's division and Hoke's men extended the new Confederate line, facing Cold Harbor. This curved position, interrupted by a ravine, became the Army of Northern Virginia's main line of battle for the coming fight, which was improvised under fire instead of being carefully selected and meticulously constructed like the Totopotomoy Creek line had been.[33]

Torbert's troopers had held. "The Rebs gave up in disgust," remarked Custer's aide Granger.[34] The Union troopers made excellent use of the high ground and exploited the poor decisions that the inexperienced Keitt had made. "Perhaps more vigor might have been put into our offensive," Alexander remarked. Had they done so, the outcome might well have been different, as the Confederates had an entire division of isolated, unsupported Union cavalry in their sights—an opportunity that they failed to exploit.[35] Sheridan was also fortunate that Hoke committed only one brigade to the battle, leaving Sheridan's left with nothing to do. Had Hoke committed his entire

---

31 Edward Porter Alexander, *Military Memoirs of a Confederate: A Critical Narrative* (New York: Charles Scribner's Sons, 1907), 536.
32 Ibid.; Gallagher, *Fighting for the Confederacy*, 399.
33 For a detailed description of the formation and alignment of the Confederate line of battle, see Rhea, *Cold Harbor*, 202–3.
34 Barnard, *An Aide to Custer*, 245.
35 Gallagher, *Fighting for the Confederacy*, 399.

division to the fighting, Sheridan might not have been able to hold the line.

About 9:00 a.m., Col. Thomas W. Hyde, who served on Wright's VI Corps staff, arrived at the Old Cold Harbor intersection with the welcome news that the VI Corps was nearby. Hyde located Sheridan near the front lines and found him to be "the most nervy, wiry incarnation of business, and business only, I had yet met." Hyde conveyed Wright's message, borrowed a carbine from a wounded cavalryman, and took his place along Torbert's line. "We had a belief in the infantry that those carbines would not hit anything, and I confirmed the belief so far as I was concerned," Hyde recalled. "To be sure there was nothing but smoke to fire at as a general thing, and though in dead earnest then, I am happy in the conviction that I did not hurt anybody."[36]

Word of the VI Corps' imminent arrival spread quickly. "About ten o'clock and when the men were becoming quite worn out besides being generally out of ammunition, word was passed along the line that the [VI] Corps was coming up in our rear to relieve us," Capt. George Sanford, Torbert's staffer, said. "It was time."[37] Periodic fire rang out on both sides of the line as the Union cavalry waited for the infantry to arrive.[38]

"In obedience to your instructions I am holding Cold Harbor," Sheridan reported to Meade's chief of staff Humphreys. "The enemy assaulted the right of my lines this morning, but were handsomely repulsed. I have been very apprehensive, but General Wright is now coming up," he acknowledged.[39] Sheridan also scribbled a note to Wright, advising him that his cavalry faced at least a division of infantry and that he was worried more might be on the way. Wright told Humphreys that he thought he could hold the Old Cold Harbor intersection with his troops unless Lee launched a major offensive, which Wright considered unlikely in the wake of Keitt's defeat. "I shall cover the road intersections at Cold Harbor, and refuse my left somewhat," Wright said, "but as I can't connect with [Maj. Gen. Gouverneur K.] Warren, I could wish that Smith, who I understand is to fill the gap, could come up."[40]

Leading the VI Corps, Brig. Gen. James Ricketts' infantry division arrived at Cold Harbor to the sounds of Custer's brigade band playing "Hail Columbia." The foot soldiers filed into the trenches that

36 Hyde, *Following the Greek Cross*, 208.
37 Hagemann, *Fighting Rebels and Redskins*, 241.
38 Hall, *History of the Sixth New York Cavalry*, 195.
39 *OR* 36, 3:470.
40 Ibid., 454.

Torbert's troopers held.[41] "Never were reinforcements more cordially welcomed," a relieved Major Kidd observed. "In solid array and with quick step [the VI Corps] marched out of the woods in rear of the line, and took our place. The tension was relaxed and for the first time since midnight the cavalrymen drew a long breath."[42] In a report to the adjutant general of Michigan, Kidd noted, "About 12 p.m. we were relieved by the [IV] Corps, to our great relief, for officers and men were worn out with incessant marching and fighting by night and day."[43]

Major General "Baldy" Smith's XVIII Corps was, in fact, on the way. However, Smith believed that Grant and Meade had failed to send help to Sheridan as quickly as they should have. "When the concentration upon Cold Harbor was determined upon," he wrote years after the war, "had the [XVIII] Corps been ordered to join Sheridan it would have reached him on the night of the 31st, with about the same length of march it did make, and would have been fresh for battle early on the morning of the 1st." Smith also remarked that Grant's logistics were "terrible."[44]

Regardless, Sheridan and his troopers had done just fine without being reinforced; assisted by Hoke's inactivity, they had held on against Confederate infantry until the VI Corps arrived and relieved them. "With our carbines alone we repulsed Hoke's division of infantry, who charged upon us with fixed bayonets," a member of Merritt's 6th Pennsylvania Cavalry proudly declared.[45] "Just after daylight June 1 [the enemy] marched to the attack, and was permitted to come close in to our little works, when he received the fire of our batteries and repeating carbines, which were used with terrible effect, and was driven back in confusion," Sheridan said. "[S]till determined to get the place, after reorganizing, he attacked again, but with the same result."[46] The Union cavalrymen's hard work was finished for the time being.

"Therefore, wishing the [VI] Corps God-speed, we rode off towards New Kent Church, on the New Castle Road, in exceedingly good humor with ourselves and the rest of the world," Capt. Charles Loeser, 2nd U.S. Cavalry, declared, "although, after the tussle of the

41 Edwin M. Haynes, *History of the Tenth Regiment, Vermont Volunteers, with Biographical Sketches of the Officers Who Fell in Battle* (Lewiston, ME: Tenth Vermont Regimental Assoc., 1870), 134.
42 Kidd, *Personal Recollections*, 335.
43 *OR* Supplement, 6:622.
44 William F. Smith, "The Eighteenth Corps at Cold Harbor," in Robert U. Johnson and Clarence C. Buel, eds., *Battles and Leaders of the Civil War*, 4 vols. (New York: Century Publishing Co., 1884–1888), 4:230.
45 Gracey, *Annals of the Sixth Pennsylvania Cavalry*, 256.
46 *OR* 36, 1:794.

last few days, we were sadly lessened in numbers, and all of us had left good friends under those trees. We got into camp about five p.m., and, having the assurance that we were not to be disturbed before morning, we rested very well indeed."[47] The Reserve Brigade's hungry, fought-out men savored their first regular meal in three days.[48] They were serenaded by the severe fighting raging at Cold Harbor. "The roar of artillery and musketry was continuous until long after dark and was kept up at intervals, the greater part of the night," a member of the 6th New York Cavalry recalled.[49] Matthew W. King of the 6th Ohio Cavalry, whose regiment was on picket that night, noted, "Indications all point to doings on a big scale tomorrow."[50]

As the Union cavalrymen plainly heard, the gates of hell had swung open at the Cold Harbor intersection, and they would not slam shut again for an additional two long, brutal, and bloody days.

---

47 Loeser, "Loeser's Recollections," 311.
48 Hagemann, *Fighting Rebels and Redskins*, 241.
49 Hall, *History of the Sixth New York Cavalry*, 195.
50 Matthew W. King, *To Horse: With the Cavalry of the Army of the Potomac 1861–65* (Cheboygan, MI: n.p., 1926), entry for June 1, 1864.

CONCLUSION

Torbert's and Gregg's divisions spent the night of June 1 encamped around Prospect Church. The next day, the two divisions moved farther down the Chickahominy River, taking a position on the north bank at Bottom's Bridge. Devin's brigade arrived first. "The Sixth New York, in the advance, came up with a force of the enemy, and after considerable skirmishing drove them across the bridge," a member of the 6th New York noted. "As the regiment approached the bridge to reconnoiter, it was greeted with a few shells from the enemy's fortifications beyond the Chickahominy, one of which killed their horses and took off a man's foot."[1] Fitzhugh Lee's division occupied the south side, with artillery support at the fords. "We had a slight skirmish with them, when both parties brought strong batteries in position, and a very loud and not very damaging artillery conversation took place, continuing until night," a member of the 6th Pennsylvania Cavalry recounted.[2] The men were hungry. "Our stock of provisions was so far exhausted that hard-tack was selling at a dollar a cracker," an officer of the 1st U.S. Cavalry complained.[3]

"We still held our post to keep any of the enemy from getting around and a strong force of cavalry was on the left of our infantry to prevent Grant from sending any troops around that way," Rufus Peck, 2nd Virginia Cavalry of Wickham's brigade, recalled. "He was known as the old left flanker. The cavalry was not in any of the hottest of this battle, as we occupied the extreme ends of the line."[4]

On June 2, Gregg's troopers commenced a reconnaissance in force at 8:00 a.m. His division ran into the enemy on the extreme left of the Union line along the Chickahominy River, where they had a severe fight with the Confederates, an encounter Sgt. Samuel Cormany, 16th Pennsylvania Cavalry, described as "savage." Cormany noted in his diary that the chaplain of the 1st Maine Cavalry was shot and killed instantly while waving his hat and encouraging the men, "who were making a good charge." That night, infantry relieved Gregg's men, and his troopers camped at Bottom's Bridge.[5] On June 3, Confederate horse artillery shelled Sheridan's positions at long range, serving as an annoyance, but doing little damage.[6]

---

1 Hall, *History of the Sixth New York Cavalry*, 195.
2 Gracey, *Annals of the Sixth Pennsylvania Cavalry*, 257.
3 Loeser, "Loeser's Recollections," 311.
4 Peck, *Reminiscences of a Confederate*, 51.
5 Mohr, *The Cormany Diaries*, 432. On June 6, Cormany received a promotion to second lieutenant.
6 *OR* 36, 1:794–95.

Also on June 3, Butler's South Carolina brigade, which now included the newly arrived 6th South Carolina Cavalry, established a picket line nine miles south of Savage's Station, at White Oak Swamp, to cover other crossing points along the Chickahominy. Much of the 1862 Seven Days Battles took place there, and evidence of those severe engagements remained. "We are now on one of the great battle fields of McClellan's retreat and the bones of two dead Yankees that were never buried are lying near here," Lt. Col. William Stokes of the 4th South Carolina recounted.[7] Private James Barr of the 5th South Carolina noted, "It does not seem that [Grant] can get as far as McClellan got. I have passed over the ground where [McClellan] fought and camped. Plenty of old clothing and everything thrown away. I hope this [w]ar will end soon."[8]

"After so much hard fighting and marching the boys naturally expected a little rest," a member of the 5th New York Cavalry of Wilson's Third Division griped. The Third Division continued operating separately from the First and Second Divisions. "Well, they got a little, and a very little rest it was. The time for an abundance of that luxury had not yet come."[9] Wilson's division spent June 2 on the march after learning that the army's main body had moved to Cold Harbor. After awaiting the arrival of about 500 reinforcements commanded by Col. Luigi Palma di Cesnola and marching from Port Royal, Wilson crossed Totopotomoy Creek, but failed to establish contact with the right wing of the Army of the Potomac. On June 3, Wilson received orders to cross to the west side of the Totopotomoy, drive Hampton from Haw's Shop, swing to the left again, re-cross the creek near its source, and attack the left of the Confederate infantry line.[10]

About noon that day, Wilson's command marched, struck Hampton's pickets near Haw's Shop, and engaged in another slugging match on the fields of the May 28 battle. "We had a warm and spirited artillery duel with them of a couple hours' duration," Sgt. George Neese of Thomson's battery of horse artillery noted.[11] Wilson's dismounted troopers drove the Confederate cavalry from three consecutive lines of breastworks, and a small mounted force pursued the retreating Southerners. "The [R]ebels fought stubbornly," Wilson admitted. Lieutenant Colonel Addison W. Preston and the intrepid Capt. Oliver W. Cushman of the 1st Vermont Cavalry were both killed in this fighting, and Lt. Col. William H. Benjamin of the 8th

---

7 Halliburton, *Saddle Soldiers*, 145.
8 Mays, "Let Us Meet in Heaven," 236.
9 Boudrye, *Historic Records of the Fifth New York Cavalry*, 137–38.
10 *OR* 36, 1:882.
11 Neese, *Three Years in the Confederate Horse Artillery*, 280.

New York Cavalry was severely wounded in the thigh.[12] "In the course of an hour or so of skirmishing, I was pleased to hear General Hampton give the order to withdraw," a relieved Capt. Theodore S. Garnett, Maj. Gen. Rooney Lee's staffer, said.[13]

After driving off the Confederate cavalry, Wilson and his division crossed the Totopotomoy, placed a section of horse artillery there, dismounted, and crossed the creek. They found enemy infantry in position along the brow of a ridge and attacked, supported by their horse artillery. "The [R]ebels after firing a few shots broke and fled, leaving 10 or 15 prisoners in our hands," Wilson reported. By then it was nearly dark, and General Lee, fearing his flank was about to be turned, withdrew his left wing from its position fronting the IX Corps. "For its gallant conduct the division received the congratulations of [Maj. Gen. George G.] Meade," Wilson proudly declared. "The operations were hazardous, and although entirely successful, cost us the lives of quite a number of brave officers and men." The Third Division returned to the junction of the roads leading to Haw's Shop and Hanover Court House, bivouacking and keeping watch on the roads in all directions.[14]

The second battle of Haw's Shop was a small engagement that ultimately had strategic implications for the entire Overland campaign. Even though Burnside called off his anticipated attack on the left flank of the Army of Northern Virginia, Wilson's pressure against Heth's position on the Confederate left flank helped persuade Lee to pull back that exposed flank, ending the battle of Cold Harbor.

On June 4, Wilson's division marched to a spot near New Castle Ferry and picketed off the infantry's right flank to the Pamunkey River. Part of the Third Division remained there until June 12.[15] Also on June 4, Torbert's First Division marched back to Old Church, while Gregg's Second Division remained at Bottom's Bridge. "Though constantly in the saddle, [we] were given a few days' respite from severe fighting," a member of the 1st New York Dragoons remarked.[16] "Before we had time to feed our horses and make coffee, the Johnnies put one over on us by shelling our camp, which was not a nice way to treat a lot of mighty tired cavalrymen," Matthew W. King, 6th Ohio Cavalry, quipped in his diary. "With this gentle hint we moved camp out of range of their guns."[17]

---

12 *OR* 36, 1:882.
13 Trout, *Riding with Stuart*, 79.
14 Ibid.
15 *OR* 36, 1:883.
16 Bowen, *History of the First New York Dragoons*, 183.
17 King, *To Horse*, entry for June 4, 1864.

On June 6, part of Wilson's division relieved Gregg's command at Bottom's Bridge. Gregg and Torbert then marched to New Castle Ferry, where the Cavalry Corps' wagon trains and fresh supplies awaited them.[18] "Saddled up before daylight and moved to the picket reserve," King recounted. "Dismounted, formed skirmish line and advanced to the river. Held this position all day; exchanged shots with the Johnnies on the opposite side of the river."[19] The Reserve Brigade occupied Edmund Ruffin's plantation again, ensuring that its crops were completely ruined.[20] "June 6th, again return to Old Church, where we take a bath in the Pamunkey River, a great treat which the whole regiment enjoyed," Sgt. Henry Avery of the 5th Michigan remembered.[21]

Also on June 6, Meade directed Sheridan to proceed with two divisions—Torbert's and Gregg's—to Charlottesville to cut the Virginia Central Railroad and meet up with Maj. Gen. David Hunter's army, which had been operating in the Shenandoah Valley, and escort Hunter's troops to the Army of the Potomac. "There also appeared to be another object," Sheridan said, "to remove the enemy's cavalry from the south side of the Chickahominy, as, in case we attempted to cross the James River, this large cavalry force could make such resistance at the difficult crossings as to give the enemy time to transfer his force to oppose the movement." Grant and Meade had apparently learned their lesson from Sheridan's Richmond Raid in May, because they retained Wilson's Third Division to escort the Army of the Potomac once it moved.[22]

On June 7, Sheridan, with Torbert's and Gregg's divisions and several batteries of horse artillery, began their march along the north bank of the North Anna River, headed toward the anticipated rendezvous with Hunter's army at Charlottesville.[23] Thus began the

---

18 *OR* 36, 1:795.
19 King, *To Horse*, entry for June 6, 1864.
20 Loeser, "Loeser's Recollections," 311.
21 Wittenberg and Husby, *Under Custer's Command*, 82.
22 Ibid.
23 On June 5, Hunter's army defeated the command of Brig. Gen. William E. "Grumble" Jones in the battle of Piedmont, during which Jones was killed. Hunter then marched to Lexington, where his army burned part of the Virginia Military Institute on June 11, in retaliation for sending its cadets to fight at the May battle of New Market. Hunter lingered in Lexington for three days, burning the home of Virginia governor John Letcher. By June 19, his army had reached Lynchburg. Lieutenant General Jubal A. Early, whose II Corps of the Army of Northern Virginia had been sent to meet Hunter's advance, arrived just in time to repulse Hunter, who then fled to West Virginia, effectively out of the war for the next month. Sheridan would not have been able to accomplish his mission of meeting Hunter at Charlottesville, because Hunter never got there. For a detailed discussion of Hunter's operations, see Duncan, *Lee's Endangered Left*.

Trevilian Raid, which lasted until June 24. At 2:00 a.m. on June 9, Hampton, with his own division and Fitz Lee's, pursued. The Confederate cavalry surpassed Sheridan's line of march a few miles west of Louisa Court House, along the Gordonsville Road, late in the day on June 10. Hampton then thrashed Sheridan in the harsh two-day battle of Trevilian Station, fought on June 11 and 12, near an obscure depot along the Virginia Central Railroad in Louisa County, about 65 miles from Richmond. Thwarted in his attempt to reach Hunter's army, Sheridan turned back. It took him until June 24 to rejoin the Army of the Potomac, which was now operating at Petersburg, 25 miles south of Richmond.[24]

Since June 1, the Union and Confederate infantry had been slugging it out at Cold Harbor. Encouraged by Sheridan's success that morning, Grant ordered up "Baldy" Smith's XVIII Corps and Wright's VI Corps to attack the Confederate defenses. However, confusing orders and bad roads delayed the attack until 5 p.m. The Union offensive briefly pierced the Confederate line, but a strong counterattack shoved the Federals back. While this attack was playing out, Meade ordered Hancock's II Corps to march the 12 miles to Cold Harbor that night to support another attack.

The Union high command ordered an early morning attack for June 2, but the II Corps got lost during its grueling night march and did not arrive until about 6:30 a.m. Deciding to give Hancock's exhausted troops a chance to rest, Meade postponed the offensive until 5 p.m. However, Grant, concerned that Hancock's men would not be ready to attack, suggested that Meade wait until the next morning. General Lee took advantage of the delay by having his troops construct extensive and intricate earthworks to strengthen their position on the heavily wooded and rolling battlefield. By the time they were finished, the Confederate works resembled the terrain of World War I's Western Front.

At 4:30 a.m. on June 3, the Union II, VI, and XVIII corps launched their assault through the inky darkness and thick fog. The attack bogged down in swamps, ravines, and dense woods, and the various units lost contact with each other. The design of the Confederate earthworks permitted the Southerners to enfilade the Northerners as they approached. The Army of the Potomac lost several thousand men killed and wounded in the assault, and severe bloodletting lasted for the entire morning. Elements of the II Corps briefly captured some of the Confederate earthworks, but Southern

---

24 A detailed discussion of the Trevilian Raid and of the battle of Trevilian Station strays far beyond the scope of this study. For that detailed discussion, see Wittenberg, *Glory Enough for All.*

artillery quickly turned those works into bloody traps. The terrain funneled the XVIII Corps into two ravines, where the Confederates mowed them down.

Unable to advance, and in no position to retreat, the Union soldiers did the only thing they could do—they built earthworks, sometimes using their comrades' corpses as components of their hastily constructed breastworks. Grant finally called off any further attacks after riding the lines and seeing for himself that further assaults would also end with bloody repulses.[25] The battle's management "would have shamed a cadet in his first year at West Point," an officer of the VI Corps lamented.[26] "I have always regretted that the last assault at Cold Harbor was ever made," Grant wrote in his memoirs at the end of his life. "No advantage whatever was gained to compensate for the heavy loss we sustained."[27]

The horse soldiers of both sides plainly heard the frightful cataclysm at Cold Harbor. "The successive advances and recoils could be numbered by a listener," Edward Wells of the Charleston Light Dragoons declared, "from the awful roar of musketry and artillery, and then the comparative cessation for short intervals." Then, the sudden silence that fell over the battlefield signaled the end of the "fruitless butchery of twenty [Federals] to every one Confederate."[28] Lieutenant Colonel Stokes, 4th South Carolina, echoed a similar note. "I was not very far from the battle field and the roar of musketry was terrific in the extreme, and having recently passed through such trying ordeals, I deeply sympathize with our brave soldiers in the trenches," he wrote.[29]

With Grant's decision to call off further assaults, the gates of hell swung shut again on June 3. The butcher's bill had come due once again, and the Army of the Potomac, in particular, had paid it, suffering 12,738 casualties, including 1,845 killed, 9,077 wounded, and 1,816 missing or captured.[30] Lee's army, which had the advantages of a strong position behind stout earthworks and was fighting on the defensive, suffered less than half as many casualties, with 788 killed, 3,376 wounded, and 1,123 missing or captured, for total losses of 5,287.[31]

Assistant Secretary of War Charles A. Dana, who traveled with Grant's headquarters, wrote, "Grant was disappointed, and talked to

25 For a detailed discussion of the bloody infantry combat at Cold Harbor, see Rhea, *Cold Harbor*, 224–395.
26 Hyde, *Following the Greek Cross*, 211.
27 Grant, *Personal Memoirs*, 2:276.
28 Quoted in Edward G. Longacre, *Gentleman and Scholar: A Biography of Wade Hampton* (Nashville, TN: Rutledge Hill Press, 2003), 191.
29 Halliburton, *Saddle Soldiers*, 144.
30 *OR* 36, 1:180.
31 Young, *Lee's Army During the Overland Campaign*, 240.

Union pontoon bridges across the James River.

(Library of Congress)

me a good deal about the failure to get at Lee in an open battle which would wind up the Confederacy. The general was constantly revolving plans to turn Lee out of his entrenchments."[32] If the plan to steal a march on Lee and cross the James River succeeded, Grant would accomplish just that.

The period between June 4 and 12 featured minor attacks, protracted artillery duels, and occasional sniping along the lines. After arguing about it for several days, Lee and Grant agreed to a two-hour truce to permit the Army of the Potomac to recover its wounded on June 7. However, nearly five days of suffering under the hot spring sun meant that few of the wounded were still alive, and hundreds of men died needlessly. Much like George B. McClellan had discovered two years earlier, Grant realized he was hemmed in at Cold Harbor and could not force his way through to Richmond. He came up with a new plan: steal another march on Lee's army, cross the James River, and move on the critical railroad town of Petersburg, 25 miles south of the Confederate capital. Most of the Army of Northern Virginia's

32 Dana, *Recollections of the Civil War,* 214–15.

supplies from the Deep South came to Richmond via the Southside and Weldon railroads, which joined at Petersburg. If Grant could cut these critical supply lines, Lee would either have to come out and fight Grant on ground of his choosing or eventually surrender.

The fighting at Cold Harbor was finally over, and the focus of the war in the East was about to shift to Petersburg.

*   *   *

"The fight on the part of our officers and men was very gallant; they were now beginning to accept nothing less than victory," Sheridan said of his command's struggle to hold Cold Harbor.[33] The Union horsemen came to believe in themselves. "In the Army of the Potomac the men that had been spoken of with contempt were now emerging from their lurking obscurity to be the heroes of victory, and were now striking terror to the hearts of their foes," Isaac Gause of the 2nd Ohio Cavalry proclaimed.[34]

"Since starting on May fourth there had been more or less fighting every day," Lt. Robert C. Wallace of the 5th Michigan Cavalry recalled. "During all that time we had been separated from our baggage with no change of clothing, not even socks. The cavalry top boots, covering heavy woolen socks, formed a nice, warm breeding place for graybacks and they made the most of it until we reached the James River, where they went to feed the fishes."[35]

Sheridan had good reason to be proud of his command. His troopers performed admirably, fighting and marching constantly and getting the better of their foes in all of the engagements discussed in this book. Haw's Shop, in particular, was a decisive victory for his command, succeeding in driving the Southern horsemen away. At the same time, defeating the Confederate cavalry was not Sheridan's mission on May 28; his mission was to find the main body of the Army of Northern Virginia, and in that he utterly failed.

These battles gave Sheridan an opportunity to test out his theories about using cavalry as a mounted strike force instead of limiting his cavalry to its traditional roles of scouting and screening. Using their technological advantages in both carbines and horse artillery, his troopers performed more as mounted infantry than as cavalry, using their horses to move from place to place, dismounting, and then employing infantry tactics. Torbert's and Sheridan's backgrounds as infantry officers paid dividends here, as they thought more like foot soldiers than they did like cavalrymen. Likewise, Wesley Merritt was

33 *OR* 36, 1:794.
34 Gause, *Four Years with Five Armies*, 271.
35 Wallace, *A Few Memories of a Long Life*, 58–59. "Graybacks" was slang for lice.

trained as a dragoon, so he was equally comfortable fighting either mounted or dismounted.[36] Most importantly, this evolution in tactics made mounted charges less and less likely, and of the Union cavalry commanders, only George Custer remained enamored of mounted combat. This was a sea change for the Army of the Potomac's cavalry, and their Confederate counterparts had to catch up. This evolution may explain some of the success that the Northern horsemen enjoyed during those six bloody days of campaigning in the spring of 1864.

The fighting at Cold Harbor marked an especially significant development in the Union cavalry's tactics. "This is the first time in all my experience that cavalry dismounted, entrenched, and fought the rebel infantry from a fortified position," Lt. Thomas B. Lucas of the 1st Pennsylvania Cavalry correctly observed. "But we whipped them handsomely."[37] Lieutenant Colonel Theodore Lyman, who served on Meade's staff, agreed. "Sheridan had been ordered to hold on with all his might," he noted in his diary on June 1, "and he accordingly did so, though it had otherwise been his idea to withdraw. And he had, this morning, a sharp engagement from behind breastworks! A notable fact, as the first instance, that I have observed, where the cavalry have used field works on a large scale. He repulsed the enemy."[38]

At the same time, Sheridan was an infantry officer. Since he had no formal training in cavalry tactics and very little experience in commanding large bodies of cavalry—roughly a month of experience doing so in the field—his tactics were unimaginative and relied heavily on the combination of an advantage in manpower and the superior technology of the Spencer carbines, which part of his Cavalry Corps carried. The dismounted fighting in these engagements closely resembled infantry combat, so the employment of infantry tactics did not necessarily negatively impact the success of the Union cavalry. His insistence upon treating his cavalry as a mounted strike force, instead of acting in the traditional roles of cavalry, meant that the infantry of the Army of the Potomac often acted without a screen, which offered the Confederates opportunities to attack. Luckily, none of those opportunities led to disaster for Grant's army.

---

36 Dragoons were originally a class of mounted infantry who used their horses to move from place to place and then dismounted to fight. However, U.S. army doctrine during the nineteenth century utilized dragoons to fight both mounted and dismounted. The antebellum U.S. army had two regiments of dragoons, the 1st and 2nd Dragoons. They were later reclassified and renumbered as the 1st and 2nd U.S. Cavalry in 1861.

37 Sauerburger and Bayard, *I Seat Myself to Write You a Few Lines*, 226.

38 Lowe, *Meade's Army*, 184.

Torbert, also an infantry officer with no formal training in cavalry tactics, likewise performed capably. Again, the dismounted fighting closely resembled infantry tactics, and Torbert, as an experienced commander of infantry, was in his element. As was so often the case during the campaigns of the spring and summer of 1864, Torbert's First Division bore the brunt of the fighting, and the Reserve Brigade and Custer's Michigan Cavalry Brigade did most of the hard work. Merritt and Custer were the workhorses, and they carried the burden admirably.

Typically, David Gregg was an anomaly. Sheridan simply did not rely on Gregg or his steadfast veteran division for the most difficult tasks, so other than joining the intense combat at Haw's Shop, Gregg's troopers played little part in the drama that unfolded at Hanover County in late May and early June 1864. The same held true at Trevilian Station two weeks later. Why Sheridan tended to avoid giving more difficult tasks to Gregg is a mystery—and Sheridan never divulged his reason—but their uncomfortable working relationship unquestionably led to Gregg's resigning his commission in February 1865, prematurely ending his tenure as the longest-serving cavalry division commander in Union service during the Civil War. Although their role was limited during these engagements, Gregg's veterans fought hard and well, effectively bearing the brunt of the fighting at Haw's Shop.

James Wilson had the most difficult task of the three Union division commanders. Assigned to operate as a detached, independent command, Wilson and his troopers spent those six critical days isolated and without support, fighting hard at Hanover Court House on May 31 and at Ashland on June 1, knowing that if they did not prevail, they would be surrounded, cut off, and either be forced to surrender or be destroyed on the battlefield by their foes. Despite his inexperience, Wilson managed his troopers very capably and fulfilled his orders, including the destruction of two important railroad bridges across the South Anna River on June 1. Colonels George Chapman and John McIntosh, Wilson's two brigade commanders, also performed well, playing integral roles in the two critical victories that the Third Division enjoyed at Hanover Court House and Ashland.

Wilson's troopers bore their burdens with good humor. "We met them at Mechumps Creek, where we took our morning exercise," William James Smith, 2nd Ohio Cavalry, remembered of the division's travails during the month of May. "Then not having had much exercise during the merry month of May, we finished up the month by giving them another dose in the afternoon at Hanover Court House. On

June 1st we had a hot time at Ashland, where we ran up against a heavy force and got rather the worst of it, and had to retire."[39]

Even though three of the four ranking officers of the Army of the Potomac's Cavalry Corps had minimal experience commanding horse soldiers, and two of them had no formal training in cavalry tactics as former infantry officers, Sheridan, Torbert, Gregg, and Wilson admirably served during those six long, hard days of marching and fighting. Torbert's men, particularly, had the most difficult assignments. These six days amply proved that the worm had turned—no longer was the Army of the Potomac's Cavalry Corps outmatched by its Confederate counterparts; it was now a formidable force to be reckoned with.

Their adversaries faced different challenges. The Confederates had recently lost their beloved leader, Jeb Stuart, which created an awkward and ultimately untenable command structure in the wake of his death. They had a senior officer who lacked formal military training or battlefield experience in commanding more than two brigades at a time. The lack of systematic remounts caused logistical difficulties, and they also faced serious technological disadvantages. In spite of these challenges, the Southern army's performance continued at the same level that had brought them fame during the first three years of the war.

"During the whole month of May we have been in a whirl," Capt. Richard Watkins of the 3rd Virginia Cavalry wrote to his wife on June 1. "In the saddle at least sixteen hours a day, watching, skirmishing, fighting. In our Regiment about one fourth of those who reported for duty the 1st of May have been killed wounded or captured... The rest are well hearty in fine spirits and bountifully supplied with rations of excellent bacon and hard bread and plenty of ammunition." He concluded, "This seems to be the crisis, the turning point of the war."[40] Lieutenant Allen Edens of the 4th South Carolina Cavalry of Butler's brigade sounded a similar note. "We are nearly broak [sic] down," he penned on June 5. "We have been marching and fighting for 10 days with hardly time to eat—I am better satisfied than I expected to be but I am tired of war—some think it will end soon but it will not end as long as the Yankees can find a man to fight."[41]

---

39 Robert W. Hatton, ed., *William James Smith's Memoirs of the 2nd Ohio Volunteer Cavalry, Company M* (Milford, OH: Little Miami Press, 2008), 17–18.

40 Jeff Toalson, ed., *Send Me a Pair of Old Boots & Kiss My Little Girls: The Civil War Letters of Richard and Mary Watkins, 1861–1865* (Bloomington, IN: iUniverse, 2009), 279–80.

41 Swank, *Confederate Letters and Diaries*, 147.

On June 3, Capt. Alfred B. Mulligan, 5th South Carolina, said, "Today finds me well only pretty well worn out with fatigue. We are certainly on the go. I have this morning for the second time since I have been in Virginia washed [and] put on clean clothing."[42] Two days later, he elaborated further. "I have under gone the extremist exposure ever since I came to [Virginia.] I did not think it possible for men to undergo so much exposure without breaking down," he wrote home. "We take rain, [and] sunshine and are getting so that we can lye [sic] down in a mud hole [and] sleep about as well as we used to in our beds. We who are just from North [and] South Carolina have just begun to realize the war." He continued, "Our horses suffer more than we do as we get enough to eat and they do not. We get bacon [and] cornbread generally ... [and] then some rice [and] sometimes hard bread."[43] There would be no rest—the ordeal of the Trevilian Raid remained ahead.

Regardless of these travails, the Confederate cavalry's morale remained high. "Everything is going on gloriously for us," Pvt. Thomas E. Bryant, 13th Virginia Cavalry, remarked on June 5. "The day before yesterday the Yanks charged our works several times, [and] were repulsed with the loss of about 8,000 in killed and wounded while ours was only 500. At such odds, I think we shall exterminate them instead of their exterminating us."[44] While Bryant obviously understated the magnitude of the Confederate army's losses at Cold Harbor, his statement demonstrates that Southern morale remained as high as ever.

The North Carolina Cavalry Brigade got a new commander on June 4. The Confederate States Congress approved the promotion of Lt. Col. Rufus Barringer of the 1st North Carolina Cavalry to brigadier general, and once he learned of the promotion, Barringer took command of the brigade. Barringer capably led the brigade until his capture during the final week of the war in the East.[45] Colonel Baker reverted to command of the 3rd North Carolina Cavalry, and Brigadier General Pierce Young, whom Barringer replaced as the head of the Tar Heels, was missed during his lengthy recuperation from the severe wound he had suffered at Ashland on June 1. Young eventually received a promotion to major general and divisional command.

The six days covered by this narrative, beginning on May 27, 1864, and ending on June 1, 1864, mark Wade Hampton's debut as commander of the Army of Northern Virginia's Cavalry Corps. Although not formally appointed to corps command until August 1864, Hampton took charge of the Cavalry Corps in its first return to

42 Hutchinson, *My Dear Mother and Sisters*, 121.
43 Ibid., 122–23.
44 Quoted in Balfour, *13th Virginia Cavalry*, 33.
45 Barringer, *Fighting for General Lee*, 147.

action since the death of the sorely missed Jeb Stuart on May 12, 1864, by virtue of seniority. Hampton had never commanded anything larger than a division in battle, so he had to learn on the job. While his handling of the deployment and control of his troopers at Haw's Shop left something to be desired—troops were fed into the battle piecemeal and without clear direction—Hampton learned from his mistakes, quickly growing into an extremely competent commander of large bodies of men. At the same time, by taking the fight to the Union cavalry at Haw's Shop, Hampton prevented Sheridan from fulfilling his mission, which was to locate the main body of the Army of Northern Virginia. "Hampton was now commander of all the cavalry and the way he managed affairs at Haws Shop and Cold Harbor over Sheridan, gave him quite a prestige, and one to be dreaded by his adversary," Charles Calhoun of Butler's brigade said.[46]

While he lacked Stuart's flair and élan, Hampton nevertheless showed great competence in commanding dismounted cavalry combat, something at which Stuart never excelled. His skill at fighting dismounted helped to even the steep odds facing the Army of Northern Virginia's Cavalry Corps. With the likes of no-nonsense Hampton commanding the Cavalry Corps, Confederate horse soldiers became extremely effective at fighting dismounted, something they demonstrated beyond any doubt at Trevilian Station a few days later.

Although supposedly co-equal with Fitz Lee and Rooney Lee under the awkward command structure that General Lee had imposed after Stuart's death, Hampton nevertheless demonstrated a real ability to work well with his fellow division commanders, even though Fitz Lee was unhappy about not being appointed Stuart's successor in command of the Cavalry Corps. Steely, but always with impeccable manners, Hampton not only found a way to work with his rivals, he found a way to work with them in a cooperative and effective fashion. This meant that, until Hampton's formal appointment as Cavalry Corps commander in August 1864, the Confederate cavalry generally acted in a cohesive and coordinated fashion, even though the command structure that General Lee installed technically treated the three division heads as independent commanders reporting directly to him. It was a recipe for disaster, but Hampton found a way to make it work effectively and efficiently.

Both Fitz Lee and Rooney Lee handled their troopers as well as possible under the circumstances. Neither was accustomed to having anyone but Stuart in command, and such adjustments take time. In particular, Rooney Lee's cavalrymen fought very effectively in the twin bloody slugging matches with Wilson at Hanover Court House

---

46 Calhoun, *Liberty Dethroned*, 122–23.

and Ashland, but his handling of the division at Haw's Shop left a lot to be desired. By insisting that his command should retreat, Rooney opened the door for the Union cavalry to drive Hampton's command from the field. Had Rooney not panicked at Haw's Shop, the Confederate cavalry easily could have maintained its strong defensive position there.

Fitz Lee performed capably during these engagements. His troopers were in an extremely difficult position of having to hold Cold Harbor against determined Union assaults, forcing his horse soldiers to fight like infantry behind breastworks, something they were not accustomed to doing. They fought stubbornly against superior numbers, ultimately forcing Sheridan to abandon the Old Cold Harbor intersection after seizing it. Sheridan was ordered to return and hold the intersection; otherwise, the battle of Cold Harbor likely would not have occurred where it did, overlapping the 1862 Gaine's Mill battlefield.

Brigadier General Butler and his rugged brigade of South Carolinians played the most significant role of any Southern command during this time. These untried rookies not only stood their ground and fought stubbornly, they earned the grudging respect of their gray-clad comrades and of the Union troopers who faced them. Despite taking heavy losses in their first combat, they quickly became a mainstay of the Army of Northern Virginia's Cavalry Corps. These Palmetto men and their one-legged commander made two remarkable stands at Trevilian Station, including the repulse of seven frontal assaults on the second day of the battle, prompting Hampton to declare, "Butler's defense at Trevilian was never surpassed." He added that Butler "was as good a soldier as we had."[47] When Hampton became the Army of Northern Virginia's cavalry corps permanent commander in August 1864, Butler was promoted to major general and assumed command of Hampton's division. Despite a lack of formal military training, Butler handled his troopers extremely effectively and soon distinguished himself as the rising star of the Confederate cavalry in the Eastern Theater.

Finally, we must address the performance of the Confederate cavalry's rank and file. Despite appalling losses of both enlisted men and officers, the Southern horse soldiers performed remarkably during these engagements. Often outgunned by the superior Union technology that Spencer repeating carbines embodied, which much of the Union Cavalry Corps carried, and despite the problems of resupplying mounts, the Confederate cavalry remained full of fight,

47 Brooks, *Butler and His Cavalry*, 254.

always prepared to do its duty and ready to conduct superior defensive actions when called upon to do so. They remained defiant and indomitable until the end of the Civil War, a tribute to the men themselves and to the officers who led them into battle.[48]

Plenty of hard work remained for the cavalries of both armies in the months ahead. Hampton and Sheridan would tangle numerous times before Sheridan was transferred to command the Union army is the Shenandoah Valley on August 8, 1864. The Union cavalry reached the zenith of its power in the Valley, dominating its Confederate foes and devastating Jubal Early's infantry at Third Winchester and then at Cedar Creek a month later. Those successes had their roots in the actions at Hanover County during the spring of 1864.

48 As just one example, Col. Thomas T. Munford, the final commander of Fitzhugh Lee's division, refused to surrender at Appomattox in April 1865, and led his troopers away instead of capitulating. He intended to go to North Carolina to join Gen. Joseph E. Johnston's army during the Carolinas campaign, but when Munford learned that Johnston had surrendered to Maj. Gen. William T. Sherman, he led his men to his hometown of Lynchburg, Virginia, and then dispersed his command. He never did surrender. See Bruce S. Allardice, *More Generals in Gray* (Baton Rouge: Louisiana State University Press, 1995), 171.

Epilogue

With most of the Confederate cavalry pursuing Maj. Gen. Philip H. Sheridan's raiders, Gen. Robert E. Lee was left largely blinded, without sufficient horse soldiers to watch the movements of the Army of the Potomac. Lieutenant General Ulysses S. Grant had already resolved to cross the James River, and he and his staff put together an excellent and intricate plan for doing so. About the same time that Sheridan was being routed at Trevilian Station on June 12, the Army of the Potomac left its works at Cold Harbor, with its regimental bands playing loudly to cover the sounds of the movement. Unlike so many other instances during the Overland campaign, this movement went off without a hitch, prompting Maj. Gen. George G. Meade's chief of staff, Maj. Gen. Andrew A. Humphreys, to praise the lack of "interruptions or delays."[1]

Major General Gouverneur K. Warren's V Corps crossed the Chickahominy River early on the morning of June 13, and then turned west, with Col. George H. Chapman's brigade of Brig. Gen. James H. Wilson's Third Cavalry Division leading the infantry's advance. Chapman's troopers found enemy cavalry at Riddell's Shop and drove them off after heavy skirmishing. Brigadier General Samuel W. Crawford's V Corps division arrived to support Chapman's troopers, blocking the routes to Riddell's Shop and a nearby bridge across White Oak Swamp.[2]

Lee's cavalry videttes learned that the Army of the Potomac was gone on the morning of June 13, leaving the Confederate commander to wonder whether Grant intended to strike Richmond from the south or cross the James and then fall on Petersburg. "Marse Robert, who knew everything knowable, did not appear to know just what his old enemy proposed to do or where he would be most likely to find him," pithy Confederate artillerist Robert Stiles observed.[3] In order to cover the southern approaches to Richmond, Lee immediately set his army in motion across the Chickahominy, along the Charles City Road. Before long, reports of the presence of Union soldiers at Riddell's Shop filtered in. Elements of Lt. Gen. A. P. Hill's III Corps drove Chapman's dismounted troopers away from Riddell's Shop and back upon their infantry supports. However, darkness halted the Confederate attack and saved the V Corps, which faced the entire

---

1 Humphreys, *The Virginia Campaign of 1864 and 1865*, 201–2.
2 *OR* 36, 1:883 and 902.
3 Stiles, *Four Years Under Marse Robert*, 308.

Army of Northern Virginia, without any support. Instead, the Confederates deployed in a position to control the approaches to Richmond and did not attack Warren.[4]

Meanwhile, the rest of the Army of the Potomac reached Wilcox's Landing on the James River late in the day on June 13. By the morning of June 14, Lee knew that only the V Corps was at Riddell's Shop, so he ordered Hill to attack Warren there. However, Warren had also slipped away, marching southeast to Samaria Church. Caught off guard, Lee was left to guess about Grant's intentions. About noon, he told President Jefferson Davis that he believed Grant "must be preparing to move south of James River."[5]

Later that day, he reported additional information to Davis. "As far as I can judge from the information I have received," Lee wrote, "Genl. Grant has moved his army to James River." Lee now assumed that Grant intended to cross the James and advance on Petersburg, so he ordered Maj. Gen. Robert F. Hoke's division to Drewry's Bluff, south of Richmond, to cross the James on a pontoon bridge and go to Petersburg to assist Gen. P. G. T. Beauregard in defending the Cockade City, while the rest of the Army of Northern Virginia waited near Malvern Hill to react once more intelligence came in confirming Grant's intentions.[6]

Grant made the best of the rare opportunity that Lee's confusion presented. During the night of June 14 and 15, boats ferried the entire II Corps across the James while the Army of the Potomac's engineers built a 2,100-foot pontoon bridge—an engineering marvel—across the James at Weyanoke. The balance of the Army of the Potomac crossed the river on this long, narrow bridge on June 15, miraculously stealing a march on Robert E. Lee.[7]

Meanwhile, Ulysses S. Grant stood on the bluffs, watching his army cross the wide James River, hands clasped behind his back. "The great bridge was the scene of a continuous movement of infantry columns, batteries of artillery, and wagon-trains," Grant's staff officer, Col. Horace Porter, recalled. "The approaches to the river on both banks were covered with masses of troops moving briskly to their positions or waiting patiently their turn to cross." The spectacle, Porter said, presented "a matchless pageant that could not fail to inspire all beholders with the grandeur of achievement and the majesty

4 For a detailed discussion, see Gordon C. Rhea, *On to Petersburg: Grant and Lee June 4–15, 1864* (Baton Rouge: Louisiana State University Press, 2017), 197–222.
5 Freeman, *Lee's Dispatches*, 227–29.
6 Ibid., 232–33.
7 Rhea, *On to Petersburg*, 223–50.

of military power."[8] Later that night, Grant told Meade's aide, Lt. Col. Theodore Lyman, "I think it is pretty well to get across a great river, and come up here and attack Lee in his rear before he is ready for us."[9]

And with that, the scourge of war left Hanover County for the second and final time. "We passed to-day *[sic]* many and extensive earthworks that were constructed and occupied a few days ago by the enemy," Confederate horse artillerist Sgt. George Neese recorded in his diary on June 3. "The whole country along the south side of the Pamunkey is literally dug up and covered with breastworks, breastworks from which there never was a shot fired, and which have been abandoned in that oft-repeated movement on his right flank and rear."[10]

"To be sure the stock of the country seems to suffer badly, and I see more dead pelts than I do live sheep, more feathers by the roads than fowls in the yards," Capt. Charles Francis Adams Jr. of the 1st Massachusetts Cavalry, who served on Meade's staff, told his father on June 4. "The country ... is terribly devastated. This Army is, I presume, no worse than others, but it certainly leaves no friends behind it. I fear that the inhabitants are stripped of everything except that which can neither be stolen or destroyed. This is the work of the stragglers, the shirks and the cowards, the bullies and ruffians of the Army."[11]

Judith Maguire was the sister of Dr. William S. R. Brockenbrough, whose farm hosted much of the fighting at Hanovertown Ferry. On June 1, she wrote in her diary, "Dr. B. was at home, with several Confederate wounded from the battle of 'Haw's Shop' in the house. Being absent a mile or two from home when they arrived, they so quickly threw out pickets, spread their tents over the [surrounding] fields and hills, that he could not return to his house, where his wife and only child were alone, until he had obtained a pass from a Yankee officer. As he approached the house, thousands and tens of thousands of horses and cattle were roaming over the fine wheat fields on his and the adjoining estate ... which were now ripe for the sickle. The clover fields and fields of young corn were sharing the same fate."

She continued, "On these highly cultivated plantations not a fence is left, except mutilated garden enclosures. The fields were as free from vegetation after a few days as the Arabian desert; the very roots seemed eradicated from the earth. A fortification stretched across [Williams Wickham's estate, Hickory Hill Plantation] in which were embedded

8 Porter, *Campaigning with Grant*, 199–200.
9 Agassiz, *Meade's Headquarters*, 166.
10 Neese, *Three Years in the Confederate Horse Artillery*, 280.
11 Ford, *A Cycle of Adams Letters*, 2:139–40.

the fence rails of that and the adjoining farms. Ten thousand cavalry were drawn up in line of battle for two days on the two plantations, expecting the approach of the Confederates; bands of music were constantly playing martial airs in all parts of the premises; and whiskey flowed freely."

Then, she noted what happened to the local slave population. "The poor servants could not resist these intoxicating influences, particularly as Abolition preachers were constantly collecting immense crowds, preaching to them the cruelty of the servitude which had been so long imposed upon them, and that Abraham Lincoln was the Moses sent by God to deliver them from the 'land of Egypt and the house of bondage,' and to lead them to the promised land." Finally, she commented on the state of things after the Army of the Potomac finally departed. "After the eight days were accomplished, the army moved off, leaving not a quadruped, except two pigs, which had ensconced themselves under the ruins of a servant's house, and perhaps a dog to one plantation; to the other, by some miraculous oversight, two cows and a few pigs were left. Not a wheeled vehicle of any kind was to be found; all the grain, flour, meat, and other supplies were swept off, except the few things hid in those wonderful places which could not be fathomed even by the 'Grand Army.'"[12]

Fortunately for the local citizenry, the seat of the war shifted south to Petersburg, leaving the blood-soaked terrain of Hanover County behind for good. The extensive earthworks that both armies had dug scarred the landscape. Unexploded ordnance threatened farmers as they tried to coax crops to grow from the damaged ground. The emancipation of the slaves eliminated a large percentage of farm labor from the local economy. The hardships imposed by Reconstruction only made things worse for the local civilians, who had to fend for themselves. Hanover County would never be the same again. But at least the war had finally moved on to Petersburg, leaving Hanover County's residents to do their best to rebuild their shattered lives and homes.

---

12 Judith White McGuire, *Diary of a Southern Refugee, During the War* (New York: E. J. Hale & Son, 1868), 277–78.

APPENDIX A

Order of Battle
Battle of Hanovertown Ferry
May 27, 1864

UNION FORCES

CAVALRY CORPS, ARMY OF THE POTOMAC
Maj. Gen. Philip H. Sheridan

FIRST CAVALRY DIVISION
Brig. Gen. Alfred T. A. Torbert

FIRST BRIGADE
Brig. Gen. George A. Custer

1st Michigan Cavalry (Lt. Col. Peter Stagg)
5th Michigan Cavalry (Capt. William T. Magoffin)
6th Michigan Cavalry (Maj. James H. Kidd)
7th Michigan Cavalry (Maj. Alexander Walker)

SECOND BRIGADE
Col. Thomas C. Devin

9th New York Cavalry (Col. William Sackett)
17th Pennsylvania Cavalry
(Lt. Col. James Q. Anderson)

HORSE ARTILLERY BATTALION

Batteries B and L, 2nd U.S. Artillery
(Lt. Edward Heaton)

CONFEDERATE FORCES

CAVALRY CORPS, ARMY OF NORTHERN VIRGINIA
MAJ. GEN. WADE HAMPTON

W. H. F. LEE'S DIVISION
Maj. Gen. W. H. F. Lee

NORTH CAROLINA CAVALRY BRIGADE
Col. John A. Baker

1st North Carolina Cavalry (Lt. Col. Rufus Barringer)
2nd North Carolina Cavalry (Maj. William P. Roberts)
3rd North Carolina Cavalry (Lt. Col. Alfred Waddell)
5th North Carolina Virginia Cavalry
(Col. James H. McNeill)

MARYLAND LINE
Col. Bradley T. Johnson

1st Maryland Cavalry (Lt. Col. Ridgely Brown–W)
Baltimore Light Artillery (Lt. John McNulty)

APPENDIX B

Order of Battle
Battle of Haw's Shop
May 28, 1864

UNION FORCES

CAVALRY CORPS, ARMY OF THE POTOMAC
Maj. Gen. Philip H. Sheridan

FIRST CAVALRY DIVISION
Brig. Gen. Alfred T. A. Torbert

FIRST BRIGADE
Brig. Gen. George A. Custer

1st Michigan Cavalry (Lt. Col. Peter Stagg)
5th Michigan Cavalry (Capt. William T. Magoffin)
6th Michigan Cavalry (Maj. James H. Kidd)
7th Michigan Cavalry (Maj. Alexander Walker)

SECOND BRIGADE
Col. Thomas C. Devin

6th New York Cavalry (Lt. Col. William H. Crocker)
9th New York Cavalry (Col. William Sackett)
17th Pennsylvania Cavalry (Lt. Col. James Q. Anderson)

RESERVE BRIGADE
Brig. Gen. Wesley Merritt

1st U.S. Cavalry (Capt. Nelson B. Sweitzer)
2nd U.S. Cavalry (Capt. Theophilus F. Rodenbough)
6th Pennsylvania Cavalry (Capt. Charles L. Leiper)
1st New York Dragoons (Col. Alfred Gibbs)

SECOND CAVALRY DIVISION
Brig. Gen. David M. Gregg

FIRST BRIGADE
Brig. Gen. Henry E. Davies Jr.
1st Massachusetts Cavalry (Lt. Col. Greely S. Curtis)
1st New Jersey Cavalry (Col. John W. Kester)
10th New York Cavalry (Maj. Matthew Avery)
6th Ohio Cavalry (Col. William Stedman)
1st Pennsylvania Cavalry (Col. John P. Taylor)

SECOND BRIGADE
Col. J. Irvin Gregg

1st Maine Cavalry (Col. Charles H. Smith)
4th Pennsylvania Cavalry (Col. George H. Covode)
8th Pennsylvania Cavalry (Col. Pennock Huey)
16th Pennsylvania Cavalry (Lt. Col. John K. Robison)

HORSE ARTILLERY

Battery M, 2nd U.S. Artillery
(Lt. Alexander C. M. Pennington)
Batteries H and I, 1st U.S. Artillery
(Lt. Edward Heaton)

CONFEDERATE FORCES

CAVALRY CORPS, ARMY OF NORTHERN VIRGINIA

MAJ. GEN. WADE HAMPTON

HAMPTON'S DIVISION
Maj. Gen. Wade Hampton

ROSSER'S BRIGADE
Brig. Gen. Thomas L. Rosser

7th Virginia Cavalry (Col. Richard H. Dulany)
11th Virginia Cavalry (Col. Oliver R. Funston)
12th Virginia Cavalry (Lt. Col. Thomas B. Massie)
35th Battalion Virginia Cavalry
(Lt. Col. Elijah V. White)

BUTLER'S BRIGADE
Col. Benjamin H. Rutledge
4th South Carolina Cavalry (Lt. Col. William Stokes)
5th South Carolina Cavalry
(Col. John Dunovant–W; Lt. Col. Robert J. Jeffords)

FITZHUGH LEE'S DIVISION
Maj. Gen. Fitzhugh Lee

WICKHAM'S BRIGADE
Brig. Gen. Williams Wickham

1st Virginia Cavalry (Lt. Col. William A. Morgan)
2nd Virginia Cavalry (Col. Thomas T. Munford)
3rd Virginia Cavalry (Col. Thomas H. Owen)
4th Virginia Cavalry (Col. William B. Wooldridge)

W. H. F. LEE'S DIVISION
Maj. Gen. W. H. F. Lee

CHAMBLISS' BRIGADE
Brig. Gen. John R. Chambliss Jr.

9th Virginia Cavalry (Col. Richard L. T. Beale)
10th Virginia Cavalry (Col. J. Lucius Davis)
13th Virginia Cavalry (Col. Jefferson C. Phillips)

UNASSIGNED

20th Georgia Battalion (Lt. Col. John M. Millen–KIA)
Love's Alabama Battalion (Capt. Andrew Love)

APPENDIX C

Order of Battle
Battle of Old Church
(Matadequin Creek)
May 30, 1864

UNION FORCES

CAVALRY CORPS, ARMY OF THE POTOMAC
MAJ. GEN. PHILIP H. SHERIDAN

FIRST CAVALRY DIVISION
Brig. Gen. Alfred T. A. Torbert

FIRST BRIGADE
Brig. Gen. George A. Custer

1st Michigan Cavalry (Col. Peter Stagg)
5th Michigan Cavalry (Col. Russell A. Alger)
6th Michigan Cavalry (Maj. James H. Kidd)
7th Michigan Cavalry (Maj. Alexander Walker)

SECOND BRIGADE
Col. Thomas C. Devin

6th New York Cavalry (Lt. Col. William H. Crocker)
9th New York Cavalry (Col. William Sackett)
17th Pennsylvania Cavalry
(Lt. Col. James Q. Anderson)

RESERVE BRIGADE
Brig. Gen. Wesley Merritt

1st U.S. Cavalry (Capt. Nelson B. Sweitzer)
2nd U.S. Cavalry (Capt. Theophilus F. Rodenbough)
6th Pennsylvania Cavalry
(Capt. Charles L. Leiper–W; Capt. J. Hinckley Clark)
1st New York Dragoons (Col. Alfred Gibbs)

CONFEDERATE FORCES

CAVALRY CORPS, ARMY OF NORTHERN VIRGINIA
MAJ. GEN. WADE HAMPTON

HAMPTON'S DIVISION
Maj. Gen. Wade Hampton

BUTLER'S BRIGADE
Brig. Gen. Matthew C. Butler

4th South Carolina Cavalry
(Col. Benjamin H. Rutledge)
5th South Carolina Cavalry (Lt. Col. Robert J. Jeffords)

GARY'S BRIGADE
Brig. Gen. Martin W. Gary

7th South Carolina Cavalry
(Maj. Alexander C. Haskell–W)

Appendix D

Order of Battle
Battle of Hanover Court House
May 31, 1864

UNION FORCES

CAVALRY CORPS, ARMY OF THE POTOMAC
Maj. Gen. Philip H. Sheridan

THIRD CAVALRY DIVISION
Brig. Gen. James H. Wilson

FIRST BRIGADE
Col. George H. Chapman

3rd Indiana Cavalry (6 cos.) (Maj. William Patton)
8th New York Cavalry (Capt. William T. Magoffin)
1st Vermont Cavalry (Lt. Col. Addison W. Preston)

SECOND BRIGADE
Col. John B. McIntosh

1st Connecticut Cavalry (Lt. Col. Erastus Blakeslee)
2nd New York Cavalry (Col. Otto Harhaus)
5th New York Cavalry (Col. John Hammond)
2nd Ohio Cavalry (Col. George Purington)
18th Pennsylvania Cavalry (Lt. Col. William P. Brinton)

HORSE ARTILLERY BATTALION

Batteries C and E, 4th U.S. Artillery
(Lt. Charles L. Fitzhugh)

CONFEDERATE FORCES

CAVALRY CORPS, ARMY OF NORTHERN VIRGINIA
MAJ. GEN. WADE HAMPTON

W. H. F. LEE'S DIVISION
Maj. Gen. W. H. F. Lee

NORTH CAROLINA CAVALRY BRIGADE
Brig. Gen. Pierce M. B. Young

1st North Carolina Cavalry (Lt. Col. Rufus Barringer)
2nd North Carolina Cavalry (Maj. William P. Roberts)
3rd North Carolina Cavalry (Lt. Col. Alfred Waddell)
5th North Carolina Virginia Cavalry
(Col. James H. McNeill)

CHAMBLISS' BRIGADE
Brig. Gen. John R. Chambliss Jr.

9th Virginia Cavalry (Col. Richard L. T. Beale)
10th Virginia Cavalry (Col. J. Lucius Davis)
13th Virginia Cavalry (Col. Jefferson C. Phillips)

HORSE ARTILLERY BATTALION

McGregor's Virginia Battery
(Capt. William M. McGregor)

Appendix E

Order of Battle
Cold Harbor
May 31, 1864

UNION FORCES

CAVALRY CORPS, ARMY OF THE POTOMAC
MAJ. GEN. PHILIP H. SHERIDAN
FIRST CAVALRY DIVISION
Brig. Gen. Alfred T. A. Torbert

FIRST BRIGADE
Brig. Gen. George A. Custer

1st Michigan Cavalry (Col. Peter Stagg)
5th Michigan Cavalry (Col. Russell A. Alger)
6th Michigan Cavalry (Maj. James H. Kidd)
7th Michigan Cavalry (Maj. Alexander Walker)

SECOND BRIGADE
Col. Thomas C. Devin

6th New York Cavalry (Lt. Col. William H. Crocker)
9th New York Cavalry (Col. William Sackett)
17th Pennsylvania Cavalry
(Lt. Col. James Q. Anderson)

RESERVE BRIGADE
Brig. Gen. Wesley Merritt

1st U.S. Cavalry (Capt. Nelson B. Sweitzer)
2nd U.S. Cavalry (Capt. Theophilus F. Rodenbough)
6th Pennsylvania Cavalry (Capt. J. Hinckley Clark)
1st New York Dragoons (Col. Alfred Gibbs)

CONFEDERATE FORCES

CAVALRY CORPS, ARMY OF NORTHERN VIRGINIA
MAJ. GEN. WADE HAMPTON

FITZHUGH LEE'S DIVISION
Maj. Gen. Fitzhugh Lee

WICKHAM'S BRIGADE
Brig. Gen. Williams Wickham

1st Virginia Cavalry (Lt. Col. William A. Morgan)
2nd Virginia Cavalry (Col. Thomas T. Munford)
3rd Virginia Cavalry (Col. Thomas H. Owen)
4th Virginia Cavalry (Col. William B. Wooldridge)

LOMAX'S BRIGADE
Brig. Gen. Lunsford L. Lomax

5th Virginia Cavalry (Capt. Reuben Boston)
6th Virginia Cavalry (Maj. Cabell E. Flournoy–KIA)
15th Virginia Cavalry (Lt. Col. John R. Critcher)

HORSE ARTILLERY

BREATHED'S BATTALION
Maj. James Breathed

Lynchburg Beauregards (Capt. John J. Shoemaker)
First Stuart Horse Artillery of Virginia
(Capt. Phillip P. Johnston)

DEFENSES OF RICHMOND
GEN. P. G. T. BEAUREGARD

HOKE'S DIVISION
Maj. Gen. Robert F. Hoke

CLINGMAN'S BRIGADE
Brig. Gen. Thomas L. Clingman

8th North Carolina Infantry
(Lt. Col. John R. Murchison–KIA)
31st North Carolina Infantry
(Lt. Col. Charles W. Knight)
51st North Carolina Infantry (Col. Hector McKethan)

Appendix F

Order of Battle
Battle of Ashland
June 1, 1864

UNION FORCES

CAVALRY CORPS, ARMY OF THE POTOMAC
Maj. Gen. Philip H. Sheridan

THIRD CAVALRY DIVISION
Brig. Gen. James H. Wilson

FIRST BRIGADE
Col. George H. Chapman

3rd Indiana Cavalry (6 cos.) (Maj. William Patton)
8th New York Cavalry (Capt. William T. Magoffin)
1st Vermont Cavalry (Lt. Col. Addison W. Preston)

SECOND BRIGADE
Col. John B. McIntosh

1st Connecticut Cavalry (Lt. Col. Erastus Blakeslee–W)
2nd New York Cavalry (Col. Otto Harhaus)
5th New York Cavalry (Col. John Hammond)
2nd Ohio Cavalry (Col. George Purington)
18th Pennsylvania Cavalry (Lt. Col. William P. Brinton)

HORSE ARTILLERY BATTALION

Batteries C and E, 4th U.S. Artillery
(Lt. Charles L. Fitzhugh)

CONFEDERATE FORCES

CAVALRY CORPS, ARMY OF NORTHERN VIRGINIA
MAJ. GEN. WADE HAMPTON

HAMPTON'S DIVISION
Maj. Gen. Wade Hampton

ROSSER'S BRIGADE
Brig. Gen. Thomas L. Rosser

7th Virginia Cavalry (Col. Richard H. Dulany)
11th Virginia Cavalry (Col. Oliver R. Funston)
12th Virginia Cavalry (Lt. Col. Thomas B. Massie)

W. H. F. LEE'S DIVISION
Maj. Gen. W. H. F. Lee

NORTH CAROLINA CAVALRY BRIGADE
Brig. Gen. Pierce M. B. Young–W
Col. John A. Baker

1st North Carolina Cavalry (Lt. Col. Rufus Barringer)
2nd North Carolina Cavalry (Maj. William P. Roberts)
3rd North Carolina Cavalry
(Col. John A. Baker; Lt. Col. Alfred Waddell)
5th North Carolina Cavalry (Col. James H. McNeill)

CHAMBLISS' BRIGADE
Brig. Gen. John R. Chambliss Jr.

9th Virginia Cavalry (Col. Richard L. T. Beale)
10th Virginia Cavalry (Col. J. Lucius Davis)
13th Virginia Cavalry (Col. Jefferson C. Phillips)

MARYLAND LINE
Col. Bradley T. Johnson

1st Maryland Cavalry (Lt. Col. Ridgely Brown–KIA)
Baltimore Light Artillery (Lt. John McNulty)

HORSE ARTILLERY BATTALION

McGregor's Virginia Battery
(Capt. William M. McGregor)
Washington Artillery of South Carolina
(Maj. James Hart)

Appendix G

Order of Battle
Cold Harbor
June 1, 1864

UNION FORCES

CAVALRY CORPS, ARMY OF THE POTOMAC
MAJ. GEN. PHILIP H. SHERIDAN

FIRST CAVALRY DIVISION
Brig. Gen. Alfred T. A. Torbert

FIRST BRIGADE
Brig. Gen. George A. Custer

1st Michigan Cavalry (Col. Peter Stagg)
5th Michigan Cavalry (Col. Russell A. Alger)
6th Michigan Cavalry (Maj. James H. Kidd)
7th Michigan Cavalry (Maj. Alexander Walker)

SECOND BRIGADE
Col. Thomas C. Devin

6th New York Cavalry (Lt. Col. William H. Crocker)
9th New York Cavalry (Col. William Sackett)
17th Pennsylvania Cavalry (Lt. Col. James Q.
Anderson)

RESERVE BRIGADE
Brig. Gen. Wesley Merritt

1st U.S. Cavalry (Capt. Nelson B. Sweitzer)
2nd U.S. Cavalry (Capt. Theophilus F. Rodenbough)
6th Pennsylvania Cavalry (Capt. J. Hinckley Clark)
1st New York Dragoons (Col. Alfred Gibbs)

SECOND CAVALRY DIVISION
Brig. Gen. David M. Gregg

FIRST BRIGADE
Brig. Gen. Henry E. Davies Jr.

1st Massachusetts Cavalry (Lt. Col. Greely S. Curtis)
6th Ohio Cavalry (Col. William Stedman)
1st Pennsylvania Cavalry (Col. John P. Taylor)

HORSE ARTILLERY

Battery D, 2nd U.S. Artillery (Lt. Edward B. Williston)

CONFEDERATE FORCES

ARMY OF NORTHERN VIRGINIA
GEN. ROBERT E. LEE

FIRST CORPS
MAJ. GEN. RICHARD H. ANDERSON

KERSHAW'S DIVISION
Maj. Gen. Joseph Kershaw

KERSHAW'S BRIGADE
Col. Laurence M. Keitt–MW
Col. John W. Henegan

2nd South Carolina Infantry (Lt. Col. William Wallace)
3rd South Carolina Infantry
(Col. William D. Rutherford)
7th South Carolina Infantry (Capt. James McNeill)
8th South Carolina Infantry (Col. John W. Henegan)
15th South Carolina Infantry (Col. John B. Davis)
20th South Carolina Infantry
(Col. Laurence M. Keitt–KIA)
3rd South Carolina Battalion (Maj. Daniel B. Miller)

BIBLIOGRAPHY

PRIMARY SOURCES

NEWSPAPERS:

Adviser and Tribune
Alexandria Gazette
Atlanta Constitution
Atlanta Daily Intelligencer
Charleston Daily Courier
Charleston Mercury
Columbia South Carolinian
Daily Morning Chronicle (Washington, DC)
Detroit Advertiser and Tribune
Detroit Free Press
Evening Star (Washington, DC)
Lexington Dispatch (Lexington, South Carolina)
National Tribune
New Haven Palladium (New Haven, Connecticut)
New York Herald
New York Times
New York Tribune
Painesville Telegraph (Painesville, Ohio)
Philadelphia Inquirer
Philadelphia Weekly Times
Raleigh Daily Confederate (Raleigh, North Carolina)
Richmond Daily Dispatch
Richmond Enquirer
Richmond Examiner
Richmond Times-Dispatch
Rutland Weekly Herald (Rutland, Vermont)
The Daily Progress (Raleigh, North Carolina)
The Herald and News (Newberry, South Carolina)
The Ledger (Lancasterville, South Carolina)

The Sunny South (Atlanta, Georgia)
The Weekly Confederate (Raleigh, North Carolina)
United Service
Western Reserve Chronicle (Warren, Ohio)
Wilmington Journal (Wilmington, North Carolina)
Windham County Transcript (West Killingly, Connecticut)

MANUSCRIPT SOURCES:

Clarke Historical Library,
  Central Michigan University, Mount Pleasant, Michigan:
    Dexter Macomber Diary

Archives, Charleston Library Society, Charleston, South Carolina:
    Edward Laight Wells Correspondence

Special Collections, Addlestone Library,
  College of Charleston, Charleston, South Carolina:
    B. H. Rutledge Letter Book
    Middleton Family Correspondence
    Thomas L. Pinckney Diary

Special Collections, Dartmouth University Library, Hanover, New Hampshire:
    Eri Davidson Woodbury Papers

Archives, Perkins Library, Duke University, Durham, North Carolina:
    John M. Cummings Papers
    Bradley T. Johnson Papers
    Munford–Ellis Family Papers
    J. L. Sperry Papers

Georgia Department of Archives and History, Atlanta, Georgia:
    W. W. Abercrombie letter of June 1, 1864
    Dickey Family Papers
    Charles P. Hansell Manuscript,
        "History of the 20th Georgia Battalion of Cavalry"

Manuscripts Division, Library of Congress, Washington, DC:
    Samuel L. Gilpin Diary
    Jedediah Hotchkiss Papers
    Howard Malcolm Smith Papers
    Gilbert Thompson Memoirs
    James H. Wilson Papers

Archives, Library of Virginia, Richmond, Virginia:
    Carter Family Papers
    Irvin Cross Wills Papers

Special Collections, Mary Ball Washington Library, Lancaster, Virginia:
    John W. Chowning Diary

Archives, Maryland Historical Society, Baltimore, Maryland:
    Charles E. Phelps Papers
        "Recollections of the Wilderness Campaign"

Archives, Museum of the Confederacy, Richmond, Virginia:
    John D. Imboden Papers
    Fitzhugh Lee Report

National Archives and Records Administration, Washington, DC:
    M266, Carded Records Showing Military Service of Soldiers Who Fought in
        Confederate Organizations, Compiled March 19, 1927, Documenting the
        Period 1861–1865
    Holmes Conrad Combined Service Records, Roll 61

Archives, Historical Society of Pennsylvania, Philadelphia, Pennsylvania:
    Louis Henry Carpenter Letters from the Field

Copies in Archives, Richmond National Battlefield Park, Richmond, Virginia:
    George T. Brooke Letter of July 30, 1903
    James F. Bryant Letters
    William L. Heermance Papers
    A. J. McBride, "Some War Experiences"
    James L. McCrorey Letter
    John J. Woodall Diary

Archives, United States Army History and Education Center, Carlisle,
    Pennsylvania:
    Isaac Rothermel Dunkelberger Diary
    Lewis Leigh Collection
        Report of Roger Preston Chew
    Isaac Ressler Diary

Archives, William L. Clements Library, University of Michigan, Ann Arbor, Michigan:
James S. Schoff Collection
Nathan B. Webb Diaries

Southern Historical Collection, Wilson Library,
University of North Carolina, Chapel Hill, North Carolina:
Edward Porter Alexander Papers
Rufus Barringer Papers
James Breathed Report
J. Frederick Waring Diary

Archives, South Caroliniana Library,
University of South Carolina, Columbia, South Carolina:
Paul Gervais Bell Papers
"The Battles of Hawes Shop and Cold Harbor and William Bell's Involvement in Them"
Hampton Family Papers
Connected Narrative of Wade Hampton III
Gabriel Manigault Autobiography

Special Collections, Alderman Library,
University of Virginia, Charlottesville, Virginia:
William H. Locke Letters

Archives, Virginia Historical Society, Richmond, Virginia:
George Brooke Memoir
Jasper Hawes Diary

Special Collections, Library, Virginia Military Institute, Lexington, Virginia:
William Black Diary
Report of John J. Shoemaker

Special Collections, Virginia Polytechnic Institute, Blacksburg, Virginia:
John R. Mayburg diary for 1864

Archives, Virginia State Library, Richmond, Virginia:
St. George Tucker Brooke Autobiography

Archives, Western Reserve Historical Society, Cleveland, Ohio:
Palmer Regimental Papers
Wells A. Bushnell Memoir

Special Collections, Yale University Library, New Haven, Connecticut:
  Brinecke Barnitz Papers
    Albert Barnitz's Field Notes

PUBLISHED SOURCES:

"A Cavalry Fight." *Charleston Daily Courier*, June 3, 1864.

Acken, J. Gregory, ed. *Blue-Blooded Cavalryman: Captain William Brooke Rawle in the Army of the Potomac, May 1863–August 1865*. Kent, OH: Kent State University Press, 2019.

Adams, Charles Francis. *Charles Francis Adams 1835–1915: An Autobiography*. Boston: Houghton-Mifflin, 1916.

Agassiz, George R., ed. *Meade's Headquarters, 1863–1865: Letters of Col. Theodore Lyman from the Wilderness to Appomattox*. Boston: Atlantic Monthly Press, 1922.

Ahearn, Robert G., ed. "The Civil War Diary of John Wilson Phillips." *Virginia Magazine of History and Biography* 62 (1954): 98–104.

Alexander, Edward Porter. *Military Memoirs of a Confederate: A Critical Narrative*. New York: Charles Scribner's Sons, 1907.

Allen, Stanton P. *Down in Dixie: Life in a Cavalry Regiment in the War Days from the Wilderness to Appomattox*. Boston: D. Lothrop & Co., 1893.

"Amos O. Banks." *Lexington Dispatch*, May 10, 1911.

Annual Report of the Adjutant General of the State of Connecticut for the Year Ending March 31, 1865. New Haven, CT: A. N. Clark & Co., 1865.

"Army Correspondence." *Painesville Telegraph*, June 23, 1864.

Barnard, Sandy, ed. *An Aide to Custer: The Civil War Letters of Lt. Edward G. Granger*. Norman: University of Oklahoma Press, 2018.

Barrett, N. A. "Sixth Ohio Cavalry." *Western Reserve Chronicle*, June 22, 1864.

Baylor, George. *Bull Run to Bull Run: Four Years in the Army of Northern Virginia*. Richmond: B. F. Johnson Publishing Co., 1900.

Beale, George W. A *Lieutenant of Cavalry in Lee's Army*. Boston: Gorham, 1888.

——————. "Spirited Cavalry Battle at Ashland." *Richmond Times-Dispatch*, September 12, 1915.

Beale, Richard L. T. *History of the Ninth Virginia Cavalry in the War Between the States*. Richmond. B. F. Johnson Publishing Co., 1899.

Bearss, Edwin C., ed. *Campaigning with Sgt. Truman Reeves and Company G, Sixth Ohio Volunteer Cavalry: From Orwell to Haw's Shop*. Privately published, n.d.

Beatty, John. *The Citizen Soldier: The Memoirs of a Civil War Volunteer*. Cincinnati: Wilstach, Baldwin & Co., 1879.

Beaudry, Richard E., ed. *War Journal of Louis N. Beaudry, Fifth New York Cavalry*. Jefferson, NC: McFarland Publishing, 1996.

Benedict, George G. *Vermont in the Civil War: A History of the Part Taken by the Vermont Soldiers and Sailors in the War for the Union.* 2 vols. Burlington, VT: Free Press Association, 1882.

Blakeslee, Erastus. "Addenda to the History and Roster of the Connecticut Cavalry Volunteers: 1861–1865." Included in *The Connecticut Cavalry Volunteers in the War of the Rebellion, 1861–1865.* Hartford, CT: Case, Lockwood & Brainard, 1889.

Booth, George W. *Personal Reminiscences of a Maryland Soldier in the War Between the States, 1861–1865.* Baltimore: Fleet, McGinley & Co., 1898.

Boudrye, Louis N. *Historic Records of the Fifth New York Cavalry, First Ira Harris Guard.* Albany, NY: J. Munsell, 1868.

Bowen, J. R. *Regimental History of the First New York Dragoons.* Privately published, 1910.

Brooks, Ulysses R. *Butler and His Cavalry.* Columbia, SC: The State Co., 1909.

--------------------. "Cavalry Stories from Recollections of War." *Richmond Times-Dispatch*, January 28, 1912.

Burton, Delos S. "Spotsylvania: Letters From the Field: An Eyewitness." *Civil War Times* 22 (1983): 22–27.

Butler, Matthew C. "The Cavalry Fight at Trevilian Station." Robert U. Johnson and Clarence C. Buel, eds. *Battles and Leaders of the Civil War.* 4 vols. New York: Century Publishing Co., 1884–1888. 4:237–39.

Calhoun, Charles M. *Liberty Dethroned.* n.p., 1903.

Cardwell, David. "Where the Gallant Lieutenant Ford was Killed." *Confederate Veteran* 26 (1918): 207–8.

Carpenter, Louis Henry. "Sheridan's Expedition Around Richmond May 9–25, 1864." *Journal of the United States Cavalry Association* 1 (1888): 300–24.

"Cavalry Engagement," *The Weekly Confederate*, June 8, 1864.

Cheney, Newel. *History of the Ninth Regiment, New York Volunteer Cavalry, War of 1861 to 1865.* Poland Center, NY: Martin Mere & Son, 1901.

Chester, H. W. *Recollections of the War of the Rebellion.* Alberta R. Adamson, Robert I. Girardi, and Roger E. Bohn, eds. Wheaton, IL: Wheaton History Center, 1996.

Clingman, Thomas L. "Second Cold Harbor." Included in Walter Clark, ed. *Histories of the Several Regiments and Battalions from North Carolina in the Great War, 1861–65.* 5 vols. Raleigh: E. M. Uzzell, 1901, 5:197–205.

"Connecticut." "The First Connecticut Cavalry." *New Haven Daily Palladium*, June 21, 1864.

Conrad, Thomas Nelson. *The Rebel Scout: A Thrilling History of Scouting Life in the Southern Army.* Washington, DC: The National Publishing Co., 1904.

Cralle, G. T. "The Bold Horsemen." *Richmond Dispatch*, January 7, 1900.

Croffut, William A. and John M. Morris. *The Military and Civil History of Connecticut During the Recent War of 1861.* New York: Ledyard Bill, 1868.

Crowninshield, Benjamin W. *A History of the First Regiment of Massachusetts Cavalry Volunteers.* Boston: Houghton, Mifflin & Co., 1891.

Cullum, George W. *Biographical Register of the Officers and Graduates of the U.S. Military Academy at West Point, N.Y., from Its Establishment, in 1802, to 1890.* 3rd ed. 3 vols. Boston: Houghton Mifflin, 1891.

"Custer's Cavalry Brigade." *Detroit Advertiser and Tribune*, June 16, 1864.

Dana, Charles A. *Recollections of the Civil War.* New York: D. Appleton, 1898.

"David McMurtrie Gregg." Circular No. 6, Series of 1917. Military Order of the Loyal Legion of the United States, Commandery of Pennsylvania. May 3, 1917.

Davies, Henry E. *General Sheridan.* New York: D. Appleton & Co., 1895.

Davis, Cameron, ed. *The Better Part of Valor: Albert Drury & His 1st Vermont Cavalry at Gettysburg, the Shenandoah Valley, and Beyond During the Civil War.* Self-published, 2017.

Davis, Paul, ed. *I Rode with Custer: The Civil War Diary of Charles H. Safford, Bvt. Major, 5th Michigan Cavalry.* Detroit: Ashton Z Publishing, 2014.

Dawson, Francis W. *Reminiscences of Confederate Service, 1861–1865.* Baton Rouge: Louisiana State University Press, 1980.

D. B. R. "Barringer's North Carolina Brigade of Cavalry." *Raleigh Daily Confederate*, February 22, 1865.

Dickert, D. Augustus. *History of Kershaw's Brigade.* Newberry, SC: E. H. Aull Co., 1899.

"Died at Post of Duty: Policeman Stanton, Gallant Veteran who Saved Life of Justice McIver at Haw's Shop Dead." *The Herald and News*, August 27, 1909.

Dowdey, Clifford, ed. *Wartime Papers of Robert E. Lee.* New York: Little, Brown, 1961.

Dunovant, Adelia A. "Gen. John Dunovant, Houston, Tex." *Confederate Veteran* 16 (1908): 183–84.

Early, Jubal A. *Autobiographical Sketch and Narrative of the War Between the States.* Philadelphia: J. B. Lippincott, 1912.

Eckert, Edward K. and Nicholas J. Amato, eds. *Ten Years in the Saddle: The Memoir of William Woods Averell, 1851–1862.* San Rafael, CA: Presidio Press, 1978.

Elmore, Albert Rhett. "Incidents of Service with the Charleston Light Dragoons." *Confederate Veteran* 24 (1916): 541.

Elson, Henry W. "Cold Harbor." In Francis Trevelyan Miller, ed. *The Photographic History of the Civil War.* 10 vols. New York: Review of Reviews Co., 1911, 3:82–92.

Floyd, Dale E., ed. "Dear Friends at Home . . .": *The Letters and Diary of Thomas James Owen, Fiftieth New York Volunteer Engineer Regiment, During the Civil War.* U.S. Army Corps of Engineers Historical Studies, No. 4. Washington, DC: U.S. Government Printing Office, 1985.

Ford, Worthington C., ed. *A Cycle of Adams Letters.* 2 vols. Boston: Houghton-Mifflin, 1920.

Fortieth Annual Reunion of the Sixth Ohio Volunteer Veteran Cavalry. n.p., 1905.

Foster, Alonzo V. *Reminiscences and Record of the 6th New York V. V. Cavalry.* Brooklyn, NY: privately published, 1892.

Foster, John Y. *New Jersey and the Rebellion: A History of the Service of the Troops and People of New Jersey in Aid of the Union Cause*. Newark, NJ: M. R. Dennis, 1868.

"From the Army of Northern Virginia." *Richmond Enquirer*, May 31, 1864.

"From the Vermont Cavalry." *Rutland Weekly Herald*, June 21, 1864.

Gallagher, Gary W., ed. *Fighting for the Confederacy: The Personal Recollections of General Edward Porter Alexander*. Chapel Hill: University of North Carolina Press, 1989.

Galloway, John M. "Sixty-Third Regiment (Fifth Cavalry)." In Walter Clark, ed., *Histories of the Several Regiments and Battalions from North Carolina in the Great War, 1861–1865*. 5 vols. Raleigh: E. M. Uzzell, 1901, 529–43.

Gause, Isaac. *Four Years with Five Armies*. New York: Neale Publishing Co., 1908.

"General Custer." *Washington Daily Chronicle*, June 7, 1864.

Gill, John. *Reminiscences of Four Years as a Private Soldier in the Confederate Army, 1861–1865*. Baltimore: Sun Printing Office, 1904.

"Gills Creek." "Letter to the Editor." *The Ledger*, June 14, 1864.

Goldsborough, William W. *The Maryland Line in the Confederate Army 1861–1865*. Baltimore: Guggenheimer, Weil, and Co., 1900.

Gracey, Samuel L. *Annals of the Sixth Pennsylvania Cavalry*. Philadelphia: E. H. Butler & Co., 1868.

Grant, Ulysses S. *Personal Memoirs of Ulysses S. Grant*. 2 vols. New York: Charles L. Webster & Co., 1885.

Griffin, Richard N., ed. *Three Years a Soldier: The Diary and Newspaper Correspondence of Private George Perkins, Sixth New York Independent Battery, 1861–1864*. Knoxville: University of Tennessee Press, 2006.

Hagemann, E. R., ed. *Fighting Rebels and Redskins: Experiences in Army Life of Colonel George B. Sanford, 1861–1892*. Norman: University of Oklahoma Press, 1969.

Hagood, Johnson. *Memoirs of the War of Secession*. Columbia, SC: The State Co., 1910.

Hall, Hillman A., ed. *History of the Sixth New York Cavalry (Second Ira Harris Guard)*. Worcester, MA: The Blanchard Press, 1908.

Halliburton, Lloyd, ed. *Saddle Soldiers: The Civil War Correspondence of General William Stokes of the 4th South Carolina Cavalry*. Orangeburg, SC: Sandlapper Publishing Co., 1993.

Hanks, Richard A., ed. *Vermont's Proper Son: The Letters of Soldier and Scholar Edwin Hall Higley, 1861–1871*. Riverside, CA: Coyote Hill Press, 2014.

Harris, Samuel. *Personal Reminiscences of Samuel Harris*. Chicago: The Robinson Press, 1897.

Hart, James F., Levi C. Stephens, Louis Sherfesee, and Charles H. Schwing. "The History of Hart's Battery." Included in Robert J. Trout, ed., *Memoirs of the Stuart Horse Artillery Battalion: Moorman's and Hart's Batteries*. Knoxville: University of Tennessee Press, 1998: 179–249.

Hatton, Robert W., ed. *William James Smith's Memoirs of the 2nd Ohio Volunteer Cavalry, Company M*. Milford, OH: Little Miami Press, 2008.

Haw, Joseph R. "Haw's Shop Community of Virginia." *Confederate Veteran* 33 (1925): 340–41.

————. "The Battle of Haw's Shop." *Confederate Veteran* 33 (1925): 373–76.

Haynes, Edwin M. *History of the Tenth Regiment, Vermont Volunteers, with Biographical Sketches of the Officers Who Fell in Battle*. Lewiston, ME: Tenth Vermont Regimental Assoc., 1870.

Heitman, Francis B. *Historical Register and Dictionary of the United States Army*. 2 vols. Washington, DC: U.S. Government Printing Office, 1903.

Hoffman, Elliott W., ed. *A Vermont Cavalryman in War & Love: The Civil War Letters of Brevet Major General William Wells and Anna Richardson*. Lynchburg, VA: Schroeder Publications, 2007.

Holmes, James G. "The Fighting Qualities of Generals Hampton, Butler, and Others Related by Adjutant-General Holmes of Charleston." *The Sunny South*, June 13, 1896.

Howard, Harold E., Jr., ed. "If I am Killed on this Trip, I Want My Horse Kept for My Brothers": *The Diary of the Last Weeks of a Young Confederate Cavalryman*. Manassas, VA: United Daughters of the Confederacy, 1980.

Humphreys, Andrew A. *The Virginia Campaign of 1864 and 1865: The Army of the Potomac and the Army of the James*. 2 vols. New York: Charles Scribner's Sons, 1883.

Hunt, H. Draper, ed. *Dearest Father: The Civil War Letters of Lt. Frank Dickerson, a Son of Belfast, Maine*. Unity, ME: North County Press, 1992.

Hursh, Warren C. "Battle of Hawes's Shop." *National Tribune*, November 11, 1886.

Husby, Karla Jean, comp. and Eric J. Wittenberg, ed. *Under Custer's Command: The Civil War Journal of James Henry Avery*. Washington, DC: Brassey's, 2000.

Hutchinson, Olin Fulmer, Jr., ed. "My Dear Mother & Sisters": *Civil War Letters of Capt. A. B. Mulligan, Co. B 5th South Carolina Cavalry—Butler's Division—Hampton's Corps 1861–1865*. Spartanburg, SC: The Reprint Co., 1992.

Hyde, Thomas W. *Following the Greek Cross, or Memories of the Sixth Army Corps*. Boston: Houghton Mifflin, 1894.

Hyndman, William. History of a Cavalry Company: A Complete Record of Company "A", *4th Pennsylvania Cavalry*. Philadelphia: J. B. Rodgers Co., 1870.

Ide, Horace K. *History of the First Vermont Cavalry Volunteers in the War of the Great Rebellion*. Baltimore: Butternut & Blue, 2000.

Isham, Asa B. *An Historical Sketch of the Seventh Regiment Michigan Volunteer Cavalry from Its Organization, in 1862, to Its Muster Out, in 1865*. New York: Town Topics Publishing Co., 1893.

John Hammond. Died May 28, 1889, at his Home, Crown Point, N.Y. Chicago: F. F. Pettibone & Co., 1890.

Journal of the Executive Proceedings of the Senate of the United States of America from February 13, 1866 to July 28, 1866, Inclusive. Vol. XIV, in two parts. Washington, DC: U.S. Govt. Printing Office, 1866.

Kidd, James H. *Personal Recollections of a Cavalryman in Custer's Michigan Brigade.* Ionia, MI: Sentinel Printing Co., 1908.

King, Matthew W. *To Horse: With the Cavalry of the Army of the Potomac, 1861–1865.* Cheboygan, MI: n.p., 1926.

Koempel, Phillip. *Phil Koempel's Diary 1861–1865.* n.p., 1923.

Lee, William O., comp. *Personal and Historical Sketches and Facial History of and by Members of the Seventh Regiment Michigan Volunteer Cavalry, 1862–1865.* Detroit: Ralston Co., 1901.

Lloyd, William P. *History of the First Regiment Pennsylvania Reserve Cavalry, From Its Organization, August 1861, to September 1864.* Philadelphia: King & Baird, 1864.

Loeser, Charles McK. "Personal Recollections—A Ride to Richmond in 1864." Included in Theophilus F. Rodenbough, ed. *From Everglade to Cañon with the Second Dragoons.* New York: D. van Nostrand, 1875: 304–28.

Lowden, J. K. "A Gallant Record: Michigan's 5th Cav. in the Latter Period of the War." *National Tribune,* July 30, 1896.

Lowe, David W., ed. *Meade's Army: The Private Notebooks of Lt. Col. Theodore Lyman.* Kent, OH: Kent State University Press, 2007.

Mahan, Dennis Hart. *Elementary Treatise on Advance-Guard, Out-Post, and Detachment Service of Troops and the Manner of Posting and Handling Them in the Presence of the Enemy.* New York: Wiley, 1847.

Martin, Isabella D. and Myrta Lockett Avary, eds., *A Diary from Dixie, as Written by Mary Boykin Chesnut.* New York. D. Appleton, 1906.

Mays, Thomas D., ed. *Let Us Meet in Heaven: The Civil War Letters of James Michael Barr, 5th South Carolina Cavalry.* Abilene, TX: McWhiney Foundation Press, 2001.

McClellan, Carswell. *Notes on the Personal Memoirs of P. H. Sheridan.* St. Paul, MN: Press of Wm. E. Banning Jr., 1889.

McDonald, William N. *A History of the Laurel Brigade.* Baltimore, MD: Sun Job Printing Office, 1907.

McGuire, Judith White. *Diary of a Southern Refugee, During the War.* New York: E. J. Hale & Son, 1868.

McKinney, E. P. *Life in Tent and Field 1861–1865.* Boston: The Gorham Press, 1922.

McMahon, Martin T. "Cold Harbor." In Robert U. Johnson and Clarence C. Buel, eds., *Battles and Leaders of the Civil War.* 4 vols. New York: Century Publishing Co., 1884–1888, 4:213–20.

McMakin, Lewis. "Custer in Action." *National Tribune,* September 8, 1910.

Meade, George, ed. *The Life and Letters of George Gordon Meade.* 2 vols. New York: Charles Scribner's Sons, 1913.

Merrington, Marguerite, ed. *The Custer Story: The Life and Letters of General George A. Custer and his Wife Elizabeth.* New York: Devin-Adair Co., 1950.

Miller, Samuel H., ed. "The Civil War Memoirs of the First Maryland Cavalry, C.S.A., by Henry Clay Mettam." *Maryland Historical Magazine* 58 (1963): 137–69.

Milling, James A. "Recollections." *Confederate Veteran* 6 (1897): 6–18.

Mohr, James C., ed. *The Cormany Diaries: A Northern Family in the Civil War.* Pittsburgh, PA: University of Pittsburgh Press, 1982.

Morton, T. C. "Incidents of the Skirmish at Totopotomoy Creek, Hanover County, Virginia, May 30, 1864." *Southern Historical Society Papers* 16 (1908): 47–56.

Moyer, Henry P. *History of the Seventeenth Regiment Pennsylvania Volunteer Cavalry.* Lebanon, PA: n.p., 1911.

"Mr. N. Davidson's Dispatches." *New York Herald*, June 2, 1864.

Myers, Frank M. *The Comanches: A History of White's Battalion, Virginia Cavalry, Laurel Brigade, Hampton's Division, A.N.V., C.S.A.* Baltimore, MD: Kelly, Piet & Co., 1871.

Nanzig, Thomas P., ed. *The Civil War Memoirs of a Virginia Cavalryman: Lt. Robert T. Hubard, Jr.* Tuscaloosa, AL: University of Alabama Press, 2007.

Neese, George M. *Three Years in the Confederate Horse Artillery.* New York: Neale Publishing Co., 1911.

Nevins, Alan, ed. *A Diary of Battle: The Personal Journals of Colonel Charles S. Wainwright, 1861–1865.* New York: Harcourt, Brace & World, 1962.

Newhall, Frederic C. *With General Sheridan Lee's Last Campaign.* Philadelphia: J. B. Lippincott, 1866.

"Old Po'Keepsie," to the editor, *Painesville Telegraph*, June 23, 1864.

"Orlando." "Butler's Cavalry," *Charleston Daily Courier*, September 21, 1864.

Page, Charles A. *Letters of a War Correspondent.* Boston: L. C. Page & Co., 1899.

Peck, Rufus H. *Reminiscences of a Confederate Soldier of Company C, 2nd Virginia Cavalry.* Fincastle, VA: privately published, 1913.

Pollard, Harry T. "Some War Events in Hanover County." *Hanover County Historical Society Bulletin* 52 (1995): 2–5.

Porter, Horace. *Campaigning with Grant.* New York: The Century Co., 1906.

Preston, Noble D. "Hawes's Shop." *National Tribune*, April 21, 1887.

——————. *History of the Tenth Regiment of Cavalry, New York State Volunteers.* New York: D. Appleton & Co., 1892.

"Progress of the Campaign in Virginia." *Charleston Mercury*, June 4, 1864.

"Progress of the War," *The Daily Progress*, June 6, 1864.

Publication Committee of the Regiment. *History of the Eighteenth Regiment of Pennsylvania Cavalry, Pennsylvania Volunteers 1862–1865.* New York: Winkoop Hallenbeck Crawford Co., 1909.

Pyne, Henry R. *Ride to War: The History of the First New Jersey Cavalry.* Trenton, NJ: J. A. Beecher, 1871.

Rea, Lillian, ed. *War Record and Personal Experiences of Walter Raleigh Robbins from April 22, 1861, to August 4, 1865.* n.p., n.d.

"Recent Cavalry Operations." *Atlanta Daily Intelligencer,* June 14, 1864.

"Recent Cavalry Operations." *Richmond Enquirer,* June 17, 1864.

"Record of Hart's Battery from Its Organization to the End of the War." Included in Ulysses R. Brooks. *Stories of the Confederacy.* Columbia, SC: The State Co., 1912: 246–72.

Regimental History of the First New York Dragoons. Washington, DC: Gibson Brothers, 1865.

Report of the Thirty-Third Annual Reunion, Sixth Ohio Veteran Volunteer Cavalry Association, Held at Warren, Ohio, October 4th, 1898. Garrettville, OH: The Journal Printing Co., 1898.

Rhodes, Charles D. "Cavalry Battles and Charges." In Francis Trevelyan Miller, ed. *The Photographic History of the Civil War.* 10 vols. New York: Review of Reviews Co., 1911: 4:220–58.

——————. *History of the Cavalry of the Army of the Potomac, Including that of the Army of Virginia (Pope's), and also the History of the Operations of the Federal Cavalry in West Virginia During the War.* Kansas City, MO: Hudson–Kimberly Publishing Co., 1900.

Roberts, William P. "Additional Sketch Nineteenth Regiment." Included in Walter Clark, ed. *Histories of the Several Regiments and Battalions from North Carolina in the Great War, 1861–65.* 5 vols. Raleigh: E. M. Uzzell, 1901, 2:99–109.

Robertson, James I., ed. *The Civil War Letters of General Robert McAllister.* New Brunswick, NJ: Rutgers University Press, 1965.

Rockwell, Alphonso D. *Rambling Recollections: An Autobiography.* New York: P. B. Hoeber, 1920.

Rodenbough, Theophilus F., ed. *From Everglade to Cañon with the Second Dragoons.* New York: D. van Nostrand, 1875.

——————. "Sheridan's Richmond Raid," in Robert U. Johnson and Clarence C. Buel, eds. *Battles and Leaders of the Civil War.* 4 vols. New York: Century Publishing Co., 1884–1888. 4:188–93.

——————. "Some Cavalry Leaders," in Francis Trevelyan Miller, ed. *The Photographic History of the Civil War.* 10 vols. New York: Review of Reviews Co., 1911. 4:262–88.

Rosser, Thomas L. "Annals of the War; Rosser and His Men." *Philadelphia Weekly Times,* April 19, 1884.

——————. "Promotion for Extraordinary Valor and Skill." *Lost Cause: A Confederate War Record* 1 (1898): 53–54.

Russell, David B., ed. *Tough & Hearty: Kimball Pearsons, Civil War Cavalryman, Co. L, 10th Regiment of Cavalry, New York State Volunteers.* Bowie, MD: Heritage Books, 2012.

Sauerburger, Donna Bayard and Thomas Lucas Bayard, eds. *I Seat Myself to Write You a Few Lines: Civil War and Homestead Letters from Thomas Lucas and Family.* Bowie, MD: Heritage Books, 2002.

Shaffer, Michael K., ed. *In Memory of Self and Comrades: Thomas Wallace Colley's Recollections of Civil War Service in the 1st Virginia Cavalry.* Knoxville: University of Tennessee Press, 2018.

Sheridan, Philip H. *Personal Memoirs of P. H. Sheridan.* 2 vols. New York: Charles L. Webster & Co., 1888.

Shreve, George W. "Reminiscences in the History of the Stuart Horse Artillery, C.S.A." Included in Robert J. Trout, ed., *Memoirs of the Stuart Horse Artillery Battalion*, Vol. 2. Knoxville: University of Tennessee Press, 2010: 291–313.

Smith, William F. "The Eighteenth Corps at Cold Harbor." In Robert U. Johnson and Clarence C. Buel, eds. *Battles and Leaders of the Civil War.* 4 vols. New York: Century Publishing Co., 1884–1888, 4:221–30.

Sorrell, G. Moxley. *Recollections of a Confederate Staff Officer.* New York: Neale Publishing Co., 1905.

Stanley, David S. *Personal Memoirs of Major-General David S. Stanley.* Cambridge, MA: Harvard University Press, 1917.

Stiles, Robert. *Four Years Under Marse Robert.* New York: Neale, 1903.

Summers, Festus P., ed. *A Borderland Confederate.* Pittsburgh, PA: University of Pittsburgh Press, 1962.

Supplement to the Official Records of the Union and Confederate Armies. 100 vols. Wilmington, NC: Broadfoot Publishing, 1994.

Swank, Walbrook D., ed. *Confederate Letters and Diaries, 1861–1865.* Mineral, VA: self-published, 1988.

Taylor, Gray Nelson, ed. *Saddle and Saber: Civil War Letters of Corporal Nelson Taylor.* Bowie, MD: Heritage Books, 1993.

Tenney, Luman Harris. *War Diary of Luman Harris Tenney, 1861–1865.* Cleveland: Evangelical Publishing House, 1914.

"The Battle of Hawes's Shop." *Philadelphia Inquirer,* June 3, 1864.

"The Michigan Cavalry Brigade." *Detroit Free Press,* June 15, 1864.

"The Recent Cavalry Operations." *Richmond Enquirer,* June 9, 1864.

"The Scene of the Impending Battle." *Evening Star,* June 2, 1864.

"The War News," *Richmond Daily Dispatch,* June 2, 1864.

The War of the Rebellion: A Compilation of the Official Records of the Union and Confederate Armies. 128 volumes in 3 series. Washington, DC: United States Government Printing Office, 1889.

Thomas, Hampton S. *Some Personal Reminiscences of Service in the Cavalry of the Army of the Potomac.* Philadelphia: R. Hamersly & Co., 1889.

Toalson, Jeff, ed. *Send Me a Pair of Old Boots & Kiss My Little Girls: The Civil War Letters of Richard and Mary Watkins, 1861–1865.* Bloomington, IN: iUniverse, 2009.

Tobie, Edward P. *History of the First Maine Cavalry.* Boston: Press of Emery & Hughes, 1887.

——————————. *Service of the Cavalry in the Army of the Potomac.* Providence, RI: N. Bangs Williams & Co., 1882.

Townsend, George Alfred. *Campaigns of a Non-Combatant, and His Remaunt Abroad During the War.* New York: Blelock & Co., 1866.

Tremain, Lyman. *Memorial of Frederick Lyman Tremain, Late Lieut. Col. of the 10th N.Y. Cavalry, Who was Mortally Wounded at the Battle of Hatcher's Run, Va., February 6th, and Died at City Point Hospital, February 8th, 1865.* Albany: Van Benthuysen's Steam Printing House, 1865.

Trout, Robert J., ed. *Riding with Stuart: Reminiscences of an Aide-de-Camp, by Captain Theodore S. Garnett.* Shippensburg, PA: White Mane, 1994.

Viola, Herman J., ed. *The Memoirs of Charles Henry Veil: A Soldier's Recollections of the Civil War and the Arizona Territories.* New York: Orion Books, 1993.

Vogtsberger, Margaret Ann. *The Dulanys of Welbourne: A Family in Mosby's Confederacy.* Lexington, VA: Rockbridge Publishing, 1995.

Wainwright, R. P. Page. "First Regiment of Cavalry." In Theophilus F. Rodenbough and William L. Haskin, eds. *The Army of the U.S.: Historical Sketches of Staff and Line with Portraits of Generals in Chief.* New York: Merrill, Maynard & Co., 1896: 153–172.

Wallace, Robert C. *A Few Memories of a Long Life.* Fairfield, WA: Ye Galleon Press, 1988.

Waring, Joseph I., ed. "The Diary of William G. Hinson During the War of Secession." *South Carolina Historical Magazine* 75 (1974): 14–23.

Wells, Edward L. "A Morning Call on Kilpatrick." *Southern Historical Society Papers* 12 (March 1884): 144–48.

————. *A Sketch of the Charleston Light Dragoons, from the Earliest Formation of the Corps.* Charleston, SC: Lucas, Richardson & Co., 1888.

————. *Hampton and His Cavalry in '64.* Richmond, VA: B. F. Johnson Publishing Co., 1899.

West, Robert Jerald L., ed. *Found Among the Privates, Recollections of the Holcomb's Legion 1861-1864.* Sharon, SC: privately published, 1997.

Wilkeson, Frank. *Recollections of a Private Soldier in the Army of the Potomac.* New York: G. P. Putnam's Sons, 1887.

Wilson, James H. *Under the Old Flag: Recollections of Military Operations in the War for the Union, the Spanish War, the Boxer Rebellion, etc.* 2 vols. Westport, CT: Greenwood Press, 1912.

Wittenberg, Eric J., ed. *One of Custer's Wolverines: The Civil War Letters of Brevet Brigadier General James Harvey Kidd, Sixth Michigan Cavalry.* Kent, OH: Kent State University Press, 2000.

Wolcott, Charles F. "Army Stories." In *Report of the Proceedings of the Sixth Ohio Cavalry.* Privately published, 1911: 40–41.

————. "The Cavalry Arm." *National Tribune*, September 8, 1910.

Woodward, C. Vann, ed. *Mary Chesnut's Civil War.* New Haven, CT: Yale University Press, 1981.

Wright, J. Russell. "Battle of Trevilian." *Recollections and Reminiscences 1861–1865.* 12 vols. Charleston: South Carolina Division of the United Daughters of the Confederacy, 1995, 6:372.

SECONDARY SOURCES:

Albert, Don. *Brandy Station to Manila Bay: A Biography of General Wesley Merritt.* Austin, TX: Presidial Press, 1980.

Allardice, Bruce S. *Confederate Colonels: A Biographical Register.* Columbia: University of Missouri Press, 2008.

———————————. *More Generals in Gray.* Baton Rouge: Louisiana State University Press, 1995.

Andrew, Rod. *Wade Hampton: Confederate Warrior to Southern Redeemer.* Chapel Hill: University of North Carolina Press, 2008.

Angelovich, Robert B. *Riding for Uncle Samuel: The Civil War History of the 1st Connecticut Cavalry Volunteers.* Gettysburg, PA: privately published, 2014.

Armstrong, Richard L. *11th Virginia Cavalry.* Lynchburg, VA: H. E. Howard Co., 1989.

———————————. *7th Virginia Cavalry.* Lynchburg, VA: H. E. Howard Co., 1992.

Arnold, James R. *Jeff Davis's Own: Cavalry, Comanches, and the Battle for the Texas Frontier.* New York: John Wiley & Sons, 2007.

Balfour, Daniel T. *13th Virginia Cavalry.* Lynchburg, VA: H. E. Howard Co., 1986.

Ballard, James Buchanan. *William Edmonson "Grumble" Jones: The Life of a Cantankerous Confederate.* Jefferson, NC: McFarland & Co., 2017.

Baltz, Louis J., III. *The Battle of Cold Harbor: May 27–June 13, 1864.* Lynchburg, VA: H. E. Howard, 1994.

Barefoot, Daniel W. *General Robert F. Hoke: Lee's Modest Warrior.* Winston-Salem, NC: John F. Blair Publisher, 1996.

Barringer, Sheridan R. *Custer's Gray Rival: The Life of Confederate Major General Thomas Lafayette Rosser.* Burlington, NC: Fox Run, 2019.

———————————. *Fighting for General Lee: Confederate General Rufus Barringer and the North Carolina Cavalry Brigade.* El Dorado Hills, CA: Savas–Beatie, 2016.

Bates, Samuel P. *Martial Deeds of Pennsylvania.* Philadelphia: T. H. Davis & Co., 1875.

Beckendorf, John Peter. "Finding Major Wallace of the 5th Michigan Cavalry." *Military Images* Vol. XXVI, No. 5 (March–April 2005): 20–24.

Bergeron, Arthur W., Jr. "John Randolph Chambliss, Jr." Included in William C. Davis and Julie Hoffman, eds. *The Confederate General.* 6 vols. New York: National Historical Society, 1991, 1:172–73.

Beyer, F. F. and O. F. Keydel. *Deeds of Valor: How America's Civil War Heroes Won the Congressional Medal of Honor.* 2 vols. Detroit: The Perrien–Keydel Co., 1907.

Bluford, Robert, Jr. *The Battle of Totopotomoy Creek: Pole Green Church and the Prelude to Cold Harbor.* Charleston, SC: The History Press, 2014.

Boatner, Mark M., III. *Civil War Dictionary.* New York: David McKay, 1959.

Brown, R. Shepard. *Stringfellow of the Fourth.* New York: Crown, 1960.

Burgess, Milton. *David Gregg: Pennsylvania Cavalryman.* Privately published, 1984.

Burns, Vincent. *The Fifth New York Cavalry in the Civil War.* Jefferson, NC: McFarland, 2014.

Catton, Bruce. *Grant Takes Command.* Boston: Little, Brown & Co., 1968.

Collea, Joseph D. *The First Vermont Cavalry in the Civil War: A History.* Jefferson, NC: McFarland, 2010.

Daughtry, Mary. *Gray Cavalier: The Life and Wars General William H. F. "Rooney" Lee.* New York: Da Capo, 2002.

Dietrich, Richard Kevin. *To Virginia and Back with Rutledge's Cavalry: A History of the 4th South Carolina Cavalry Regiment.* Wilmington, NC: Broadfoot, 2015.

Divine, John E. *35th Battalion Virginia Cavalry.* Lynchburg, VA: H. E. Howard Co., 1985.

Driver, Robert J., Jr. *1st Virginia Cavalry.* Lynchburg, VA: H. E. Howard Co., 1991.

----------------. *First and Second Maryland Cavalry, C.S.A.* Charlottesville, VA: Rockbridge Publishing, 1999.

----------------. *10th Virginia Cavalry.* Lynchburg, VA: H. E. Howard, 1992.

Driver, Robert J., Jr. and H. E. Howard. *2nd Virginia Cavalry.* Lynchburg, VA: H. E. Howard Co., 1995.

Duncan, Richard R. *Lee's Endangered Left: The Civil War in Western Virginia, Spring of 1864.* Baton Rouge: Louisiana State University Press, 1999.

Emerson, W. Eric. *Sons of Privilege: The Charleston Light Dragoons in the Civil War.* Columbia: University of South Carolina Press, 2005.

Franklin, Ellis and Austin N. Hungerford, comps. *History of that Part of the Susquehanna and Juniata Valleys Embraced in the Counties of Mifflin, Juniata, Perry, Union, and Snyder, in the Commonwealth of Pennsylvania.* 2 vols. Philadelphia: Everts, Peck & Richards, 1886.

Frye, Dennis E. *12th Virginia Cavalry.* Lynchburg, VA: H. E. Howard Co., 1988.

Furgurson, Ernest B. *Not War but Murder: Cold Harbor 1864.* New York: Alfred Knopf, 2000.

Gabbert, John M. *Military Operations in Hanover County Virginia 1861-1865.* Roanoke, VA: Gurtner Graphics & Printing Co., 1989.

Hand, Harold, Jr. *One Good Regiment: The 13th Pennsylvania Cavalry in the Civil War, 1861-1865.* Victoria, BC: Trafford, 2000.

Hanover County Historical Society. *Old Homes of Hanover County, Virginia.* Hanover, VA: Hanover County Historical Society, 1983.

Hardy, Michael C. *The Battle of Hanover Court House: Turning Point of the Peninsula Campaign, May 27, 1862.* Jefferson, NC: McFarland, 2006.

Harrell, Roger H. *The Second North Carolina Cavalry.* Jefferson, NC: McFarland & Co., 2004.

Helm, Lewis Marshall. *Black Horse Cavalry: Defend Our Beloved Country.* Falls Church, VA: Higher Education Publications, 1999.

Hewitt, Lawrence L. "Matthew Calbraith Butler." Included in William C. Davis and Julie Hoffman, eds. *The Confederate General*. 6 vols. New York: National Historical Society, 1991, 1:150–53.

Holland, Lynwood Mathis. *Pierce M. B. Young: The Warwick of the South*. Athens: University of Georgia Press, 1964.

Holmes, Torlief S. *Horse Soldiers in Blue: First Maine Cavalry*. Gaithersburg, MD: Butternut Press, 1985.

Hopkins, Donald A. *The Little Jeff: The Jeff Davis Legion, Cavalry, Army of Northern Virginia*. Shippensburg, PA: White Mane, 1999.

Hunt, Roger D. *Colonels in Blue: Union Colonels of the Civil War, Pennsylvania, New Jersey, Maryland, Delaware and the District of Columbia*. Mechanicsburg, PA: Stackpole, 2007.

Hunt, Roger D. and Jack R. Brown. *Brevet Brigadier Generals in Blue*. Gaithersburg, MD: Olde Soldier Books, 1990.

Kester, Donald E. *Cavalryman in Blue: Colonel John Wood Kester of the First New Jersey Cavalry in the Civil War*. Hightstown, NJ: Longstreet House, 1997.

Knudsen, Lewis K., Jr. *A History of the 5th South Carolina Cavalry, 1861–1865*. Wilmington, NC: Broadfoot, 2016.

Krick, Robert E. L. "Repairing an Army: A Look at the New Troops in the Army of Northern Virginia in May and June 1864." Included in Gary W. Gallagher and Caroline E. Janney, eds., *Cold Harbor to the Crater: The End of the Overland Campaign*. Chapel Hill: University of North Carolina Press, 2015: 33–72.

————————. "Stuart's Last Ride: A Confederate View of Sheridan's Raid." Included in Gary W. Gallagher, ed., *The Spotsylvania Campaign*. Chapel Hill: University of North Carolina Press, 1998: 127–69.

Krick, Robert K. *Lee's Colonels: A Biographical Register of the Field Officers of the Army of Northern Virginia*. Dayton, OH: Morningside, 1992.

————————. *9th Virginia Cavalry*. Lynchburg, VA: H. E. Howard, 1982.

————————. "Thomas Lafayette Rosser." Included in William C. Davis and Julie Hoffman, eds. *The Confederate General*. 6 vols. New York: National Historical Society, 1991, 5:112–15.

Lewis, Michael J. *Frank Furness: Architecture and the Violent Mind*. New York: W. W. Norton, 2001.

Longacre, Edward G. *Custer and His Wolverines: The Michigan Cavalry Brigade 1861–1865*. Conshohocken, PA: Combined Books, 1997.

————————. *Fitz Lee: A Military Biography of Major General Fitzhugh Lee, C.S.A.* New York: Da Capo Press, 2004.

————————. *From Union Stars to Top Hat: A Biography of the Extraordinary General James Harrison Wilson*. Mechanicsburg, PA: Stackpole Books, 1972.

————————. *Gentleman and Scholar: A Biography of Wade Hampton*. Nashville, TN: Rutledge Hill Press, 2003.

————————. *Jersey Cavaliers: A History of the First New Jersey Volunteer Cavalry, 1861–1865*. Hightstown, NJ: Longstreet House, 1992.

——————————. *Lee's Cavalrymen: A History of the Mounted Forces of the Army of Northern Virginia, 1861-1865*. Mechanicsburg, PA: Stackpole Books, 2002.

——————————. *The Cavalry at Gettysburg: A Tactical Study of Mounted Operations during the Civil War's Pivotal Campaign, 9 June-14 July 1863*. Rutherford, NJ: Fairleigh Dickinson University Press, 1986.

Lubrecht, Peter T. *New Jersey Butterfly Boys in the Civil War: The Hussars of the Union Army*. Charleston, SC: The History Press, 2011.

Maney, R. Wayne. *Marching to Cold Harbor: Victory & Failure, 1864*. Shippensburg, PA: White Mane, 1995.

Martin, Samuel J. *Southern Hero: Matthew Calbraith Butler, Confederate General, Hampton Red Shirt, and U.S. Senator*. Mechanicsburg, PA: Stackpole, 2001.

McCartney, Martha W. *Nature's Bounty, Nation's Glory: The Heritage and History of Hanover County, Virginia*. Hanover County, VA: Heritage and History of Hanover County, Inc., 2009.

McFeely, William S. *Grant: A Biography*. New York: W. W. Norton & Co., 1982.

Mesic, Harriet Bey. *Cobb's Legion Cavalry: A History and Roster of the Ninth Georgia Volunteers in the Civil War*. Jefferson, NC: McFarland, 2009.

Moore, Robert H., Jr. *Chew's Ashby, Shoemaker's Lynchburg and the Newtown Artillery*. Lynchburg, VA: H. E. Howard Co., 1995.

——————————. *The 1st and 2nd Stuart Horse Artillery*. Lynchburg, VA: H. E. Howard Co., 1985.

Morris, Roy, Jr. *Sheridan: The Life and Wars of General Phil Sheridan*. New York: Crown Publishers, Inc., 1992.

Nanzig, Thomas P. *3rd Virginia Cavalry*. Lynchburg, VA: H. E. Howard Co., 1989.

Northern, William J., ed. *Men of Mark in Georgia*. 3 vols. Atlanta: A. B. Chapman, 1907-1912.

O'Neill, Robert F., Jr. *The Cavalry Battles of Aldie, Middleburg and Upperville: Small but Important Riots, June 10-27, 1863*. Lynchburg, VA: H. E. Howard, 1993.

Page, Rosewell. *Hanover County: Its History and Legends*. Richmond, VA: privately published, 1926.

Power, Tracy. *Lee's Miserables: Life in the Army of Northern Virginia from the Wilderness to Appomattox*. Chapel Hill: University of North Carolina Press, 1998.

Ramsey, Marc. *The 7th South Carolina Cavalry: To the Defense of Richmond*. Wilmington, NC: Broadfoot, 2011.

Rhea, Gordon C. *Cold Harbor: Grant and Lee May 26–June 3, 1864*. Baton Rouge: Louisiana State University Press, 2002.

——————————. *On to Petersburg: Grant and Lee, June 4–15, 1864*. Baton Rouge: Louisiana State University Press, 2017.

——————————. *The Battle of the Wilderness, May 5-6, 1864*. Baton Rouge: Louisiana State University Press, 1994.

————. *To the North Anna River: Grant and Lee, May 13–25, 1864.* Baton Rouge: Louisiana State University Press, 2000.

Snellgrove, Benjamin E. "Williams Carter Wickham." Included in William C. Davis and Julie Hoffman, eds. *The Confederate General.* 6 vols. New York: National Historical Society, 1991, 6:134–35.

Sommers, Richard J. "Thomas Lanier Clingman." Included in William C. Davis and Julie Hoffman, eds. *The Confederate General.* 6 vols. New York: National Historical Society, 1991, 1:202–5.

————. "John Dunovant." Included in William C. Davis and Julie Hoffman, eds. *The Confederate General.* 6 vols. New York: National Historical Society, 1991, 2:86–875.

————. "Martin Witherspoon Gary." Included in William C. Davis and Julie Hoffman, eds. *The Confederate General.* 6 vols. New York: National Historical Society, 1991, 2:176–79.

Sondley, Forster A. *A History of Buncombe County.* 2 vols. Asheville, NC: Advocate Print Co., 1930.

Staats, Richard J. *The History of the Sixth Ohio Volunteer Cavalry 1861–1865.* 2 vols. Westminster, MD: Heritage Books, 2006.

Stiles, Kenneth L. *4th Virginia Cavalry.* Lynchburg, VA: H. E. Howard Co., 1985.

Swank, Walbrook D. *The Battle of Trevilian Station: The Civil War's Greatest and Bloodiest All Cavalry Battle.* Shippensburg, PA: Burd Street Press, 1994.

Sword, Wiley. *Mountains Touched with Fire.* New York: St. Martin's Press, 1995.

Thomas, D. Michael. *Wade Hampton's Iron Scouts: Confederate Special Forces.* Charleston, SC: The History Press, 2018.

Thomas, Emory N. *Bold Dragoon: The Life of J. E. B. Stuart.* New York: Random House, 1986.

Urwin, Gregory J. W. *Custer Victorious: The Civil War Battle of George Armstrong Custer.* East Brunswick, NJ: Associated University Presses, 1983.

Venter, Bruce M. *Kill Jeff Davis: The Union Raid on Richmond 1864.* Norman: University of Oklahoma Press, 2016.

Warner, Ezra J. *Generals in Blue: Lives of the Union Commanders.* Baton Rouge: Louisiana State University Press, 1964.

————. *Generals in Gray: Lives of the Confederate Commanders.* Baton Rouge: Louisiana State University Press, 1959.

Webber, Mabel L. "Dr. John Rutledge and His Descendants." *The South Carolina Historical and Genealogical Magazine.* Vol. 31, No. 1 (Jan. 1930): 7–25.

Wellman, Manly Wade. *Giant in Gray: A Biography of Wade Hampton of South Carolina.* New York: Charles Scribner's Sons, 1949.

Welsh, Jack D. *Medical Histories of Confederate Generals.* Kent, OH: Kent State University Press, 1995.

Wert, Jeffry D. "Bradley Tyler Johnson." Included in William C. Davis and Julie Hoffman, eds. *The Confederate General.* 6 vols. New York: National Historical Society, 1991, 3:172–79.

--------------. *Custer: The Controversial Life of George Armstrong Custer.* New York: Simon & Schuster, 1996.

--------------. "Lunsford Lindsay Lomax." Included in William C. Davis and Julie Hoffman, eds. *The Confederate General.* 6 vols. New York: National Historical Society, 1991, 4:85.

--------------. "Pierce Manning Butler Young." Included in William C. Davis and Julie Hoffman, eds. *The Confederate General.* 6 vols. New York: National Historical Society, 1991, 6:169–70.

--------------. "Robert Frederick Hoke." Included in William C. Davis and Julie Hoffman, eds. *The Confederate General.* 6 vols. New York: National Historical Society, 1991, 3:114–15.

Williams, Robert A. "Haw's Shop: A 'Storm of Shot and Shell'." *Civil War Times Illustrated* 9 (January 1971): 12–19.

Wittenberg, Eric J. *Glory Enough for All: Sheridan's Second Raid and the Battle of Trevilian Station.* Washington, DC: Brassey's, 2001.

--------------. *Rush's Lancers: The Sixth Pennsylvania Cavalry in the Civil War.* Yardley, PA: Westholme, 2007.

--------------. *The Union Cavalry Comes of Age: Hartwood Church to Brandy Station, 1863.* 2nd ed. Charleston, SC: The History Press, 2017.

Young, Alfred C., III. *Lee's Army During the Overland Campaign: A Numerical Study.* Baton Rouge: Louisiana State University Press, 2013.

WEBSITES:

"Erastus Blakeslee." https://prabook.com/web/erastus.blakeslee/1080478

David Hamilton Find-a-Grave page,
 https://www.findagrave.com/memorial/10926204/david-hamilton

"Hanover's History." https://www.hanovercounty.gov/684/Hanovers-History

"History and Culture of Ashland."
 https://www.ashlandva.gov/177/History-Culture

"History of Hanover Tavern." https://hanovertavern.org/tavern/history/

John R. Maybury Diary for 1864,
 https://www.civilwardigital.com/CWDiaries/John%20R.%20Maybury.pdf

Pvt. Oliver Hering Middleton Jr. Find-a-Grave page,
 https://www.findagrave.com/memorial/33447334/oliver-hering-middleton

John MacPherson Millen Find-a-Grave page,
 https://www.findagrave.com/memorial/8746304/john-macpherson-millen

Benjamin Huger Rutledge Sr. biography page,
 https://www.litchfieldhistoricalsociety.org/ledger/students/2194

Benjamin Huger Rutledge Sr. Find-a-Grave Page,
 https://www.findagrave.com/memorial/59189362/benjamin-huger-rutledge

Index

Photograph by Scott Cunningham

About the Author

E ric J. Wittenberg is an award-winning Civil War historian, speaker and tour guide. A native of southeastern Pennsylvania, he has been hooked on the Civil War since a third-grade trip to Gettysburg. Wittenberg is deeply involved in battlefield preservation efforts with the Civil War Trust. He is a graduate of Dickinson College and the University of Pittsburgh School of Law. He is an attorney in private practice in Columbus, Ohio, where he resides with his wife Susan and their three golden retrievers.

CPSIA information can be obtained
at www.ICGtesting.com
Printed in the USA
BVHW040213130921
616651BV00019B/456